The First Fleet Marines

The First Fleet Marines
1786-1792

John Moore

University of Queensland Press
ST LUCIA • LONDON • NEW YORK

First published 1987 by University of Queensland Press
Box 42, St Lucia, Queensland, Australia

© John Moore 1987

This book is copyright. Apart from any fair dealing for the
purposes of private study, research, criticism or review, as
permitted under the Copyright Act, no part may be reproduced
by any process without written permission. Enquiries should
be made to the publisher.

Typeset by University of Queensland Press
Printed in Australia by The Book Printer, Melbourne

Distributed in the UK and Europe by University of Queensland Press
Dunhams Lane, Letchworth, Herts. SG6 1LF England

Distributed in the USA and Canada by University of Queensland Press
250 Commercial Street, Manchester, NH 03101 USA

Cataloguing in Publication Data

National Library of Australia

Moore, J.H. (John Harwood), 1929– .
   The First Fleet marines 1786–1792.

   Bibliography.
   Includes index.

   [1]. First Fleet, 1787–1788. 2. Australia — History,
   Military — 1788–1851. 3. Great Britain. Marine Corps —
   History — 18th century. I. Title.

994.02

British Library (data available)

Library of Congress

Moore, John, 1929–
   The first fleet marines, 1786–1792.

   Bibliography: p.
   Includes index.
      1. Great Britain. Royal Marines—History—18th
   century. 2. Great Britain. Royal Navy. Fleet,
   First—History. 3. Australia—History—1788–1851.
   4. Phillip, Arthur, 1738–1814. 5. Ross, Robert,
   b. 1740? 6. Clark, Ralph, d. 1794. I. Title.

VE57.M66   1987   994.4'1'02   86-30904

ISBN 0 7022 2065 5

To my wife Rita, daughters Janet and Roslyn,
and in memory of Betty and Robyn

Contents

Illustrations *ix*
Tables *x*
Preface *xi*

Historical Introduction *1*
1 Preparations for the Great Adventure *18*
2 The Voyage Out *46*
3 Botany Bay to Sydney Cove *77*
4 Sleeping on the Ground *88*
5 Early Crimes and Punishments *97*
6 The Manly Aborigine *108*
7 Little Journeys — Hard Climbs *124*
8 Hardship in Sydneytown *132*
9 The Reluctant Hangman *143*
10 Rations and Supplies *147*
11 Marines under the Lash *158*
12 Parramatta *165*
13 God Save the King *168*
14 Staying On: Family and Land *172*
15 Major Robert Ross *182*
16 Norfolk Island *227*
17 Phillip's Dispute with Dawes *256*
18 The Second Fleet *261*

19 The New South Wales Corps   *269*
20 Homeward Bound   *274*
Conclusion   *284*

Appendix A — Children of Marines 1787–1792   *290*
         B — Officer Biographies   *294*
         C — Order of Battle   *303*
Notes to the Text   *308*
Bibliography   *334*
Index   *339*

Illustrations

Following page 180

Uniforms worn by British Marines, 1755–1807
A marine marksman, 1799
An officer of marines, 1799
Lord Sydney, 1787
Governor Phillip, 1787
Captain John Hunter
David Collins, Judge Advocate of New South Wales
Captain Watkin Tench
Lieutenant George Johnston
Alicia Clark
Entrance of Port Jackson, 1788
Settlement at Sydney, 1788
Sydney Cove, Port Jackson, 1788
John Hunter, David Collins, Lieutenant Johnson,
    Governor Phillip, Surgeon White and an
    Aboriginal woman and child
Governor Phillip's house, 1791
Sketch of the explorations of the Sydney Plain
Norfolk Island locations   *page 228*

Tables

1. Marine Corps daily rates of pay   8
2. Weekly ration: Ship and Shore   28
3. Distribution of marines and convicts, 1786   32
4. Distribution of officers and marines off Portsmouth, 1787   40
5. Paysheet for tradesmen employed to build military accommodation   136
6. Quartermaster's report on clothing stocks   148
7. Livestock ownership, 1788   150
8. Marine marriages, 1788–1792   177
9. Marine deaths, 1787–1791   178
10. Land grants to marines in Sydney   180
11. Sample of marines in New South Wales Corps   181
12. Sixty acre land grants to marines, Norfolk Island, 1791   246
13. Death and sickness rates, Second Fleet convicts, June 1790   266

Preface

I have written this work mainly to provide an account of life in the first four years of Sydney from the viewpoint of the First Fleet marines. These naval soldiers were sent to protect the British colony in Australia and maintain its law and order. The tour of duty to Botany Bay was out of the usual run of military service, and called for considerable relaxation of regimentalism. Marines shared with the convicts the hunger, loneliness and fear of an unfamiliar and unrelenting environment. Yet they did not become tyrannical and oppressive as did later military units. Their explorations opened up much of the Sydney Plain.

The British Marines' contribution to the settlement's establishment was a sound one which even the carping behaviour of their commandant could not undo, and yet they have suffered the injustice of becoming incorporated in the tarnished reputation which seems to rest upon some military units of the colony's early era. The fault is one of blurring and generalizing. In an attempt to present their story as truthfully as possible, I have accumulated the evidence as it exists to let it speak for itself; and I believe the evidence supports my contention that whatever the early military's reputation might be, the First Fleet marines are entitled to one of their own — a reputation for sound service marred only by the incorrigibility of their commandant. I hope that readers will confirm the judgment.

In the last decade or so, a quiet revolution has occurred in which historical research, once largely the preserve of universities, is now pursued by unlettered thousands who in it have found an absorbing fascination and a productive use of leisure time. I am sure that some of this surge of interest comes from the enchantment of historical anecdotes. Thus, where anecdotal incidents have been pertinent to the present topic, I have deliberately included them in the hope that teachers in particular might find these helpful in animating for their students the otherwise dry-bones of text book history.

I would like to thank a number of people who, directly or indirectly, have contributed to this book. Firstly I shall always be indebted to Macquarie University, Sydney, for the benefit I gained from the erudition and enthusiasm of its Australian History Department. Lecturers such as Professor Duncan Waterson, Dr Portia Robinson, and Dr Frank Clarke (who suggested I write this book), showed me the enjoyment inherent in investigating Australia's historical origins. I also owe thanks to the staff of the Mitchell Library, Sydney, for their ready assistance in locating obscure references; to Mr Allan Faragher, principal of Fairholme College, Toowoomba, for the availability of leave; to Miss B. Spiers of the Royal Marines Museum, Portsmouth, UK, for many letters answering my questions; and to Lt Col. Ted Marshall, B.Ed., MA., formerly of the Royal Australian Army Education Corps, whose friendship and knowledge of Australian history I have valued and enjoyed.

Finally, but not least, I owe a considerable debt to my wife Rita not only for her typing of the manuscript, but also for her encouragement and support during the long preparation of it.

Historical Introduction

The British Marines Before 1788

The first troops to serve in Australia were four companies of the British Marine Corps who arrived in New South Wales with the First Fleet in 1788. They were not soldiers in the strict meaning of the word because soldiers belong to an army: the first army unit in Australia was actually the New South Wales Corps which took over from the marines in 1791. Unfortunately that corps damaged much of the military's good reputation which had been established by the marines during their four-year service. It is regrettable therefore, largely because the marines and the New South Wales Corps were both military units, that in the minds of many since, the excesses and dubious reputation of the New South Wales Corps have come also to be applied to the Marine Corps. This blurring of the facts has done an injustice, if not a libel, to the marines: in an unorthodox and difficult situation, they never imposed on society the suffering and injustice which their army successors inflicted. Consequently, the wrong done to the marines should be redressed, and it is this which, hopefully, this book achieves.

Britain's Marine Corps had been in existence for over 123 years before its New South Wales detachment embarked on its tour of duty. The Marine Corps had been founded by Charles II on 28 October 1664,[1] when a regiment was raised called "The Duke of York and Albany's Maritime Regiment of Foot" to produce the type of soldier whose capacity to fight was not diminished by the debilitating effects of long and arduous voyages. This new military requirement made traditional soldiers unsuitable because these tended to be still suffering from seasickness when their active duty ashore was required.[2]

The marines quickly showed their mettle, and in an age when Britain was expanding her empire, they added the important territories of Gibraltar and Nova Scotia to the Empire in the War of Spanish Succession. In the War of Austrian Succession they saw extensive service in the West Indies, assisted in the seizure of Louisberg in North America in 1744, and captured Pondicherry from the French in India in 1748. In conformity with the custom of the day, the marines were disbanded when the war finished in 1748.

Seven years later, a war between Britain and France became inevitable, and Britain realized that it would be a worldwide contest for empire. Thus she embarked upon an immediate expansion of her forces. On 5 April 1755, the marines were raised for the fourth time and have remained on the Order of Battle ever since.[3] Some fifty companies were formed and organized into three divisions with headquarters at Chatham, Plymouth and Portsmouth in the south of England. The new force was placed under control of the Admiralty, and the Marine Mutiny Act was passed for its regulation while serving on shore.[4] Though officers could move between the British Army and the Marine Corps, the sale of Marine Corps commissions was abolished (unlike the army).[5] Possibly this was designed to remove any barrier to suitable applicants of limited means in the urgency of the 1755 re-establishment and to conform more closely to naval practice. Before this, army commissions had been more expensive than marine commissions because they were more highly regarded. Thus a lieutenant's commission could have been purchased for £250 in the marine corps, but £400 in the army.[6]

It was into this newly organized Marine Corps that Robert Ross, later the Lieutenant Governor of New South Wales, was commissioned in 1756. On 18 May that year France declared war on Britain and the Seven Years' War (1756-1763) had begun. For the next four years extensive and heavy use was made of the marines. In an amphibious operation combined with the Royal Navy, they captured Senegal in 1758; and in the same year, led by one of their most famous officers, James Wolfe, who had been commissioned in the marines in 1741,[7] they fought at Cape Breton and St Johns. From there they took almost six thousand French prisoners of war. In doing so, they gave the French good reason to doubt their own future in Canada. In 1759, one of the busiest years in the corps' history, marines were committed in the Caribbean, where they captured Barbados, Martinique and Guadaloupe. Meanwhile in an action of considerable audacity, marines landed on the French coast itself to convince France that she was incapable of protecting her own shores, let alone of invading England. In September 1759, a marine detachment (including Robert Ross) was part of a force led by General Wolfe which scaled the Heights of Abraham, captured Quebec, and thus secured Canada for Britain. Meanwhile, those marines employed in the American theatre had captured Belle Isle on the Detroit River, and before the war ended in 1763 these were to see further action at Martinique, Cuba and the eastern American seaboard.

In the meantime, France had retaken Pondicherry, but in 1761 the British Marines recaptured it and this ruined the French East India Company in India, to the considerable advantage of British commerce.[8] Their final action in the war took them to the Philippines where a force which included three hundred marines captured Manila from the Spanish on 6 October 1762, thereby opening tremendous commercial possibilities in the East and China for Britain.

Peace in 1763 saw the usual reduction in marine strengths

but the Seven Years' War had secured for Britain an enormous empire, in the procurement of which the marines had played a significant and successful part.

Peace however was short lived and by the mid-1770s the English colonists in North America were becoming increasingly resentful at Britain's treatment of them. War loomed, and on 18 April 1775 a body of marines under Major Pitcairne was employed in the first hostile act in a war which ultimately resulted in American independence.[9] The fateful action occurred at Concord where the Provincial Congress had established a military stores dump which Pitcairne's marines were ordered to destroy. Their approach to Concord was arrested by the American militia who then pushed them back to Lexington. This British action immediately aroused the whole countryside to arms and the marines withdrew to Bunker's Hill, where in the ensuing action their performance was commended in Orders on 20 May 1775. Amongst individuals singled out for commendation were Captain Robert Ross, who commanded 5 Company, and Second Lieutenant David Collins of 3 Company, the future Judge Advocate of New South Wales.[10] The next year, the marines earned a further commendation from General Massey at Halifax.[11] Massey was to command the Marine Corps in America for another two years, after which he recorded in his General Orders of 27 February 1778 that he had not had to rebuke a single officer or marine, nor had there been a court martial in those two years. This was a rare claim and reflected the higher quality of men in the Marine Corps, for the marines contrasted to the often dissolute and abandoned type of soldier who could be found in the ranks of the British Army. It was this type of soldier whom Wellington would later describe as "the scum of the earth".[12]

The war against the American colonists became more dogged than was initially anticipated, and frequently necessitated increases in British military strength. Consequently in the six years from 1776 to 1782, the Marine

Corps had a threefold rise in strength[13] which presumably accelerated officer promotion. Yet Robert Ross remained a captain and stayed so till the American war was over.

As many had predicted, the war in America eventually went against Britain. Even before it began, Hervey, the Adjutant General, had displayed no illusions about its ultimate failure and in blunt terms he had said, "To attempt to conquer [America] internally by our land force is as wild an idea as ever controverted common sense".[14] After a succession of failures, the British Commander, Cornwallis, eventually had to surrender on 5 September 1781, and the peace treaty of Versailles was signed two years later.

By 1783 therefore, the marines had completed their first 120 years. They had served on most continents, under a variety of conditions, with mainly successful results, and could point proudly to parts of the British Empire which had been won by their fortitude and ability. Even so, their standing in the British military world was still not to be envied. In many ways they competed with the army because of similarities in their land-fighting role, organization and rank structure. To understand the relationship between Britain's long established army and her youngest service, the contemporary standing and reputation of the British Army itself needs to be viewed.

The British Army had established its reputation during the first century or so of the marines' existence, in the campaigns of three outstanding commanders: Marlborough, Wolfe and Clive. Under them, it had laid the foundations of the British Empire and, in conjunction with the Royal Navy, had demonstrated to the world a growing British ascendance in world affairs. It could point to an increasing list of outstanding achievements unparalleled in its age. Not least among these was the brilliance of Blenheim in 1704, the daring of Clive at Plassey in 1757 by which Britain gained the "jewel" of her empire, and the epoch-changing defeat of her arch-enemy the French at Quebec in 1759, by which Canada was won. The year 1759 had proved to be a brilliant one for the army. Even before that year, the run of army successes suggested, if not an invincibility, then at least a dominance among other contemporary forces. But 1759 had topped it all and rightly came to be called the British Army's "year of victories".[15] In 1759 the army captured the French possessions in West Africa and the Caribbean; and in Europe at Minden it had astonished that continent's military powers by defeating Marshal Contades' French army with a meagre six regiments of British infantry which forced Contades to remark, "I have seen what I never thought to be possible; a single line of infantry break through three lines of cavalry ranked in order of battle, and tumble them to ruin."[16]

A month after Minden, Wolfe's army had captured Quebec, a success which Lord Amherst's army quickly followed in a matter of weeks with the complete subjugation of French Canada. By the year's end, the army had won for Britain a large portion of her empire. Everywhere her army had triumphed, and humiliated her enemies. Its prestige rose even higher when, within another three years, it defeated the French in India and the Spanish in the Philippines. Its fighting reputation remained untarnished till its defeat by the American colonists in 1781, the cause of which was more the stupidity of the British government than any failure by the army; yet even that reverse was ameliorated by the existence of the rest of the Empire which the British Army could rightly claim to have won.

For the Marine Corps to compete against this catalogue of achievement was very difficult, if not impossible.

Admittedly, marines had played their part in the achievement of Britain's supremacy but both their relative recency and smaller strength militated against them, for their 120-year existence had not been without its difficulties and objections. They had faced the usual opposition to things new and innovative, and their re-raising in 1755 had been strongly opposed by the army, which felt that any increase in strength should be fully allocated to it. Instead the Prime Minister, the Duke of Newcastle, gave half the increase to the Marine Corps largely because of a personal animosity which existed between himself and the army's Commander-in-Chief, the Duke of Cumberland.[17] When the re-raised Marine Corps was then placed under command of the Admiralty's Lord High Admiral,[18] Cumberland objected to Newcastle, who disregarded him and remained firmly committed to the re-raising of the marines. This incident could not have improved army-marine relationships.

However if the army planned any reprisals against the newly re-raised corps, it would have suffered certain rebuff from the strong man of Newcastle's cabinet, Lord Anson. As the Admiralty's First Lord, he took the fledgling corps under his protection.[19] It was as well that he did because unscrupulous politicians, eager to dispense patronage to their supporters, saw the corps as a handy place from which to offer officer appointments to their clients. Though entirely typical of the period, this quite ignored the recipient's suitability or military competence and would have saddled the new corps with an officer dross which would have militated against its efficiency and reputation. Anson remained firm in resisting all such attempts to misuse the corps,[20] and, as Robert Ross was commissioned into the corps at this time (1756), Anson's policy would indicate that Ross must have been regarded as a young man of promise.

Upon the 1755 re-formation of the corps, twenty companies were allocated to Portsmouth, eighteen to Plymouth, and twelve to Chatham. These were called the Portsmouth, Plymouth, and Chatham "Divisions" and it was from these divisions that the Botany Bay detachment would volunteer thirty-two years later. The companies were numbered in rotation between the three divisions, number one being allocated to the Chatham Division, number two to the Portsmouth, number three to Plymouth, and so on. Thereafter, a marine was known by the number of his parent company and this number always appeared after his name in official documents.[21] Officers were gazetted to companies, their commissions being King's commissions signed personally by the sovereign and tenable only in the company nominated in the commission. A fresh commission was issued if the officer was transferred to another company, a practice which remained in force till 1815.[22] Those desiring to be second lieutenants applied to the Admiralty for a commission, the qualifications for which were that the applicant was to be a gentleman between the age of fifteen and twenty-one,[23] though occasionally men were promoted from the ranks.[24]

The marine privates were gained by recruiting squads which consisted of an officer, a sergeant, a corporal, a drummer, and a private, and these visited various parts of the kingdom. Men were enlisted for life,[25] although discharge by purchase was allowed on the payment of ten guineas.[26] The marines who came to New South Wales, however, were subject to special conditions in that they were given the option of discharge after three years. Bounty money of two guineas each was paid to recruits as inducement to join,[27] and the Marine Corps' daily rate of pay (see Table 1) included a food and clothing allowance.[28] Corps dress was colourful by today's standards and consisted of a red long-tailed doublet, white trousers, black headdress, black shoes, and gaiters. Insignia was worn to distinguish

Table 1 Marine Corps daily rate of pay

Rank	Pay	Subsistence*	Total
Major	15s	11s.6d	£1.6s.6d
Captain	10s	7s.6d	17s.6d
First Lieutenant	4s.8d	3s.6d	8s.2d
Second Lieutenant	3s.8d	3s	6s.8d
Quartermaster	4s.8d	3s.6d	8s.2d
Adjutant	4s	3s	7s.0d
Sergeant	1s.6d	1s	2s.6d
Corporal	1s	8d	1s.8d
Private	8d	6d	1s.2d
Drummer	1s	8d	1s.8d

Source: Cyril Field, *Britain's Sea Soldiers*, 134. Based on Millan's Succession of Colonels, 1743
* a food and clothing allowance

rank: officers wore an epaulette which differed according to the rank held, and they carried a sword.

It would appear that the army's antipathy towards the Marine Corps continued, concealed so barely that it took only minor incidents to demonstrate its covert existence. Such an incident occurred in 1764 when marines were sent to Haslar Hospital, Portsmouth, to relieve the army's Thirty-first Regiment. They were to combine garrison duties at the hospital with shipboard duty in the harbour as and when required by the local admiral. When the marines' commanding officer attempted to deploy his men in compliance with these instructions, he was appalled to find that his orders were countermanded by Colonel Welldon who as the army's local commander asserted what he conceived to be the army's superior right to deploy and use marines in whatever way it best suited army requirements. The army's negation of a Marine Corps' order was a serious matter and was referred by the corps to the Admiralty for decision, whereupon the Admiralty requested the Secretary for War to prevent Colonel Welldon "interfering with the Commanding Officer of the Marine Forces in the disposition of the Marines".[29] The instance is not an isolated one. Some eight years previously, the Secretary for War had had to censure Colonel Anstruther's Seventh Regiment over some difficulty in taking over guards from the marines. On that occasion, the Secretary had thought it necessary, as a way of bolstering the status of marine commissions, to rule that: "Officers of Marines have rank according to the date of their Commissions".[30] Clearly army officers had been deprecating marine commissions, and probably interpreting the relative cheapness of marine commissions before 1755 as an illustration of their inferiority.[31] Nor was the desire for parity helped by the government decision of 1759 to reward successful admirals by making them generals of marines on salaries of up to £1,200 a year. This irksome practice continued till 1837 and denied marine officers, no matter how meritorious their service, the top postings in their corps. Not only did it frustrate the individual, but it demeaned the corps, and certainly for its part the British Army would never have tolerated such an insult: there was no way any government could have foisted admirals on the army in such a manner.[32] Clearly this and the practice at demobilization of transfering marine regiments to the army as if they were unwanted once they had done their duty, indicated a diminished status for the Marine Corps.

It appears that this struggle for parity of recognition was keenly felt by marine officers, and this probably explains Ross's acute awareness in 1787, not only of the honour being done the Marine Corps in permitting it rather than the army to provide the Botany Bay detachment, but also of the absolute necessity for the corps to perform well to justify its selection.[33] Ross stated quite openly in his letter of gratitude to Evan Nepean, Under Secretary for the Colonies, that the corps occupied a "subordinate obscurity" from which Ross hoped it would be rescued by its performance at Botany Bay to become "an active Corps".[34] The government also was aware of the British Marines' inferior status because Ross in the same letter confirmed that it had been Nepean who had gained the New South Wales' tour of duty for the marines so that the corps could lift itself. Nepean, now that he was part of the government, was doubtlessly moved by affection for the Marine Corps, with which he had served during the American War of Independence.

This review of marine and army relations should not be concluded without citing two other illustrations of a lack of cordiality between the two services. When the New South Wales Corps arrived at Port Jackson in 1791 to relieve the marines, the two formations clashed almost immediately, and Ross, within a few days of his return to Sydney from Norfolk Island, had a violent disagreement with Captain Hill of the New South Wales Corps.[35] This in itself would not be so extraordinary, for Ross had a propensity for rancorous behaviour, but others including Lieutenant Ralph Clark also expressed a dislike of the army personnel.[36]

The second illustration is significant because it illustrates a lessened rapport between the lower ranks of both services. When the American war ended, British Army units in Plymouth and Portsmouth rioted; the riots were appalling and both towns were so menaced that for a while the situation was out of control. Such fear did the mayor and aldermen of Barnstaple have of a unit commanded by Major Fish that they requested the Secretary for War to arrange a speedy departure of the unit once it was disbanded because they were apprehensive of the "dangerous consequences" of such men being left at large.[37] However, the marine privates, far from joining their army counterparts, so distanced themselves from them that they were used as sentries to put down the mutinous army.[38] Had there been any strong affinity between marine and soldier, especially in the unsettled recriminatory period which followed the Treaty of Versailles, their use in this way would not have been possible. The marines' loyalty so pleased the Lords of the Admiralty that they commended them for it and it might well have been their good reputation in 1783 and not only their usefulness during the long sea voyage, which caused Matra (as will be seen) to suggest marines rather than the army soldiers in his "Proposal for Establishing a Settlement in New South Wales" in that same year.[39]

Marine Corps behaviour and discipline during the 1783 riots suggests again that the calibre of the ordinary marine was superior to that of his British Army counterpart in the 1780s, and this contention was later to be borne out by the unfavourable disciplinary record of the New South Wales Corps at Norfolk Island during that common period when both army and marine detachments were serving there.

Meanwhile, within the Marine Corps itself, so satisfied was Admiral Lord Howe with the standard and discipline of the marines in the Plymouth division during his inspection in

October 1785, that he ordered each marine to be granted a pint of beer. A few years later, an inspection by the Prince of Wales also resulted in a commendation of the marines for their personal appearance and the cleanliness of their barracks.[40] The soundness of the marines' esprit de corps was illustrated by the endeavours made to improve the calibre of the lower ranks — such as the establishment of a school at the Plymouth orderly room to teach reading and writing not only to men wishing to qualify for promotion, but also to their children.[41] That a military organization in a Britain of the 1780s should provide an educational service for the children of its lowest ranks was not only innovative, but indicated a social concern within the corps for both its troops and their families' welfare. This also evidenced itself later when families were permitted to accompany the troops to Botany Bay, and by a concern for the discipline of members' children, about whom orders were issued which laconically stated that "children who want flogging [are] to be reported to the Adjutant".[42] Corps discipline was strengthened when a system was instituted for entering minor infractions on regimental defaulter sheets and filing them in what the marines called "The Black book" — a description which carried its own censorious connotation. After 1784, these sheets were issued to captains commanding companies and so brought the level of responsibility for discipline and efficiency closer to the men.[43] Company pride, usually competitive, was doubtlessly served as a result. Though small in themselves, all these procedures are means by which morale and discipline are furthered, and an esprit de corps established.

On the other hand, the discipline of the British Army's lower ranks was not earning for it the praise which was being bestowed upon the British Marines, for it was not to be so many years after 1788 that Wellington felt constrained to describe his troops in scathing terms. After the battle of Badajos, his troops not only plundered, raped, and murdered, but also tore off women's ear lobes to acquire gold earrings, and wrenched fingers from live hands so as to procure more quickly gold rings from nuns, women and children alike.[44] Even under Wellington's own stern control, his army's discipline after the battle of Vittoria degenerated to such licentious anarchy that he had to advise Lord Bathurst that until discipline amongst "our vagabond soldiers" could be restored, the army would "do no good" even by its greatest victories.[45] Three days later he would reinforce his disgust for the "common soldier" by advising Bathurst that it was quite impossible for him or anyone else to command a British army when it was impossible to keep "such men as some of our soldiers are" in order.[46] One of the causes of this state of affairs lay in the type of man recruited into the eighteenth century British Army. Its recruits were drawn from the poorer sections of society. Criminals made up a proportion of it. Recruiting squads found the readiest response from the semi-employed unskilled portion of the population who were attracted by the bounty paid to recruits. It has been estimated that the average army battalion contained fifty drunkards, plunderers, stragglers, and criminals.[47] It does not surprise then that when Wellington in 1813 asked his colonels to find him men who could mint French currency, forty counterfeiters were discovered at St Jean de Luz alone.[48] When magistrates gave the choice of a jail term or military service to convicted criminals, they were impressing criminals into the services. If the Marine Corps received its share of recruits in this way, its more wholesome ethos appears to have exercised a regenerative influence, for nowhere did the corps have the disciplinary problems which the army was experiencing. Australia's first army unit, the New South Wales Corps, illustrated the problem. In 1797, a detachment of the New South Wales Corps travelling out to Sydney on the *Lady Shore* seized the ship. The guard, which included six offenders from London's Savoy Military Prison plus some French and Irish deserters, murdered the captain and mate. After the mutiny, the troops handed over the vessel to Spanish authorities in Rio de Janeiro. This incident evaporated all trust that shipowners had in using soldiers of the New South Wales Corps as guards and in 1798 they began to recruit their own.[49]

It is strange therefore that, considering the respective standards of the two services, the British Marines appear to have been Britain's military underdogs. They had a sound fighting record, and were without the disciplinary aberrations which were bedevilling the British Army. But in the stultifying atmosphere of military hierarchy, new services and other innovations were then, as now, resisted. And so it was with the marines: they were a smaller and relatively new service being made to serve a tough apprenticeship to obtain recognition. It was for this reason that Ross was initially so mindful of the need for them to do well at Botany Bay. He saw the corps' service there as being partly a public relations exercise which if successful would do something to lift its reputation and move it to a somewhat closer parity with the army. In the circumstances it was a pity that the greatest obstacle to that desirable aim was to be the behaviour of Major Robert Ross himself.

Another cause of the Marine Corps' inferior status was its attempt to break into what had been hitherto the closed military community of the navy and army. In the eighteenth century this was tantamount to an outsider breaking into Britain's integrated social system. It was a society which had its boundaries, margins, and internal structure of church, county society, and aristocracy. As the Empire expanded, the need to expand that society also increased but in such a way that the old order could be retained. One way in which this was achieved was by increasing the availability of officer commissions. Thus the "marginal man"[50] was drawn into the circle of honour. But such marginal intruders were graded: Irish peers were not the equal of English peers; Edinburgh Doctors of Laws were not the equal of their Oxford counterparts; and marine officers were not the equal of Guards' officers because the Marine Corps was not the equal of the army. The corps had been admitted to the military class but with an inferior status, an illustration of which was that in 1780 it possessed only one officer with an inherited title whereas the Life Guards, Grenadier Guards, and Coldstream Guards together had forty-seven.[51]

The 1780s saw the first contacts between marine and convict. As early as 1784 marines had guarded convicts in the prison ship *Dunkirk* at Plymouth,[52] and in a number of ways the two groups had much in common. They both came from the lower orders, shared the same impecunious backgrounds, as well as the lack of an adequate education and the franchise. In the lives of both, endurance, suffering, patience, and submission were common experiences and although the similarities ought not to be exaggerated, neither ought they be overlooked as causing at least a part of the relative tolerance which developed between the two groups at Port Jackson.

Punishment too was an experience common to both, though as eighteenth century military punishment was more severe than civil punishment, it was harsher for marine than convict. At a court martial in 1765, a marine was found guilty of theft and desertion, for which he was shot by firing squad; for desertion only, another received a thousand lashes, as did another for striking a sergeant. Sentences of a thousand lashes were not uncommon. It was not without reason therefore that Americans during their war referred to British soldiers as "lobsters" and "Bloody-backs".[53] Convict sentences at Port Jackson were considerably lighter than these.[54]

The conclusion of the American War of Independence by the Treaty of Versailles in 1783 brought to Britain an interlude of ten years' peace before France would declare war on 1 February 1793. The Marine Corps used the period to adjust to the usual reduction after demobilization by retaining only those marines who were the "stoutest, fittest, and healthiest men", in excess of 5 feet 6 inches tall (1.68 m) and under forty years of age.⁵⁵ It was as well for the New South Wales colony that such a culling occurred because it was from these soldiers that the volunteers for the rigours of the place would come. The reduction in strengths was a severe one: ten of the seventy companies were removed from the corps Order of Battle, whilst the remaining sixty companies were each reduced in strength to three sergeants, three corporals, two drummers and fifty privates,⁵⁶ which would be the strength of the Botany Bay companies. Officer strengths were also pruned and some forty-six officers were placed on half pay as from 30 April 1786.⁵⁷ The purpose of establishing a pool of half-pay officers was to retain their availability to supply the needs of future contingencies, and the officers from this pool would have been used to make up any shortfall in officer requirements for the Botany Bay tour of duty if full-time officers had been unwilling to volunteer.⁵⁸

The peacetime period after 1783 was also used by the corps to turn its attention to such "household" matters as introducing a system of time-expired clothing issues,⁵⁹ deciding not to issue NCOs or marines with greatcoats, but to continue with the issue of watchcoats, and with issuing capes for sentry duty only. For the first time, Standing Orders were issued for the divisions,⁶⁰ and regulations were promulgated for marines ashore and afloat. The lack of pensions had for a long time been a matter of concern to officers. Pensions did not exist because there was no retiring age for officers, their service continuing till they died or went on half pay. An Officers' Widows Fund existed to help the wives and families of those officers killed in action,⁶¹ but this did not allay a widespread concern amongst officers about their retirement benefits. Consequently, in March 1787 a memorial was prepared by officers of the three divisions and presented by General MacKenzie to the Lords of the Admiralty. It met with some success, for on 5 November 1791 the Earl of Chatham gained from the government permission for aged officers to retire on full pay,[62] and many took advantage of this breakthrough.

Such then were the mundane matters that occupied the attention of the corps in the dreary period of the mid-1780s. No prospect of war was apparent to enliven the doleful and deadening experience of peacetime soldiering and so the corps resigned itself to its rather unexciting existence.

It was whilst the corps languished in this torpor that the government announced its decision to solve the problem of overcrowding in its jails and prison hulks by sending convicts to Botany Bay, where a penal settlement was to be established. Such a venture would require a military presence for which the British Marines would be chosen. Why they and not the army were selected was not stated by Lord Sydney, but factors such as the long voyage, the current favourable reputation of the marines after their exemplary performance during the army riots of 1783, Matra's preference for them in his Botany Bay plan of the same year, and the marines' previous experience in guarding convicts on prison hulks, would all have had their influence. Major Ross believed that the corps' opportunity was "entirely owing" to the desire of Evan Nepean to redress the marines' inferior status.[63] The Botany Bay service was to be the first instance of the Marine Corps being employed outside its usual line of duty. Even so Ross entertained no doubt that it would perform creditably for he intended the detachment to strain every nerve "in the faithful and diligent discharge" of its duty.

Good intentions therefore were not lacking. A unique opportunity had been given the marines to prove themselves worthy of the confidence Nepean and the government had placed in them. Nor, as will be seen, was there any lack of enthusiasm within the corps itself to join the Botany Bay detachment. Consequently, with hopes high and expectations confident, the Marine Corps set about forming and preparing its detachment for a new type of service in a new land, remote, lonely, and mostly unknown.

1

Preparations for the Great Adventure

The first mention of a detachment of British Marines for New South Wales appeared in James Maria Matra's 1783 plan to establish a colony at Botany Bay. Matra had formed a close association with that man of wealth and influence, Sir Joseph Banks, while serving as a midshipman on Cook's *Endeavour* in 1770.[1] In the following years, neither had forgotten the favourable impression both had formed of New South Wales, and now that Matra had himself become a man of influence as Britain's consular representative for Morocco and was associated politically with Fox, who was in coalition government with Lord North, he put on paper a plan entitled "A Proposal for Establishing a Settlement in New South Wales" which he sent to the government on 23 August 1783. In it, he foresaw the colony as fulfilling two purposes: firstly to be a base from which commerce could be conducted, and secondly to be a haven for those American loyalists who, now that Britain had lost the American War of Independence, were dispossessed. Britain, he felt, owed them relocation. Initially therefore, he did not envisage the colony as a penal one, and for that reason he estimated that only two companies of marines would be necessary. These, he suggested, should be selected from such of that corps as best understood "husbandry, or manufactures".[2] He planned that they should be the vanguard to go ahead of the main body of colonists to prepare for their reception.

Fox and North however had little time to consider the plan because their government fell a few months later and they were replaced by the government of Pitt the Younger. Pitt's Secretary of State for Home Affairs was Lord Sydney, a man of inadequate ability whose successor, Lord Grenville, said of him that he was "unequal to the most ordinary business of his office".[3] The Home Affairs portfolio included responsibility not only for Colonial Affairs but also for the nation's penal system which was being strained to its limits. Edmund Burke highlighted this to the House of Commons in March 1785 when he revealed that there were one hundred thousand prisoners in English jails.[4] The system's problems had been exacerbated when transportation of Britain's convicts to America had ceased with the loss of the American colonies. As a result, England's jails had become so overcrowded that ships which had become unseaworthy were being pressed into commission as prison hulks to accommodate the overflow. As these hulks were moored up rivers in full view of the adjacent population, there arose a mounting public concern at the possibility of prison breaks and the subsequent threat not only to public safety but also to community health. This concern was not without basis: convicts aboard the prison hulk at Plymouth rose on 24 March 1786 and were not subdued till eight had been shot dead and thirty-six wounded.[5] This politically sensitive issue confronted Lord Sydney just at the time when Matra, urged no doubt by Sir Joseph Banks, arrived with his plan. The discussion between the two was to have great significance for Australia because Lord Sydney apparently observed that Botany Bay, if established as a penal settlement, could provide the solution to his jail problem.[6] Matra in all probability was encouraged by the promising reception Lord Sydney had given his scheme and so he added an addendum to the effect that a further use for Botany Bay could be its utilization as a colony for transported convicts. This addition failed to produce an immediate government response. But Matra's resolve was not lessened for he appears to have explained his scheme to Admiral Sir George Young who incorporated its most salient points in his own recommendation which the Attorney General, Pepper Arden, then submitted to Lord Sydney on 13 January 1785.[7]

But Lord Sydney again chose to shelve the proposal and to await the recommendations of a committee which the government had set up to enquire into the feasibility of establishing a penal colony on Lemaine Island, four hundred miles up the Gambia River in Africa.[8] This was not the first time that Gambia had been assessed for its suitability as a penal colony: in 1775 and 1776, when the American war had interrupted transportation, 746 convicts had been sent to Gambia, of which 334 had died, 271 had deserted, and nothing definite had become known of the rest.[9] The debacle caused a "perpetual commotion".[10] Consequently the fact that in 1785 Gambia could again be considered as a place for a penal colony demonstrated the desperate situation which the overcrowded jails and prison hulks were posing. The government's committee of enquiry was told on 9 May 1785 by Evan Nepean that the government plan envisaged the despatch to Lemaine of 200 convicts "too dangerous to remain in this country".[11] They were to become self-supporting; their number was to increase by annual increments; and they were to be visited occasionally by a guard ship stationed down river at Yannimaroo.[12] The government's plan received a setback when Captain John Nevan of the African trade told the committee that he had been on the Gambia River opposite Yannimaroo the previous year and had found the place so unhealthy that he had lost six of his twenty-one crew with fever. He had seen five European traders there but they were so ill and emaciated that they were hardly able to crawl.[13] He went on to express the opinion that the whole of his crew would have died within a year had they stayed there, and he felt that if fever failed to claim those convicts which the government was considering sending there, then murder by natives certainly would. Captain Nevan's testimony was followed by that of Captain Thomas Nesbitt who also had been there on a ship in 1780: he confirmed what Nevan had said and went on to report that he had met a captain there who actually had lost the whole of his crew in a year.[14] With such damning evidence, the government's interest cooled, though it did respond to a recommendation of the committee that the southern coast of Africa around the Das Voltas Bay area be reconnoitred for a suitable location. The sloop *Nautilus* was sent to investigate and report.

Meanwhile public apprehension continued to grow. In March 1786, the lord mayor and aldermen of London, reflecting public concern at the current crime wave and the threat to public health and safety posed by the overflowing jails, petitioned the government to restore transportation.[15] The press took up the public concern: the *Daily Universal Register* (later renamed *The Times*) complained that Londoners were victims of a crime wave.[16] The same paper tended more to eulogize Botany Bay than to present it as a place of horror and dread: consequently one sailor ostentatiously stole from a shop in Piccadilly and thereafter appeared in court "with every mark of joy on his countenance, and twirling his hat over his head, hollowed [sic] out, 'Botany Bay, a hoy!'" In later cases a young forger begged to join the First Fleet, and a soldier, tired of serving, committed a robbery so that he could be sent to the penal settlement.[17] Accordingly, such was the threat to public safety that an increasing concern from a variety of quarters forced the issue; the government could vacillate no longer, and midway through 1786 it apparently began planning a final resolution of the problem, for the press reported that a plan was being formed for settling a colony at Botany Bay "for the reception of felons".

Whether or not the return of HMS *Nautilus* from Das

Voltas Bay at the end of July with the news of its unsuitability for a penal colony,[18] or the warning sent on 1 August by Sir James Harris, British Ambassador to The Hague, that the French intended establishing colonies in the East Indies,[19] or the announcement by Colonel Cathcart upon his arrival from Mauritius on 14 August that the French had the capacity to send considerable naval forces to the East Indies[20] — whether or not these tilted the balance is unknown. Whatever the reasons for the decision, on 18 August 1786 Lord Sydney wrote to the Lords Commissioners of the Treasury at Whitehall. After acknowledging the overcrowding of the jails, the possibility of prisoner escapes and the spread of infections which would result, he advised that "His Majesty has thought it advisable to fix upon Botany Bay" as a likely place for a penal colony. He then went on to ask the Treasury to provide a proper number of vessels to convey 750 convicts, and three companies of British Marines whose role would be to exert "a proper degree of subordination and regularity" in the new settlement.[21] Matra's plan had provided for two companies only; Lord Sydney's current proposal was for three companies; in the finish however, four companies were despatched. Lord Sydney called the detachment "the Marine Corps", which was a loose use of the word "corps", and he advised the Treasury that during the voyage and after disembarkation, its troops were to be victualled by the Royal Navy. His preliminary estimate of the detachment's strength was that it would be about 180 in addition to a command staff of 15, which was a close estimate, for 212 would be its final strength. As well, Lord Sydney felt it advisable that 200 island women be procured from nearby islands as companions for the men.[22] He apparently thought better of this proposal, omitting it from his final plan.

To his letter, Lord Sydney attached an enclosure titled "Heads of a Plan" which, amongst other things, expanded on the role of the marines.[23] A warship together with a two-hundred-ton tender was to accompany the fleet and it appears that the original intention was for the marines to travel in these two ships, until the need for convict surveillance suggested that some marines should be put on each transport as guards during the voyage. After the fleet had arrived at New South Wales, the Marine Corps detachment was to form a military establishment on shore for the dual purpose of preserving order and protecting the settlement against the natives. As many marines as possible were to be tradesmen such as carpenters, sawyers, smiths, and potters.[24] Whether Lord Sydney intended these artificers to perform some of the civil construction work of the colony, or whether they were to use their expertise to guide the convict labourers, he did not state. It was unfortunate that he failed to do so because clearer instructions would have clarified the position when Ross later refused to allow the marines to supervise convicts.

Thirteen days later, on 31 August, Lord Sydney sent his next letter to the Admiralty reiterating the need for a force of 160 marine privates to preserve order, and authorizing the Commissary of the colony to issue tools and all utensils needed to erect the marines' barracks to provide for their comfort. He stipulated that their term of service was not to exceed three years, and he felt that the service ought to prove attractive to NCOs and men, though if this failed to be so, he authorized the further inducement of bounties. Discharge after three years' service was to be calculated, not from the date of leaving England, but from the date of landing in the colony.[25] Such a short term would be an attractive alternative to the normal requirement of service for life.

Tenders to procure the necessary ships for the fleet were then called in the form of Admiralty advertisements posted in coffee houses frequented by shipowners.[26] From the response, tenders for the charter of six transports and three storeships were accepted.[27] The transports were the *Alexander* (452 tons), *Charlotte* (345 tons), *Friendship* (278 tons), *Lady Penrhyn* (338 tons), *Scarborough* (418 tons), and *Prince of Wales*

(333 tons); the storeships were the *Borrowdale* (272 tons), *Fishburn* (378 tons), and *Golden Grove* (331) tons. They were all comparatively new vessels and had been built after 1780.[28] To these nine ships were added two warships: the *Berwick*, renamed the *Sirius*, and a small naval tender, the *Supply*. The *Berwick* had originally been built as a storeship for the East India Company but before leaving the dockyard she had been destroyed by fire down to the waterline. The burnt out hulk had been purchased by the government, fitted out with the "refuse of the yards",[29] and sent on two voyages as a victualler to America and the West Indies. It was upon her return from these two voyages that she was again sent to the dockyard at Deptford and fitted out as the *Sirius* of 610 tons with a crew of 160 men. Six weeks later, Captain Arthur Phillip was appointed to her command with instructions to prepare her for sea.[30] Meanwhile, the *Supply*, a much too small naval transport of 170 tons, was similarly ordered to Deptford for preparation.[31]

Phillip, fifty years of age in 1788, had been born in London of an English mother and a German father who was a language teacher. In 1755 he had joined the Royal Navy as a mishipman, and saw service in the Mediterranean and West Indies. In 1763 he had retired on half pay to take up farming, but when Portugal went to war with Spain in 1774, he had been appointed to serve the Portuguese navy, which he did with such distinction that the Portuguese long remained grateful to him. When the American war broke out, he returned to the Royal Navy and rose to the rank of captain. At the war's end, he again returned to farming until 1786 when he was appointed Governor of New South Wales.[32] He had been married, though not happily, and had no children. He was not a flamboyant person but rather retiring and this might have accounted for Admiral Lord Howe's opinion that he himself would not have chosen Phillip for the governorship.[33] Significantly however, a neighbour to Phillip's farm was George Rose, Secretary to the Treasury, and as the Treasury was heavily involved in the Botany Bay project, it might well have been Rose who influenced the appointment. Possible further evidence for this contention was provided later when Phillip named the second settlement at New South Wales, Rose Hill.[34] (It was later renamed Parramatta.) Whoever selected Phillip made a choice most beneficial to the colony.

With Phillip's appointment decided, preparations were then begun to form the marine detachment for the colony. On 8 October, Stephens, as Secretary to the Admiralty, wrote to the commanders of the marine divisions at Chatham, Plymouth and Portsmouth in the south of England asking them to provide their proportion of volunteers for the detachment.[35] Portsmouth in particular was to provide eighty men: volunteers were preferred but any shortfall was to be obtained by compulsion if necessary. Those volunteering were offered the choice of discharge in England or New South Wales provided they served the full three years and earned a record of good behaviour. If a discharge in New South Wales was chosen, permission to settle there would be granted and the marine settler would be placed upon relief so as to enable himself to become established. Further details for those wishing to remain in the colony were promised later. In the same letter, Stephens instructed the divisional commanders to send him the names of those officers who volunteered, though the proviso was added that if the required number could not be obtained from volunteers amongst officers on full pay, the Admiralty then would call on officers on half pay.[36] That the Admiralty should doubt their willingness to serve wherever and whenever wanted, considerably angered the full-pay officers and as things turned out, there was a quick response from them. The Admiralty had not meant to impugn them but had intended giving those on full pay the option of preferring a posting of a more military nature than Botany Bay.[37] The response from those eager to serve was immediate: within six days — that is by 14 October 1786 — two hundred men had volunteered from which the commandant at Plymouth chose a "fine detachment" amongst which were men from "all trades". By 8 November, so heavy had been the response that the Admiralty was forced to publish that no more were required.[38] In fact, such was the eagerness of the men to volunteer that recourse to a ballot was necessary.[39] By the same date, the response from officers had been similarly overwhelming, and late officer applicants were advised that there was now "no room".[40] This rush to join the Botany Bay detachment so severely depleted the strength of the Portsmouth garrison that those remaining were forced to do guard duty two nights out of every three.[41] That the Plymouth commandant had been able to gain so many soldiers who were also tradesmen was not simply fortuitous: at the time, a growing number of soldiers were unemployed tradesmen who had been made redundant by technological change.[42] A high degree of fitness was demanded from volunteer officers and consequently, applications from those who were not fit, such as Lieutenant Coutts who lacked a right hand, were refused. Coutts was replaced by Captain James Campbell, then serving on the guardship *Carnatic*, who shortly became second-in-command of the detachment.[43]

After Stephens' call for volunteers went out on 8 October, Brevet Major Robert Ross of the Chatham Division lost no time in applying, and four days after the advertisement he was appointed commander of the detachment.[44] As such, he was to play a leading and controversial role in the colony's affairs during its first four years. The officers who volunteered next after Ross were Captain Tench and Lieutenant Timins.[45]

A week later the divisions were advised that the marines' request for their wives and children to accompany them had been agreed to in principle though Stephens stipulated that their numbers would be regulated by prevailing circumstances, which left everyone wondering.[46] Those officers who had volunteered for the tour of duty were then alerted to hold themselves in readiness, and Stephens asked that the two captains junior to Major Ross, and the next six lieutenants on the sea duty roster, whose names he asked be sent to him, be alerted for embarkation. To establish uniform policy, he stipulated that once an officer had been selected for Botany Bay service, the Admiralty alone would adjudicate on any requests for change or variation.[47]

On 15 November, whilst applications from officers were being processed, Stephens requisitioned the weapons and ammunition for the detachment from the Board of Ordnance. These included one hundred new weapons,[48] ten thousand musket flints and one thousand carbines.[49] On Stephens' orders, these were to be loaded on the *Sirius* which was still fitting out on the Thames at Deptford.[50] Unfortunately however, the *Sirius* was to sail without the ammunition.

Preparation gained momentum on 21 November. On that day the government was asked to raise the manpower ceiling of the Marine Corps to compensate it for the loss of its four companies going to Botany Bay.[51] As well, the Admiralty advised Lord Sydney of the ship and shore ration scales which would be applicable to the Botany Bay marines, although circumstances were to prevent any compliance with the shore scale two months after Port Jackson was reached.[52] However, the Block Ration Scale (see Table 2) was laid down.[53] To ensure the availability of adequate stocks, Lord Sydney requested two years' reserve of provisions.[54] Also on the same day, because nothing more had been heard about the number of wives who would be permitted to accompany the detachment, a request from the detachment

Table 2 Marines' weekly ship ration (1786)

Day	Bread (lb)	Beef (lb)	Pork (lb)	Peas (pt)	Oatmeal (pt)	Rum (pt)	Butter (oz)	Cheese (lb)	Vinegar (pt)
Sun.	1		1	½		½			
Mon.	1				1	½	2	¼	
Tues.	1	2				½			
Wed.	1			½	1	½	2	¼	
Thurs.	1		1	½		½			
Fri.	1			½	1	½	2	¼	
Sat.	1	2				½			½
	7 (3.2 kg)*	4 (1.8 kg)	2 (900 g)	2 (1.1 l)	3 (1.7 l)	3½ (2 l)	6 (170 g)	¾ (340 g)	½ (284 ml)

Marines' weekly shore ration (1786)

Bread or flour 7 lb (3.2 kg)
Beef 7 lb or **pork** 4 lb (1.8 kg)
Peas 3 pt (1.7 l)
Butter 6 oz (170 g)
Rice ½ lb (227 g) or a further 1 lb (454 g) of flour

Source: *Historical Records of New South Wales*, vol 1, part 2, 29
* approximate metric conversion in brackets

was sent by the Admiralty to Lord Sydney, suggesting that ten wives per company be allowed.[55] This number was felt to be reasonable.[56] In the event, twenty-eight wives and seventeen children went.[57] In the same letter, the Admiralty sought clarification on whether or not the marines would be expected to pay for their rations whilst ashore in New South Wales. The query arose because it was usual practice for marines whilst serving on ships to be victualled similarly to seamen without any deduction from pay; ultimately, it was decided that their rations would be free.[58]

Up to this point, arrangements for raising the detachment had lacked legal sanction, but the situation was regularized on 24 November when the Privy Council gave its sanction.[59]

Late in November and during December, the officers began to be posted. On 28 November, Lieutenant George Johnston — later the Lieutenant Colonel Johnston of the New South Wales Corps who arrested Governor Bligh in 1808 — was ordered to board the transports *Lady Penrhyn* and *Alexander* at Woolwich with thirty NCOs and privates. There they guarded convicts, of which those who boarded the *Alexander* at Woolwich on 6 January 1787 were the first convicts to board the First Fleet.[60] A day after Johnston's posting, Captain David Collins — son of the General Collins who was commanding the Plymouth Division[61] — was appointed Judge Advocate both to the colony and to the marine detachment.[62] He had had no training in the law. In the days following, other officers were given their embarkation orders.

In the meantime, preparations at Deptford aboard the *Sirius* were nearing completion, and on 5 December, Captain John Hunter RN boarded her as post captain, taking over command of her from Phillip.[63] On the 9th she sailed down the Thames from Deptford to Longreach, mooring the same afternoon to load her naval ammunition. About the same time, the fitting out of three of the five transports at Deptford was completed, and on 15 and 21 November they sailed, passing the *Sirius* at Longreach on their way to the fleet rendezvous on the Mother Bank anchorage off Portsmouth. By then, only the *Lady Penrhyn* and *Alexander* remained in the Thames, and these were detained to await their full complement of convicts from Woolwich and Newgate. It would be another two months before the whole fleet would be concentrated on the Mother Bank off Portsmouth on 22 February. By then, Lieutenant George Johnston's party had given seventy-five days' guard duty of convicts on *Lady Penrhyn* and *Alexander* even before fleet duty began. This demonstrates the fact that service for the marines began in varying periods of up to six months before the fleet sailed.

Because security aboard the *Alexander* was causing concern, Ross inspected it and ordered alterations to the convicts' handcuffs. Even so, some convicts managed to slip theirs off. Escape however was impossible because every hatchway was guarded by marines who occasionally entered the holds crammed full of convicts by way of a ladder lowered specially and temporarily for the purpose. On these occasions, in spite of the increased vigilance of the sentries, additional precautions were judged necessary and pairs of convicts were handcuffed and chained together. Their every movement thereafter had to be concerted in tandem.

Before the year ended, Pitt asked Nepean the likely cost of the Botany Bay project "including the expenses incurred in the detachment of Marines".[64] Nepean advised that the overall cost for the three-year tour of duty would be £15,971.14s.6d which consisted of £14,089 for pay and clothing, and £1,882.14s.6d for ordnance items. His estimate however turned out to be a considerable understatement: one item alone, the marines' pay, had by 1791 amounted to £18,784.[65] In addition to the figures supplied, Major Ross was to receive £250 for the lieutenant governorship. Bearing in mind that annual allowances paid to the Judge Advocate, chaplain, and surgeon were £182.10s, the allowance paid to Ross was not only the highest in the colony except for the

£1,000 paid to the Governor,[66] but also it appeared on the Civil List rather than the Military List. This ought to have indicated clearly enough to Ross, that he was to fulfill the dual roles of Lieutenant Governor and commander of the marines, both of which subordinated him to the Governor. Events will show that Ross at times failed to appreciate the subordinate nature of his situation.

As the year drew to a close, Phillip wrote to Stephens for direction on a host of contingencies.[67] As a result, Stephens told him that for disciplinary purposes, he could exchange marines from the four companies on a one-for-one basis from the reserve of thirty-four held aboard the *Sirius* or *Supply*. Phillip was told that when sick marines were landed in a foreign port, they were to be treated in the same manner as sick seamen, and that treatment would be paid for by the Commissioners for the Sick and Hurt. He asked whether marines were to be supplied with fresh meat when the crew of the *Sirius* was similarly supplied, but in a typically bureaucratic reply his implied suggestion was denied, even though he raised the matter twice.[68] This angered him and he replied that as the Navy Board had failed to consult him on the matter of the marines' rations, he declined to accept responsibility for any discord or consequence which might follow.[69] This remonstrance appears to have had the desired effect because marines (and convicts) were supplied during the voyage with fresh meat when in port. Phillip also asked whether the wives of marines were to be victualled as supernumaries, and he was told that they were to be victualled on the same scale as soldiers' wives travelling on transports.

The year closed with consideration being given to the distribution of marines and convicts throughout the fleet. Nepean asked Mr Thomas, the victualler's agent, to make the necessary allocations, which Thomas did.[70] (See Table 3.) These figures were to be amended before sailing day to make provision for a marine guard aboard the *Lady Penrhyn*. As only 174 marines could travel aboard the transports, 34

Table 3 Distribution of marines and convicts, 1786

Ship	Convicts		Marines	
	Men	Women	Men	Women*
Scarborough (at Portsmouth)	210	–	32	4
Friendship (at Plymouth)	80	24	40	3
Charlotte (at Plymouth)	100	24	40	3
Alexander (at Deptford)	210	–	32	4
Lady Penrhyn (at Deptford)	–	102	–	4
Ship to be supplied				
(*Prince of Wales*)		30	30	30
	600	180	174	48

Source: *Historical Records of New South Wales*, vol 1, part 2, 42
* wives of marines

plus Ross, Dawes, Long and Furzer were to travel on the *Sirius* and the *Supply* and embarkation orders for these were issued on 11 January.[71] It is unclear whether those who travelled by *Sirius* and *Supply* were in the nature of a reserve or a "left out of battle" (LOB) element. On the one hand, their numbers were needed to make up the companies' strengths, but on the other, some sort of "reserve" remained on board the *Sirius* after her arrival at Port Jackson, and this was called upon to supply replacements for those who were sick.[72] In any case all 34 privates came from the Portsmouth Division.[73]

The first day of 1787 saw the warrant issued which confirmed the appointment of Captain David Collins as Judge Advocate to the marines.[74] His appointment, for which he was to be paid an allowance of ten shillings per day, was by a warrant specially issued by the Admiralty. He was authorized to officiate at courts martial and general courts martial for the trial of officers, NCOs, and Marine Other Ranks, according to the rules and regulations of the Admiralty. This stipulation was significant in that he was being required to perform his office in strict accord with those Admiralty regulations applicable to the Marine Corps. Consequently, when a question arose later as to Phillip's legal competence to issue warrants for general courts martial (the courts martial which try officers), Collins was to decide the point by a strict adherence to Admiralty law and precedence.

January also saw the detachment starting to come together as a unit, completing those many incidental arrangements involved in a unit's formation. Consequently on 2 January the Commanding Officer of the Plymouth Division was ordered to supply Ross with a set of colours if they could be "spared".[75] These colours were probably those which were presented to the corps in 1760 and seem to have been those carried at the battle for Belle Isle in 1761 and subsequently taken to America in 1775.[76] The design of the regimental colour was a wreath of thistles and roses on a white background.[77]

By mid January, embarkation stores were arriving daily and a stock reserve was gradually assembled aboard the *Sirius*.[78] Many of the items came from the various divisions and were in such poor condition that on 22 January, Captain Shea condemned many of the arms and accoutrements, and ordered their replacement.[79] Moreover, deficiencies in quite important items were observed by Phillip who complained that no medical stores for either marines or convicts had yet arrived.[80] He requested that the scale of medical issues for the marines be the same as that for the navy.[81]

Meanwhile batches of convicts were arriving aboard the various transports and required surveillance by marines. Consequently Captain Shea, Lieutenants Kellow and Morrison, and 31 Other Ranks, were aboard the *Scarborough* waiting for their complement of convicts who were walking to Portsmouth from Woolwich.[82] They arrived on 2 March and were amongst a party of 210 who arrived at the dockside under guard of a troop of Light Horse. The seas however were too rough for them to be conveyed out to the transports, so they were temporarily placed aboard HMS *Gorgon*, then lying in Blackhouse Hole in Plymouth Bay where surveillance was provided by guardships moored alongside.[83] The seas abated on 4 March, enabling the convicts to be transhipped from the *Gorgon* by sailing lighters to the *Alexander* and *Scarborough*, where surveillance was taken over by marine guards, Private John Easty included.[84] Their surveillance must have been thorough, for next day they detected a convict with a hidden knife in his shoe, for which he received twelve lashes.[85] By now the *Alexander* convicts had been aboard for three months and were showing increased sickness as a result; it was decided therefore to smoke and whitewash between her decks using two decked lighters from the dockyard.

By mid March the final composition of the fleet was completed when the *Friendship* and *Charlotte* arrived with the Plymouth convicts on the 13th and 14th respectively.[86] Captain Watkin Tench commanded the marine detachment aboard the *Charlotte*,[87] and Captain-Lieutenant James Meredith commanded that aboard the *Friendship*.[88] The arrival of Adjutant Long and Quartermaster Furzer aboard *Sirius* in late February had completed the officer complement, and the Admiralty's fear that sufficient officers might not volunteer for such an unusual tour of duty proved groundless.[89]

The officer who was going to have the most prominent influence on the colony's affairs was Major Robert Ross. He had been born in 1740 and at the age of sixteen had been commissioned into a company of the British Marines division at Chatham. During the Seven Years' War he had served in North America at the siege of Louisbourg in 1758 and a year later was present at the capture of Quebec. He returned to Chatham and was promoted to first lieutenant in 1759 but in spite of the war lasting another four years, he received no further promotion during it. In 1773, he had been promoted to captain-lieutenant and despatched to America where, as the commander of 5 Company, 1st Battalion of Marines,[90] such was his performance that he was mentioned in orders.[91] When Captain Stephen Ellis, the commander of 39 Company, was killed at the Battle of Bunker's Hill on 17 June 1775, Ross replaced him. In 1779 he returned to England in HMS *Ardent*, but in the English Channel the ship was captured by the French on 17 August and Ross was taken prisoner of war from which he was later released in exchange for some French prisoners.[92] His next service was in the Mediterranean and West Indies from 1781–82, and on 19 March 1783 he was promoted to brevet major, which is to say that he was promoted to the honorary rank of major but without major's pay.[93] Brevet rank was not substantive, or actual, rank; it was honorary rank usually given as a charitable gesture for lengthy rather than outstanding service. Yet to reach even that substituted rank Ross had taken twenty-seven years. His promotion therefore had been very slow and his twenty-seven years to reach brevet major rank compared with the eighteen it took James Meredith[94] and Watkin Tench.[95] Consequently, it would appear on the dual evidence of an inordinately sluggish promotion as well as the award even then of only brevet rank, that Ross's military career had been both mediocre and unpromising. In addition, of the twenty officers who ultimately served with the detachment during its tour of duty, only four were not promoted after their return to England. Ross was one of them.[96]

The question arises then as to why such an officer was chosen not only to command the detachment but also to be the Lieutenant Governor of New South Wales. Those who appointed him have not left us with their reasons for doing so, but his was an age of patronage. To gain preferment, people needed patrons and the benefits of alliance to avoid being an impotent outsider. The use of patrons was widespread: Bligh had two, Sir Joseph Banks and the Earl of Vincent; John Macarthur's patron was a family friend, George Watson, who was private secretary to the Secretary of State for the Colonies, Lord Camden; George Johnston of the marines was attached to the Duke of Northumberland; and Major Robert Ross used the patronage of Evan Nepean, with whom he had served in the American war and who had since become Under Secretary in the Home Office.[97] Ross's use of Nepean's help was apparently widely known, for in an article in the *London Chronicle* of 23 June 1789, the claim was made that Ross owed his civil appointment as Lieutenant Governor to both Nepean and Sir John Jervis, respectively former purser and former captain of HMS *Fondroyant*.[98] Whether Nepean had a similar influence on Ross's military appointment is difficult to establish, but it was very likely. Ross was forty-eight years old when he assumed command of the detachment, and he had had thirty-two years' service. He was therefore, above all else, a very experienced officer, and that fact must be given considerable weight in assessing his future performance.

The company commanders were Captain-Lieutenants James Meredith and Watkin Tench, and Captains John Shea and James Campbell.[99] As well as being a company commander, Campbell became second-in-command to Ross. Initially at least, they had been friends, and when Campbell was appointed, Ross laboured hard with Nepean to gain him an additional preferment.[100] Nepean however did not respond even though Campbell had then served thirty years. Officially at least, Nepean gave no reason for his disinclination, but as Campbell had attained only the rank of captain in those thirty years, he had probably provided Nepean with little cause to grant anything, let alone preferment. New South Wales, to which Campbell travelled aboard the *Lady Penrhyn*, was to be his first service outside England. This might have been a reason for his joining the detachment and another might have been that both he and Ross were mutual friends from the west country.[101]

John Shea came from a Marine Corps family.[102] His father, a marine lieutenant, had been killed in action at Bunkers Hill in 1775 whilst serving in the same battalion as Ross: they would probably have known each other. At the time of his father's death, John Shea was a lieutenant who had been commissioned in 1773. Within eight years, and after service in America, he had been promoted to captain. He was well connected: his wife was related to Admiral Lord Hood. He had a young family of four when the fleet sailed, the eldest of whom was only seven. During the voyage, in which illness attacked him, he commanded aboard *Scarborough*.

James Meredith had been commissioned eleven years and had been a captain-lieutenant for five when the fleet sailed. His promotion had been more rapid than that of Ross or Campbell and he had probably displayed the early promise which enabled him ultimately to become a general, the highest rank of any of the Botany Bay officers.

Watkin Tench, the other company commander, had also been commissioned eleven years and had been promoted captain-lieutenant five days after Meredith. Consequently, he too had had a promotion much more rapid than his superiors. He was twenty-nine years of age when the fleet sailed and was a most cultured man. His father had owned a respected boarding school and this was probably the source of his sound education, for he possessed an impressive knowledge of latin and Milton. His has been described as "the most cultivated mind in the young settlement" and from the time he was appointed to command the marines aboard *Charlotte* for the voyage, he kept a diary, now known as Tench's Narrative, which has become one of the most valuable contributions to the early history of the colony.[103] He had a pleasant manner and seems to have been well liked: Southwell, a midshipman who kept a journal of the times, found him to be "polite and sensible";[104] later, Elizabeth Macarthur was so pleased to number him among her exclusive circle of friends that few days passed without their meeting;[105] and as will be seen, there developed a most useful friendship between him and the other well-educated member of the military, Lieutenant William Dawes. Tench was to serve the British Marines for forty years before retiring with the rank of lieutenant general.[106]

Of the other officers, Second Lieutenant John Long was appointed Adjutant and Lieutenant James Furzer was made Quartermaster. Lieutenant William Dawes went to Port Jackson in the dual capacities of an engineer officer and an astronomer. He did not join the unit till he replaced Lieutenant William Collins at Port Jackson. Long, Furzer and Dawes served on the detachment's headquarters and all three travelled aboard *Sirius* to the colony. The lieutenants were Robert Kellow, John Poulden, Thomas Davey, Thomas Timins, John Johnson, James Maitland Shairp, and James Maxwell. The second lieutenants were Ralph Clark, John Faddy, John Creswell, and William Collins. Of these, some introduction should be given to Ralph Clark for he was the most homesick of the officers, and, like Tench kept a diary. He left in England his wife, Alicia (whom he nicknamed Betsy), and a baby son, Ralph. To both, he was utterly devoted, and to assuage his pining for them, he poured out his love and his homesickness into his diary. Because at times his thoughts verge on the mawkish, he obviously meant the diary to be personal and private. It now however has become a public and valuable chronicle of the colony's early events.

The career details of the officers reveal that as a group they were an experienced lot. Their commanding officer had had thirty-two years' commissioned service by the time the fleet reached Port Jackson; the most junior company commander had been in that posting for at least five years; and the first lieutenants had all seen at least nine years' commissioned service and had held first lieutenancies for a minimum of seven years before sailing. Even the most junior lieutenant, Faddy, had seven years' commissioned service to his credit. In addition, the group contained two officers whose scholarship was quite above the average — Watkin Tench and William Dawes. Consequently, the Admiralty, and especially Evan Nepean, would have been justified in holding high hopes for their success.

By early March 1787 the fleet was congregated off Portsmouth.[107] (See Table 4.) In addition the marines were accompanied by twenty-eight wives and seventeen children.[108] During March and April 1787, the convicts endured their harsh conditions below deck. Overcrowded, impoverished, and denied even the elementary comfort of sunlight, they languished in the gloom of their foetid existence. The plight of those so housed on the *Alexander* did not go unnoticed by Surgeon White who, on 10 March, asked Lieutenant Johnson and the ship's master if the convicts could come up on deck for half an hour at a time in daylight to "breathe a purer air". Both agreed and went further by granting permission for the convicts to come up immediately if White thought this necessary.[109] Johnson's ready acquiescence is early evidence of a reasonable attitude which was to typify marine-convict relations.

Phillip also worked for convict welfare by asking Lord Sydney for a more liberal ration, and for both marine and convict to receive fresh meat and vegetables whilst at anchor off Spithead.[110] Not prepared to accept inaction, he followed this with a letter to Nepean requesting power himself to improve ration allocations to both marine and convict, the need for which was illustrated by the fact that already in the two months since troops had been embarked, one in every six had been sent to hospital.[111] Stephens agreed to provide adequate rations in future.[112] But when a fortnight passed and no improvement had occurred, Phillip again wrote to Nepean, saying that troops were being sent out in a worse state "than ever troops were sent out of the Kingdom".[113] By mid April marine sickness became so serious a problem that the Portsmouth commandant had to disembark some troops who were too ill to make the voyage.[114] Ross told Stephens that since embarkation on the *Alexander*, sixteen marines had

Table 4 Distribution of officers off Portsmouth, 1787

Sirius	Maj. Robert Ross	Lt John Johnson
	Capt. David Collins	Lt James Maitland Shairp
	Lt John Long	
	Lt James Furzer	*Alexander*
		Lt Thomas Davey
Lady Penrhyn	Capt. James Campbell	Lt Thomas Timmins
	Lt George Johnston	
	Lt William Collins	*Prince of Wales*
		Capt. James Meredith
Scarborough	Capt. John Shea	Lt Ralph Clark
	Lt Robert Kellow	Lt John Faddy
	Lt James Maxwell	
		Friendship
		Capt. Watkin Tench
		Lt John Creswell
		Lt John Poulden
		Charlotte

Distribution of marines off Portsmouth, 1787

Ship	Major	Captain	Lieutenant	Sergeant	Corporal	Drummer	Private	Total
Sirius	1	1	2	1	—	3	6	14
Lady Penrhyn	—	1	2	—	—	—	3	6
Scarborough	—	1	2	2	2	1	26	34
Alexander	—	—	2	2	2	1	30	37
Prince of Wales	—	—	2	2	2	1	25	32
Friendship	—	1	2	2	3	1	36	45
Charlotte	—	1	2	3	3	1	34	44
	1	5	14	12	12	8	160	212

Source: *Historical Records of New South Wales*, vol 2, 384

had to be medically evacuated, and some of these had died. As the ship had thirty-four marines aboard, this was an evacuation rate of forty-seven per cent. Ross attributed the cause to accommodating the marines between decks, where the air was putrid. He had discussed the problem with the agent, who had agreed but who could see no solution other than to shift some of the convicts and give the space to the marines. This would relieve congestion and the space the marines had occupied could then be used to store personal effects — "the only thing it is fit for".[115] In the same letter, Ross brought to notice the plight of the children who, with their mothers, were accompanying their soldier fathers on the voyage. These children were not being rationed, but were required to exist on their parents' ration, which was a complete ration for the father and half a ration for the mother. He cited the case of one family of a father, mother and two children, who were living on one-and-a-half rations.[116] The problem was resolved by giving the same scale of rations to women and children as was laid down for military families on passage.

As part of the preparations, Ross had indented for a small supply of ammunition "for present use of the detachment". Stephens in his reply pointed out to Ross that he would require additional ammunition for the voyage and consequently Stephens had authorized General Smith "to supply you therewith accordingly".[117] However, the detachment's ammunition was not supplied, and the fleet sailed without it. In doing so, the security of the fleet and all aboard was placed in jeopardy during the first leg of the voyage. It was a serious oversight and as the ultimate responsibility for so important a commodity rests with the commanding officer, Ross must be blamed. It put Phillip to the inconvenience of having to purchase ammunition from the Portuguese at Rio de Janeiro.

Meanwhile, still anchored off Portsmouth, the marines continued their guard over the convicts and attended to those chores inherent in garrison life: thus Private Easty from his ship *Scarborough* had to accompany a convict who was to become the surgeon's mate on the *Lady Penrhyn*; some days later Easty helped to smoke and wash the *Scarborough*'s decks, and after two marines were transferred to the *Prince of Wales*, Easty's group was able to spread their hammocks. He noted that the surgeon left the ship drunk; and on the last day of the month, Easty was confined for dropping his cutlass. Also confined that day was convict Luke Haines (Haynes) for disobedience of orders. He was a bad character who was to give much trouble.

Lieutenant Ralph Clark was by now in an advanced stage of emotional distress at his impending separation from his family and sought to lessen his sorrow by writing to Phillip, who was then staying at Haymarket in London, seeking permission for his family to accompany him on the voyage. Phillip apparently raised the request with Lord Howe, who refused it. Two days later, on 12 April, Clark tried again, arguing that the refusal to allow officers to be accompanied by their families was unfair and discriminatory because it did not apply to others: privates could take families, and the Reverend Richard Johnson, the chaplain, was taking his wife. Phillip only reiterated that the decision had been a government one and not his. On 16 April, Lord Howe advised that his reason for refusing the request was that the extent and demands of Clark's duties would be as much as if he was on war service. Clark thereupon decided on one more ploy: he applied to Phillip for ten days' leave to visit Plymouth so as to complete his affairs now that his wife could not accompany him. Next day, Phillip refused his request, and Clark at last accepted the reality of his failure, though not of his situation.[118]

On 2 April, Phillip received power by Letters Patent to convene the Criminal Court. It was to consist of the Judge Advocate (Collins) "together with six officers of His Majesty's forces by sea or land", of whom five had to concur in capital cases.[119] The obligation of marine officers to serve on the court was clearly covered by the Letters Patent, and yet, as will be seen, Ross later chose to oppose officers serving on it.

As April passed, some children accompanying their convict parents on the long and arduous voyage became so ill that when Surgeon Arndell of the *Friendship* saw them, he felt they could not live till morning. Lieutenant Clark, who was an enthusiastic member of the Church of England, asked Reverend Johnson to come aboard from the *Sirius* and baptise them.[120] The motive for Clark's concern is not known; either it sprang from a compassionate concern for the children, or from a compunction to conform to ecclesiastical requirement, or possibly from both. Uppermost in his mind at the time was the tender feeling he felt for his own family, and, in such a frame of mind, the love he felt for his own child quite probably extended in some degree at least to the convicts' sick and ailing offspring. It is however much too early to be positive about him; the evidence of future actions will be significant in deciding whether he lacked compassion for convicts, especially the females, or whether his later caustic criticism of them was justified under the circumstances.

It is timely to note that already some of the convict women had proved difficult. At ten o'clock on the evening of 19 April aboard *Lady Penrhyn*, the roll call by Lieutenants George Johnston and William Collins revealed that five convict women were missing. In the ensuing search, one was found with Squires, the second mate, and four were with sailors. The officers ordered all five convicts to be put in irons and moved forward, and Johnston reported Squires to Ross, who had him removed.[121] On another day a bystander in a street leading to the docks was watching a group of women convicts being walked to their ship. One woman appeared remarkably handsome and the bystander felt much pity for her until she began making lewd gestures, which appalled him and "precluded in great measure that degree of pity ... which beauty in apparent distress will ever excite".[122]

Phillip had been authorized to spend up to £200 on spirits for the marines during the voyage, but no finance had been allocated for spirits thereafter, when liquor would have to be paid for by the user. On 2 December, Phillip asked Nepean for a free ration of spirits for the marines whilst serving at Botany Bay. Phillip feared there would be discontent if the marines did not get free rum — particularly as the naval ratings aboard the *Sirius* and *Supply*, who were also on king's service, would be receiving their usual entitlement.[123] He pointed out that it would take time for beer production to get under way in the new colony. No reply had been received by 7 May when the *Scarborough* marines, realizing the imminence of departure, again raised the matter. They sent Ross a memorial expressing their "grief" that the spirit ration was to be discontinued after arrival. Ross, referring the matter to Phillip, said he inferred from the Admiralty instruction that the marines would be "properly victualled by a Commissary" at Botany Bay, and that this properly included spirits.[124] Phillip took it up with Nepean on this basis, but Nepean replied on 10 May that Ross was mistaken: it had been expressly stated that the usual rations should be given, "excepting wine and spirits". However, as Lord Sydney wished to remove every possible cause of dissatisfaction, he had, ex gratia, authorized a free issue of spirits for three years.

Ross's part in this matter deserves investigation. Obviously he saw that free spirits at Botany Bay would improve morale, and he had received two instructions which he contrived to interpret as being in disagreement. He chose to use the one which most favoured his purpose, and thus he tried to subtly force Lord Sydney's hand. If this appears an uncharitable view, it ought to be considered alongside those future occasions when Ross again placed his own interpretation on words to suit his own, sometimes preverse, ends.

Such occasions were to include the general courts martial and criminal court controversies. (See chapter 15.)

At last the month of departure arrived. On 7 May, Phillip boarded the *Sirius*, bringing with him a clock which he ordered be wound daily at noon. Because this was to be the official timepiece of the fleet, he further ordered that it was to be wound in the presence of either Hunter or Dawes, to whom responsibility for its welfare was given. Also to be present was the marine duty officer and duty sentry, neither of whom were to be relieved till they had seen the timepiece wound.[125] In the few days remaining, final preparations were undertaken, with watering and provisioning being completed on the 11th. All NCOs and privates who had not recovered from their sicknesses were returned to their divisions on Ross's orders.[126] These did not include the seventeen marines and convicts who a day or so before departure got mumps. These were kept aboard in anticipation of their early recovery which did occur a few days after sailing, probably because of the improved ventilation.[127] It was only at this late hour that Phillip learned that a considerable part of the women's clothing had been left behind but it was too late now for anything to be done.[128] The women, together with their children, born or unborn, would have to make do with what little clothing they possessed for the next three years. Then, just as the ships were ready to sail, the seamen on the transports and storeships went on strike and refused to sail till they had been paid.[129] With that problem solved, Saturday 12 May dawned and Phillip ordered the departure pennant be flown from *Sirius* to alert the fleet to prepare for sea. The great adventure was about to begin.

2

The Voyage Out

Early on Saturday 12 May, the fleet of eleven ships then lying off Portsmouth's Mother Bank was joined by HMS *Hyaena* which was to act as fleet escort down the English Channel till the ships reached the Atlantic. Later that morning *Sirius* unmoored to lead the fleet around St Helens before nightfall but the wind dropped, forcing the ships to anchor for the night between the Mother Bank and Spithead. At four o'clock next morning, a fine day with a light southeasterly breeze, *Sirius* made signal for the fleet to get under way and by nine o'clock its ships had sailed through The Needles till by noon they were six miles from St Albans.[1] Ensconced in his misery aboard the *Friendship* was the now inconsolable Ralph Clark. He had risen early that morning, and noticing the ominous signal from the *Sirius*, he knew that his dreaded departure had now moved from inevitability to reality. And yet in his desperation for one last glimpse of his Alicia and Ralph he forlornly hoped that the fleet would call into either Plymouth or Torbay. This was so very unlikely that he sat down and wrote a letter to his "dear and fond affectioned Alicia and our sweet Son". Miserable beyond description, but still hopeful of one last chance of seeing his wife, he closed his diary for the day with the entry, "Oh my fond heart lay still for you may be dispointed [sic]".

While Clark was in the depths of this misery, diarist Watkin Tench aboard the *Charlotte* was more curious to observe the reactions of the convicts at leaving their native country. He strolled amongst them, and contrary to what he had expected, he heard hardly any "lamentations"; in fact their universal feeling seemed to be "an ardent wish for the hour of departure".[2] What distress he did see was more evident amongst the men than the women, only one of whom was crying and even her tears were fleeting for she soon wiped them away — an action which evoked from the educated Tench a line of Milton's *Paradise Lost*: "Some natural tears she dropp'd, but wip'd them soon".[3] However, beyond this lone example, he saw no further distress, but rather a "cheerfulness and acquiescence".[4] That people could leave their native land with such little regret was a telling indictment of the harsh and unappealing lives that these people had led, to depart from which was felt to be more of a lucky escape than a heart-rending wrench.

On the 14th, a foul wind blew and many of the women were seasick.[5] In spite of the many months of waiting for departure, a roll-check revealed that the Provost Marshal, together with the third mate of the *Charlotte* and five crewmen of the *Fishburn*, had been left behind.[6] Clark continued as disconsolate as ever and concluded his diary for the day with the sad entry, "dear happy spot adieu wher[e] all my treasure is on earth dear stocke adieu".[7] By the 15th, the ships were off Falmouth. Progress was so slow that they suffered the ignominy of being passed at 2 p.m. by a ship sailing from London to Lisbon.[8] The slowness was caused, at least in part, by the heavy loading of the ships. This is illustrated by what happened when Corporal Baker, in grounding his musket, caused it to discharge. Apart from shattering the bones of his right foot, so many stores cluttered his area that the bullet then ricochetted through a cask of beef and was not spent till it had penetrated two geese. Fortunately for Baker, Surgeon White's skill had him repaired and back on duty in three months.[9]

On the 16th, the seamen went on a short strike for an increased ration of beef, which Clark felt was a ruse to enable them to supply it to "the damned whores" of women convicts in return for their sexual favours. Some of the women and seamen had already broken through a bulkhead and had had "connections", and Clark, strongly disapproving the women's behaviour, said that he had not realized there were so many "abandoned wretches" in England. His assessment was that they were "ten thousand times" worse than the male convicts and he forecast that they would cause a great deal of trouble on the voyage.[10] His attitude was typical of many of his class, and though he was well meaning, he was typically hardened to convict suffering. When the women eventually were transferred to another ship at the Cape of Good Hope, and the area they vacated was filled with sheep, Clark's retort was that he expected the sheep to be the better shipmates.[11] But by then, as will be seen, his patience had long been expended. On the next night, he had his first dream of Alicia, a dream which was to be the first of many for he was still dreaming of her four months later.[12] In spite of the stern warning given to the convicts that instant death would be the penalty for escape or mutiny, those aboard *Scarborough* attempted to seize her on 18 May. They were unsuccessful and after one had been given twenty-four lashes, and others put in double irons, particulars of each convict's name, age, trade, and crime were recorded.[13] A few days later, the *Hyaena* bade farewell to the fleet and on the 21st the ships left the familiar coastline of England for the unknown vicissitudes of the wild Atlantic. Orders were given to remove irons from all convicts other than those under punishment, but the hard core of *Scarborough*'s perverse and incorrigible felons, unchastened by their failure three days previously, again attempted to seize the ship. Again they failed but Captain Shea had the two ringleaders transferred to *Sirius* where they were lashed and sent to the *Prince of Wales* to be heavily ironed and subject to the discipline of Lieutenants Davey and Timins.[14]

The Atlantic greeted the little fleet with strong winds and a heavy swell which continued unabated till the 31st. Sea sickness was widespread: Ralph Clark on the day the *Hyaena* left the fleet was very sick but still able to rejoice that the wind which was a head wind for the fleet would at least be a tailwind for the *Hyaena*, enabling it to convey more quickly the letter he had written to his wife.

His despondency increased, and what with depression and seasickness, he could do nothing on the night of the 23rd but dream of his wife and son, and in one of those passionate heaves that can spring unbidden from the human heart, he poured forth his wretchedness: "Oh my God, never did a man long so much after anything than I do to know how they both are. What would I give for a letter from her dear hand; but why do I think of impossibilities — because I love them tenderly with a sincere heart as ever man loved woman."[15]

Another young man aboard *Friendship* was, however, in a mood more artful than emotional. Either to gain freedom from his convict shackles or for some other reason forever to be unknown, John Bennett broke out of his irons, for which he received a flogging of thirty-seven lashes. The incident in itself would be of little consequence except for some light it throws on Ralph Clark's perceptiveness, for his opinion of Bennett was that, though young, he was well schooled in roguery.[16] His assessment was later vindicated when, at the Cape, Bennett stole all the provisions owned by those convicts who had liberty to walk the decks, then hid himself in a long boat, and ate the lot.[17]

The marines continued their surveillance of the convicts who were allowed on deck in small, well-guarded groups;[18] the officers made visits, weather permitting, to fellow officers aboard other ships to indulge in drinking; Ralph Clark pursued a loftier recreation by reading "The Story of the Humble Friend" from a 1775 edition of the *Lady Magazine*, and was "much taken with it".[19] His chief hope however was to arrive at Teneriffe to find some ship returning to England by which he could send a letter to his "dear heavenly woman".[20]

The weather abated to the extent that on 2 June the ships were almost becalmed and the sea so flat that Ross was rowed from *Sirius* to the *Scarborough*, where he spoke to the convicts and let them out of the irons in which they had been placed since their mutiny.[21] Shortly, on the horizon, the Canary Islands were seen and next day, when about twelve leagues from the island of Teneriffe, Governor Phillip ordered all ships to get into line. By 8 p.m., all were in the harbour of Santa Cruz. Phillip's purpose in calling at Teneriffe was to gain fresh water and vegetables to prevent scurvy: the daily ration by now had become monotonous, marines receiving 1 pound (454 g) of bread, 1 pound of beef and 1 pint (568 ml) of wine per day compared with the convicts' ¾ pound of bread, ¾ pound of beef and no wine.[22]

Captain Meredith and Lieutenant Clark declined an invitation to be presented to the Governor of the Canarys, but Lieutenant Faddy, with his propensity for socializing, accepted. During the morning, local traders came aboard to sell fresh vegetables, which Private Easy, and no doubt other marines, eagerly purchased.[23] Ross also boarded *Friendship* that day to enquire about two sergeants whom Meredith had confined for a court martial because of unsoldierly behaviour. After hearing Meredith's story, Ross decided not to try them, but went on to say that they "deserved hanging", a statement which brought forth the wry comment from Clark that that was a "very pretty way of carrying out service, I must own".[24] Ross then joined Phillip in inspecting the marine and convict quarters on the *Friendship* and ordered all convicts out of irons with the warning that they would be re-shackled immediately upon the slightest offence. Phillip gave permission for all marines to disembark, enabling Sergeant Scott and his wife to have a pleasant stroll and picnic ashore.[25] To the great delight of both marines and convicts, Phillip permitted wine and fresh beef to be available whilst the fleet was at Santa Cruz, and advised that letters for England could be sent by a Spanish ship which was sailing the following afternoon for Spain. Such news alerted Ralph Clark and he straightaway sat down and wrote to his "sincere and affectioned wife". Sergeant Scott wrote to his mother-in-law.[26]

At the end of this first leg of the long voyage, Phillip had reason to be satisfied with the health of all on board. In a return prepared on 4 June, only 74 convicts and 7 marines had been reported sick, an incidence of 1:10. Assuming the marines were privates, this represented a sickness rate of 10 per cent convicts and 4 per cent marines. So far, no marine had died, but there were seven deaths out of the 750 convicts being transported. The only case of venereal disease amongst marines were two reported on the *Alexander*, which carried male-only convicts. However the *Scarborough* also carried males only and none of its marines had contracted the disease.[27] Sickness among the marines increased as the voyage progressed. Some 17 marines reported sick from Teneriffe to Rio compared with 64 convicts (1:4), whilst from Rio to the Cape of Good Hope, the contrast was 20 marines compared with 93 convicts (1:4).[28] Meanwhile, on board the *Alexander*, Lieutenant John Johnson had made a complaint against two of his marines, including Private Richard Askew. Ross ordered Clark to conduct a preliminary investigation to establish whether charges should be laid. He decided that a case existed against Askew concerning liquor and the court martial was held on the 8th.[29] It is not clear whether he was acquitted, but Easty says he was found guilty and sentenced to three hundred lashes, of which he received only fifty.[30]

During the fleet's weak-long stay at Santa Cruz, the marine officers entertained themselves in various ways. Ralph Clark, lacking money, remained aboard, though on the 6th he and Doctor Arndell, also of the *Friendship*, enjoyed a convivial time in the mess aboard the *Scarborough* with Captain Shea and Lieutenants Kellow and Davey. Others attended to their own recreation: Lieutenant Philip Gidley King RN formed a party of fourteen including some marine officers to visit Laguna, an inland town on Teneriffe.[31] The initial stages of the journey passed through barren, rocky country, until a fertile plain was reached, picturesque with vineyards and fields of corn, mulberries, figs, pumpkins, and onions. Wine was cheap and plentiful at twenty-two pence a gallon, and although beef too was plentiful, it was of poor quality and expensive.[32] After a pleasant though very hot day, King's party returned tired but refreshed. Watkin Tench, who went ashore a number of times to watch the lifestyle and habitat of the local people, was surprised that in so hot a place, flavoured ices were served plentifully as dessert at the Governor's banquet. He found that they were obtained from the perpetual natural ice formed in the caverns of the island's peak. He was bothered by beggars; disgusted by the immodesty of low class women; discouraged from conversation by the taciturnity of the Spanish; surprised that the European decline in the Catholic Church was not reflected at Teneriffe; impressed by the affection which the people had for their bishop; and struck by the financial contrast of the bishop being paid ten thousand per year, whilst the Governor received only two thousand.[33]

On board the fleet riding at anchor in the bay, the marines continued their guard of the convicts. However, in spite of every precaution, John Powers, who had been allowed to help seamen water the *Alexander*, managed one night to hide himself on deck when the others were returned below. He remained hidden for some hours, and then, lowering himself over the bow of the ship, floated quietly to a boat that lay astern. This he boarded, cut adrift, and allowed the current to carry it away from the ship. When out of earshot, he rowed to a Dutch ship but his request to be taken on board was rejected. He then decided to row to the Grand Canary

Island, some ten leagues away. But meanwhile, to gather strength for the attempt, he sought refuge for the night amongst some rocks on the shore, setting the rowing boat adrift lest it reveal his whereabouts. Unfortunately for him, a party of marines from the *Alexander* saw the boat, deduced that he was in its vicinity, and apprehended him. He was taken to the *Sirius* and then transferred to the *Alexander* under orders to be heavily ironed.[34]

On Saturday 9 June, when the fleet had completed its watering, Phillip flew the blue flag with a yellow cross to indicate that no more boats were to go ashore.[35] Before the fleet left, a fight broke out on the *Friendship* involving four convict women — Elizabeth Dudgeon, Margaret Hall, Elizabeth Pully and Charlotte Ware — for which Ralph Clark had them put in irons.[36]

At last everything was ready for the Atlantic voyage to Rio de Janeiro, and at 5 a.m. on Sunday 10 June, Phillip signalled from the *Sirius* to weigh anchor and set sail on this hot and languid day. For the next two days the fleet was almost becalmed and Teneriffe remained clearly in sight, but on the 13th a good breeze sprang up and they set a southwesterly course. For the next week good progress was made and all was well except that Ralph Clark took ill. He recovered after taking an emetic and some bark, only to become quite angered to see Captain Meredith releasing from their shackles the four women whom he had placed in irons ten days previously.[37] He strongly disapproved of Meredith's clemency, for he felt there were no greater "whores" living than these four: the same women who had broken through a bulkhead to get to the seamen whilst their ship was on the Mother Bank. He predicted that it would not be long before they would again be in trouble, and after describing them as "bastards" and a "disgrace" to their sex, he yearned for all women to be out of his ship.[38] Although Clark was reflecting the contemporary disdain of his class towards convicts, it must be admitted that the women convicts on the *Friendship* do appear to have been the most troublesome in the fleet, for it was they who had to be transferred to another ship at the Cape of Good Hope.

Whilst Clark nursed his melancholy, the fleet crossed the Tropic of Cancer at 2 p.m. on 15 June. Sergeant Scott of the *Prince of Wales* records that the frivolity of the crossing — which included ducking, shaving and lathering with tar and grease — was restricted to the seamen because Lieutenant Maxwell would not permit his marines to take part.[39]

The 23rd of June was Ralph Clark's third wedding anniversary, which brought to him a mixture of anguish and happiness. After describing his wife as "the most tender, best, and Beautifulest of her Sex" and pledging to keep every anniversary of his marriage as long as he had breath in his body, he reiterated that no man possessed such treasure as centred in his Betsy. He longed for the months to fly so that he could again kiss his loved ones, and lashed himself with recrimination that he had ever allowed "gains" to induce him to leave them, revealing in that comment that he had joined the expedition to improve his status in life so that his family could benefit. Consequently, though he deeply regretted separation from the two he loved most, nevertheless, he had embarked upon his tour of duty to further their interests. The day was of such special significance to him that he broke from his usual custom and invited the ship's captain, both mates, and fellow officer James Meredith, to join him in a small celebration. But the function was no sooner over and the guests had no sooner gone than he lapsed again into remorseful melancholy, contriving in it to imagine that he heard his son call out "Pappa, Pappa" which he confided to his diary was "dear sweet music" to his "poor ears".[40]

Whilst Clark was thus turning his thoughts to loved ones, the *Charlotte*'s female convicts below her battened hatches were fainting in droves in the foetid and stifling heat. Many fainted so repeatedly that they fell into fits, and yet the hatches, according to Surgeon White, could not be removed to permit circulation of fresh air "without a promiscuous intercourse immediately taking place between the women and the seamen and marines".[41] If, as White says, marines were also offending, their lack of discipline was partly to blame for the women's distress. How general this situation was throughout the fleet is not mentioned by other writers on the First Fleet but even for it to occur on the *Charlotte* reflects adversely on her marines and their officers, Watkin Tench, John Poulden and John Creswell.

At about the same time, glimpses of events aboard the *Prince of Wales* suggest that the long voyage and the cramped conditions were telling on marine performance and relationships. Privates Arthur Dougherty and Robert Ryan were charged on 24 June by Lieutenant Maxwell for disobeying orders. Maxwell apparently took so serious a view of the incidents that he and Sergeant Scott took Dougherty and Ryan to the *Sirius* where they remained for the night. Next day, Ross formed a court martial aboard the *Prince of Wales*, where Dougherty was acquitted, but Ryan received three hundred lashes given immediately.[42]

Strained human relationships were also appearing. On 30 June, Sergeant Scott ceased sitting at the same table as Sergeant Hume because Mrs Hume had, for some reason, take exception to Scott.[43] Then some days later Sergeant Kennedy of the *Prince of Wales* got thoroughly drunk, and after abusing several people and making a general nuisance of himself, jumped down a hatchway, falling heavily on Sergeant Scott's wife, who was in her seventh month of pregnancy. Her husband recorded that she got a severe fright for it "hurt her greatley". Lieutenant Maxwell had Kennedy placed under guard whilst awaiting his court martial.[44]

Meanwhile, Ralph Clark was spending his leisure time reading a play called *The Death of Douglas*, in which a child becomes lost. For Clark, that was sufficient stimulus to remind him of his virtuous Alicia and Ralphie which brought a quiet cry.⁴⁵ A few nights later, he spent an evening after dinner talking to Lieutenant Faddy and eventually the conversation got around to the affairs of a family which they both knew back home. It appears that Hannah Courdry, the daughter of the family, once stayed at Mrs Fuge's house in which a Mr Perry was also a guest. According to Faddy, Perry seduced Hannah and told Faddy that he had done so. Clark was shocked by the revelation. At first, he refused to believe it but Faddy insisted that "if ever woman was [seduced], Hannah was". Clark had known that familiarities had taken place but the version he had been told before leaving England was that Perry, a married man and a father, had not seduced her. In fact, Clark told Faddy that after he had heard of the incident, he had gone home and roundly condemned Perry for his tasteless behaviour because he felt that a girl as virtuous as Hannah ought not to have suffered such unpleasant attentions. And so it was, that thousands of miles from home, in the middle of a vast ocean, two marine officers were deep in discussion of the age-old question of who was responsible in illicit love-making. From the discussion, we can glean some glimpses of character: Faddy seems to have relished Hannah's fate, whereas Clark was appalled that womanly virtue could be so violated. He held not only an idealized view of womanhood, but also, at that time at least, a firm conviction that extramarital relations were wrong, and it was the conjugal status of Perry as much as his lustful action which bothered him.⁴⁶

On 5 July all aboard the fleet except doctors and the sick were restricted to a water ration of three pints (1.7 l) a day. In future all water issues were to be supervised by a lieutenant or NCO who was to stand at the water coppers.⁴⁷ On the same day, Captain John Shea fell seriously ill with what was probably tuberculosis.⁴⁸ Clark was full of pity for Shea's wife and young family, and during the next week when Shea's condition worsened, Clark spent sleepless hours worrying about what would happen to his own "beloved

Alicia and dear sweet boy" should he himself suffer illness.[49] By the 13th, however, Clark spoke in mid ocean to Lieutenant Kellow aboard the *Scarborough* and when told that Shea was improving, he was genuinely relieved and thanked God for the sake of Shea's wife and family.[50]

Meanwhile, a bout of troublesome behaviour broke out amongst some of the women convicts. On 3 July, Clark was called up by the *Friendship*'s master, Captain Walton, and told that some of the ship's seamen had broken through a bulkhead to the women's area and that four women, Elizabeth Dudgeon, Elizabeth Pully, Elizabeth Thackerly, and Sarah McCormick, had been found in the seamen's quarters. Dudgeon and Pully had previously committed the same offence on the Mother Bank,[51] and were among the four placed in irons for fighting at Teneriffe. Clark's low opinion of women convicts was thus, to him, confirmed. It was a feature of his condemnation to blame the women rather than the men, but in so doing he was displaying the typical male attitude of his day. On this occasion, however, the offending seamen were sent to the *Sirius* for flogging and the women ordered into irons for the rest of the voyage, which Clark felt was too lenient: if he had had his way, they would have been flogged as well.[52] Two days later, Elizabeth Dudgeon again transgressed by being impertinent to Captain Meredith; she was flogged and Clark was pleased to observe that the corporal who administered the flogging "laid it home" and did not "play with her". When she was then tied to a pump, Clark was again pleased, for he felt that she had at last got what she had been "fishing for" for a long time. Dudgeon had now committed four offences — more than any other woman on the ship — and her incorrigibility was demonstrated by the need later to leg-iron her and Elizabeth Hall for fighting.[53]

But Clark's woman-troubles were not finished. On 18 July, Elizabeth Barber uncontrollably abused Doctor Arndell. She began by accusing him in lurid and fiery language of wanting to seduce her, which he denied. The matter was reported to Meredith who, after dinner that night, decided that in the interests of justice he ought to enquire into her allegation. When he did so, she turned her venom on him and "called him everything except a gentleman", adding that she was no more a whore than his own wife. She then became violently abusive, and such was her screaming tirade that Meredith ordered her to be leg-ironed, though even this restraint did not prevent her incorporating Lieutenant Faddy into her outburst. Clark, who was in earshot, had never in all his life heard such expletives or expressions come from anyone's mouth. Her screaming continued for she refused to be silenced and finally crowned her effort by both asking Meredith to "come and kiss her c . . ." and calling him a "lousy rascal". That was as much as Meredith was prepared to endure and he ordered her to be gagged and leg-ironed with her hands tied behind her back. For two days her hands remained tied, when they were freed for a while and then tied again. Her outburst reinforced the view Clark held of the women and he expressed a preference to have a hundred men on board rather than a single woman.[54] He no doubt felt this view was vindicated a few days later when Meredith had to put Margaret Hall in irons for defecating on the floor between decks. As punishment, he handcuffed her to Elizabeth Barber, whose leg irons he removed, for Hall had not only been one of the offenders on the Mother Bank but had been one of those punished by Clark at Teneriffe. She did not stay long in irons, for next day Doctor Arndell ordered her out of them as she was very unwell. On 24 July, leg irons had to be put on Elizabeth Pully, but as they caused her to blister, they too were removed two days later. None of this group was contrite, for on 1 August, Barber, Thackerly, Dudgeon, and Pully had to be put back into irons by Meredith because "the damned whores", the moment they got below, started fighting one another. Meredith told the sergeant to let them fight it out, and not to part them.[55] Obviously he had had enough, particularly when two days later Sarah McCormick, who so recently had been one of those who broke through to the seamen, fell so ill that Doctor Arndell did not expect her to survive the night and had to bleed her twice. She was "eaten up" with venereal disease. With singular vindictiveness Clark hoped that she had given the seaman "something to remember her by", for he considered that the seamen were "ten thousand times" worse than the male convicts. However, McCormick recovered to continue in trouble later at Port Jackson.[56] Eventually the incorrigibility of these women was beaten when, at Rio, the *Friendship*'s six worst women were exchanged for the *Charlotte*'s six best.[57]

In spite of the troubles which these few had caused, the day-to-day affairs of others in the fleet had continued. Private Arthur Dougherty, so recently acquitted of his crime, received a son, Daniel, born on 10 July;[58] and Lieutenant Ball, commander of the *Supply*, boarded the *Scarborough* on the 12th to check her cleanliness in compliance with Phillip's insistence on ship hygiene as a type of preventative medicine.[59] Even so, Lieutenant Faddy was kept awake one night by bugs, a hundred of which he killed next morning with oil of tar, claiming that the *Friendship* swarmed with them.[60] Clark continued to dream of his Alicia sitting by the fire in her night cap, and worked himself into a panic lest the dream indicated that something could be wrong with her.[61] Eventually, on 28 July, Phillip sent the *Supply* around the fleet to warn of a small island ahead — a use to which he often put that ship.[62] As the eight weeks' crossing of the Atlantic was nearing its end, he sent the *Supply* ahead on 2 August to look out for land. Such was the accuracy of his navigation that she returned within four hours having found Rio harbour, and on 6 August, giving a thirteen gun salute as it moved up the harbour, the fleet anchored at 8 p.m. Because Phillip was held in high regard by the Portuguese for the service he had previously rendered their navy, he received that night a grand illumination of fireworks.[63]

Phillip lost no time on 8 August in taking the officers, less Ralph Clark, to pay their respects to the Viceroy, who received them with kindness and gave them unrestricted access to the area. This was in sharp contrast to the restrictions placed on Captain Cook when he called there — a further indication of Phillip's high standing with the Portuguese.[64] Clark did not accompany the group: both the Adjutant and the Quartermaster visited his ship to ask him to do so but he told them that he had no "particular desire", and, as Faddy was keen to go, he and Meredith went instead.[65] This was the second occasion that Clark had chosen not to accompany brother officers ashore, and he was to refuse a third invitation by Long to visit the Viceroy on 21 August, which suggests that he was becoming solitary and unsociable.[66] At Rio, his thoughts about his wife were becoming obsessive, and when the weather prevented his walking ashore on the 9th he wrote yet another letter, addressing her as his "adorable, sweet, and sincere Alicia".[67] At last on the 20th he went ashore, but by himself, to collect butterflies for Alicia. Whilst doing so, he visited a house to rest when the owner's daughter noticed that Clark's pendant picture of Alicia had fallen. She picked it up and asked to look at it, but such was the obsessiveness with which he valued the picture that he agreed to her doing so only very reluctantly, and for as long as the daughter held it, his hands shook "like a little bird when schoolboys handle its young".[68] His melancholy was leading to a type of neurotic depression and by late October, it would bring him to the verge of a nervous breakdown. To while away the time, he had used the voyage thus far to make a desk for his "dear sweet woman", and his stay at Rio seems to have been dominated by a desire to get it covered in green cloth for her.[69]

Whilst Clark was absorbed with his joinery, Sergeant Kennedy continued to languish in those irons in which, since his drunken spree on 14 July, he had been awaiting court martial aboard the *Prince of Wales*. On 9 August, Ross transferred him to the *Alexander* and replaced him with Sergeant Clayfield.[70] Generally speaking, the discipline among the marines during the three months' voyage from England had been sound, five infractions only having occurred: on 31 July, Privates John Easty and William Douglas had been confined for one week for being drunk on duty;[71] at Rio on 10 August, Private James Lee, in drunkeness, had been confined and given 100 lashes for being insolent to Corporal Nicholas;[72] the next day Private Luke Haynes, a violent man of whom we shall hear more, was confined for fighting Private Bullmore and received 150 of a 200-lash sentence;[73] and on 31 August, also at Rio, Corporal Baker received 200 lashes for inducing a seaman whilst ashore to pass a counterfeit dollar manufactured by a convict.[74] With the detachment strength at 212, these few infractions indicate a good discipline.

Richard Johnson, whose practice it was to conduct Divine Service aboard one ship each Sunday whilst in port, preached aboard the *Lady Penrhyn*, selecting as his text Psalm 107, verse 23: "They that go down to the sea in ships and occupy their business in great waters".[75] The day was pleasantly concluded by a dinner aboard the *Lady Penrhyn* during which Ross seemed rather affable to Clark and asked if he expected Alicia to come out to Botany Bay.[76] Unfortunately Clark's reply was not recorded, but in any case she never came. The following Wednesday, two marines fought a vigorous fight: Privates Michael Toulon and John Barrisford went for one another with a relish. Both were drunk, and when an officer ordered them to stop, Toulon abused him. Both were court martialled, Toulon receiving 175 lashes of a 300-lash sentence, and Barrisford 50 lashes for a lesser crime of fighting.[77]

For some, the boredom of the long voyage needed diversion, and from Rio until they arrived at the Cape of Good Hope, Meredith, Faddy and Doctor Arndell managed to hold nine parties in which their heavy drinking and roisterous singing of dubious mess songs ran on late into the night.[78] Such occasions held little attraction to Clark: he seems to have attended two only, and even then he restricted himself to lemonade before retiring at nine o'clock. He was critical of Meredith for not setting a better example, and predicted that these drinking bouts would end in discord. In this, as in his prophecy about the convict women, he was vindicated: on both 5 September and 10 November, Meredith and Arndell quarrelled over trivialities. The trouble was that in drink they became cantankerous; especially did Meredith become obdurate; but when sober, they settled their imagined differences and resumed their convenient alliance. It was all natural enough considering their unusual situation, but it was not good for military discipline because Meredith, when in drink, was not only falling out with Doctor Arndell over infantile trivialities, but when sober, he would quarrel with Faddy, his subordinate, and then effect a reconciliation by drinking with him all night.[79] These infractions went on so long than eventually Ross had to intervene. He did not handle the situation very well, however, for he not only reprimanded Meredith in public, but did so, in Clark's opinion, in language unbecoming an officer.[80] Even this failed to end the periodic animosity between Meredith and Faddy and on 3 and 4 January they engaged in a bitter two-day quarrel. On that occasion Clark blamed Faddy, whom he described as the "most selfish, grumbling, and bad hearted man I was ever mess mates with".[81]

But in tracing the antics of these two, we have digressed from other events aboard the fleet which still lay at Rio, and where 13 August was proving a busy day for courts martial. Privates Cornelius Connell, Thomas Jones, John Jones, and James Reiley were charged "for having an improper intercourse with some of the female convicts contrary to orders". Connell was found guilty and received one hundred lashes;[82] but John Jones and Reiley were acquitted through lack of evidence even though there were witnesses to their crime.

Those witnesses, however, were convicts, and convict evidence was not admissible. Thomas Jones was further charged with attempting to corrupt a sentry so as to gain his connivance for an illicit visit to the women; he was found guilty and sentenced to three hundred lashes, but Major Ross cancelled the punishment because of his previous good character.[83] These charges arose because a military order had been issued to the marines forbidding intercourse with the convicts. On the same day, Phillip and Ross both gave Meredith orders that when irons failed to prove adequate dissuasion to the women convicts they were to be flogged, the same as the men.[84] The day however was not all gloom. Phillip in the evening hosted an excellent dinner for Hunter, Ross, David Collins, Meredith, Clark, King, and Arndell (who, as usual, got "tipsy"), though Clark, perhaps a little unctiously, hastened with his assurance that he himself had never been drunk — and then on second thoughts modified his disclaimer when he took into account his wedding day.[85] And lest it should be thought that Clark was at last getting over his homesickness, he remained on board a few days later when Meredith and Arndell went ashore. He suffered a fit of such homesickness that he was reduced to being "the most unhappy of men living". However, his spirits revived sufficiently next day for him to accompany those two turbulent friends ashore. As usual, the two of them went on a drinking spree and after returning "tipsy", proceeded to make a great racket that night, to which Clark left them and went to bed.[86]

But all was not given over to diversion and amusement: a variety of duties called for attention. Thus when a corporal on the *Friendship* was demoted, Private Thomas Chapman was promoted in his place;[87] four days later, on 21 August, it being the custom for the military to pay their respects to the Viceroy, Phillip and the marine officers complied, and the *Sirius* gave a royal salute.[88] Phillip, who had been concerned by the lack of ammunition on board because of the oversight before leaving Portsmouth, now rectified the omission by purchasing ten thousand musket balls from the Viceroy.[89]

August closed with two events involving children of marines. Little Ralph, Clark's "beautiful and beloved son", was two years old on the 23rd, and Clark, after thanking God for the boy's preservation, dined aboard *Sirius* with the Adjutant, though he declined to stay for supper so as to return to the *Friendship* to drink a private toast in lemonade to his "little Ralphie". During the voyage, Clark appears to have been a teetotaller, and even later, when he sat up till 2 a.m. to accompany Meredith, Faddy and Arndell during one of their roisterous drinking and singing bouts, he himself drank lemonade only.[90] The other child event of late August at Rio was that, after a twenty-seven-hour labour, Sergeant Scott's wife, June, at 1 p.m. on the 29th was safely delivered of a daughter — neither mother nor child being the worse for Sergeant Kennedy's drunken fall on Mrs Scott some seven weeks previously. Richard Johnson christened the baby, Elizabeth, on board the *Prince of Wales* five days later.[91] Scott had been a dutiful husband: he and June had gone for prenatal walks ashore, and a week or so before the baby's birth he had procured fresh beef and oranges for his wife. Unfortunately, his labour of love was not without its hazards: he had fallen and injured his arm whilst doing so.[92]

Phillip, too, had been shopping. He was concerned that he would have an insufficient supply of rum for the marines whilst at Botany Bay and, possibly because the Rio authorities were so cooperative towards him, he purchased the rum there and had it loaded into the *Fishburn*.[93]

In the early days of September, the fleet prepared for sea. These preparations were noticed by a Portuguese soldier who had been absent without leave from his unit for five or six days. Fearful of the punishment which awaited him, he dreaded to return, and instead boarded *Sirius* to sail away in her. Phillip, displaying great humanity, had him rowed ashore to a spot where the soldier's landing would be unobserved so he could return to duty unnoticed.[94] Phillip acted with similar compassion at the Cape of Good Hope when a Swiss soldier also tried to stow away: Phillip would not put him ashore until he had extracted a promise of pardon from the man's regiment.[95] Phillip was a most humane man whose long military service gave him a fatherly understanding of the harshness of the soldier's lot.

At six o'clock on the morning of 4 September, the fleet departed for the cross-Atlantic voyage to the Cape of Good Hope. As he left Rio, Phillip was given a twenty-one gun salute, which he returned. His stay at Rio, and indeed that of the whole fleet, had been most pleasant: relations with the authorities had been cordial; the convicts and marines had received oranges, bananas, pineapples, apples, and fresh beef in abundance; and the marines had enjoyed the freedom ashore given them by the Viceroy. Phillip's plan to avoid scurvy by a balanced diet for all whilst in port had proved highly successful, for, up till sailing from Rio, he was able to report to Nepean that only fifteen convicts and one marine child had died since leaving England.[96] Everyone had eaten extremely well at Rio: both marine and convicts had had fresh rations since arriving, marines receiving 1¼ pounds (568 g) of beef and 1 pound (454 g) of rice per day, whilst their children had received ¾ pound of beef plus 1 pound of rice and an issue of vegetables each day.[97] In all probability the marines and convicts were eating much better during the voyage than they would have done in England.

But scarcely was the fleet out of Rio when storms struck with an awful fury; huge seas several times broke over the *Friendship*, and hatch covers above the convicts had to be battened.[98] During the twenty days to 25 September, gales and rain lashed the ships mercilessly; many marines, particularly on the *Alexander*, were seasick.[99] So terrified were the convict women aboard *Friendship* that they read the Collect and Lessons for the day from the Book of Common Prayer, and sang psalms. That they should have resorted to religion is cause for some reflection. Firstly, it demonstrated that there existed, probably throughout the fleet generally, an adherence to the church's liturgy. This would suggest that many of those who succumbed to promiscuity did so out of circumstance rather than abandonment; for it ought not to be forgotten that these women were Australia's founding mothers. In spite of the famine and destitution of the first two years of the colony these women were to bear, nurse, and care for the nation's first children against hardship unparalleled since in Australia's history. Secondly, their resort to the Book of Common Prayer suggests that the church's educational system was more effective than is often acknowledged. These women who were at the bottom of the social scale had at least a passing familiarity with its practices and teachings. This is not to suggest a convict saintliness, for just as it was wrong for Clark to brand them all as "abandoned wretches", so is it wrong to see them as paragons of saintly perfection. Their recitation of the liturgy did not prevent one woman aboard the *Prince of Wales* from stealing whilst the others were engaged in their prayers, for which she received six lashes. She was, however, the first to be flogged on that ship in the almost nine months that its women had been aboard.

And as for Clark, he was tortured not only by the storms but also by an eight-day bout of persistent toothache which lasted till the 17th.[100] His suffering seems to have made him temporarily aware of the suffering of others, for he gave an old coat to Private Thomas Williams to keep him warm in the biting cold, and to Mrs Young, wife of Sergeant Thomas Young, he gave some tea because she had none.[101]

The spirit of magnanimity however was not universal: hemmed in, in the confined space, Meredith and his drinking partner, Doctor Arndell, drunkenly quarrelled over a piece of wood; convicts Sarah McCormick and Elizabeth Pully who had spent many occasions with both seaman and marine alike, now told Arndell that they were pregnant

(McCormick had venereal disease);[102] and to top everything, the long hard voyage was breeding mutinous discontent on both the *Prince of Wales* and *Alexander*.

The trouble came to a head on 6 October, one week short of the Cape of Good Hope. On the *Prince of Wales*, Sergeant Scott heard it rumoured that four seamen intended assisting its convicts to seize the ship. On the *Alexander*, some marine officers reported that some crew and convicts had arranged to escape at the Cape: taking advantage of a widespread sickness amongst the marine guards, they had stolen an iron crowbar.[103] Phillip's reaction was immediate: he ordered four of the offending seamen to transfer to the *Sirius* and replaced them with four of her own men, thus aborting their nefarious plans.[104]

Four days short of port, Mary Richards, the wife of Private Lawrence Richards, gave birth to a son, William.[105] For some unexplained reason William appears not to have been baptised till Christmas Day 1790.[106]

During the afternoon of 12 October, as was the custom when nearing land, Phillip sent the *Supply* ahead to reconnoitre.[107] Next day at 5 p.m., after a voyage from Rio of five weeks and four days, the fleet anchored in Table Bay. The reception by the Dutch at the Cape of Good Hope was more restrained than that given by the Portuguese at Rio, and Phillip and his principal officers made only one visit to Government House. The severe Atlantic crossing had taken its toll, and the fleet arrived with twenty marines and ninety-three convicts sick.[108]

Lieutenant Faddy marked the arrival with a display of conduct unbecoming an officer. On 14 October, as Clark's tooth was still proving troublesome, Faddy accompanied him aboard *Scarborough* to have the tooth extracted. They stayed late, and when they returned to the *Friendship* Faddy, who was well under the influence of liquor, publicly abused Clark in front of Meredith, accusing him of behaviour unbecoming an officer and a gentleman. Clark took exception to this and, using normal military procedure, he wrote to Meredith applying for a Redress of Wrongs to be heard by a general court martial. Meredith gave the application next day to Ross, who refused it and asked Clark to settle the affair privately. Clark refused, so Ross suggested that the matter be heard unofficially by a panel of brother officers. Still Clark would not agree. Meanwhile Faddy, sick with a heavy hangover, tried to convince Clark that at the time of his indiscretion he was so drunk that he did not know what he was saying. But his appeal to Clark was unavailing. On 17 October, Ross, Shea, Tench, George Johnston, and five other officers came on board the *Friendship* at 10 a.m. to resolve the dispute. The enquiry that followed did not pronounce Faddy unequivocally guilty, which suggests that its members thought the matter a minor one. Instead they requested Faddy to acknowledge his use of the words claimed; apparently Faddy did, for there the matter seems to have died.[109] This incident suggests that officer relationships were becoming less harmonious, and that, even before arriving at Botany Bay, the detachment lacked a close homogeneity. We are not sure why Clark pressed the issue so strongly. He may have wished to uphold military discipline. Faddy had committed a serious military indiscretion in criticizing a fellow officer publicly, especially if junior rank was present. Or the incident may have originated in an antipathy between these two disparate characters: Faddy, the heavy drinking, carousing, man of the world; Clark, the sensitive, family-loving, teetotaller.

Clark at the time of this incident was under severe nervous pressure. He was in the depths of constantly recurring homesickness which by 27 October became so extreme that in one of his constant dreams about Alicia and Ralph, he dreamt that Ralphie was dead. Involuntarily, he screamed so loudly in his sleep that he woke Meredith. He knew that his nervous condition was serious and he recognized the danger of breakdown, admitting that the stress of his pining was "too much" for his health. Every Sunday he kissed Alicia's portrait and, as a man basically of a religious bent, he read, for solace, the Lessons, prayers, and psalms set for the day in the Book of Common Prayer.[110] His emotional torture continued for the whole stay at Table Bay: on 1 November, when he was told of the arrival of a ship from London, he so desperately hoped for a letter from Alicia that his diary entry for the day became disjointed, exclaiming, "Oh my God, how my heart goes pitte-patty ... almost half mad." But when no letter arrived, such was his abject despondency that he went to bed to see if he could get "any ease" from crying in his pillow.[111]

Whilst the officers were occupied with settling their squabbles, and Clark was tearing himself apart with remorse, life for the ordinary marines was happier. On 15 October, after fresh supplies had been brought aboard, marines and their families, as well as the convicts, tucked into a hearty meal of beef, mutton, soft brown bread, unlimited greens, and the usual ration of wine.[112] During their stay at the Cape, all ships had such ample meat, bread and fresh vegetables, that Phillip did not land the twenty marines and ninety-three convicts who were sick, but kept them on board for their recuperation.[113] As if to illustrate the verities of life, two days later, Private Matthew Wright's wife had a daughter,[114] whilst Drummer Benjamin Cook's wife, Mary, died and was, in the words of Easty, "hove overbord" at 6.30 p.m.[115] Even so, military chores had to continue, and when an inspection of the fleet's magazine by Lieutenant Maxwell revealed 196 damaged cartridges, they were dried and put into horns and paper.[116]

A few days later Lieutenants Maxwell and Timins were transferred from the *Charlotte* to the *Prince of Wales* in place of Lieutenants Creswell and Poulden.[117] This transfer was ordered by Ross, who had received complaints about Maxwell from the soldiers. After the transfer, Ross boarded the *Prince of Wales* unexpectedly to discuss these with Maxwell, and caught him in a state of such drunkeness that his incoherence prevented his holding any discussion. Ross immediately ordered him to transfer back to the *Charlotte* to be replaced by Creswell. Poulden, however, wished to remain with Creswell (no doubt he did not relish the thought of spending the next nine weeks with the alcoholic Maxwell) and so he changed ships with Timins.[118] Ross had not acted peremptorily for it was not the first occasion he had found Maxwell incapable of duty because of drink: at Rio he had spoken to him about the problem and had hoped to reform him by then transferring him to the *Charlotte* but Maxwell had asked for another chance.[119] Ross had given him this in a spirit of compassion for a brother officer, but his incapacity at the Cape now left Ross with no alternative. Initially, in a spirit of consideration, Ross advised him to apply for repatriation home on grounds of sickness. Then, as if to jolt some sense into the man, he threatened not to allow him to land with the detachment at Botany Bay.[120] Maxwell's behaviour thereafter improved.

But drink was bedevilling other officers during those later days at the Cape. Lieutenant John Johnson's excessive drinking was such that his supercession was necessary, and consequently Lieutenant Furzer was ordered by Ross to transfer to the *Alexander* and take command of Johnson's detachment — a disgrace for any officer.[121] General discipline also received attention: on 20 October, Privates Thomas Bullmore and John Woods were confined for fighting, Bullmore recently having a fight with Private Haynes, and two days later, Private Patrick Connelly was court martialled for insolence to a sergeant.[122]

Such necessary, though mundane, chores were relieved at times by occasions of sheer pleasure. Walks ashore offered the most pleasant diversion, for Table Bay was a place both of beauty and cosmopolitan interest. Its botanical gardens with their many varieties of birds were a delightful spot for a picnic, and it was to them that Sergeants Scott, Perry and

Dwan together with their wives and Scott's baby daughter Elizabeth, now almost eight weeks old, went on the 24th to spend a "very agreeable day".[123] They found much to interest them even apart from the gardens, for ships from all quarters of the globe were passing through the port: they watched one from Holland; another proceeding from China to Denmark; an East Indiaman from England to Bengal; and an American, the *Friendship*, en route from Boston to India, having just completed a leg of eighty-two days from Madeira.[124] Life ashore was not without its dangers however for the picknickers learnt that just prior to the fleet's arrival, a Malay who had been refused permission by the Governor to be repatriated to Batavia, had gone berserk under the influence of opium, and, grabbing what weapons he could, had rushed out into the night, killing and maiming men indiscriminately. It had taken two days to capture him by which time he had killed fourteen and wounded almost double that number. As punishment his body had been broken on a wheel and after execution his head and limbs had been severed to be distributed in various parts of the country. The incident had caused widespread community consternation.[125]

On board the *Friendship*, Ross decided at last to act on complaints from marines against the convict women, and on 26 October he ordered all her women convicts to be transferred to other ships, their place to be taken by thirty sheep.

On 8 November, after the carpenters had erected stalls for their voyage, many animals, including bulls, seven cows, one stallion, three mares, three colts, and "a great number" of rams, ewes, goats, boars, and sows, were stowed aboard the *Sirius* and some of the transports.[126] The ships must have resembled Noah's Ark, and for marine and convict alike, must have smelt like it.

A day before sailing, Sergeant Isaac Knight of the *Alexander* was reduced in rank and remained reduced till his arrival at Botany Bay.[127] On the same day, Ross boarded the

Friendship to give Meredith a warning to improve his conduct. His admonition was given publicly and in intemperate and arrogant language such as Clark felt one officer ought not to use to another.[128] As will be seen, this would not be the only occasion that Ross would act in this improper way, even though in this instance Meredith's drinking habits deserved severe, though private, censure.

At last, arrangements for the last leg of the voyage were completed and on 12 November the fleet set sail to cross the Indian Ocean for Botany Bay. All had eaten well at the Cape — in fact it was Clark's opinion that the convicts had been treated more like children than prisoners.[129] But from now on, all communication with the outside world would be cut, and the pleasures of the Cape would give way to the "coarse fare and hard labour" of Botany Bay; for many must have felt, as Bradley did, that they were leaving the last abode of civilized people for a "residence of savages".[130]

Phillip gave no salute on leaving the Cape lest it frighten the stock he had on board, but on their way out of the harbour they spoke to the *Kent* which was inward bound from London and were told that the Second Fleet for Botany Bay was being prepared.[131] The news reassured them, but falsely so, for the Second Fleet would meet with disaster.

The wind blew so hard for the first two days that huge seas broke over the ships.[132] On the 14th, water was rationed at three quarts (3.3 l) a day, and dysentery broke out amongst the convicts, who transmitted it to the marines with whom the epidemic raged till Christmas. Private Daniel Creswell, who contracted it on 19 November, died eleven days later, the only marine to die on the voyage.[133] It had produced in him an agony more acute than anything Surgeon White had previously witnessed.[134]

The appalling weather with its increasing cold and rain together with widespread sickness of a particularly virulent kind were not conducive to lifting the spirits of Ralph Clark. Since shortly before leaving the Cape, the obsession with his loneliness had strengthened its effect on him: he had grasped his wife's picture and kissed it a "thousand times"; he had fallen into uncontrolled crying, and such was the depth of his melancholy that he constantly dreamt of his family — in fact, only ever of his family. In one such dream, he dreamt of his mother, and that was more than he could take, for it produced such a mental agony that his condition deteriorated to irrational desperation. He thought how willing he would be for the doctor to cut off any two of his fingers if, by such mutilation, he could hear from Alicia. Desperate for her, he fossicked out one of her previous letters and began reading it, but it was more than his condition could take: he had to put it aside for so profoundly did it upset him that he thought he would go "mad". He now experienced long fits of crying, and when one night he had a tortuous nightmare in which both Alicia and his mother died, he buried his head in his pillow and cried for hours.[135] His self-torture had made him at times quite misanthropic: when a convict woman lost seven pairs of Doctor Arndell's stockings overboard, Clark doubted the truthfulness of her story. He felt that other convicts had stolen them, and in a vituperative outburst he poured out his loathing of them. "There never was a greater number of D . . . d B . . . s in one place as there is in this ship", he railed, and then, in giving full vent to his rancour, he let it be known that if any one of them was to lose any of his washing, he would willingly "cut them to pieces".[136] There was an ambivalence in his nature: on the one hand, he could be a man of touching sensitivity; on the other, especially where convict women were concerned, he could be heartless. And as far as Faddy was concerned, his disliking had become so firm that he had decided not to share a tent with him at Botany Bay.[137] To what extent these reactions were exacerbated by his mental condition it is hard to say, though such a condition would hardly have been conducive to benevolence.

Meanwhile, Phillip had decided to divide the fleet by

forming a vanguard to push ahead of the main fleet to reach Botany Bay earlier to prepare reception arrangements. He announced his decision on 16 November; David Collins, his secretary, knew of it on that day, and the evidence strongly suggests that Ross also knew of it on the same day. But Ross took two exceptions to the decision. Firstly, he felt "hurt" that Phillip had not confided in him prior to leaving the Cape. (It apparently never occurred to him that Phillip might not have made the decision then.) And secondly, Ross alleged that others had known of it before he had because the first he had heard of the vanguard was from someone in the mess of the *Sirius*. He was to nurse this grievance for nine months until, in July 1788, he would add it to his other complaints against Phillip.[138]

An examination of the facts, however, does not justify Ross's reaction. A few days out of the Cape, probably on the 16th, when Phillip asked Ross if he wished to join the vanguard, Ross felt aggrieved that he had not been told earlier. But even if Phillip, whilst at the Cape, had privately considered the possibility of dividing the fleet, he was under no obligation to transmit his private musings on possible contingencies to Ross who was not the Lieutenant Governor, in the terms of his commission, until the settlement at Botany Bay was established.[139] At the Cape therefore, he was merely the officer commanding the marines. Consequently, Ross erred in assuming that during the voyage Phillip was obliged to make him his confidant. Ross's piqued reaction revealed either his failure to understand his position, or his determination to elevate himself to an unauthorized equality with Phillip. As for Ross's other complaint — that the information had come to him indirectly from some conversation in the *Sirius* mess — no evidence exists to suggest that Phillip conspired or contrived to deny Ross the knowledge. Collins states that Phillip merely "signified his intention" which gives the impression that there and then, it was for public consumption.[140] It would be quite normal and entirely feasible that Ross would hear of the plan from "mess talk", because, as it was primarily a naval and navigational decision, Phillip probably discussed it with officers such as Hunter and Ball before he came to a firm conclusion. After all, as Hunter's *Sirius* was to lead the main fleet, and Ball's *Supply* was to lead the vanguard, they were involved in a technical way that Ross was not. In all probability, Ross learnt of the decision from others who had heard of it from Hunter and Ball. But for Ross to expect consultation on such a matter was for him to assume an authority and a standing which, as a major, he did not possess; for him later to report Phillip to the Admiralty on the matter, was indefensible. However, in spite of feeling aggrieved, Ross transferred on the 25th to the *Scarborough* with his quartermaster and adjutant to be part of the vanguard.[141] The other transports in the vanguard of four were the *Alexander* and the *Friendship*; and the remaining seven ships of the main body came under the command of Hunter.

The first days of December were days of fierce winds and a dreadful rolling swell. The further south both fleets sailed, the more intense the cold became, and frightful seas broke over them. Clark and probably others became more seasick than ever before.[142] It was into these tortuous conditions that John was born to Private and Mrs Harmsworth at 3.30 a.m. on 1 December.[143] In spite of the uninviting physical circumstances surrounding his arrival, he did at least have the advantage of spending his early days on a clean ship, for the greatest service which the marines did the First Fleet was to maintain strict shipboard cleanliness. Doctor Bowes, surgeon of the *Lady Penrhyn*, confirmed this in acknowledging their strict attention to cleanliness and airing of berths;[144] King also attributed the excellent state of health of the First Fleet to "the activity and vigilance of the officers of marines"; whilst Private Easty wrote that marines were ordered to scrub their own hammocks every fortnight.[145]

As the *Friendship* ploughed through the cold and tremendous seas of the southern Indian Ocean with the rest of the vanguard, Ralph Clark's despair continued undiminished, and he described 7 and 8 December as his blackest days. On the 7th he thought so incessantly about Alicia that he looked forward to going to bed for "a hearty cry" to relieve the heavy load he felt round his heart.[146] The 8th was even worse for him as he fought back tears, and even reading about Lady Jane Grey sent him crying. In the extremes of his misery that day, he revealed that his reason for leaving his loves ones had been to gain promotion. It was rank that he had been after: he even dreamt once that he had been made a first lieutenant.[147] Writing later from Norfolk Island to his friend Kempster in 1790, he confirmed the point by stipulating that the only inducements for which he would stay would be promotion and to be joined by his family.[148] In his sadness however he could still be kind, albeit to men only, for on 10 December he took pity on convict John Best who was very cold and gave him some rum, an action he repeated a week later to other cold seamen.[149]

Some ration items were becoming scarce, and when flour was expended on the *Prince of Wales* her marines were given beef in lieu;[150] even so, Christmas day saw a reasonably traditional meal enjoyed: Sergeant Scott's dinner comprised pork, apple sauce, beef, and plum pudding. He crowned the day with four bottles of rum which he said was the best "we veterans could afford".[151] On the *Lady Penrhyn*, Doctor Bowes gave three marines currants to make a plum pudding, and "to cheer their hearts and to distinguish this day as being the most remarkable in the year", the captain gave them a reasonable quantity of grog.[152] On the other hand, Clark aboard the *Friendship*, kissed Alicia's picture and, contrary to the adequacies of the above meals, he had only a "poor dinner", during which he drank her health in water. His abstinence however was not embraced by other marines, several of whom got drunk.[153]

3

Botany Bay to Sydney Cove

The year 1788 began with the fleet 44° south, 135° east, in a howling gale.[1] Next day, the incorrigible Private Luke Haynes was ordered to an immediate court martial by Ross for unsoldierly-like behaviour. Captain Shea presided, and though Haynes was found guilty, his sentence of one hundred lashes was cancelled. Whilst Haynes was transgressing, the convicts aboard the *Scarborough* made a play and sang songs — an indication of their happiness.[2] On 3 January the vanguard saw the coast of Australia for the first time.[3] By 7 January the main fleet was off Tasmania.[4] On the day following, with the long voyage nearing its end, Ross told Meredith to prepare the weapons and stores ready for landing.[5] And at 2.15 p.m. on Friday 18 January, the *Supply* entered Botany Bay, anchoring on the north side so that her following ships could see her.[6] Phillip lost no time in landing, and at three o'clock, accompanied by Dawes, King and some officers of the *Supply*, he was rowed to the north shore. Standing on the beach, non-plussed, were some Aborigines, to whom Phillip advanced using kind and reassuring gestures. He offered them coloured beads, but, being too frightened to allow him to come up to them, they retreated; whereupon he laid the beads on the shore and retired a little. A trembling Aborigine took them up and hurried back to the safety of the group, and Phillip returned on board having conducted this first meeting between Aborigines and the First Fleet.[7]

Next day, Saturday the 19th, nineteen hours after Phillip's arrival, the three transports of the vanguard, *Scarborough*, *Alexander*, and *Friendship*, anchored in the bay at 9 a.m. As Collins went on to write, "Thus under the blessing of God was happily completed in eight months and one week, a voyage which before it was undertaken, the mind hardly dared venture to contemplate ... without some apprehensions as to its termination."[8]

Botany Bay that day became the scene of considerable activity. At daylight a party had gone ashore to catch fish. At half past ten a long boat from the *Supply* transferred much needed hay for sheep on the *Friendship*; Meredith of the *Friendship* visited the *Scarborough* and stayed all day; John Johnson from the *Alexander* was entertained to tea by Ralph Clark on the *Friendship* and they caught a great many fish; and Ross, who visited Phillip in the *Supply*, was added to an exploration party which was to consist of some marines together with Phillip, Dawes, Ross, Ball, Long, and King in three boats.

They left at 11 a.m. and travelled along the bay's northern shore to Cook's River, along which they sailed for about six miles, and from thence to George's River where the group went ashore for a lunch of corned beef and beer in which they drank to the healths "of our friends in England".[9] After walking a little distance along the shore from where they saw some Aboriginal huts, they returned to the *Supply* at six o'clock that evening. Much later, after midnight, Meredith and Doctor Arndell returned to the *Friendship*, again slightly drunk, and informed Clark, who long since had gone to bed, that Ross now required a duty officer to be on deck day and night. Instinctively Clark knew that Meredith would not do much of the new duty and that consequently most of it would fall to himself and Faddy.[10]

Sunday 20 January dawned a lovely day of light southwest winds and a temperature of 74 °F (23 °C). At 4 a.m., the *Prince of Wales*, which was part of the main fleet, lay off the bay: Sergeant Scott thought the land looked "exceeding well".[11] An hour or so later, Clark rose and began the day by kissing his wife's picture, and read, as was his custom, the Collect for the day from the Prayer Book. It was the third Sunday after Epiphany, and the Collect was singularly appropriate:

> Almighty and everlasting God, mercifully look upon our infirmities, and in all our dangers and necessities stretch forth thy right hand to help and defend us.

He then saw the main body of the fleet assembling for entry outside the heads. The First Fleet anchored in the bay at 9.30 a.m.[12] The voyage had taken 252 days of which 68 had been spent in port.[13] All had much for which to be thankful: the long voyage, during which one marine, a marine's wife, a marine's child, plus forty convicts and five convict children had died was now behind them.[14]

Moreover, the convicts had given less trouble than expected: Phillip felt they had behaved well;[15] Tench had found them "humble, submissive, and regular";[16] and Ross felt that they appeared "perfectly satisfied and obedient".[17] This had made the task of the marines much easier.

Work began at once and the fleet had no sooner anchored than five parties went ashore. A marine guard of five was sent ashore by Clark to protect a party from *Sirius* which cut grass for the cattle;[18] two other parties from the *Scarborough* and *Alexander* and apparently containing Private Daniel Southwell also went to the same spot to assist.[19] The Aborigines were shy and would come no closer than six or seven yards, so the marines threw them presents of beads, ribbons, mirrors, buttons, and trifles which they accepted eagerly.[20] Phillip's most urgent need was to evaluate Botany Bay as a viable site for the settlement; a thorough reconnaissance therefore was required.

At ten o'clock that morning, accompanied by Ross, Hunter, King, Dawes, and a marine party, Phillip went to Point Sutherland on the southern shore of the bay.[21] Here the party split: one group led by Phillip went off to explore a section of the southern bay whilst the other, consisting of King, Dawes and three marines, went off to explore the George's River area, in search of a fresh water supply. King's group landed at Lance Point, climbed a hill, and were confronted by Aborigines who made gestures for them to "begone". King was mindful that his protection consisted of three marines only, and so he retreated towards the shore, leaving some ribbons and beads on the ground which were collected by two Aborigines who tied them round their heads. But their group was not to be placated by gifts, and, shouting for King's party to leave, they threw a spear to hasten its departure. They had now grown to about twelve; strengthened by these reinforcements, their manner became threatening. King retreated by walking backwards down the hill, but when the natives threw a spear into the midst of his group, King ordered a marine to fire with powder only, and the Aborigines ran off in fear, ending the first display of Aboriginal resentment of Europeans. King's party returned to its boat where they were joined by Phillip's group. Phillip, who showed a genuine compassion towards Aborigines, then visited Lance Hill, met the Aborigines, gave them presents, and restored harmony. His manner seemed to them genuine, and, reassured, they fraternized and gathered round the three rowing boats. Such was the reconciliation Phillip had effected, that the Aborigines, heavy with remorse for the spear which had been thrown, sought Phillip's approval for them to kill the thrower, whom they began to prepare for death. Phillip signalled them to desist. To show the spear thrower that he had been forgiven, Phillip gave him some beads. The Europeans then sailed up another inlet, where a larger party of Aborigines approached them. The Europeans were, of course, dressed; the Aborigines were not, but they were, according to King, curious to know what sex the Europeans were. King therefore ordered "one of the people" (either a seaman or a marine) to "undeceive them" by revealing himself. King says the Aborigines then "made a great shout of admiration" and, pointing to their women standing on shore, offered them to the Europeans' "service". King's response was to offer one of the women a white handkerchief to cover her nakedness. But by now evening had come and Phillip's party was twelve miles from the fleet, so they returned at midnight.[22] Phillip was far from impressed with the viability of Botany Bay in spite of the high praise Cook had given it. Tomorrow, another site would have to be sought.

Monday the 21st was also a delightful day of northeast breezes and a temperature of 75°F. At daylight Meredith and Faddy went fishing and stayed out all day, leaving Clark to send a shore party to pitch four tents.[23] These were probably used by carpenters and sawyers sent ashore to fell trees and construct sawpits.[24] As it had not yet been finally decided to settle at Botany Bay, the convicts were not landed, and all work ashore was performed by marines and seamen, with Ross commanding all shore-side operations.[25] At 6 a.m., disappointed with the previous day's reconnaissance, Phillip set out north for Broken Bay in three open boats accompanied by Hunter, Collins, James Keltie (the master of *Sirius*) and David Blackburn (the master of *Supply*) together with a guard of marines.[26] They sailed up the coast and decided as they neared Port Jackson to enter and explore it. It had been named by Cook after Sir George Jackson who in 1770 had been Second Secretary to the Admiralty. They entered the harbour early in the afternoon and at first were not impressed, but opinions quickly changed. Hunter records: "We had not gone far in ... [when we] found ourselves perfectly land locked ... we proceeded up for two days examining every cove capable of receiving ships."[27] Phillip was thrilled with what he had found, and in his ecstasy he described Port Jackson as "the finest harbour in the world".[28] He entered one cove and found flowing into it a fresh water stream (later called the Tank Stream) which solved the problem of Botany Bay's water deficiency. Phillip named it Sydney Cove after Lord Sydney.

Meanwhile, at Botany Bay Ross was in charge with instructions to clear the area around Point Sutherland ready to land the marines and convicts should the site be chosen. A party consisting of King, Dawes and a group of marines set out in two boats to explore twelve miles of the George's River, whilst another party consisting of marines and some crew from the *Sirius* landed on the southern shore to clear ground and dig sawpits. There the natives objected to trees being felled. Apparently remembering the previous day's incident in which a marine had fired his rifle, they expressed a dislike of the soldiers, and after one Aborigine approached a marine and felt the point of his bayonet, they urged them to depart.[29] Whilst these various groups were busy in the affairs of the settlement, others had time for recreation, Doctor Bowes and several gentlemen finding time to go ashore to fish.[30]

On Tuesday 22 January, early in the morning, the Adjutant, Lieutenant Long, visited Clark aboard the *Friendship*. Clark had as yet made no visit to the shore. By contrast, Faddy and Meredith had had every day ashore, and this day was no exception: Meredith left the ship to dine out; Faddy accompanied King ashore; Clark was left to "think the more" of his Alicia;[31] and Captains Campbell and Tench received warning orders for their companies to be ready to disembark the following day.

Early on the 23rd, Private Easty went ashore at Point Sutherland as part of the guard protecting the seamen making a sawpit. Easty also noted that the land was poor, and by now no one was impressed with Botany Bay. Clark at last left the *Friendship* and went to the *Scarborough* with Doctor Arndell for breakfast, after which they collected Lieutenant

Davey to visit the proposed settlement site on the southern shore. Ross accompanied them on a long walk into the country. Clark was not impressed with Botany Bay as a site and hoped that Phillip would find a better one for otherwise, he predicted, all would perish within a year. However, by the time they returned to the *Scarborough* that evening, Phillip had returned "full of praises" for Port Jackson and announced his intention to establish the settlement there.[32] Clark was delighted and that night broke his custom of an early retirement to stay up for supper.[33] Phillip intended losing no time in relocating the settlement and told the fleet to prepare for departure next morning.[34] In anticipation of this, a work party of convicts and a marine company was put aboard *Sirius*.[35] The completed sawpit was immediately abandoned when orders were received for all to return on board for the transfer to Port Jackson.[36]

All were ready to depart at daybreak on 24 January when, to everyone's consternation, two French ships were sighted standing off the heads, waiting for the strong winds to abate so that they could enter. Phillip was alarmed, for he did not know their intentions, and he ordered a party to be sent to Point Sutherland to hoist English colours. He also stipulated that the move to Port Jackson be kept secret, and that no one was to go on board the French ships.[37] In the meantime, he thought it wise to delay the fleet's departure till the following day. Shortly, he concluded that the ships were the *Boussole* and *Astrolabe* on the round-the-world expedition of Comte de Jean-Francois de Galaup La Perouse. Whilst La Perouse had been at Kamchatka on the Russian Pacific coast, he had received orders from the French Minister of the Marine to hasten to New South Wales to assess British plans for colonization; Phillip's wariness therefore was well placed. However, two factors enabled La Perouse to deduce that the settlement would be sited not far from Botany Bay: the first was the loose talk by the English crew members, and the second was the use by Phillip of the smallest ship, the *Supply* to convey him to Port Jackson after he left Botany Bay.[38]

Although the fleet's departure was postponed, not all were idle: Clark, apparently in a very sociable mood, invited Captain Shea and Doctor Balmain for lunch, and Lieutenant Maitland Shairp for tea and supper; a party from the *Scarborough*, protected by marines, went on shore to collect grass for fodder; Private Southwell was ordered ashore to dismantle the frame of the sawpit and return it to the *Supply*; and in the evening Ross visited all ships of the fleet to convey Phillip's orders about the departure. These included the transfer, early next morning, of Lieutenants George Johnston and William Collins of the *Lady Penrhyn* to the *Supply* so as to be with *Supply*'s marine company immediately upon its arrival at Sydney Cove. By the time Ross reached the *Friendship* to tell Clark to send two corporals to the *Charlotte* and four convicts to the *Scarborough*, Clark had retired early to bed after the most social day he had had since leaving England.

Friday 25 January was a hazy day with early fog and fresh southeasterly winds which produced big rolling seas. At four o'clock in the morning, a marine sergeant boarded the *Lady Penrhyn* with orders for Johnston and Collins, with their company of marines and forty convicts, to board the *Supply*.[39] They tried to sail at daybreak, but strong winds forced *Supply* to anchor till noon.[40] At 7 p.m. *Supply* reached Sydney Cove, which had been selected as the settlement site because it had the "best spring of water", and its depth of water at the shoreline would enable ships to anchor close to shore, thus negating the need for expensive quays to be built.[41] Meanwhile, the rest of the fleet remained at Botany Bay with Phillip's order to Hunter aboard *Sirius* to bring all to Port Jackson as soon as the seas permitted.

The next day, Saturday 26 January, was the day on which Phillip would found the settlement. It was a sunny day of 70 °F (21 °C) and at daylight a marine party from the *Supply*, and everybody else who could be spared, began clearing a small area near the Tank Stream.⁴² A flagstaff was erected to its east from which the Union Jack was flown.⁴³ The clearing of this space destroyed for evermore the quiet tranquillity of that perfect spot, and the fleet was not without those who felt the twinge of regret that such a jewel could never be the same again. Collins observed that the quiet stillness of the bush was now "for the first time since creation, interrupted by the rude sound of the labourer's axe"; and that its tranquillity was giving way to "the voice of labour ... and the busy hum of its new possessors".⁴⁴ Trees were felled and bush was cleared, all in preparation of the camp site for the marines and the few convicts who that day would land and be encamped upon it by 4 p.m.⁴⁵ At sunset and apparently before the main fleet from Botany Bay had anchored, the whole party which had arrived in the *Supply*, including the Governor, the principal officers, and the marines, assembled at the spot which had been cleared that morning and at which the Union Jack now flew. A firing party of marines formed up and fired a feu de joie, in between the volleys of which, toasts were drunk to His Majesty King George III, the royal family, and success to the new colony.⁴⁶ In such manner was Australia founded.

Meanwhile at Botany Bay the seas abated sufficienly by nine that morning for La Perouse' ships to enter and anchor a mile off the northern shore. Hunter sent a lieutenant aboard to offer assistance, but in conversation with the French he avoided revealing the new site of the settlement. At noon, Hunter felt that the seas were sufficiently abated for the fleet to depart, and he signalled them to do so. As they began to sail, tragedy almost struck: the transports started to experience great difficulty in getting enough wind to stay on the course needed to get out of the bay. The *Prince of Wales* and the *Friendship* collided heavily and carried away the *Friendship*'s jib boom; then the *Charlotte* ran into the *Friendship* and both ships nearly ended up on the rocks;⁴⁷ consequently it was not till three o'clock in the afternoon that the last of the ships cleared the bay. At 7 p.m. Hunter's fleet entered Port Jackson and moved up the harbour to anchor in Sydney Cove by 8 p.m. Clark agreed Port Jackson was "one of the finest harbours in the world".[48] Phillip was on shore to greet them, and Hunter, in reporting to him, passed on what intelligence he had gained about La Perouse.

The new arrivals gaped about them, and many were deeply stirred by the untouched beauty of the place: Bowes felt its coves had a "novel and romantic appearance"; Tench enjoyed its "luxuriant" shores covered with trees to the water's edge; King, more pragmatically, noticed the dangerous shoal just inside the harbour's entrance and the quantity of labour that would be needed to clear the many trees; but the most moved appears to have been Collins who, using Milton's line "one who brings a mind not to be changed by time or place", saw the enormous responsibility placed on the newcomers not to sully the purity of nature "in her simplest, purest garb . . . by the introduction of vice, profaneness, and immorality".[49]

Phillip closed the momentous day with orders that parties of convict men, guarded by marines, would land each morning to fell trees and dig sawpits, return to their ships for lunch, and spend the afternoons ashore in labour, returning to the ships at night.

And so ended the saga of a remarkable voyage — more remarkable in some ways than any other yet made. Phillip's floating gaol had operated well; his navigational skill had brought his fleet through hitherto uncharted waters without mishap; the marines, in Phillip's opinion, had behaved well;[50] scurvy, which normally broke out on such expeditions, had been avoided by Phillip's foresight and resupply programme; marine and convict alike had arrived at Port Jackson healthy and happy in spite of nine months' incarceration aboard tiny, congested ships.

Finally, Phillip had shown profound wisdom, foresight, and decisiveness in changing the site of the settlement to

Sydney Cove. Well might everyone that night have felt grateful for their present condition, and well might Phillip had felt a quiet pride in what, so far in his life, had been his greatest achievement.

4

Sleeping on the Ground

It was one thing for the fleet to have arrived safely at its destination, but it was going to be quite another to found a colony. The task was a daunting one; problems were many, and the role of the Marine Corps would be crucial. Its willing assistance and its attitude to a convict society would largely dictate the degree of harmony and progress in the infant settlement. So far, the relationship had been reasonably amicable mainly because the convicts had been confined and the sexes separated, thus facilitating control. But those restrictions would cease after disembarkation and then the real nature of the marine-convict relationship would be asserted. The first month or two ashore would lay the foundations of that ethos in which group attitudes and relationships would develop, and in many ways the very early days would establish the social environment in which marine and convict would have to exist.

The settlement's first day ashore at Sydney Cove, Sunday 27 January, was a cloudy and windy one. Clark rose, and as usual kissed Alicia's picture and read the Lessons appointed for the day, which was the fourth Sunday after Epiphany. Its Epistle came from Romans 13:1 in which Paul outlines the Christian plan for relationships. Perhaps it would have been more beneficial if Major Ross had also pondered its message.

> Let every soul be subject unto the higher powers . . . Render therefore to all their dues; tribute to whom tribute is due; custom to whom custom, fear to whom fear, honour to whom honour.

His devotions ended, Clark surveyed the shore and was completely "charmed" by it, noting how pretty the tents looked among the trees.[1] As it was urgent that an area be cleared for the marine camp, the *Scarborough*, *Friendship* and *Charlotte* moved up that morning to the head of the cove to land a party of convicts for the purpose,[2] whilst at 2 p.m. another party of five marines and one hundred convicts landed to discharge stores and erect two marquees for the camp near the Tank Stream.[3] Activity was everywhere visible: Tench captured the scene graphically.

> Business now sat on every brow, and the scene, to an indifferent spectator, at leisure to contemplate it, would have been highly picturesque and amusing. In one place, a party cutting down the woods; a second, setting up a blacksmith's forge; a third, dragging along a load of stores or provisions; here an officer pitching his marquee, with a detachment of troops parading on one side of him, and a cook's fire blazing up on the other. Through the unwearied diligence of those at the head of the different departments, regularity was, however, soon introduced, and, as far as the unsettled state of matters would allow, confusion gave place to system.[4]

The Tank Stream divided the settlement into its eastern and western sides. On the eastern, Phillip established Government House — a prefabricated canvas marquee worth £115[5] together with accommodation for his staff, marine guard, and a few convicts. On the western side, the camps for the remaining convicts and the marine detachment were to be established. Phillip promulgated the settlement's boundaries and appointed a constable and two marine guards to apprehend all who were found outside them.[6]

At 6 a.m. on Monday the 28th, disembarkation of the male convicts began. Only the sick were retained on board, because as yet there was no hospital on shore. Clark for his part was glad to see the *Friendship* complement go. He and his marines landed at 10 a.m. complete with wives, children, and personal effects, clashing with the marines landing from the other three companies, and confusion reigned for a time. Clark and Thomas Davey shared a marquee, and as Lieutenant Timins' tent was not yet erected, they let him put his bed in with them. Clark had judged that conditions ashore for the first few days would be primitive, so he still slept aboard.[7] On the other hand, Captain Campbell on his first day ashore was so well housed in his tent as to not only entertain Doctor Bowes but also to present him with some insects and a lorikeet bird.[8] Whilst the cattle were being landed on the eastern shore, Hunter set out to survey the harbour to what is now Manly. Convicts busily cleared ground,[9] the marines pitched their tents,[10] and so by the end of the second day, everyone had been landed except the sick male convicts, the female convicts, and, presumably, those marines needed on board to guard them.

The 29th was a cloudy, hot day; Clark rose early and had a breakfast of one biscuit and a glass of water;[11] convicts were set to dig a garden;[12] and Corporal Goodall was reduced to the ranks for some infraction not mentioned.[13]

Next day, Ross issued the detachment its first Routine Orders (then called Orders of the Day) and these were entered in Captain Campbell's Orderly Book. They stipulated that one NCO and six privates were to mount guard at the hospital till further orders; patrols were to bring in stragglers and to fire on any escapee or convict out at night; the dinner mess drum was to be beaten at noon, before which no man was to be served; company rations were to be drawn Mondays and Fridays from the contractor, though spirits were to be drawn daily. As well, a sergeant was to be added to the Quarter Guard, a section of the main guard, to enforce orders against stragglers, and the next day's duty roster was published nominating Clark as guard officer, Timins as duty officer, and Faddy and Collins as officers on call.[14]

Lieutenant King, who had been aide-de-camp to Governor

Phillip, was appointed by him as Lieutenant Governor of Norfolk Island. Phillip had been instructed before leaving England to form a settlement on Norfolk Island "to prevent its being occupied by any other European power". (On 14 February 1788 Phillip sent twenty-five people under P.G. King to form the settlement.)[15] King's place at Port Jackson was filled by Lieutenant George Johnston. Johnston's competence and dignity of manner apparently had been such as to merit the appointment, and this pleased Bowes, who, though usually a severe critic, forecast that Johnston would fill his new post successfully.[16] Clark now brought ashore the last of his personal effects plus his "farm" of two hens and a pig which he hoped would "multiply fast with the assistance of God". At 10 p.m. on 30 January a "most outrageous storm" of lightning, thunder and rain struck the settlement,[17] forcing Clark, clad in shirt only, to get out of his tent to slacken its ropes.[18]

The tropical storms continued on the 31st and the sultry heat rose to 80°F (27°C). Captain Campbell issued the second group of Routine Orders, which published the next day's duty roster and ordered that the guard report was to be given to the duty officer for its transmission to Ross. To prevent straggling by soldiers, the orders also required company commanders to call rolls twice daily. Shooting and fishing areas were nominated, though officers were required to gain prior approval from Ross as they were not to leave camp without his permission. Clark was finding life hard and uncomfortable. He was sleeping on the ground, his palliasse was hard, and the only softness was a little grass underneath. He was feeling the oppressive heat and had never slept worse, for as well as spiders, ants, and every vermin crawling over him, he was reduced to using his uniform pouch as a pillow.[19] Conditions for the marines were primitive, though Clark appears to be the only one who complained. However, plenty of fresh fish was caught, and Meredith and Davey dined bountifully with Clark that evening.[20]

Heavy rain fell throughout the first day of February and added to the discomfort of those under canvas. Captain Campbell's Routine Order for that day stipulated that trees felled were to have their roots grubbed up because the stumps which were now proliferating had become a danger. Considerable inroads therefore were being made into the forest.

Because some convicts had been absconding to Botany Bay to visit the French ships, Phillip told King and Dawes to visit La Perouse in case any difficulties had arisen. The two left Port Jackson by cutter at two o'clock in the morning, and after being received courteously, stayed overnight.[21] Meanwhile back at Sydney, Clark rose at daybreak and, apparently to check his company's efficiency, ordered tents to be struck and moved twenty yards, a task which was completed in fifteen minutes.[22]

Campbell's Routine Orders also set out the arrangements for the following day's church parade: the drum roll, which was to assemble the compulsory parade, would beat at 10 a.m. to signal the battalion to form up. Ross, keen for the military to set a good example, told the Marine Corp wives to be dressed cleanly. The detachment's new guard would mount early at 7 a.m. to permit the old guard to get cleaned before joining the parade; tent flaps were to be tied back for the tents to be aired; and all paths were to be swept — details which have ever been the normal contents of Routine Orders.[23]

The colony's first Sunday was 3 February, the fifth Sunday after Epiphany. Quite early on that day, King and Dawes set out from Botany Bay on their return journey after visiting the French ships but with both wind and swell against them, they had to row all the way and did not board *Sirius* till 7 p.m.[24] For Clark, however, it was a special day, his wife's birthday. He began it by inviting William Collins to breakfast, and later invited Meredith, Davey and Timins to drink her health in punch.[25] Campbell's orders that day required that no seaman was to enter convict camps without permission from the guard officer. This was designed to forestall problems when the women would be landed in a few days' time. Another order required the Surveyor General to supervise convicts clearing ground: Ross would not permit marines to supervise convict labour — a stand which had the unanimous support of the officers.[26] In spite of these trivialities, however, the day was to be most remembered as the day of the settlement's first church service. It was held "on the grass"[27] under a "great tree"[28] and though the contents of Johnson's sermon have not survived, he preached from Psalm 116, verse 12: "What shall I render unto the Lord for all his benefits towards me". It was an appropriate text for those who had survived the ordeal of the voyage but possibly Johnson selected it not so much with the past in mind as with the present, surrounded as they were by a scenically beautiful situation, and with the hope it offered to convicts of a lifestyle better than that of the hulks and gaols from which they had come. But whatever Johnson's reason, Clark found it a "good" sermon, and it was well received by both marines and convicts, whose behaviour was, according to Tench, "equally regular and attentive".[29] Their forebearance was all the more commendable because the service must have been a lengthy one, including as it did the baptism of James Thomas, the son of Private Samuel and Ann Thomas.

Wednesday 6 February was the day the convict women disembarked. They were ready by 5 a.m., and after being fruitlessly searched for stolen property,[30] they were landed by rowing boats between 6 a.m. and 6 p.m. The male convicts reacted immediately and, according to Doctor Bowes, "got to them very soon after they landed", producing scenes of riot and debauchery beyond his capacity to describe. Ralph Clark, however, on whom the new surroundings were having an agreeable effect, went shooting with Lieutenant John Johnson and bagged a duck and some birds. He sent these to Ross, then joined him for supper. During the meal a most severe electrical storm struck, knocking down a sentry who was standing outside the major's tent. The storm persisted and at midnight, lightning split a tree which killed five sheep belonging to Ross.[31] So vicious were these early storms that during the next night, a sentry was blinded by lightning.[32]

The 7th of February was the memorable day on which Phillip's commission was read to the public. It was a ceremonial occasion in which the detachment took a prominent part. The day began with the detachment busying itself during the early morning with the usual "spit-and-polish" which precedes ceremonial parades — Clark himself being up early to dress for it.[33] At 11 a.m. the detachment, under arms and with colours flying and band playing, formed a guard of honour to receive the Governor. Phillip was accompanied by Ross, the Chaplain, and other principal officers. As Phillip approached the colours, they were dipped in respect to him, and he saluted them by removing his hat. The marines then marched past accompanied by the band which played several pieces "suited to the business".[34] After the parade had re-formed, Phillip complimented the officers on a fine parade and then addressed the troops, commending their soldierly bearing and behaviour since boarding their ships a year earlier.[35] These comments so pleased Major Ross that he ordered them to be recorded in the General Orders Book. The troops then marched to an adjoining ground which had been cleared for the occasion, and formed a circle around the convicts, who were ordered to sit down. Phillip, accompanied by Ross, David Collins, the chaplain, and other dignitaries, moved to the centre. There they stood behind a camp table upon which had been laid two red leather cases containing the commissions of Phillip and the judiciary, both of which Collins read aloud. They informed the assembly that these commissions had been embodied in the Act of Parliament by which the colony had been founded, and which empowered Phillip to convene a criminal court consisting of the Judge Advocate and six officers of His Majesty's forces. Its decisions were to be by majority vote except in capital cases where five of the six had to concur. Its judgment would then be executed by the Provost Marshal. At this point Collins, having completed his part of the proceedings, handed over to Phillip. Addressing his remarks to the convicts, Phillip said that whilst he did not doubt that there were many among them who would display a "disposition to amendment", neither did he doubt that there were others who would be incorrigible. To these he promised the full "rigour of the law". Accordingly, thieving of poultry and stock, so essential to the colony's survival, would be punishable by death; those men attempting at night to steal into the women's tents would be fired upon, and death by starvation would be the lot of those who would not work. He explained that the harsh difficulties facing the settlement necessitated these harsh penalties, and although no one would be worked beyond his capacity, everyone would have to contribute his share if all were to survive. He indicated that their first task would be the erection of houses for the principal officers, followed by houses for the marines, and finally houses for themselves. These remarks concluded the proceedings and the convicts were then dismissed.[36] The marines marched back to their parade ground, formed up in inspection order, and after being reviewed by Phillip who marched along their front rank, they gave him the general salute due to a captain-general.[37] Three volleys were then fired as the band played the first part of God Save the King between each volley.[38] All officers then attended a cold collation which was held in a large marquee specially erected for the occasion. Clark however was in a glum mood for not only did he find the mutton to be maggot-ridden, but he was unhappy about the powers vested in Phillip. Never before had he heard of any British officer having such authority.[39] Captain Meredith closed the day appropriately that evening by reading to the marines the letter addressed to them from the King when they first joined the tour of duty.[40]

During the next few days, the women's camp continued as a place of debauchery: Clark was appalled at its scenes and observed that "no sooner has a man gone in with a woman than another goes in with her".[41] He called the place "a whore camp" and a "Sodom" in which more sin was committed "than in any other part of the world". Tench agreed with him and said that though licentiousness and the old habits of depravity had begun to recur, prevention of it was impossible.[42] Bowes confirmed these reports and on 9 and 11 February referred to illicit visits by men to the camp, though the percentage of women involved is not stated. Even so, it is apparent that during a good part of February, the colony was close to a breakdown of morality and order: convicts were breaking bounds, thieving was rife, as was drunkeness caused by the smuggling ashore of spirits by unscrupulous seamen; and the convict men, feeling a self-appointed responsibility for the convict women, took on a vigilante role against any seamen they found loitering near the women's camp. Such seamen were assaulted most brutally. Well might Bowes describe the situation as one of "chaos and confusion" for lawlessness was uncontrolled. And yet Phillip was powerless to do anything about it, for two reasons: the British government had failed to provide overseers for the convicts, and Ross had refused to allow the marines to act in their stead — a matter which will be investigated later.

5

Early Crimes and Punishments

The early days of the colony had produced widespread licence and disorder from which it was imperative that the military be distanced so as not to be infected by it. In this era a military force could quickly and easily degenerate into a rabble: after the battle of Badajos, Wellington's British Army troops plundered, raped, and murdered, and he was to describe them as "the scum of the earth".[1] A latent capacity for this prevailed at Port Jackson. Consequently, maintenance not only of military discipline but also of convict respect for their military supervisors was essential if a general chaos was to be avoided. Two sets of problems therefore existed: one was to maintain normal military discipline within the detachment itself; the other was to find a way of handling convict insubordination and the snide, contumely taunts which increasingly came from them. The forms for enforcing military discipline were readily available under the Mutiny Act and were well understood by the marines to whom they applied; but the new experience of dealing with the sauciness and veiled impertinence of civilians not subject to military law, was to be, at times, vexing; the necessary retention of the marines' superior position in society was difficult to maintain.

These challenges came from seaman and convict alike. A

precursor of what was to come occurred as early as 5 February, the day before the convict women landed, when a drunken seaman from the *Alexander* entered the marine camp and arrogantly affronted some of the officers, who had him seized and drummed out. Four days later, faced with the need to dissuade illicit visits by seamen to the women's camp, the whole marine band was called upon to play the "Rogues March" to drum out a sailor who had entered the women's tents. Not two more days were to pass before the process had to be repeated for a seaman and a boy from the *Prince of Wales* who were caught in a woman's tent. To increase the ignominy, the boy was dressed in petticoats.[2] The drumming however had little success though the humiliation it bestowed greatly pleased Clark who used the occasion to declare his complete marital fidelity to his wife, a resolution which was later to come unstuck at Norfolk Island.[3]

So far, any disregard for military orders had come from seamen, but it did not take long for their example to be followed by convicts. On 8 February, Samuel Barsby, a convict, was charged with abusing the drum major, Benjamin Cook, striking Drummer John West with an adze, putting him in fear of his life, and repeatedly abusing the sentry guard whilst in custody. His offences arose when, working as a cooper on the eastern side, he broke his adze. Walking across to the western side he met two seamen who, whilst enquiring for the women's camp, gave him three-quarters of a bottle of rum. He drank this before meeting another convict, Thomas Acres, with whom he quarrelled. Cook saw them and ordered them back to work. Acres complied, but Barsby hit Cook with his adze and Cook retaliated by hitting him with his cane. Lieutenants Clark and William Collins happened to be passing and intervened, ordering Drummer West to take Barsby to the guard. This convulsed Barsby to such an anger that he again struck Cook with his adze. Cook had had enough, and, assisted by West, he overpowered Barsby until the guard came and took him to the lockup. But

Barsby's fury continued and that evening he became so violent that he had to be bound and gagged.[4] At his ensuing trial, which was to be the first in the colony, the Criminal Court assembled and sentenced him to 150 lashes. The case was important from two points of view. Firstly it indicated the beginnings of a new audacity by convicts towards the military, and secondly it demonstrated the lightness of convict sentences compared with those being given to marines.

For example, Private Bramwell of Campbell's company had received 200 lashes from a court martial for striking Elizabeth Needham, a convict who was, according to Clark, "a most infamous huzzy". She had refused to go into the bush with Bramwell to be seduced by him, though he had had "connections" with her during the voyage.[5] Bramwell's crime was less serious than that of Barsby and yet his punishment was greater. These disparities caused discontent and "great murmuring" in the detachment.[6] However, the marines ought not to have been surprised, for eighteenth century military punishments were harsher than those under civil law. Sentences of 1,000 lashes were not uncommon in the British Army. It was not without reason therefore that Americans during their war referred to British soldiers as "lobsters" and "Bloodybacks".[7] The Port Jackson marines, in fact, were under the discipline of their own officers, not the Criminal Court. Any complaints therefore which they harboured about the severity of their sentences ought to have been against their own officers and not against supposed inequities in the system.

The discontent generated by the incident was not lessened however when further instances occurred. On 20 February, Privates Green, McDonald and Godfrey were convicted for "going to these D --- B --- of convict women" (Clark's description). Green received 100 lashes, and McDonald and Godfrey 50 each.[8] And on 10 March, two privates who brought a convict woman into their tents in the camp were each sentenced to 150 lashes. A common member of each of these courts martial was Ralph Clark, whose harsh attitude to anything associated with convict women might have induced the harsher penalty. The problem was exacerbated by the growing indifference and precocity of some of the convicts towards military personnel. Late in February, two women who were called back by the perimeter sentries, contemptuously refused to comply and kept walking till the sentries shot at them. Neither was hurt — much to Clark's disappointment.[9] Other instances showed a growing convict determination not to be cowered by the marines: convict James Cullen had an argument with Sergeant Thomas Smith about felling a tree, during which Cullen became insolent and aggressive. Two privates who were witnesses gave evidence to the Criminal Court, which found Cullen guilty but sentenced him lightly with 25 lashes.[10] Incidents of convict insolence occurred throughout the year. At midnight on 1 August, Corporal James Baker and Private William Godfrey were sent to the women's camp to investigate a disturbance and bring the culprit to the guardhouse. When they arrived, they found Anne Farmer lying drunkenly in the corner of her tent. She refused to accompany them, and as they could not budge her they informed an officer. He found her too drunk to be moved and ordered her to be left there till the morning, when she was brought for trial before Hunter and David Collins. Her defence was that when a tree had fallen on her hut and destroyed it, some convicts had looted some of her provisions, and she had therefore disobeyed the marines' order to go to the guardhouse because she feared more would be stolen. She then accused Corporal Baker of taking indecent liberties with her. Hunter and Collins found her not guilty.

Because the colony lacked a civil police force to deal with petty convict crime, this function fell to the marines whose guardhouse (normally a detention centre for erring soldiers) had now to be used as a police station. Thus at midnight on 3 July 1788, Mr White, the surgeon, was awakened by the sound outside his tent of Joshua Peck vomiting from drunkenness. He found Peck to be too drunk to stand and called the guard corporal, who searched Peck's tent and found a tea kettle of red wine which, White suspected, had been filled from the hospital's cask. He woke Surgeon Balmain, and together they went to the hospital laboratory tent where they found John Small incoherently lying in a state of "beastly drunkenness", and Chadwick "staggering with intoxication". Chadwick and Peck were sent to the guardhouse, as Small would have been except that he was too drunk to be moved.[11] The incident illustrated the civil nature of much of the marines' duty. They were military being used in the role of civil police and a propensity existed for a highly acrimonious relationship to develop between them and the convicts. The fact that it did not do so was due to the moderate and accommodating attitude of the marines towards their convict prisoners. Such forbearance of course was given short shrift in cases where, as opposed to jousting with the system, convicts deliberately committed personal offences against marines. Thus on 4 June 1788, convict Samuel Peyton,[12] knowing that Lieutenant Furzer was attending the bonfire festivities in celebration of the King's birthday, entered Furzer's tent and was in the act of stealing some shirts, stockings and a comb when the officer returned unexpectedly and caught him. Furzer hit him on the head with such force that he knocked him unconscious and forced his hospitalization. But worse was to follow for Peyton: it was discovered that in league with a convict named Corbett he had entered Captain Meredith's tent, also with the intention of robbery. Retribution was salutary: both convicts were sentenced to be hanged. Peyton acknowledged the justice of his sentence, and at the fatal tree, both burglars prayed for forgiveness "that they might be received into that bliss which the good and virtuous only can either deserve or expect". They were then "turned off" in front of the assembled convicts, upon whom their hanging made a deep impression.[13] Peyton left a deeply moving letter for his mother which again showed the surprising influence of the Book of Common Prayer on England's most ordinary people.[14] The deaths of Peyton and Corbett demonstrated that whilst the marines were prepared to tolerate a convict's vexation with the transportation system, they would not tolerate direct assaults upon marine possessions — such was the sanctity of property in the eighteenth century.

On another occasion, David Collins, the Judge Advocate, and Augustus Alt, the Surveyor General, sat in judgment on Mary and William Thompson for being drunk and insolent to the marine guard on 28 August. From the line up of strong witnesses, including Lieutenant Creswell, Sergeant Thomas Smith and Private Thomas Haswell, it was justifiable to expect a strong sentence. But William received only thirty lashes, and Mary, twenty-five.[15] Then there was the convict bystander, George Eccleston, who witnessed a fight between a marine and a male convict. Having observed apparently that the marine was getting the worst of it, Eccleston expressed the wish for a similar fate to befall all marines, whom he described as "bloody buggers".[16] He received fifty lashes for this utterance, which was inconsistent with the thirty that William Thompson had received for the same offence. The significance of both cases is that they illustrate a readiness amongst some convicts to be insolent to marines, and as convicts do not appear to have dauntingly feared the marines, the degree of convict alacrity towards them was probably more general than limited. When one convict, Fraser, was asked by Sergeant Connor to cease wandering through the Marine Corps lines and to leave, he moved two paces, turned to Sergeant Connor and said, "You may kiss my arse". His punishment was only twenty-five lashes.[17] This light sentence may have been obtained because of mitigating circumstances, because a fortnight later the notorious Samuel Barsby was also charged with drunkenness and insolence to a sentry, for which he received three hundred lashes.[18] Even so, a twenty-five-lash sentence for insolence to a marine compared mildly to sentences of up to two thousand for other offences, and in the mind of convicts, made the act of insolence to marine guards appear a trivial offence.

The problem of military control over the convict population was exacerbated by the inexperience of the soldiers in controlling women — a task not only quite new to the marines, but also one which at times baffled them to the point of bewilderment. This was well demonstrated in the affair involving Sarah Bellamy and Captain Meredith in August 1789.[19] Bellamy, a red-haired seventeen-year-old who already had had an illegitimate son, lived in a small hut in which a propped up wooden shutter acted as a window. Her bed was beneath the shutter, which opened out on to the street. One night after a heavy drinking session Meredith and Captain Keltie, master of the *Sirius*, were walking down Bridge Street — so named because it crossed the Tank Stream — when they hit upon the idea of visiting Bellamy. They arrived at her house, and, prompted by the euphoria of drink, Meredith put his hand inside the shutter and grabbed a handful of Sarah's red hair. She began screaming and kept it up until a considerable crowd gathered, for she intended extracting from the incident the maximum indignity for Meredith. The gathering crowd much discomfited Meredith who realized that he was now in an embarrassing predicatment. He tried to quieten the screaming Sarah by "pulling rank" and calling the town watch to take her away, but the watch consisted of convicts, and Harris, its leader, decided first to get her side of the story. This he obtained, and at the ensuing magistrate's court he produced it as evidence, reporting further that Sarah had alleged that after the incident, Meredith had entered her house and ordered her to the watch house, which she refused because it had been Captain Meredith and not she who had disturbed the peace. When she was pressed to reveal why she had created such a din, she revealed that she had decided "in her own breast to do it — that she was determined not to put up with such unmerited treatment from Captain Meredith or anyone else", thereby displaying no fear of the military, or, for that matter, of anyone else who transgressed her personal rights. The colony was subject to British civil law which strongly safeguarded civil liberty and protected personal rights. Combined with lingering notions of chivalry, this gave women a special position and made it difficult and at times impossible for an unsure military to deal with them; for the marines knew that Phillip would uphold the rule of law in all cases.

From the instances of the male convicts assuming an obligation to protect convict women from the seamen, as well as a refusal to be overawed by the military, convict society began to display the nascent beginnings of a distinctive Australian characteristic in which authority, pomp, and power are regarded with a light and flippant irreverence. Moreover convict society was beginning to see itself as a society in itself — a society different from those who would return "home". For the convicts, New South Wales was "home", and in that realization, the concept of an Australian society was born. From their new environment, convicts developed a growing self-confidence which by the latter part of 1789 had grown first to a lessened fear, and then to a familiarity with the marines. Accordingly, the notorious Sarah McCormick showed her contempt for marine status by abusing Private George Fleming; Elizabeth Mason felt sufficiently emboldened to bring a frivolous complaint against Drummer Abbott; male convicts Harrogan and Russell did not hesitate to fight Corporal Daniel Standfield, for which Russell was not even punished;[20] and when convict Herbert Keeling abused Private Arthur Dougherty, the court merely ordered an apology.[21] Admittedly, sentences were not always uniform: whilst McCormick, Mason and Harrogan could receive the light punishment of twenty-five lashes, others, for the same offence of insolence, could receive double that amount. Such was the sentence suffered by William Edwards in October 1789, and also by Amelia Levy, in spite of her mitigating evidence that Sergeant Clayfield had done nothing to stop stones being thrown at her by members of a work party for which he was responsible, and for which she had felt sufficiently aggrieved to chide him with "scandalous and abusive language".[22]

These recorded instances involve a small percentage only of the convicts, and even then some affected are from the more abandoned of them; but the fact that they judged the relationship between convict and marine to be sufficiently lacking in fear or oppressive cruelty as to permit such an alacrity, indicated that the marine yoke was a light one, and one at which tilts could be made. Tench confirmed this by saying that marine severity was "rarely exercised" on convicts, and this in spite of convict behaviour which at times was quite exasperating.[23]

Thus, while Phillip was absent from Sydney on an exploration expedition in August 1788, a convict named Daley told Ross that he had discovered a gold mine near the entrance to Sydney Harbour. Ross told him to take Captain Campbell to its location. The two took a boat from the *Sirius*, rowed to near the entrance, and landed. Daley then asked if he could withdraw a little into the bush, to which Campbell agreed. Having duped Campbell, Daley then returned to Sydney where he announced that he had put Campbell in possession of the mine and that Campbell now wanted an officer and a guard of marines to secure its safety. This produced great excitement and whilst Daley was feted and well fed, Lieutenant Poulden and the guard were prepared for departure. But before they could set out, Campbell returned to expose the hoax. The imposter was taken into custody and ordered to be whipped, but, endeavouring to maintain the fiction, Daley reiterated that if another officer was sent with him, he guaranteed to show him the mine. So well did he dissemble that none could judge whether he was genuine or not. Lieutenant George Johnston was deputed to accompany Daley but he decided on a strategy to test his honesty: Johnston told him that if he was deceiving him, he would shoot him dead. This frightened Daley, who confessed his hoax and was punished. Surgeon White felt that Daley might have been insane, but others were not convinced.[24] In any case, the incident showed that, for Daley at least, the marines held little fear.

Even where an infraction came from the worst type of convict, punishment was not excessive: Elizabeth Fowles was of so abandoned a character that her four-year-old daughter was made a state ward and sent to Norfolk Island to be cared for by Governor King. And yet such a woman received only twenty-five lashes when convicted of abusing a marine guard.

To supervise the labour of the convicts, Phillip had appointed some of the more reliable convicts as overseers. Official convict labour superintendents did not arrive until June 1790, and even then the five who came on the *Lady Juliana*[25] were not much use because they did not know enough about agriculture.[26] The situation for Phillip's convict overseers was almost intolerable: on the one hand they were disliked by other convicts, from whom they had to wrest a fair day's effort, and on the other they had to be very careful not to offend the marine officers, who were sensitive to any display of independence or attempted equality. This latter aspect is illustrated by the incident involving convict James White and convict overseer Henry Abrams. After an argument with White over where to put some timber, Abrams was charged with having said "Damn and bugger Captain Tench and Mr Long", and with having threatened to knock their heads off. Abrams denied the allegations and was found not guilty. But he was warned that if he had used those disrespectful words, he would have received the "severest punishment".[27] The implication was that overseers should be submissive to officers. Confirmation of this expectation seems implicit in Collins' eulogy for H.E. Dodd, the

Superintendent of Convicts at Rose Hill (later renamed Parramatta), who died on 28 January 1791.[28] Collins says that Dodd had gained the "approbation and countenance of the different officers" who had been on duty at Rose Hill, which was another way of saying that he had known his place in relation to them.

Unfortunately, very few comments by convicts on early marine-convict relations have come to light, but two letters are significant. One was written by a female convict on 14 November 1788. She did not mention any fear of the marines, and on the contrary, felt sorry that attacks by Aborigines had made their duty so "very hard". She revealed that all convict letters were examined by an officer, though a friend was taking hers privately to England.[29] The other letter was written by a young convict on 9 April 1790 when news of the loss of *Sirius* had reached Port Jackson, forcing Phillip to take the severest measures to save the colony from starvation. These measures demanded increased vigilance from the marines and according to the letter writer, this produced a fear of them among the convicts. He described the wretched condition of all at Port Jackson and went on to say, "We fear the troops for they are not contented with seeing those who live better than themselves, nor with us who live worse".[30] He was apprehensive about the fate of all convicts; he felt the marines would desert by returning to England, thus leaving them to perish by themselves. However, in assessing these sentiments it must be remembered that the letter was written when the colony's predicament was at its greatest peril, necessitating measures which, though extremely severe, were nevertheless temporary and unrepresentative.

6

The Manly Aborigine

The Marine Corps' relationship with the Aborigines was in accordance with Phillip's humane Aboriginal policy. Before leaving England, he had been instructed to ensure that there was no unnecessary interference with the Aborigines' way of life, and those who did so were to be punished "according to the degree of the offence".[1] The Aboriginal policy was therefore that they were to be protected without having any formal legal rights themselves.

The subject of the treatment of indigenous subject people had received wide publicity just before the First Fleet left England, because of the impeachment of Warren Hastings. That impeachment began in the spring of 1786 whilst ministers were considering Botany Bay, and Edmund Burke, who led the impeachment, began his impassioned speeches to the House of Commons in early 1787. The cause of Hasting's indictment was that whilst he had been highly successful as the Governor General of India, he had not always exercised his authority in strict conformity with British constitutional practice. His defence was that this was not always possible when dealing with indigenous subject peoples, but Burke opposed this notion with great vehemence by defending the right of Indians to be treated in the strictest conformity with the highest principles of British humanitarianism. In one speech to Parliament delivered just before the Botany Bay fleet sailed, he said that "their blood, their opinions, and the soil of their country make one consistent piece, admitting no mixture, no adulteration, no improvement".[2] This sentiment was taken up by correspondents to British newspapers who applied it to the Aborigines at Botany Bay. One correspondent to the *Morning Chronicle* hoped that English annals would not be stained "with shedding innocent blood; others, writing to the *Daily Universal Register*, thought they ought to be civilized; one writer to the *Public Advertiser* suggested that the Aborigines be incorporated into the local scene, and another warned that those in charge of the settlement would have to exercise much "circumspection" over the reaction of troops towards them.[3] This sensitive public debate on Aboriginal welfare would have presented clear guidelines to Phillip on how to formulate his local Aboriginal policy — and not only to Phillip but to those marine officers who would come face to face with the Aborigines.

The marines made their initial contact with the Aborigines during the week spent at Botany Bay. There, though intrigued by the Europeans, the Aborigines had urged them to leave and consequently must have rejoiced when they saw the British fleet depart on 26 January. But Sydney Cove was only a long afternoon's sail away, and consequently the Aborigines' problem had been merely relocated.

When Phillip was examining the various coves of Port Jackson between 21 and 23 January, the initial Aboriginal reaction had been hostile, for they were armed and vociferous. But in one of the coves where Phillip landed after gaining the confidence of an Aborigine who appeared to be of some importance, the man approached to where the Europeans were boiling their meat for lunch. Before the spot could be reached, he realized that in passing the marines who were drawn up near the place, he would be separated from his companions. Instead of showing fear, however, he displayed "great firmness" by indicating that he would not hesitate to protect himself if any treachery was shown towards him. He then proceeded with Phillip to inspect the boiling meat, and though lacking an eating utensil himself, indicated that he would like a taste. Phillip, seeing some oyster shells nearby which could fill the role of plates, gave them to him and the meal was eaten.[4] Such was Phillip's Aboriginal policy of friendship and compassion.[5] Phillip was so impressed by the confident bearing and manly behaviour of the Aborigines in one of the harbour's coves that he named the place Manly Cove.[6] A relationship of rapport quickly developed between the Manly Aborigines and Phillip's party, so much so, that when the Europeans began preparing their lunch there, the Aborigines could not restrain their curiosity and joined them; but they became such a nuisance, Phillip drew a circular boundary on the ground, which the Aborigines quickly realized was a demarcation and thereafter sat down nearby, very quietly.

Even after the main fleet arrived at Sydney Cove, Doctor Worgan records on 27 January that when some fishing boats went to haul in their catch, some Aborigines "who behaved very friendly", helped pull in the seine, which, for their "kind office", they were liberally rewarded with a portion of the catch.[7] Hunter experienced the same friendliness next day on a survey of the harbour. His party landed at Camp Cove and was preparing a meal when some Aborigines arrived. Laying down their weapons some distance away, the blacks fraternized with the Europeans (including marines), looked at their boat, and watched the way the meal was cooked.[8] At another point, the natives directed the boat to the best place to land by pointing sticks, and then met the group most cheerfully when it landed.[9] On 29 January, Hunter's survey party at Shell Cove found the Aborigines to be "quite sociable", and though he encountered another group later in the day who were armed and took defensive precautions to protect their women, the relationship which characterized these early contacts was one of friendly apprehension rather than animosity. However as European activity increased and began to show signs that the whites had come to stay, the Aborigines saw that their land and hunting grounds had been invaded and taken from them, and by 4 February, Bradley recorded that during an exploratory voyage up the harbour, the party was confronted by such "an astonishing number" of Aborigines on the shores that Hunter judged it prudent not to land.[10] Next day, Doctor Bowes described a confrontation with the natives in which a European fishing party that wished to land was pelted with stones and threatened with lances.[11]

Thus by mid February, relationships between the two groups had begun to deteriorate. The Marine Corps detachment had no part in this process. They were a strictly disciplined group who understood clearly not only Phillip's policy of friendship towards the Aborigines, but also his orders not to use ball ammunition against them.[12] As a result, the marines perpetrated no unprovoked attack upon Aborigines during the whole of their term in the colony, in spite of the requirement for them to provide defence against Aboriginal attacks.

During March and April, incidents of actual violence began to occur. The first of these arose when, after Phillip had given a large number of presents to a group of Aborigines, one of them took a spade, for which Phillip chastised him. The Aborigine broke into a fury and returned with an armed party which was soon checked when a musket was fired.[13] Incidents then began to proliferate: several convicts eloped from Port Jackson to Botany Bay and were killed by natives;[14] A seaman who had been missing for days was found by the Governor's gamekeeper, half-starved and nearly dead. Natives had stripped him naked and pelted him with stones, and the only way he had saved himself was by hiding in a swamp up to his neck.[15] On the other occasions, a spear was thrown near Captain Meredith, and a convict out collecting vegetables was beaten severely by Aborigines.[16]

By April, a detectable Aboriginal behaviour pattern was emerging. Phillip had become popular with them, as was illustrated by the friendly reception received on his various trips: on one journey in particular, an Aborigine showed his welt marks on his shoulder made by blows from a stick.[17] But in contrast to this was the fear and hostility which the blacks felt towards the convicts, and in this Collins felt they were justified because of the attacks made by convicts on them.[18] By April the earlier rapport at Sydney was being replaced by Aboriginal fear of whites, and instead of approaching them, the blacks now tended to run away.[19] And yet the Botany Bay Aborigines remained friendly to the officers who visited there on 27 April to confirm that the French ships had departed. On that occasion, both groups slept near each other, the Aborigines gave the officers fish, and both groups parted "very friendly".[20] It was therefore at Sydney only that relationships had turned sour. And it was only a matter of time before a serious reprisal occurred.

That reprisal came on 30 May 1788.[21] Captain Campbell had used two convicts, William Okey and Samuel Davis, to cut rushes for thatching his roof. He had taken them to the South West Arm of the harbour and had left them there with a tent. When he returned to collect them, the tent was still standing but both convicts had been killed. Okey had three spears through the chest, his skull was split open, his brains dashed out, and one eye seemed to have been cut out by an axe.[22] Davis, a youth, had been hit on the forehead, though White felt that he had died from fear and exposure.[23] It was Phillip's opinion that the convicts themselves had provoked the fatal reprisal.[24] Next morning he set out with a dozen armed marines, together with White and Lieutenants Johnston and Kellow, to apprehend the Aboriginal culprits, but no trace of them could be found, even though the party pushed on to the burial place at Botany Bay of Abbe Louis Receveur, the Franciscan priest from the *Astrolabe* who had died there during La Perouse's visit.[25]

Four months later, on 4 October, convict Cooper Handley was out with an armed party of marines collecting wild vegetables and sweet tea when he strayed. Aborigines murdered and mutilated him.[26] The marines heard the commotion, gave chase, but could not catch the culprits. In the evening a marine party went out to bury his body, the head of which had been beaten to a "jelly". One spear was driven through his head, and another through his body, and one arm had been broken.[27]

Up till now, no soldier had been attacked by Aborigines. But by mid December 1788 a soldier and several convicts had disappeared and were not heard of again; three convicts had been wounded and one had been killed near Botany Bay.[28] Early on 18 December an exaggerated report reached the settlement at Sydney Cove that two thousand Aborigines were gathering at Brick Kilns, a clay area about a mile from the settlement. A marine detachment commanded by an officer was ordered to march immediately from The Rocks area of the settlement at Sydney Cove to reconnoitre the force, but it soon returned, reporting the Aborigines to number only fifty who, when the convicts pointed their shovel at them in the manner of muskets, had fled into the bush.[29]

By late December 1788, Phillip was in two minds about the Aboriginal problem: on the one hand he felt sorry for the obvious incursions which the settlement had made into their lives and hunting grounds, and he was under no illusions that some of his own convicts had exacerbated the situation. He knew this had forced the Aborigines into murderous reprisals. On the other hand, according to Tench, Phillip had become tired of the petty warfare which the Aborigines were now mounting against the settlement.[30] Concerned by the dilemma, he decided to capture some Aborigines to attempt a process of reconciliation. Accordingly, on 31 December, Phillip sent two boats of marines under Lieutenant George Johnston down the harbour "to seize and carry off some of the natives".[31]

The party reached Manly, and after landing, it lulled the Aborigines by giving them a few presents. When the natives were thus occupied, the marines rushed them, and although most Aborigines fled, two were caught. The captives were terrified and screamed their fear and appeals to be freed, whereupon the Aborigines who had escaped now charged the marines. Then followed Australia's first "battle" during which one of the captive Aboriginals escaped; the other, Arabanoo, was tied up and put in the bottom of a boat. Both boats then pushed off from the shore just as the Aborigines began a shore attack by throwing spears, stones, and any other handy missile. To gain a clean break from the enraged attackers, the Europeans fired muskets into the air. Meanwhile, Arabanoo, securely fastened by ropes, "set up the most piercing and lamentable cries of distress", but once the boat was out of range of the shore, he was somewhat assuaged by being given some broiled fish, after which he relaxed and accepted his fate.[32]

When they reached Sydney Cove a crowd (including Tench) turned out to see the Aborigine. He was about thirty years of age, not tall but robust, and though of a manly dignity, was fearful of the crowd. His agitation was great. He was awestruck at all he saw and showed a courtesy to women. He was taken to Phillip's house and at first even the smallest things frightened him, such as the bell over Phillip's front door. But the Governor's intention was to befriend him, and by familiarizing him with European ways, he hoped to allay his fears so that he could ultimately return to his people and likewise allay theirs. Consequently, Phillip had him dine with him at his own table; Arabanoo was selective in the foods which he ate, enjoying fish and duck but refusing bread and salted meat. Phillip must have found Arabanoo's practice of eating his own head lice rather disconcerting. He had his hair cut and was given a bath in which he was scrubbed "from head to foot". Then, dressed in a shirt, jacket and trousers, he was handcuffed and roped around the left wrist to prevent his escape, and a convict was deputed to attend him.[33] He was led about on the end of this rope but a house was to be built for him and his keeper.[34] Next day, 1 January 1789, as if the mores of centuries could be changed in a single day, he was taken back to Manly Cove and fettered by a foot to the boat. Trying to talk to his kinsfolk, he broke down and cried.[35] He returned disconsolately to Sydney Cove.

There he eventually became an avid tea drinker though he could not bring himself to like alcohol. White children were a delight to him and he loved to cuddle them. On 17 February, whilst Phillip was taking him down the harbour, he jumped overboard. Quickly his clothes began to fill and he had to be saved. On 18 May 1789, he died of smallpox, reposing a confidence in Europeans till the end. Phillip was distressed at his passing and after attending his funeral had him buried in his own garden.[36] Arabanoo's manly demeanour and his impatience with any indignity, even though he knew he was in the power of others, never forsook him, and far from being craven, his refusal to allow a superiority on the part of his captors made a strong impression on them. His death stopped all attempts to capture and train Aborigines. Phillip tacitly admitted the failure of his well-intentioned attempt at racial reconciliation.

It appears that the greatest enemies to such attempts were the convicts themselves, and incidents between the two groups invariably necessitated the intervention of the marines. Such a state of affairs occurred in March 1789 — before Arabanoo's death — when sixteen convicts absconding from their work at Brick Kilns and arming themselves with clubs, made for Botany Bay with the deliberate intention of attacking Aborigines and stealing their fishing gear. But their plan went astray, for when they arrived in Botany Bay, there were themselves scattered by the Aborigines. Running in all directions, they invited piecemeal retaliation and shortly one convict was killed and seven were wounded.

Some managed to return to the Brick Kilns and raise the alarm, and a marine detachment commanded by an officer marched out to restore the peace. The detachment arrived too late to prevent the casualties, though it did bring back the dead body. When Phillip heard of the convicts' provocation, he was furious, and, rounding up those who had taken part, he ordered them to be flogged in front of Arabanoo. Arabanoo was told of their offence against his people, but even so, the flogging so revolted him that he could show only "disgust and terror".[37] Physical punishment appalled the Aborigines, and they felt deep sympathy with the sufferer. The women were particularly affected and would cry at the pain being inflicted. When one convict was caught stealing fishing tackle from Daringa, the wife of the Aborigine Colbee, Phillip ordered him to be flogged in front of a group of blacks. But Phillip's good intention was not understood. They were appalled at the inhumanity to which they had been invited; Daringa cried, and another Aboriginal woman, Barangaroo, took a stick and menaced the flogger.[38]

Thus the Europeans could not always predict what the blacks would do. An example of this was the Baneelon Affair. Baneelon, an Aborigine, came to Phillip full of anger one day in November 1790, and said that he was going to kill the sixteen-year-old daughter of an Aborigine who had injured him. Phillip was considerably alarmed at Baneelon's wild gestures, and so with David Collins and the marine orderly sergeant, he accompanied him. Shortly they reached the Aboriginal hut in which the young girl was lying, but on seeing her, Baneelon ran at her with a spear wounding her head and shoulder before Phillip's party could disarm him. Phillip tried to soothe him but in vain; then the sergeant tried pointing his dreaded musket at him, but this too was in vain, for Baneelon shouted his intention to behead the girl. At this, a large group of Aborigines gathered to support him, thus placing the European party in some danger. Fortunately, the *Supply* was nearby and the party was rescued by it. Meanwhile Phillip had ordered that the girl be taken to hospital, but Baneelon, refusing to be placated threatened to retrieve her even from there. In case he might be serious, a marine sentry was posted at the hospital. Shortly Baneelon arrived; the sentry at once pointed his rifle at him; Baneelon was heedless and entered the hospital. But there, his wrath having subsided, he apologized to the girl and spoke kindly to her.[39]

Confrontations between the English and the Aboriginal ways of life were not every time so pleasingly resolved. The British Marines were ordered to mount another expedition against the Aborigines after the McEntire incident.[40] On 9 December 1790, a marine sergeant with three convicts, including the Governor's gamekeeper, McEntire, went shooting kangaroos near Cook's River which ran into Botany Bay. They put up for the night in a hut recently built for sportsmen, and at 1 a.m., the sergeant was awakened by a rustling noise which he thought to be a kangaroo. He woke the others, and on looking outside, they saw two Aborigines with spears approaching whilst three others watched ready nearby. McEntire told his companions that he knew these natives, and after laying down his gun, he advanced to talk to them, whereupon one, Pimelwi, threw a spear which entered McEntire's left side. One of the Europeans rushed forward and broke off the spear whilst the other two chased the Aborigine but failed to catch him. In great pain and freely losing blood, McEntire asked not to be left in the wood to perish, so accompanied by the others, he crawled back to Sydney where he died eleven days later. Phillip felt that this latest fatality called for a show of strength, and a marine party commanded by Captain Tench was ordered to Botany Bay to seek the culprit. Before it set out, Phillip called for Tench and quite uncharacteristically told him that, as the Aborigines had killed seventeen whites since the landing at Sydney Cove almost three years ago, Tench was to capture two and kill ten. These ten were then to be beheaded, and their heads brought in — hatchets and bags for the operation to be supplied.[41] At this point, records Tench, Phillip stopped his macabre instruction to ask him if he would like to propose any alteration to the orders, to which Tench suggested the compromise of capturing six but slaying none.

The patrol set out early on 14 December 1790 and consisted of Tench, Captain Hill of the New South Wales Corps, Lieutenants Poulden and Dawes, forty-six privates, and three days' rations. It was an abortive expedition however for it returned to Sydney three days later without a single captive. This first attempt having failed, Tench led a second party of thirty-nine, to the area between George's and Cook's rivers.[42] They set out before sunset on 22 December 1790, and after crossing Cook's River in pitch darkness, were confronted by a creek, probably Wolli Creek, at 2.15 a.m. As Tench wanted to get across before sunrise, he ordered the men to ford the creek. They were up to their waists in glutinous mud when a sergeant got stuck, only to be followed by many others including Tench himself. Those in the beleagured group began calling out that they were sinking. Tench's impatience had led to a sudden, critical situation to which he had no answer: "What to do, I knew not," he wrote.[43] The solution was provided by a soldier who quickly called to those on the bank to cut trees and threw them to those in the water. In this way, after half an hour's extreme effort by every available hand, the party was rescued, Tench himself saving the sergeant by ordering that ropes be tied under his armpits so that he could be pulled out. After this near-debacle, half the muskets were unserviceable, but the party pushed on till daybreak, though no natives were found.

Eventually they returned to Sydney next morning, disappointed and embarrassed by their "fruitless peregrination".[44]

Undaunted by this failure, it was decided that in future, all

Aboriginal transgressors caught committing any misdemeanour would be punished. Shortly, two Aborigines were detected taking food from a potato garden; a sergeant and a party of marines took off in pursuit but it was dark before they overtook them. Instead of capturing the offenders, the marines — contrary to Phillip's orders — fired among them, but the two escaped, leaving a blood trail. Two days later, some of the Aborigines round about said that the injured man, Bangai, had died. One of the natives, however, felt that Bangai was still breathing. Hopeful that he might be able to save him, Surgeon White immediately went to where Bangai was lying but he had died shortly before from a bullet wound in the shoulder.[45] This was the only occasion that an Aborigine was shot by a marine, and from Tench's account it appears that the chase to which Bangai had put the marines might have raised their "ardour" for retribution. Hunter places a quite different complexion on the incident and says that the two Aborigines were seized but broke away, whereupon one threw a club at the marines: only then, in self-defence, did the marines fire. Hunter's version supplies information which Tench did not record, and as Hunter was a most accurate and reliable chronicler his additional evidence places the marines' action in a more favourable light.[46]

The Aborigines often showed considerable kindness and a complete lack of treachery to marines. One such occasion occurred during the expedition of Tench and Sergeant Knight in May 1791 to ascertain whether the Hawkesbury and the Nepean, discovered in separate forays, were the same river. It became necessary to cross the river but Sergeant Knight could not swim. An Aborigine named Deedora fetched his native canoe for Knight. Tench, realizing that the canoe could not take both of them, swam over, leaving the gear and three muskets to be brought across by other Aborigines. Whilst the Aborigines were doing this, particularly as they had the rifles, they had Tench and Knight "entirely in their power", and yet, as Tench wrote, "they manifested no ungenerous sign of taking advantage of the helplessness and dependence" of the two Europeans. Nor did they pry into the packages even though they saw in them articles for which they longed. Tench was deeply impressed by their self-control and trustworthiness, and, unable to hide his feelings, he wrote of them with loving admiration: "Let him whose travels have lain among polished nations, produce me a brighter example of disinterested urbanity, than was shown by these denizens of a barbarous clime to a set of destitute wanderers on the side of the Hawkesbury."[47]

Very shortly after, there occurred a second incident which also deeply moved Tench in his admiration for Aboriginal integrity. On Richmond Hill, near the Hawkesbury, a hawk was shot which then fell into a tree. The dutiful Deedora offered to climb the tree to retrieve it, and, so as to help him, he was lent a hatchet. He was fascinated by its usefulness and asked if he could have it; however as it was required to chop the wood for the evening fire, he was told that if he cared to return next morning, it would be given to him. In reality, Tench and Knight were not genuine in their offer but Deedora accepted their refusal with such grace that again Tench could not withhold his admiration for the man's dignity, and wrote: "Not a murmur was heard; no suspicion of our insincerity; no mention of benefits conferred; no reproach of ingratitude: his good humour and cheerfulness were not clouded for a moment."[48]

It appears therefore that a harmonious relationship existed between marine and Aborigine overall, and that the only exceptions to this were the punitive reactions which the marines were, on rare occasions, ordered to mount against them. No evidence suggests that marines pursued any personal tyranny against the Aborigines, for, from the evidence already quoted, the blacks not only displayed a respect for them, but in some cases developed a friendship which could be touching in its sincerity and decency. And it appears that such was the rapport which the marines established, that the Aborigines came to give their cooperation to anyone wearing a military uniform, be he marine or not. In June 1791, such a relationship was extended to a soldier of the vanguard of the New South Wales Corps who became lost near Parramatta whilst he was looking for some sweet tea. After some hours of bewilderment, he saw some Aborigines, amongst whom was one who had frequently visited the Parramatta settlement, and who was known as "Botany Bay Colbee". Colbee and a friend joined the soldier, who asked them to show him the way back to Parramatta, but neither showed any interest to do so until the soldier, in fear and desperation, offered them the enticement of carrying his musket. This, Colbee eagerly accepted and accompanied the soldier to Sydney explaining that Sydney was closer than Parramatta. At the end of the journey, Colbee returned the soldier his musket and, asking him to tell Governor Phillip that the assistance had been rendered by Botany Bay Colbee, he departed without even accepting the gift the grateful soldier offered.[49]

Such an attitude was in contrast to the dislike which Aborigines appear to have felt for the convicts. Lacking the military discipline of marines, and being suppressed themselves, there were those convicts who enjoyed suppressing and tyrannizing the only group in the settlement subordinate to themselves. Such convicts Tench described as "savages".[50] And at times, such was the enormity of the convicts' crimes against the Aborigines that the blacks could not suppress a justified rage. Collins records an incident which happened in June 1791. A force of marines was stationed at Parramatta, where the river was mainly deficient in fish. They were being greatly convenienced by some Aborigines who, making the long row from Sydney, brought them fish in return for bread and salted meat. One such entrepreneur was young Balloodery, who after securing his canoe went to the officers' huts with his fish. During his absence some convicts sneaked down and destroyed his canoe. Balloodery was so enraged that he threatened to take revenge on all whites. The six culprits were caught, probably by marines, and were punished, but a convict who strayed away from the camp was speared by Balloodery, who then had to be warned to keep away from all white settlements. Thus ended the commercial service which he had been rendering, and Collins, incensed and disgusted with the behaviour of his own kin, wrote of them with bitter recrimination: "How much greater claim to the appellation of savages, had the wretches who were the cause of this, than the native who was the sufferer."[51]

Ralph Clark developed a particular rapport with them, and Phillip himself had noticed that the Aborigines were not as afraid of Clark as they were of others. As a father mindful of his own child in England, Clark loved the Aboriginal children, and he showed his admiration for Aboriginal parents who would not part with the children they were nursing just to allow him to cuddle them.[52] He would give the children red cloth. On one occasion he wanted to exchange a hatchet for two spears with two Aborigines named Dourrawan and Tirriwan. Landing at Lane Cove on the Parramatta River with Phillip, Clark called to them, and at first they fled until they recognized him. He talked with them and told them that he had brought some red cloth for their women. He asked both men to bring him their children, which they did. He spent two hours with them before proceeding up the river. Such was the friendship which existed between him and the Aboriginal group that upon his return its members called to him to come ashore, but as he wanted to reach Sydney before nightfall, he indicated he could not.[53]

But Ross and Campbell did not share Tench, Collins and Clark's love for the Aborigine. Ross felt that they were not as harmless or inoffensive as some represented them to be.[54] Captain Campbell, in his letter to Doctor Farr of 24 March 1791, described them as the "most abject of the human race" who had "the curiosity of a child who is no longer pleased with his rattle while he remains ignorant of the noise it makes". Although he acknowledged that the men were expert in catching fish and were physically active and of good size, he had an aversion to the women. To him, they were "an antidote to all [sexual] desire" and were the "filthiest of God's creatures". He observed that when they lay down to sleep "which they do like so many pigs one upon the other, should any of the calls of nature disturb them, they discharge whatever it is without moving from the spot". Of the young women, he wrote that their breasts resembled "two loose bags dangling" like "half filled black bladders", and then recounted that Surgeon White had resolved never to go near Aborigines again after an Aboriginal boy whom he had befriended, returned from a visit to his tribe "besmeared with excreta done on him when he was asleep".[55] When assessing the credence of Campbell's opinions, however, it is as well to remember that he is the only chronicler who describes the Aborigines with such strong disparagement and aversion.

7

Little Journeys — Hard Climbs

The Marine Corps deserves considerable recognition for its exploration of the Sydney Plain. Marines were associated with each of the fifteen exploration parties mounted during their stay, and of these, seven expeditions were exclusively marine. It was natural that Phillip should look to them for this service as their training better equipped them for it than any other group in the settlement, and they appear to have enjoyed the challenge of discovery and the respite such expeditions presented from the barrack-routine of Sydney and Parramatta. Especially was this so for Tench and Dawes.

There were three exploration expeditions which went out at different times in 1788 and each of these was accompanied by a marine guard. The first was Hunter's "up the harbour" expedition of 5 February,[1] made necessary because Phillip in his initial visit to Port Jackson between 21 and 23 January had been too busy to thoroughly examine it.[2] Hunter now carried out an accurate survey and found that the land westward was more fertile than that immediately adjacent to the settlement.

The second expedition was that by Phillip north to Broken Bay from 2 to 9 March for which marines again acted as guards.[3] It was not entirely successful: although the beautiful area of Pittwater was discovered, Phillip noted that it did not "vie with that which he had chosen for the settlement at Sydney Cove";[4] some of the party returned with dysentery;[5] and Phillip, who had embarked on this expedition before he had fully recovered from an illness, had then slept several nights on the wet ground and returned home with a pain in his side with which he had to live for the rest of his life.[6]

In spite of this ailment, Phillip led the third expedition, which included Lieutenant George Johnston and three marines. They set out northwest from Manly on 15 April and returned to Sydney on 19 April. They passed through French's Forest and observed the Carmarthen Hills (later named the Blue Mountains) and Richmond Hill from Pennant Hills.[7] Phillip suspected a large river would be found near Richmond Hill. This was a hard expedition, Phillip describing it as being "not without great labour",[8] but all that had resulted from it was the knowledge that approximately forty miles inland were lofty and blue mountains at the base of which probably ran a river.

Lured now by the need to find that river, Phillip mounted the fourth expedition from 23 to 29 April whose marine personnel were those of the previous party augmented by Lieutenant Creswell and six privates.[9] Taking seven days' rations of bread, beef, rum, and water, together with a camp kettle, two tents, and poles carried by the marine privates, they landed up harbour at Homebush Bay to explore westward in search of any river, for Phillip was becoming concerned to find water additional to that in the Tank Stream. The party was considerably encumbered, carrying packs of forty pounds (about 18 kg), and looking like a "gang of travelling gypsies".[10] As a precaution to assist their safe return, they notched trees as they went, but upon reaching a hill which Phillip named Belle Veue (now Prospect) rations began to run short, and as Phillip was suffering considerable pain in his side, they returned to the boats at Homebush Bay. This too had been a hard expedition: everyone (except Phillip) carried his own gear; the nights were very cold, and

Phillip's constant pain was at times extreme. Even so, he energetically led younger men and estimated that thirty miles had been covered.[11] Although discovery of the river had to wait till Tench's expedition of June the following year, Phillip now knew that there was good country close to the settlement, and he intended settling and cultivating it early in the spring.[12]

The fifth expedition, also led by Phillip, included from the detachment Lieutenants George Johnston, Long and Creswell, and six marines.[13] It aimed, after Phillip had taken "a few weeks' rest", to explore the coast from Manly to Broken Bay. Leaving Manly on 22 August 1788, its members reached Narrabeen Lagoon where they shot a duck for dinner. Pressing on, they reached Broken Bay where they saw Aboriginal fishing nets and fishing lines of good quality, but at McCarr's Creek they found the country impassable and returned to Manly on 25 August. There they were met by a large crowd of Aborigines, to whom Phillip gave some fishing lines and hooks. Creswell gave one of the women a handkerchief, and the party returned to Sydney that night.

From 6 to 16 June 1789, Phillip mounted an expedition to Broken Bay from which the Hawkesbury River was discovered, but this was a civil rather than a marine expedition: its sole marine member was Captain George Johnston, unless the "Two other people each armed with a gun" which Hunter mentions, were also marines.[14] After the discovery of the Hawkesbury most of the exploration of the Sydney region was handed over entirely to marine officers.

An interested but disappointed observer of that Hawkesbury expedition had been Watkin Tench. The pursuit of discovery held a strong fascination for him, and he had an ambition to acquire some distinction as an explorer, but when the Hawkesbury expedition left, he was occupied commanding the detachment at Parramatta. He was not to be daunted however and, stimulated by a desire to explore the unknown, set out on the marines' next journey. From his

Parramatta headquarters at daybreak on 26 June 1789, with a party which included Surgeon Arndell and two marines, he made for Prospect Hill, some five miles to the west. Here the party paused, and whilst pondering their next move and observing the wild virgin bush about them, Tench, the most cultured of the detachment's officers, was reminded of that "wild abyss" which Milton had described in his Paradise Lost.

> Into this wild abyss the warie fiend
> Stood on the brink of Hell and look'd awhile
> Pondering his Voyage for no narrow frith
> He had to cross.[15]

Observing the Carmarthen Hills (later the Blue Mountains) extending from north to south, the party sought the direction to be taken and, observing to the northwest a make of land which indicated the existence of a river, set out in its direction, walking all day, as Tench wrote, "through a country untrodden before by European Foot".[16] Except for the croak of a melancholy crow which occasionally flew overhead, or a kangaroo bounding at a distance, the solitude was complete and undisturbed. At 4 p.m. they stopped for the night near what is now Penrith, and after making camp, lit a fire to cook their meal of barbecued salted pork and a crow which they had shot. Next day at daylight they resumed their trek till within an hour they were on the bank of a river "nearly as broad as the Thames at Putney", and which was running slowly in a northerly direction.[17] It showed signs of having been ravaged by a rapid flood-torrent[18] and housed vast flocks of wild duck, whilst its forty-foot-high banks were peopled with many Aborigines. Pleased with their discovery, they returned to Rose Hill on the third day and reported their discovery to Phillip who named the river not the Tench, as it should have been, but the Nepean after Evan Nepean.[19] Phillip suspected that this river would empty into the Hawkesbury,[20] but this was not proved till May 1791.

In September, Tench and others accompanied Hunter on a nine-day survey of Botany Bay, the results of which Hunter set down on a map. He sent two boats with tents and provisions to Botany Bay under Mr Keltie, master of the *Sirius*, whilst he and others, including Tench, walked there from Sydney Cove. When they arrived, Keltie's party had already pitched tents for them at a base camp, from which during the next ten days they explored five miles of Cook's River, completing a meticulous survey.[21]

With the discovery of the Nepean, the next obvious step was to penetrate the Blue Mountains. Accordingly Phillip asked Lieutenant Dawes of the marines, accompanied by Lieutenant Johnston and a Mr Lowes, to cross the Nepean and probe the mountains.[22] The party was out from 9 to 14 December, but was then obliged to return, for in that time it had done nothing but struggle through gullies and up the rocky hills which everywhere confronted it. Even though Dawes reached the summit of Mount Twiss, which being fifty-four miles inland from the sea was the furthest inland yet reached by any European, the summit of the mountains seemed barred by inaccessibility.[23] Thus the seventh predominantly marine expedition ended rather unprofitably.

During August and September 1790, Tench was to mount three explorations.[24] Early in August, accompanied by Dawes and Doctor Worgan, he set out from Rose Hill on a seven-day walk in a southwesterly direction during which they discovered Pyramid Hill on the Razorback Range (now Mount Prudhoe), and came across a river which Tench felt was the Nepean near its source. He judged the land to be "only tolerably good" but felt that towards the south it would improve. This judgment was vindicated later when the cattle which strayed from Sydney Cove in 1788 were found in robust condition south at Cowpastures, the same area on which Macarthur's sheep would graze in twenty years' time.

Late in the same month, Tench made a second excursion,

this time to the northwest of Rose Hill, which again brought him to the Nepean. He traced it to the spot where he had discovered it fourteen months previously and this caused him to have very little doubt that the Hawkesbury and the Nepean were the one river.

Shortly after, probably in early September, Tench undertook an expedition to Broken Bay, and from all three expeditions brought back soil samples for analysis.

The eleventh expedition, a "strong and numerous" one, consisted of twenty-one men including Phillip, Tench, Dawes, two sergeants, and eight privates.[25] Its aim was to establish conclusively that the Hawkesbury and the Nepean were one and the same river. The plan was to move northwest from Rose Hill to the Hawkesbury River at Richmond Hill, then follow the river south to where Tench and Arndell had forded it in the previous June (near the present Penrith Railway bridge), go for a short distance westward, re-cross the river, and follow it north along its eastern bank till they were certain that it was what they had been calling the Nepean. Each man, except the Governor, carried his knapsack containing rations for ten days, together with a gun, a blanket, and a canteen; the total weight of these items was forty pounds (about 18 kg), but as a cooking kettle and a hatchet were also carried, the all up weight would have been closer to fifty.

They set out on 11 April 1791 from the Governor's house at Rose Hill in a northwesterly direction, taking frequent compass bearings and counting paces, which they estimated at 2,200 to the mile. The going was so hard that by the morning's end it was necessary for a marine to carry not only his own gear but the knapsack of a fatigued member. By 8.30 a.m. on 12 April, they had reached the Nepean, but, thinking they were too far north of Richmond Hill, they back-tracked downstream until nightfall overtook them. Next day, they climbed a rise, saw Richmond Hill in the opposite direction in which they had been walking, and before nightfall, began retracing their steps. Richmond Hill's position had been wrongly calculated by its earlier discoverers eight miles downstream from its true position. The new expedition then walked all the 14th and next day. Noticing the river now to be tidal, they knew they were below Richmond Hill. Shortly however their march was barred by South Creek and next morning, with their mission unaccomplished, they abandoned the trek and returned to Rose Hill.

But such an avid explorer had Tench now become, that failure to solve the Hawkesbury-Nepean riddle was unthinkable: consequently, with Dawes, Sergeant Knight and a private, he determined on yet another attempt to ascertain on which of the two rivers Richmond Hill was situated.[26] They set out on 24 May 1791 and reaching the bank of South Creek which was opposite the spot where a month earlier they had been stopped, they walked to Richmond Hill, climbed it, and slept that night at its base. Walking westward from the river, they reached Knight Hill (now Kurrajong), named in true companionship after the "trusty serjeant" who had been the faithfully indefatigable companion of all their travels.[27] From here they beheld the panoramic sweep of the river beneath them and saw clearly that the Hawkesbury and the Nepean were the one river. It was at the river that the previously mentioned assistance given by Deedora met with Tench's profound gratitude.

The thirteenth expedition was to be the marines' last.[28] It was made by Tench and Dawes in July 1791 when they went in search of a large river supposed to exist a few miles to the southward of Rose Hill. They did not succeed in finding anything better than a saltwater creek (now thought to have been Prospect Creek) which they thought ran into Botany Bay.[29] On its bank (probably near the present Lansdowne Bridge) they spent a miserable night in subfreezing temperatures. Their discomfort was exacerbated by a lack of water: having presumed they were going to find a river, they had not filled their water bottles before setting out. In describing that morning's scene, Tench brought into view the ornateness of his prose

> The sun arose in unclouded splendour, and presented to our sight a novel and picturesque view; the contiguous country, as white as if covered with snow, contrasted with the foliage of trees, flourishing in the verdure of tropical luxuriancy. Even the exhalation which steamed from the lake beneath, contributed to heighten the beauty of the scene ... Nothing but demonstration could have convinced me, that so severe a degree of cold ever existed in this low latitude. Drops of water on a tin pot, not altogether out of the influence of the fire, were frozen into solid ice, in less than twelve minutes.[30]

Writing in 1898 about these marine expeditions, Lieutenant Colonel Parkins Hearle, RMLI, gave proud recognition to the arduous exploration work done by his brother marines of a former era: "These little journeys undertaken from time to time may seem very small performances at the present day, but the difficulty of penetrating the country even for twenty or thirty miles inland can only be understood when we have fully realised the struggles of our hardy pioneers, to reach the great barrier which blocked the way to the unknown plains of the west."[31]

It was to take another twenty-five years to cross those mountains, but during their tour of duty, the marines' exploration of much of Sydney's immediate hinterland opened up new agricultural possibilities which would bring much advantage to the growing colony.

8

Hardship in Sydneytown

The rigour of the detachment's service at Port Jackson was more onerous and harsh than the usual marine service aboard ships, or in colonies well established. Ralph Clark's opinion was that it was much harder than war service.[1] It entailed the arduous labour of founding a colony out of virgin bush; of starting entirely from scratch, and of enduring the inconveniences and physical discomforts intrinsic in such a task. Added to these were a precarious and hungry existence during a thirty-month famine, hot weather in which temperatures in tents could reach 105 °F (40.5 °C),[2] and the loneliness and dejection which flowed from the isolation and lack of news from home. While everyone in the settlement endured these problems, the marines' job became even more arduous as conditions became harsher. Whereas the labour of convicts was reduced when famine set in, marine duty continued undiminished. The frequency of duty was added to by the number of posts which had to be manned because the detachment's barracks were located on the western side of Sydney Cove but a subaltern's guard had to be sent to the eastern side each morning to guard Government House and the principal offices.[3] As well, the Rose Hill outpost had to be manned as did the standing patrol at South Head. Reaction to these rigorous duties varied within the detachment. Ross continually complained about them. While his aversion to most things associated with the colony coloured his view, collaboration of his complaints is not lacking.

As early as July 1788, Ross was telling Stephens that the officers' duties were "severe" to the point that this was the reason for his reluctance to evacuate sick officers such as Lieutenants Maxwell and William Collins.[4] A year later he was claiming that "no troops ever had more severe duty", while at the same time he was also able to report that none did their duty "with more alacrity".[5] What Ross was claiming was that in spite of the harshness of its duties, the detachment was responding well. He was not alone in highlighting the severity of marine duty, for both Clark and Tench supported his view. Clark found his own duties unrelentingly hard from the moment he stepped ashore: on his first day he was duty officer, and a month later he had been duty officer for forty-eight consecutive hours, and had not taken off his clothes for six days.[6] Nor did the situation improve during the next five months for he noted in July that there had been no lessening in the constancy of duty: officers were seldom able to have more than two nights consecutively in bed, and the situation was worsened by the "disagreeable" requirement for officers to sit as members of the Criminal Court — a commitment superimposed on their military duties.[7] "Nothing in this country", remarked Clark, "could make a man wish to stay . . . it is the poorest country under heaven."[8] Tench was less chagrined in his assessment: he felt that if settlers were not overambitious, then New South Wales "was not without inducements".[9] For the marines, however, severity of duty continued, and by 1790 there had been no improvement. So constant had been their duties that no tactical training had been done since leaving England because their time had been spent in felling trees, ploughing, and building houses. Consequently, regimentalism had gone except for mounting a small guard by day and a piquet at night.[10]

Another factor contributing to hardship was the primitive and unhealthy state of the detachment's accommodation. The tents initially erected were supposed to be temporary accommodation until huts could be built for the officers and barracks for the men. Construction of these began on 14 February 1788 but even though the work was performed by the detachment assisted by almost one hundred convicts, Phillip was complaining in July that neither had been finished, and nor had the hospital which was to contain a marines ward. Even the storehouse which was to receive the provisions still unloaded from three of the transports was not finished. To expedite the work, Phillip allotted the labour of the ship's carpenters from the *Sirius*,[11] but their removal from ship board maintenance appears to have contributed to the leaky condition of the ship during her voyage to the Cape of Good Hope in October that year.[12] The allocation of a fifth of the male convicts to the task of construction was in part aborted by two militating factors: the unreliability of the convicts and the lack of convict overseers. The convicts lacked enthusiasm for the construction of someone else's accommodation, and within a fortnight on the job they had stolen a third of the tools issued to them.[13] Moreover, it was only with the utmost difficulty that labour was obtained from them, and this was caused largely by the unanimous refusal of the marine officers to superintend convict labour.[14] The officers had failed to notify Phillip of this refusal till after the fleet had left England, consequently preventing his hiring replacements. This gap slowed construction work considerably.[15] Overseers were not despatched till 1789,[16] and Phillip was forced to appoint his personal servant, Henry Edward Dodd, as the supervisor of convict labour on the government farms,[17] but it appears that during the construction of the military accommodation, no such official existed.

Convict indifference and thieving were not the only impediments to the work. March 1788 was a very wet month, tents had to be covered with thatch, and temporary clay huts were erected.[18] In addition, building materials lacked quality, and the local timber was found to be springy and rotten. This delayed the construction of the barracks, which were to be built of timber, one building for each of the four companies, each measuring sixty-seven by twenty-two feet (approximately 20 m by 7 m). They were to be spaced to admit plenty of air and to enclose the parade ground,[19] at the corner of which Ross's house was built.[20]

By March the marines were involved in so much of the construction work that they held a meeting on the 18th and, according to Easty, decided against any further work without additional pay.[21] Such a meeting was very unusual as it invited an allegation of mutinous conduct, but the marines had chosen the day on which the officers were fully occupied with the court martial of Private Hunt and the subsequent hiatus created by Ross's arrest of five officers. It is apparent that tension within the detachment that day was considerable: not only officers, but also the other ranks, were openly expressing their dissatisfaction, and morale was seriously sagging.

This discontent was further inflamed in April when the marines saw that although they were still living in tents, the convicts had built their own huts.[22] Winter was approaching, so realizing that little effort could be expected from the convicts, the marine privates undertook to build two barracks for themselves.[23] They established several sawpits to promote the work and even allocated four ship's carpenters from the *Sirius* to direct the project, but even with their expertise the project was too ambitious, and they had to settle for building one hut only. Even then, progress was painfully slow and quite intolerable.

On 15 May 1788 Ross decided to take action. He told Phillip that the only way to get the barracks built was to employ tradesmen who were serving with the unit, for which he recommended they receive additional pay at the same rate as that paid to marines when engaged in public

Table 5 Paysheet for tradesmen employed to build military accommodation, 1788

Artificers belonging to the Marine Detachment. Employed from the 17th May to the 30th Sept., 1788, both Days included:—

Trades.	No. of Comy.	Names.	No. of days empd.	How, & where employ'd.
Carpenters	56	Chas. Reynolds	112½	An indifferent carpenter.
	6	Patk. Connell	109½	" "
	6	Willm. Dowlan	81½	" but a very good sawyer.
	59	Edw.d Dinger	90	A very ordinary carpenter.
	61	Thos. Scott	10	Ordinary joiner & tolerable sawyer.
	35	Andw. Fishburne	101	Ordinary carpenter.
	11	Jose. Lewis	70	" " and sawyer.
	30	Robt. Stephens	55½	Labourer assisting the carpenters.
	18	Jno. Lewis	85	Ordinary carpenter.
	5	Ralph Brough	99½	" "
Masons	11	John Brown	96½	Stone cutter.
	8	Thos. Phillips	110	
	48	Jno. Folly	86½	Mason and bricklayer.
	41	Mark Hurst	100	" "
	47	Jno. Bates	27	A mason lent from the *Sirius*.
Shinglers	38	Chas. Brixey	107	Superintending the shingle makers
	41	Heny. Wright	68	
	27	Benjm. Cusley	44	
	26	Jas. Angel	29	Employ'd making shingles.
	42	Jno. Roberts	23	
	2	Willm. Hallam	61½	
	56	Jno. Brown (2d)	61½	
Sawyers	15	Jas. Rogers	59½	Tolerable sawyer.
	51	Jno. Griffiths	53½	" "
	24	Wm. Strong	97½	A good sawyer.
	35	Richd. Knight	59½	" "
	51	Heny. Rossor	45	" "
File cuttr	30	Thos. Jackson	88½	Employ'd at the publick forge.
	50	Jno. Branson	35½	Miner employ'd at the public cellar.
		Total no. of days	3,072½*	

R. Ross, Major.

Source: *Historical Records of Australia*, vol 1, 81

* Ross's total appears to be in error. The days as listed by Ross total 2067½ days

service.[24] The extra payment was also merited because ship's carpenters were being paid extra for working ashore.[25] Phillip agreed, and ten carpenters, five masons, seven shinglers, five sawyers, one file cutter, and one miner from the detachment were used to build the barracks, Ross's house, and other public works. These twenty-nine marine tradesmen worked a total of 3,072½ days during a nineteen-week period for which Ross sent home a return for pay.[26] (See Table 5.)

August was a cold, wet, frosty month, in which the brick kiln more than once fell in, huts became rain sodden, and the temperature fell to freezing point.[27] But with the marine artificers at work, all officers except one or two were living in separate huts by September, and construction of the barracks, the hospital, and the storehouses was proceeding. Though of timber, it was planned to make them more durable by later walling them up with bricks or stone if limestone could be found or sent out as ballast.[28] All officer accommodation was completed during October and, according to Phillip, the troops moved into the almost-completed barracks.[29] Ross disagreed with this claim and complained to Stephens that because Phillip had allocated all the marine tradesmen to purposes "his Excellency imagin'd to be of more importance than the getting the detachment under proper cover", the other companies would not be in their accommodation for some months.[30] His forecast was confirmed by Collins who recorded that the marines took possession of their barracks towards the end of February 1789 — a year after construction had begun.[31]

The officer huts were in a row opposite the marine barracks; the convict huts were, according to Surgeon John Harris, as good as the officers' but were interspersed throughout the region around The Rocks, that ridge on the western side of Sydney Cove. Perhaps because Phillip, Collins, and the Commissary, Andrew Miller, occupied the only three attractive houses, Surgeon Harris was unimpressed with what he saw and described the settlement as "the most miserable looking place I ever beheld".[32] A convict woman writing home about this time confirmed Harris's view: she described Sydney town as consisting of two streets of four rows of "most miserable huts" which contained no windows, but whose casements instead were filled with lattices of twigs; at the end of the rows was a cemetery. Women had no supply of clothes, and those with children were quite wretched. Some who had become pregnant to seamen had been deserted by them; there was no tea, and very little salt or sugar.[33] Both convict and marine therefore were suffering alike, and until the marines departed from the colony in December 1791, they continued to live in the incommodious housing they had built for themselves in 1788 — accommodation which their successors, the New South Wales Corps, quickly replaced by brick structures.[34]

During the year in which the marines' accommodation had been constructed, the heavy load of duty, coupled with the continuous rain, tented accommodation, and uninviting diet, had taken toll of their health. By late March 1788, sickness had weakened the detachment. To replace those incapacitated, Lieutenant Dawes, one corporal and eight privates were transferred to the detachment on land from the reserve held aboard the *Sirius*.[35] In April, widespread scurvy broke out among marine and convict alike.[36] White noted that it rose "to a most alarming height".[37] Dysentery struck some in the camp,[38] and two officers, Lieutenants James Maxwell and William Collins (the younger brother of David Collins), were seriously affected.[39] Collins fell ill on 28 February, and so virulent was his attack that within twenty-four hours Doctor Bowes did not expect him to live.[40] During March and April his condition became chronic, and duty by him was impossible. Ross requested the surgeons to examine him to decide whether he should be evacuated to England, and on 12 May, Surgeons White and Worgan reported that he was in "so weak, low, and debilitate a condition" by the three months' long dysentery that they felt his life depended upon evacuation.[41] Phillip held him in such high regard that he would not have parted with him on any other grounds.[42] Evacuation was recommended also for Maxwell who as well as dysentery had developed a blindness caused by a disease of the optic nerve.[43] Both officers left for England on 14 July

1788.[44] Their departure further reduced officer numbers and exacerbated the problem of excessive officer duty. Dawes was transferred to the detachment to replace William Collins.[45] This did not, however, solve the problem of filling Maxwell's place, whose duties during his illness had been performed, unpaid, by Ross's son, John, whom Scott stated to be only nine years of age.[46] Ross now suggested to Stephens that the boy's appointment be confirmed because it was Admiralty policy to give preference in the granting of commissions to the sons of old officers, in which category, after thirty-two years' service, Ross classed himself.[47] If Scott is to be relied on, Ross did not wait for the Admiralty's approval and gave his son the local rank of second lieutenant on 9 February 1789.[48]

The extent of marine sickness during 1788 can be gauged from the figures in Phillip's sickness returns: on 9 July 1788, there were thirty-six marines under medical treatment compared with sixty-six convicts; proportionately therefore, marine sickness was greater than convict sickness.[49] Mortality statistics however showed an opposite picture, for whereas twenty-three convicts died from sickness in the colony's first nine months, only three marines died during the same period.[50] The much higher convict mortality rate was probably due to the sick condition and the advanced age of many of them from the time they had embarked in England: in July 1788 Phillip had reported that fifty-two of them were unfit for labour because of old age or infirmity.[51] Unfortunately, later comparisons are not possible because Phillip ceased sending sickness returns to England, but seventeen members, or one in eight of the detachment, died during the four-year tour of duty. The only officer to die was Captain John Shea. His health had been poor during the voyage,[52] and he died of consumption on 2 February 1789.[53] He was buried with full military honours at a service conducted by the Reverend Richard Johnson, which the Governor and all officers attended. The only non-commissioned officer to die was Sergeant Henry Petrie,[54] and twenty-five privates also died.

Dental problems created another hardship. On 18 February 1788 Doctor Considine, in extracting one of Ralph Clark's teeth, tore away some of the jaw bone which adhered to it. Clark fainted but even though his tooth was bleeding and his pain was such that he could write to Alicia, "Oh, my God, what pain it was", he refused to allow Considine to remove him from piquet (sentry) duty that day or the two which followed.[55]

The marines also had to face the vagaries of human nature. When famine came to the settlement, members of the detachment who established gardens to grow their own vegetables had to suffer the galling irritation of the theft of their crops. On shore, the stealing was rife; even Ross's own garden was not immune,[56] and Ralph Clark therefore established his garden on an island in the harbour. Even this precaution failed, and during a ten-day period in February 1790, when his crops were ready for harvest, a bed of onions was stolen, as were all his potatoes. Furthermore, when he went to gather his corn, fifteen hundred cobs — the greater part of his crop — had also been taken. Consequently, instead of gathering six bushels, he gathered only one. Understandably, he was infuriated and wished the thieves were in "hell".[57] Finally, as will be seen, the food shortage at Sydney forced Phillip to divide the people by sending Ross and part of the detachment to Norfolk Island in February 1790.[58] Even when the Second Fleet arrived with resupply, it replaced famine with the beginnings of extortion: thus the master of the *Lady Juliana* sent a great quantity of his own personal goods and stores ashore to be sold at highly inflated prices. Scott gives some examples: the captain was selling sugar which cost three pence halfpenny a pound for eighteen pence a pound;

thread which cost fourpence per ounce he sold for two shillings an ounce; ribbon which cost eightpence a yard he sold for up to three shillings and ninepence a yard; and paper worth sixpence a quire, he sold for two shillings. In the isolated and parlous situation in which the marines existed at Sydney, there had no alternative but to submit to such an outrage.[59]

Natural calamities and the harsh nature of the bush also added to marine difficulties. To become lost in the bush was a dangerous and frightening experience: Privates Rogers, Odgers and Toulon became lost and perished and Captain Campbell, who was lost for two days in December 1788, was lucky to survive.[60] Fishing also had its dangers, and in July 1790 two marines lost their lives in extraordinary circumstances. Mr Ferguson, a seventeen-year-old midshipman from the *Sirius*, and three marines had gone fishing in a small boat off Bradley's Head in the harbour when a whale swam by and swamped their boat. They began bailing but the whale returned and swam under the boat, lifting it out of the water. It sank into the vortex created, drowning Mr Ferguson, Private John Bates and Private Thomas Harp. The other marine, Private John Wilkins, saved himself by swimming to the southern shore.[61] All three who died apparently were fine men: Southwell described Harp and Bates as two of the most worthy veterans of which the battalion could boast — Bates in particular, from his good conduct, had become a firm favourite.[62] Ferguson the midshipman, was described by Southwell as "possessing the firmest principles . . . of morality and honour".[63] As for the offending whale, it beached itself two months later on Manly beach and died, after which the Aborigines cut it up and ate it. (They invited Phillip to their repast; he went on 7 September, but was speared through the shoulder by one of them who acted independently of the others.)[64]

But perhaps even worse than death or danger was the loneliness and isolation of Port Jackson. There was, at times, a deadening sameness about the soldier's service which produced boredom. This was accentuated when the last merchant ships of the First Fleet departed in November 1788, leaving the colony without contact till the *Lady Juliana* arrived in June 1790. Desolation was widely felt from the "dreariness and dejection" of their situation.[65] They were tortured by their abandonment, and by early 1790, so great was their despondency at being cut off from home news that "men abandoned themselves to the most desponding reflections" by day, till at night, sleep mercifully transported them to "happier climes".[66] So strong became their desire for rescue that for eighteen months after arrival, a marine party walked each week to Botany Bay in the forlorn hope that a ship might have called there rather than at Port Jackson. Eventually the debilitating famine denied the physical stamina needed for such a reconnaissance and instead, on 30 January 1790, a lookout was established at South Head by Hunter and a party of six from the *Sirius* helped by Surgeons White and Worgan, all of whom lived there in tents for ten days.[67] From the lookout, every eye strained and every heart sank as the sea was searched for a ship. Tench wrote: "The misery and horror of such a situation cannot be imparted."[68] Clark wrote: "God help [us] if Some Ships don't arrive."[69] And so the tour of duty was made the more rigorously severe not only by the physical hardship of duty in a harsh country, and not only by the privations of a famine, but also by the homesickness and anguish of a two-year break in communications with home, kith, and kin — an experience not endured by marines before or since.

9

The Reluctant Hangman

A macabre requirement of marine duty was to witness all executions in the colony, and as some of these were both extremely sad and appallingly bungled, it is reasonable to assume that private soldiers at least of the sensitivity of Southwell would have regarded such duty with distaste. Although no marine recorded his feelings as he witnessed the hangings, the accounts of officers such as Clark and Tench reveal a hardened indifference to the victims, whose crimes against the struggling community they felt fully merited such retribution.

The first hanging at which the detachment was ordered to attend was that of convict Thomas Barrett on 27 February 1788. Barrett, in league with convicts Henry Lovell, Joseph Hall and John Ryan, had been brought before the Criminal Court at 1 p.m. on 27 February when all four were charged with stealing butter, peas and pork. They were found guilty in a short hearing and Barrett, Lovell and Hall were sentenced to death; Ryan was ordered to receive three hundred lashes. At 5 p.m., the marine detachment formed up with muskets, and marched to the execution site where at 5.15 p.m., the three condemned arrived. At 6 p.m. the marines, with Major Ross present, were drawn up on parade opposite the tree which was to be the gallows. All convicts were present as the execution was meant to be a deterrent. Shortly, Ross received from Phillip a twenty-four-hour respite for Lovell and Hall, but the execution of Barrett, "a most vile character"[1] and the most "notorious" of the criminals,[2] was to proceed. Barrett adopted a highly arrogant attitude until that moment when he mounted the ladder, whereupon he went very pale and seemed much shocked. At this ghastly moment, a delay occurred because the convict hangman could not bring himself to place the noose around Barrett's neck. Embarrassing moments ticked by whilst every persuasion was brought upon the reluctant and faint-hearted hangman to perform his office. At last Provost Marshal Brewer and Major Ross joined in their efforts to coerce him to his task. Together they bullied him; Ross went so far as to threaten that the marines would shoot him if he did not perform, but in spite of all threats the hangman still could not affix the noose. Consequently, Mr Brewer had to do it for him. Barrett then confessed his guilt and, indulging himself in a death-bed confession, he admitted publicly to having led a very wicked life. This he followed by asking to speak to a convict named Seddiway, also a bad type, and this was granted. He followed this with a further request to speak to a female convict, but this was refused. The chaplain then prayed fervently with him after which Barrett exhorted all present "to take warning by his unhappy fate", after which in the quaint words of Doctor Bowes, he was "launched into eternity".[3] Tench was more judgmental about Barrett's execution, observing impassively that he died "with that hard spirit, which too often is found in the worst and most abandoned class of men".[4] Barrett's body hung for an hour and then was buried near the gallows. His hanging however had had its embarrassing moments and clearly revealed the need for a less timid hangman. But before the matter could be resolved, Hall and Lovell's reprieve expired next day and they were again brought to the tree of execution. There, in the pouring rain, humidity, thunder, and storm, the marines at 3 p.m. again assembled, though needlessly as it turned out, for after standing in the rain for an hour, the Judge Advocate brought a pardon from the Governor conditional on the condemned being banished from the settlement. Only Ryan now remained to be dealt with. The convicts had sent Phillip a petition begging mercy; Phillip relented, and Ryan was taken out of irons and sent back to work.[5]

Next day, 29 February in the leap year of 1788, another execution was listed. The four condemned convicts were John Williams and Daniel Gordon (who were Negroes), William Shearman, and James Freeman. Promptly at 3.45 p.m., the detachment was again drawn up with muskets. The condemned were brought by guards to the gallows with halters around their necks. They were in the extreme of misery. "When the parson had done with them", says Clark, Phillip, taking further advantage of the convict petition for Ryan by which the convicts had promised to behave, pardoned Gordon and Williams provided they were banished. Shearman was punished by lashing, and Freeman was pardoned on condition that he became the public hangman: and so by his acceptance of the post, the problem of the reluctant hangman was resolved.[6]

Other executions included those of John Bennett and Thomas Sanderson. Bennett, a youth of seventeen,[7] was hung on 2 May 1788 for robbing the *Charlotte* stores tent. Again Tench was sententious: "He met his fate with a hardness and insensibility, which the grossest ignorance, and a most deplorable want of feeling, alone could supply".[8] Sanderson's execution presented a gory scene: he had escaped to the woods after stealing food during the famine but frequently returned to the settlement at night to repeat the offence. He was captured, tried and hanged on 10 January 1789. Collins' account suggests that while he was being hanged, at the same location, at the same time, a convict named Ruglass (who had stabbed Ann Fowles with whom he had cohabited) was receiving 350 of his 700-lash sentence.⁹ For those of ghoulish tendencies, it had been a day of heightened activity, though multiple forms of punishment at the same location were not unusual. Bradley records an occasion when some convict thieves were flogged under a tree from which another thief "was hanging over their heads".¹⁰ For marines forced to perform such gruesome duty there could have been little pleasure, for although none of the marines' accounts express any sympathy for the victims, it is reasonable to assume that as they were not of a sadistic or pitiless nature, such duty, at least for some, would have been a tasteless labour.

10

Rations and Supplies

The marines' tour of duty encountered other problems which, coupled with the famine, added to the rigour of the service. Significant amongst these was the detachment's logistic shortfall. The initial issue to the detachment quickly proved to be inadequate, and as early as July 1788, Ross had to submit supplementary indents for a great number of items which included greatcoats (these were also used as sleeping bags on patrols), bed cases, blankets, rugs, iron pots, cooking utensils, shoes (at the rate of six pairs per marine per year to meet the heavy wear suffered in such harsh country), leather soles, nails, hemp, wax, bristles, materials for making women's and children's shoes, needles, thread, thimbles, scissors, cloth for leggings, white and check shirts, wooden bowls and platters for messes, soap, and all sorts of necessities for the marines' women and children. Larger trousers were also required, for those in stock were so small that troops had to draw three from which, by tailoring, two of useful size could be made.[1] A defect of the greatcoats was that because of the winter rain and summer dew, they were constantly damp and did not keep the troops dry.[2] Money was also needed so that the men could be paid in advance. This indent by Ross was not excessive because Surgeon White not only confirmed its needs but also added items

Table 6 Quartermaster's report on clothing stocks in Port Jackson, September 1788

	Leather caps	White shirts	Check shirts	Thread hose	Trousers	Knapsacks	Gaiters	Shoes	Leather drabs
Quantity received	576	383	829	576	1726	400	576	576	384
Quantity issued	195	138	356	116	440	16	4	318	285
Balance	381	245	473	460	1286	384	572	258	99
Quantity unserviceable		4	6		34	43	19		
Balance serviceable	381	241	467	460	1252	341	553	258	99

Source: *Public Records Office, London*, Admiralty References ADM 1/3824, 66; and ML PRO Roll 412

such as sugar, barley, rice, oatmeal, currants, spices, vinegar, potable soup, and tamarinds. All of these items were needed to facilitate the recovery of sick marines and their wives and children because salt rations, which were the universal issue, were unpalatable to children, and not conducive to good nutrition.[3]

By September 1788, marine clothing stocks for issue were barely at subsistence levels. Quartermaster Furzer's Return of 30 September (see Table 6) showed the plight.[4]

Only half the shirts and a quarter of the shoes remained and yet the arrival date of the resupply fleet was not known. In August 1789 the last of the shoes had been issued to the detachment and by 1790, when the resupply fleet had been wrecked off South Africa, stocks were so short that an officer correspondent, whose letter was published in England, revealed that marines had no shoes and were mounting guards in bare feet. Tench agreed with this, for he had seen many a guard mounted in which the shoeless predominated.[5] Derisively, the officer-correspondent observed that "Pride, Pomp, and Circumstance of glorious war" were at an end, and he went on to say how chagrined he would be upon his return to England to see troops "whose only employ has been to powder their hair, polish their shoes, and go through the routine of a field day".[6]

The amount of tobacco brought out was also quite inadequate and by July 1788 it was in such short supply that Ross had to purchase 1,782 pounds of it at eighteen pence a pound from Captain Duncan Sinclair, master of the *Alexander* — a cost which was charged against the soldiers' pay.[7] The supply of alcohol, because of the loss of the resupply fleet, was exhausted by 1790, and Phillip pointed out to Nepean that though there was no alcohol in the settlement, the marines had been promised before leaving England that they would receive a spirit issue for three years.[8]

In providing two years' rations for the detachment before it left England, no difficulties either in adequacy or availability had been foreseen.[9] Upon arrival at Port Jackson, the weekly ration for marines and convicts was set at 7 pounds (3.2 kg) bread or flour, 7 pounds beef or 4 pounds (1.8 kg) pork, 3 pints (1.7 l) peas, 6 ounces (170 g) butter, and 1 pound (454 g) flour of ½ pound (227 g) rice. Marine wives were allowed two-thirds of the ration.[10] But no sooner had the ration scale been set than it became necessary to reduce it, for Scott records on 13 March 1788, that twelve pounds of beef and eight pounds of pork per hundredweight had to be cut from the scale.[11] The reason for this was that it was naval tradition for such a cut to be made to make up for loss when bulk quantities were divided into small serving quantities.[12] Thus the meagreness of the ration was to be compounded by the niceties of bureaucratic regulations. As stocks began to diminish, the livestock owned by the marines and others in the colony (see Table 7) assumed an added value.[13] Bearing in mind that the marines were approximately a quarter of the whole population, their proportion of ownership was liberal; but, as Ross was to point out in July 1788, troops whose duty was as heavy as was the detachment's, could not exist indefinitely on salted meat alone.[14] To overcome this deficiency the *Supply* had been despatched in May to Lord Howe Island, between Port Jackson and Norfolk Island, to procure fresh turtle meat, but

Table 7 Livestock ownership, May 1788

Stock	Total in colony	Number owned by marines	Percentage owned by marines
cows	5	1	20%
goats	19	12	63%
hogs	49	10	20%
pigs	25	17	68%
rabbits	5	2	40%
turkeys	18	6	33%
geese	29	9	31%
ducks	35	8	23%
fowls	122	55	45%
chickens	87	25	29%
horses	4	0	0%

Source: *Historical Records of New South Wales*, vol 1, part 2, 151

without success. Its failure was also the more keenly regretted because by now scurvy had broken out.[15] Shortages of items other than rations also began to appear by July, and Surgeon White was forced to advise Phillip that the marines' wives and children (as well as convicts) who were in hospital, lacked blankets and sheets.[16] But also Ross was asking for more stationery, clothing, and a continuation of the spirit ration.[17] The shortages were made all the worse when on 5 June the cattle and other stock which had been brought from the Cape of Good Hope were allowed to stray because of the indolence of their convict shepherd.[18]

In September, mindful of diminishing stocks, Commissary Andrew Miller made a stocktake which revealed approximately a year's supply of flour, beef, butter, and peas; two year's supply of salted pork; but only fifteen weeks' supply of rice.[19] (When Hunter took the *Sirius* to the Cape of Good Hope on 2 October 1788, Commissary Miller asked him to procure hospital stores.)[20] What Miller could not know was that the next resupply would not arrive for another twenty-two months.

By November the deteriorating condition of the detachment's weapons was causing alarm to its quartermaster, whose Return of Arms in his store showed a sixth of the muskets to be unserviceable.[21] Ross, whose antipathy to Phillip was by now well developed, blamed the situation on Phillip who he alleged had kept the blacksmith in such constant employ on other tasks, that it was taking up to three months to have weapons repaired.[22]

By Christmas 1788, all were mindful of the need to conserve the remaining rations until the anticipated arrival of the Second Fleet. Some were adding their issues from the Q store by personal supplements as Sergeant Scott had done by setting a broody hen on seventeen eggs, from which sixteen were hatched. Unfortunately, as a result of various misfortunes such as attacks by a rat and some drowning or straying, only two chickens remained by the new year.[23]

Before 1788 concluded, such was the looming shortage of flour that Phillip despatched the *Sirius* to the Cape of Good Hope to procure a replenishment. On board she carried a marine element of a sergeant, a corporal, a drummer, and fourteen privates.[24] As the voyage circumnavigated the world by proceeding from Port Jackson to the Cape of Good Hope via Cape Horn, these men appear to have been the first marines to have done so. Unfortunately, the flour obtained was infested with weevils.

By September 1789, twenty-one months had passed without any resupply, and butter was the first commodity to expire. This signalled the introduction of food rationing, and in October the marines (and the convicts) were reduced to two-thirds' rations. Accordingly, the weekly flour issue was reduced from 7 pounds to 5 pounds 5 ounces (3.6 kg to 2.4 kg), pork from 5 pounds to 3 pounds 5 ounces (2.3 kg to 1.5 kg), and peas from 3 pints to 2 pints (1.7 l to 1.1 l). No other items were available.[25] At two-thirds of an issue, the marines were receiving the same ration as their wives.

The marine and convict ration scales were identical, for Phillip would permit no discrimination between the two groups. This scale lasted for only four months till half rations had to be introduced on 27 March 1790; marines and convicts then existed on 4 pounds of flour, 2½ pounds of salted pork, and 1½ pounds of rice per week.[26]

Such a ration barely prevented starvation but the reduction was necessary because of two factors: the wrecking of the *Sirius* at Norfolk Island on 19 March 1790; and the widespread thieving by convicts of food gardens. The loss of the *Sirius* was a particularly serious blow. After her 1788 trip to the Cape of Good Hope, she had set out for China via Norfolk Island on 5 March 1790. She conveyed Major Ross, two companies of marines, and stores for Norfolk Island, but on trying to get close to shore there, she was wrecked. News of her fate was conveyed to those at Port Jackson by the *Supply*, the approach of which was signalled to Phillip and

Tench at Sydney Cove on 5 April from the flag at the South Head signal station. They checked their observation with a telescope but, Tench wrote, could only see a marine at the flagstaff strolling around "unmoved by what he saw".[27] But a hoisted flag at South Head meant to those at Sydney Cove that a ship had been sighted, and as the Second Fleet was hourly and eagerly awaited, Phillip decided to go down the harbour for information. Tench accompanied him, and when they were halfway down they saw a rowing boat coming towards them. Tench sensed misfortune and said to Phillip "Sir prepare yourself for bad news". When the two boats met, the one from the *Supply* revealed that the *Sirius* had been lost. Phillip and Tench were struck with "unspeakable consternation" and returned to Sydney Cove at once. The news there was greeted with universal dismay, particularly as it was quickly realized that the colony's only link now with the outside world was by the little, quite inadequate, *Supply*. Phillip lost no time in facing the new disaster: at six o'clock that evening he summoned a council of all officers, both civil and military, to determine what measures ought to be adopted.[28]

Phillip's action revealed how seriously he viewed the situation, for normally he neither shared his responsibility nor sought counsel from subordinates. The Commissary, John Palmer, took an inventory of stocks held in the government store which revealed that at the present rate of issue, the pork would last till July, rice till September, and flour till mid November 1790.[29] Such meagre stocks necessitated a further cut, so from 12 April 1790 issues were reduced to 2 pounds (900 g) of pork, 2½ pounds (1.1 kg) of flour, and either 2 pounds of rice or 1 quart (1.1 l) of dried peas a week.[30] It was also decided to despatch the *Supply* to Batavia for additional supplies, and so greatly were the marine officers in want of necessities that eight of them drew bills against their pay to enable the *Supply* to make purchases for them.[31] She departed on Saturday 17 April, conveying King who was to make his way from Batavia to England with Phillip's despatches. Her departure enveloped the wretched colony in further apprehension. Tench's reaction was to recall a line from Vergil's Aeneid: "In te omnis domus inclinata recumbit" (on you rests all our sinking house)[32] — for everything, including the colony's salvation, depended on that little ship and her commander, Lieutenant H.B. Ball.

The plight of the colony called for the strictest measures if survival was to be achieved: all private boats were requisitioned for public fishing at both Port Jackson and Botany Bay, and the fishing had to be performed under officer supervision. As an inducement, successful fishermen were to receive one pound of uncleaned fish for breakfast. These measures resulted in four hundredweight of fish being caught by 7 April. Others were appointed to grow vegetables. In addition, gamekeepers were appointed to shoot the kangaroos which were destroying gardens, but as such work could not be sustained by their rations, the gamekeepers received an additional quantity of flour and pork.[33] The meagreness of the ration was not the only problem, for the pork had by now been so long in brine that it had become too salty to be edible after boiling; and yet it was too precious to be wasted. Consequently, it was toasted over a fire, its drips of fat being either mopped up by bread or caught in a saucer of weevil-infested rice.[34] Well might Collins have asked, "Was this a ration for a labouring man?"[35] It became necessary when people visited one another for them to take their own bread, and such was the universal hunger that the labour expected of convicts had to be reduced to the hours from sunrise to 1 p.m., after which they spent their afternoons cultivating their gardens.[36] Consequently the greater part of public works had to cease,[37] and when the Second Fleet arrived in June 1790, by which time the convicts had slaughtered and eaten nearly all the livestock in their care, convicts were capable of only a few hours' work a day.[38] According to Tench however there was no such reduction in the duties performed by the marines, for he records that their daily tasks were unaltered — his other statement that convict duty also continued unaltered during the 1790 famine appears to be incorrect, for it is at variance with all other accounts.[39]

The famine caused an enormous increase in the pilfering of food and associated items. Whether cultivated by convict or marine, gardens continued to be robbed frequently, as Collins felt, either from the "villainy of the people" or "the necessities of the times".[40] Tench took a compassionate view: "I everyday see wretches", he wrote, "pale with disease and wasted with famine struggling against the horrors of their situation", and from this he reflected that "the throes of hunger would ever prove too powerful for integrity to withstand".[41]

Severe punishment therefore had to be inflicted on food thieves, and sentences given at this time were the most severe of Phillip's term. He ordered that culprits be neck-ironed and shackled whilst doing their daily quota of work,[42] and floggings of enormous severity had to be imposed: thus William Lane — allegedly prompted by hunger — stole thirteen pounds of biscuits and was sentenced to two thousand lashes.[43] One convict was flogged after he was caught stealing fishing tackle from Daringa, the wife of the aborigine Colbee. And yet severe deterrents were necessary if the food supply was to last. When convicts Robert Hunt and William Hand admitted stealing corn at Parramatta — an offence then so common there that the severest punishment was necessary to deter others — both were sentenced to wear a seven-pound (3.2 kg) iron collar for two years.[44] Of the judicial severity necessary, Tench lamented, "Such was the melancholy length to which we were compelled to stretch our penal system".[45]

Marines were not immune from the depredations of thieves: Thomas Osborn, the baker at Parramatta, was apprehended after absconding with the marines' flour and bread;[46] and when convict Isaac Cowden pleaded guilty to stealing vegetables from Sergeant Young's garden, he received one hundred lashes in spite of pleading hunger as the cause.[47] Convicts however were not the only thieves: a marine who robbed a garden himself received five hundred lashes.[48]

The famine produced other misfortunes: prices became inflated, a laying hen fetching twenty shillings and a roast pig ten shillings.[49] The policy of shooting kangaroos failed because so few were caught, and the supply of salt ran out, necessitating the construction of two boilers at the east point of Sydney Cove to boil sea water, from which the salt was extracted.[50] Occasionally a plentiful catch of fish brought a temporary respite, as in May 1790 when two thousand pounds of fish were caught, saving the issue of five hundred pounds of pork.[51]

When at last the storeship *Justinian* of the Second Fleet arrived on 21 June 1790, a restoration of full rations was made, and public works again resumed with the building of a road from the wharf to Phillip's house and the further development of the Rose Hill settlement. This improved rationing did not last long, for a drought during the first quarter of 1791 destroyed crops.[52] Consequently the ration again had to be reduced and Collins noted that the facial features of the labouring convicts "indicated the shortness of the ration" they were receiving.[53] As the marine ration was the same as the convict's, the marines were again suffering a similar hunger. It was not till the arrival of the storeship *Matilda* on 8 August 1791 that Phillip finally was able to increase weekly rations to 5 pounds (2.3 kg) of flour per man, and 3 ½ pounds (1.6 kg) per woman.[54] In the meantime, life was still such a struggle that convicts attempted to stowaway on the *Neptune* as she prepared to sail on 22 August 1790. They were discovered by a marine party commanded by the town adjutant, Lieutenant Long.

This attempt might have been encouraged by the earlier

epic escape of the party of William and Mary Bryant on 29 March, the day after the Dutch transport *Waaksamheyd* conveying Hunter and the crew of the *Sirius* sailed for England. On the day of their escape no ships were in the harbour, and as the Bryant party intended making for Batavia by sea, they could not be chased. At daybreak next day, a sergeant and a party of marines set out in a long boat to pursue them up the north coast. But the escapees were aided by a compass, quadrant, chart, and nautical information given them by Captain Detmer Smith, the culpable master of the *Waaksamheyd*.[55] The fugitives reached Batavia, but only Mary ultimately was to reach England. Easty felt it was an act of desperation for Bryant to take his wife and two children under the age of three on so long a voyage of seventeen hundred leagues. However, he felt sympathy for them: William and Mary's term had expired, but because of lack of documentation, they could not be freed. To them, the thought of liberty from such a place as Port Jackson was adequate reason for the tragic escape.

11

Marines under the Lash

Convicts were not the only lawbreakers in the colony. After the marines landed at Sydney, their duties largely became those of army pioneers, with surveillance and exploration comprising subsidiary tasks. Because they were not used in normal marine or military roles, the danger existed of a decline in military discipline. Such a decline is often the result of a prolonged period of non-regimental duty, and yet at no stage during their four years at Sydney Cove does the evidence suggest that discipline was anything but firm — and this in spite of the unorthodox situation in which they found themselves, and in spite of parade ground regimentalism having to yield to the pragmatic demands of founding a settlement. In this, Tench acknowledged that "attention to the parade ground duty of troops, gradually diminished"; instead, marines felled the "ponderous gum tree" or broke the stubborn clod; wheelbarrows and spades replaced the musket; and time usually devoted to martial pursuits was now used in "the sawpit, the forge and the quarry".[1] Although overall discipline remained firm, minor offences by individual marines were of course committed — but the records cite less than 20 of them for a detachment of 212 on a four-year tour of duty in circumstances of considerable privation. In this regard, the marines differed from later regiments serving in New South Wales. Those units experienced considerable problems with discipline and one of the main reasons for those problems was that soldiers became corrupted by the convict labourers with whom they had to associate in disparate groups, often in the absence of their sergeants, and in situations where captains were separated from their companies.[2] Such a decline in discipline did not occur with the marines because they did not divide into small groups but remained in companies at Port Jackson, Rose Hill, or Norfolk Island where there was no change from the strict regimental system of command; and because they did not supervise convict labour, they did not have to associate as closely with the felons.

The most common offence amongst marines was stealing, though the first instance recorded did not occur till 2 March 1789 when Corporal James Plowman was charged with stealing a shirt from Private Edward Odgers. Convicts Amelia Levy and Elizabeth Fowles gave evidence that they had been offered a shirt to spend the night with Plowman and Corporal John Wixstead. Wixstead rejected the accusation, but even so was reduced in rank, and Private William Goodall was promoted corporal in his stead. Plowman also rejected the evidence of Levy and Fowles by stating that if he had wanted to give a shirt away, he would have given one of his own. Strongly in his favour were sixteen years of unblemished service, and he was acquitted.

In the same month, the robbery of the public storehouse was discovered to have been perpetrated not by convicts, but by marines — a revelation which brought great embarrassment and shame to the detachment. The Commissary, Andrew Palmer, found upon arrival at the store on 18 March 1789, pieces of a key which had been broken in the padlock of the principal door. The pieces were sent to the convict blacksmith who revealed not only that they belonged to Private Joseph Hunt, but also that he previously had brought the key to the blacksmith to be altered. Hunt was ar-

rested but offered king's evidence in which he confessed to
Major Ross that provisions had often been stolen from the
store during previous months and that he had often heard
Private Luke Haynes threaten to murder anyone who
betrayed the thieves. Haynes had been tried previously for
the death of another soldier, Private Bullmore.[3]

The thieves' plan had been an ingenious one. The robbery
party had consisted of seven marines, each sworn to secrecy.
They had secured some keys which Hunt had had the
blacksmith alter to fit all three doors to the storehouse; then,
whenever one of the seven was sentry for the night, two or
more of the gang were to enter the store, shut the door, and
take as much liquor and provisions as they could. Any passing sentry would check the door, but finding it secure would
assume all was well and move on. The plan worked well till
the night the gang member who was sentry decided to rob
without the aid of his accomplices. He placed the key in the
lock, but hearing the approach of the patrol, he panicked.
Knowing that the corporal would check the lock, he
frantically tried to withdraw the key, but it snapped, leaving
a part inside the lock. In further panic, he then threw the
stem away. At this stage of his evidence, Hunt named his
accomplices as Privates James Baker, James Brown, Richard
Dukes, Thomas Jones, Luke Haynes, and Richard Askew.
Dukes, who was at Rose Hill, was arrested and brought to
Sydney Cove where he added the further complication of
not only admitting to having committed robberies at Rose
Hill, but also named as his accomplices there, Privates Norris
and Roberts. This escalation caused their arrest but their
cases were stood over till the other was tried.

The trial court met at 9 a.m. on Wednesday 25 March
1789. Its bench comprised the Judge Advocate, Captains
Campbell, Meredith and Tench, and Lieutenants George
Johnston, Creswell and Furzer; accordingly, it had the
number to impose the death penalty. The evidence was
heard during the morning and at 2 p.m. the court adjourned

to consider its verdict; half an hour later it announced the death sentence on all six offenders. The gallows were erected and the six marines were hanged at 10 a.m. two days later.[4]

Tench lamented the "awful and terrible example of justice", though his description of them as "the flower of our battalion" was at variance with the opinion of others.[5] Collins noted that as Baker, Haynes, Askew, and Duke had been tried previously for Private Bullmore's death, they had long been "verging towards this melancholy end".[6] But Collins' sentiment would have been at odds with that of the detachment because of the social relationships which a unit produced. A British unit of the late eighteenth and early nineteenth centuries was much more than a fighting machine; it was an intricate way of life; a closed society; a cocoon in which a private's independence was taken from him and replaced by a dependence on his regiment. He ate and slept among his messmates under the watchful eye of his corporal; his sergeant drilled him and trained him, and through him the man could pass on his grievances to his captain. It was a paternal system which brought men close together and in their unity gave them a respect for their unit and its reputation. The sadness and remorse which Tench felt therefore was closer to the detachment's reaction than was Collins' albeit more accurate observation. Those hanged were replaced by a party of marines from the reserve held aboard the *Sirius*.[7]

Collins and Ross then investigated Hunt's accusation against Roberts and Norris, who denied all knowledge of his claim. In an endeavour to test their veracity, Norris was offered a free pardon if he confessed but he persistently proclaimed his innocence so both were discharged.

Hunt had figured prominently in three controversial incidents. He was court martialled on 18 March 1788 for assaulting Private Dempsey. (This had caused dissension in the detachment and had resulted in the arrest of the officers of the court. See chapter 15.) In February 1789, he had been found guilty of being absent from his post whilst on duty as a sentry (for which he had received seven hundred lashes in two doses separated by three weeks). And a month later, still sore no doubt from his flogging, his evidence had caused six of his fellow marines to be hanged. Hunt was obviously a disreputable character frequently in trouble and was recognized as such by Private Easty who was angry at his duplicity. With intimate knowledge of what went on in the ranks, Easty claimed that each of the six had said that Hunt was the first who had robbed. Easty also said that the sense of regret throughout the detachment for those executed was so widespread that there was hardly an officer or marine who had not shed tears at the injustice of Hunt receiving a free pardon.[8]

The robbery of the public store was the most notorious case of military thieving and made a profound impression not only on the detachment, but on the colony generally. There were however other instances of marine larceny. On 31 March 1790, Private Richard Knight stole two cabbage plants worth three pence from Private Joseph Harpur, for which he received two hundred lashes;[9] Private Mark Hurst was tried for stealing rice from the public store on 27 August 1790 and received five hundred lashes.[10] Almost on the same day, Private James McManus was confined for stealing a chest belonging to Private Charles McCarthy of the New South Wales Corps but was acquitted by maintaining that he had received the articles out of the chest from Drummer John Dell of that Corps who then was also confined. McManus tried to commit suicide by cutting his throat in the guardhouse but his life was saved by Corporal Begley. His acquittal did not convince Sergeant Scott, who felt he was guilty and had won his case on a technicality.[11] Private John Pugh had been returned to Sydney Cove from the settlement at Norfolk Island for stealing potatoes from the public store. He was tried by a battalion court martial and received five hundred lashes together with six months on a ration of four pounds (1.8 kg) of flour a week without any meat or eggs.[12] Private William Godfrey, who had been posted as sentry at the public cellar at 11 p.m. on 16 July 1791, was found by Sergeant Smith to be robbing the cellar of wine an hour later. Godfrey had picked the lock with a nail. At his trial he admitted his guilt but also impeached Privates William Roberts and William Norris as having been accomplices in this act for the past three months. They were then charged with having stolen between 1 May and 17 July 1791, nine gallons (40 l) of rum and five gallons (23 l) of red wine, but again their posturings served them well and their case was dismissed because of insufficient proof. Their guilt however was widely suspected: Easty wrote that everyone thought them guilty, and with this view Collins concurred.[13] They were sent to do duty at South Head where they could not repeat their crime; Godfrey on the other hand was sentenced to eight hundred lashes, and after being drummed out of the unit "with every mark of disgrace that could be shown him",[14] received his first three hundred lashes that same day.

Other offences included assault: that by Private Hunt on Private Dempsey will be treated in chapter 15, but the attack on Private Thomas Bullmore was so severe that on 10 November 1788, he died of wounds received.[15] (His attackers, as we have seen, were hanged on 25 March 1789 for robbing the public store.)[16] The fatal attack probably occurred during a drunken brawl because its sequel was that Captain Meredith's company was taken off grog for seven days by Major Ross.[17]

Other minor offences included the one previously mentioned which resulted in the court martial of a marine for striking a female convict for refusing to accompany him into the woods for cohabitation,[18] and Private Easty's indiscretion in taking a female into the marines' camp, for which he received 150 lashes.[19] These and the charges brought against Private Henry Wright were the only sexual charges brought against marines.

Wright's misconduct was the abhorrent crime of child molestation. On 10 September 1789, he was charged with having carnal knowledge of Elizabeth Chapman, an eight-year-old girl. She was called and questioned: she acknowledged her age and told the court that she was old enough to know that those who told lies went to the devil but that heaven was the destiny of those who told the truth. She could say her catechism and repeated the Lord's Prayer to the court. A number of marines were called as witnesses and the girl's mother expressed the opinion that Wright "had the character of doing such things with children".[20] He was sentenced to death but was pardoned by Phillip and sentenced to serve the term of his natural life at Norfolk Island. Collins gives a strange reason for the lighter sentence: he says it was given because sex was so freely available from women that this crime was unlikely to be repeated.[21] His forecast however was wrong: two years later Wright sexually molested the ten-year-old Elizabeth Gregory at Norfolk Island, for which he was forced to run the gauntlet between men and women.[22] He seems to have rehabilitated himself thereafter and became a carpenter; and when he died aged eighty at Park Street, Sydney, in 1837, he was believed to be the last First Fleet marine to die in Sydney.[23]

12

Parramatta

The Rose Hill area was reconnoitred on 2 March 1788 by Bowes, Ross, Campbell, and Ross's gardener. Because they found the soil exceedingly rich,[1] it was decided early in October the same year to form a settlement there and name it after George Rose, Phillip's neighbour in England and Under Secretary to the Treasury.[2] Phillip was later to rename Rose Hill as Parramatta on 2 June 1791.[3] Captain Campbell's company was to provide a party of himself and two other officers, four NCOs, a drummer, and twenty marines to form the settlement. The advance party under command of Lieutenant John Johnson left Sydney on 2 October 1788 via the river to prepare reception arrangements for the main party which, with Captain Campbell and Lieutenant Shairp, arrived on 22 November 1788.[4] They took with them seventy convicts.[5] The most famous convict at Parramatta was to be the expiree James Ruse. He was Cornish and had been a farmer all his life. Phillip gave him a grant and ordered that two acres be cleared of timber and a house built for him. On 21 November 1789, Ruse began his farm and immediately showed himself to be an industrious and keen settler. He married Elizabeth Parry, who had been pardoned by Phillip, in September 1790. As her husband's mutual helper, she bore his child and did the backbreaking work of establishing the property. By Christmas 1791, such was the success of their joint labours, that Ruse was able to ask that he and his family be taken off the public store.[6]

By April 1790, a redoubt had been constructed at Parramatta which contained barracks for officers and one hundred men.[7] Thus the Parramatta troops occupied completed barracks before all of their Sydney counterparts occupied theirs.[8] Eventually the strength of the Parramatta detachment was reduced till it consisted of a subaltern and a small party of marines who were relieved each month.[9] The Parramatta outstation was supplied with stores carried from Sydney Cove by the first ship built in the colony. It was built by the carpenter of the *Supply* from May to October 1789, weighed twelve tons according to Bradley but fifty according to Scott, and though the convicts called her *The Rose Hill Packet*, Collins says that because of her shape, she was generally known as *The Lump*.[10]

Of great assistance to the Parramatta marines was Henry Edward Dodd. He had come out from England as a servant to Phillip, but when Ross refused to allow the detachment to supervise convicts, Phillip employed him as Superintendent of Convicts at Rose Hill where he gained the "approbation and countenance" of officers who had served there.[11] His death therefore on 28 January 1791 was widely regretted.

With the arrival of the advance party of the New South Wales Corps, the marines were relieved at Parramatta on 10 and 11 March 1791. Their relief was performed under harsh conditions as the heat on both days was unbearable at 105 °F (40.5 °C). Bushfires were roaring, birds gasping in the stifling heat, and bats were dropping dead. The marine detachment was ordered to return by boat to Sydney Cove, but such was their consumption of water in the torrid conditions that they exhausted their supply during the trip. An officer landed to search for a replenishment, but so dry was the country and its creeks that he had to walk several miles before he found any.[12]

Marine service at Parramatta had covered two-and-a-half years during a period when the main settlement at Sydney Cove was heavily dependent on Parramatta's supplementary source of food supply. The colony's survival vitally depended on it and the surveillance provided by the marines established an ethos of relative orderliness from which such a programme of agricultural productivity could proceed. In that way, the Marine Corps contribution at Parramatta was a vital one.

13

God Save the King

The celebration of royal occasions was a highlight of marine service at New South Wales; such occasions, even during the height of the famine, were times of special parades, festivities, and additional rations. The King's and Queen's birthdays were meticulously observed; other members of the royal family were occasionally honoured; and such special events as the restoration of the King's health provided the marines with occasions for royal celebration.

The first such celebration was that held to honour the birthday of King George III on 4 June 1788. It was kept as best as possible "in this country",[1] when at sunrise, at 1 p.m., and again at sunset, the *Sirius* and *Supply* acknowledged the event with twenty-one gun salutes.[2] At noon, after marching across from its barracks, the detachment was drawn up in front of Government House where it fired three volleys whilst the band played the first part of the national anthem between each volley.[3] This was followed at one o'clock by the officers proceeding to Government House to pay their respects. Phillip received them most graciously and after congratulating them on being His Majesty's first subjects to celebrate his birthday in New South Wales, they sat down to a lunch of mutton, pork, duck, fowl, fish, kangaroo, salad, pies, and preserved fruit. Wines from Portugal, Madeira and

Teneriffe were in plenty as was "good old English porter" which went "merrily round in bumpers".[4] Toasts were drunk for the King, the Queen and the royal family, and for Prince William (later William IV). Phillip then announced that, following English practice, the settlement and surrounds would be proclaimed a county, to which he gave the name Cumberland, after which he used the announcement for another toast, "The County and the Cumberland family".

Whilst such convivialities were being observed inside Government House, Phillip, always the gracious patriarch of his colonial family, had each marine given a pint of porter and each convict given half a pint of rum. And three sailors who had been confined on the island of Pinchgut were pardoned — all to celebrate the royal occasion.[5]

With the luncheon completed, Phillip had need to go into an adjacent room, and whilst he was away someone suggested a toast to him in his absence, whereupon everyone filled their glasses and drank to "The Governor and the Settlement". Three hurrahs were then given and the band played. Upon his return, Phillip acknowledged hearing the toast and thanked his guests heartily before returning their complement by himself drinking a toast to their health, promising that nothing would be lacking on his part to promote harmony and unanimity throughout the settlement.[6] At 5 p.m. the party broke up to visit bonfires which the people had made for the celebration, and as Phillip approached, the convicts gave three cheers and a party of them sang "God Save the King". He stayed twenty minutes and then returned with many of the officers to Government House for a further cold repast. At 11 p.m. the festivities of the day ended with never a sign that throughout them, Phillip had been in constant pain, which he had striven to conceal.[7] Such was the calibre of this man.

The day had been one of what Tench called widespread "loyal conviviality",[8] in which as Doctor Worgan observed "every heart beat with loyalty and joy"[9] — every heart, that is, except those officers who upon returning to their tents found that they had been burgled.[10] Captain Meredith was lucky enough to catch his burglar, a convict, in the act.[11] Worgan was disgusted that the convicts had spoilt so enjoyable a day, lamenting, "Did you ever hear of such a set of reprobates".[12]

The celebration of the Prince of Wales' birthday on 12 August 1788 was another most festive occasion which was more than welcome as a diversion from the loneliness and hardship of colonial life. As usual, all labour ceased for the day,[13] and the *Sirius*, moored on the eastern side of the cove, fired a twenty-one gun salute and displayed colours from her mainmast. The marine detachment marched to the flagstaff near the Tank Stream from where it fired three volleys,[14] as the Governor received the military compliments due to him, after which he gave a dinner.[15] For some reason however the two doctors, White and Balmain, had a falling out which they resolved with a pistol duel. Each fired five rounds before being separated without harming each other, although Balmain did sustain a small flesh wound in the right thigh. Phillip, sagacious enough not to give the incident more importance than it merited, suggested tactfully that "the two sons of Esculipious [sic] would do better to draw blood from their patients than from each other".[16] But the harsh demands of founding a settlement were beginning to affect human relationships because no sooner had the flare-up between White and Balmain been settled than another broke out between White and Adjutant Long, and a repetition of the duel would have ensued had it not been for the intervention of friends.[17] Both Clark and White acknowledged that "the seeds of animosity" were budding;[18] but their claim seems to have been somewhat too general, for apart from the animosity felt towards Ross (which will be dealt with in chapter 15), personal relationships between officers, with the exception of those occasional personality clashes always to be expected, held harmoniously.

The Queen's birthday was celebrated on 19 January 1789

and the King's birthday celebration of June that year included a play performed by a party of convicts. It was called "The Recruiting Officer" and was performed before an audience which included Phillip and sixty other people. It was the first play performed in Australia and contained much improvisation using coloured paper. Its venue was described by Tench as being a mud-walled convict hut with light provided by a dozen farthing candles. The play itself was one which had been written by George Farquhar (1678-1707) who had first produced it at Drury Lane in 1706. He based its plot on his observations of recruiting during his own service as a recruiting officer at Shrewsbury.[19]

Between the King's birthday festivities in 1789 and 1790, the ravages of debilitating famine took their toll, but with the Second Fleet arriving just before the 1790 celebration, the community feeling and morale changed to one of joyousness. Collins captured its spirit when he wrote that the King's birthday "was kept with every mark of distinction that was in our power"; to demonstrate his joy and gratitude at the recovery of George III's health, Phillip pardoned all offenders, increased the ration for the day, and, Collins wrote, "at the Governor's table, where all the officers of the settlement and garrison were met, many prosperous and happy years were fervently wished to be added to His Majesty's life".[20]

Nothing, not even famine, was permitted to prevent the celebration of these royal occasions. After the *Sirius* was wrecked at Norfolk Island, fishing boats were sent out to sea to catch sufficient fish to provide a royal banquet for everyone on the island. Unfortunately bad weather forced the boats to return, but the island colony still commemorated the regal occasion.[21]

These celebrations brightened an otherwise drab and suffering existence and as Phillip used them to dispense pardons and issue additional rations and alcohol, it is of little doubt that they were eagerly anticipated, not only for honouring the head of state, but also for the relief which they offered.

14

Staying On: Family and Land

Family Life

Some twenty-eight marine wives and seventeen marine children accompanied the detachment on the First Fleet.[1] As conditions deteriorated in the settlement, they were not to escape its hardships and privations. Although no account of a marine's family life has yet come to light, the occasional references to wives and children in official correspondence enable a picture, admittedly incomplete, to be drawn.

During the outward voyage, the families travelled in the same ship as their marine father, but whether, once they reached Sydney Cove, they lived with him in married quarters within the barracks complex, or adjacent to it, is not clear. What is clear however is that the families were providored from the public store and felt its increasing incapacity to supply them with the necessities of life. As early as 4 July 1788, Commissary Andrew Miller wrote to Phillip that marine wives and children were feeling materially the want of necessities which he listed as being 6,000 pounds of sugar, 2,000 pounds of sago, 6,000 pounds of barley, 20,000 pounds of rice, and 20,000 pounds of oatmeal.[2] These are considerable quantities and point to the drain that providoring marine families had on existing stocks. Wives originally received two-thirds of their husbands' ration,[3] but when Phillip reduced the soldier's ration to two-thirds in November 1789, he did not further reduce that of the wives.[4] Consequently from that time onwards, husband and wife received the same impoverished issue until the ration was restored after the *Matilda* arrived in August 1791, when the distinction was again restored of the husband receiving 5 pounds (2.3 kg) of flour a week to his wife's 3½ pounds (1.6 kg).[5] The children appear not to have been as underfed, for at the height of the famine in April 1790, they were receiving (except babies under eighteen months) the same ration as their parents. Babies under eighteen months received the same flour and rice ration as their parents, but only 1 pound of pork.[6]

An astonishing oversight in the supply of logistics for the settlement had been the omission of clothing for marine wives and children, and as soon as the items brought by individuals from England wore out, the want was immediately felt. By July 1788, Ross was writing to Stephens asking for materials to make women's and children's shoes as well as such items as lawn, handkerchiefs, coloured dress materials, quilts, petticoats, and stockings,[7] their cost to be debited against the husband's pay.[8] It is reasonable to believe that faced by such shortages, mothers would have made cut-down clothes for their children from their own worn-out garments.

The supply of one particular item, alcohol, ceased during the famine. For some of the marine wives who had a liking for it, the imposed abstinence must have been a great privation. Female drinking was most prominent during the outward voyage when some wives drank so heavily that action had to be taken against them. Sergeant Hume and his wife seem to have had a real "session" in late May 1787, for on the 20th his wife's rum ration had to be stopped, as was his own a week later, and that by his own order.[9] At about the same time, the wife of Private Michael Redman displayed such a propensity for drink that Lieutenant Maxwell stopped her liquor issue for a month.[10]

The drunkeness of both Private and Mrs Arthur Dougherty just prior to reaching Botany Bay was so complete that her issue had to be stopped for twelve days, and both were jailed for six.[11] At the same time, the pregnant Martha Davis, wife of Private John Davis, received a grog suspension of ten days,[12] and the women's liquor ration was suspended entirely from 26 February to 13 March 1788, so widespread was its abuse.[13] The payment for wives' liquor posed a problem for Phillip, and he wrote to Nepean on 5 July 1788 for direction. This probably resulted from Surgeon White's recommendation to him that marine wives who were sick should receive a medical liquor issue "for health reasons".[14] To regularize the situation, Phillip, on his own initiative, ordered the Commissary to issue half the husband's issue to his wife on the understanding that if Treasury refused to stand the cost, then the husband would pay.[15] This arrangement apparently brought the problem under control for it disappeared as a ration issue thereafter.

Recorded relationships between the marine women seem to have been harmonious with the single exception that Mrs Martha Davis was charged on 23 April 1791 with having scandalously abused both Sergeant and Mrs Scott by calling Mrs Scott a whore. She ascribed the outburst to provocation and was told to apologize, which she did.[16]

Births, deaths and marriages did not leave the marines in their isolated corner of the world untouched, for the itinerary of life refused submission to seclusion or isolation.[17] On the First Fleet, the marines had increased their seventeen children to twenty-one[18] by the time the fleet reached Port Jackson.[19] Until the main body of the marines departed in December 1791, forty-nine marines produced sixty-five children of which thirty-seven were legitimate and twenty-eight illegitimate. (See appendix A.) These illegitimates were produced by twenty-four marines, who represented 11 per cent of the detachment, but of this figure, 33 per cent were officers even though officers constituted only 12 per cent of the detachment's strength — that is, the officers comprising 12 per cent produced 33 per cent of the illegitimates. Moreover seven, or almost half the officers, produced illegitimate children although only one-eleventh of the other ranks did so. However, whereas seven of the other ranks refused to allow their offspring the birthright of a father's surname but gave them their mother's name instead, no officer-father refused his children so basic a right of heredity, and three of them — Meredith, Kellow and Furzer — took their son home with them, leaving daughters with their convict mothers. Private Brixey, despite his earlier description in the records as being the "putative" father of his son William, is the only marine aboard the *Gorgon* who returned with his child and its convict mother (whom he did not marry whilst in the colony). Fifteen mothers of marine children were to be abandoned to the uncertainty and harshness of a forbidding struggle for existence when the *Gorgon* sailed. In the colony's early days, few things were more impressive than the courage and unfailing service of mothers, particularly in those cases of renunciation of fatherly responsibility, which were reasonably common. But it was certainly not confined to marines, for civil officers, seamen, and even captains of ships all sailed away indifferent to the herculean burden they had imposed on impoverished women for whom even the struggle for personal survival was daunting enough without the demanding imposition of family. Such mothers coped in various ways: some battled on at Port Jackson; others, such as Elizabeth Cole, the mother of Private Ellis's son, worked at Norfolk Island for six years before moving to Hobart; Margaret Green, the mother of Private Green's son, also went to Norfolk Island where she settled with settler Private Owen Cavenaugh who farmed there till 1796 before moving back to the Hawkesbury; whilst Alice Harmsworth, widow of the Private Thomas Harmsworth who had died on 30 April 1788,[20] and by whom she had had two children, battled on till she married Corporal Daniel Standfield on 15 October 1791, by which date she had produced their son, Daniel. They too settled at Norfolk Island.

Two marines, William Brixey and William Blackburn, apparently refused to acknowledge their children, and were described in the records as "putative", and "reputed" fathers, whilst Private John Browne appears the most pitiless: his daughter's mother died at the birth, he denied his baby his name, and might even have abandoned her, for both Hunter and Collins had to sit as magistrates to decide the child's fate.[21] They appointed Frances Davis as foster mother, but she was not long troubled by the child for the girl died before she was three months old. However, not all fathers of illegitimates abandoned their responsibility: Privates Cotterill, McDonald, Ryan, and Mitchell became settlers and provided for their new families. Few marines married the women with whom they had cohabited, though Private Nash and Standfield, as well as Sergeant Perry, did marry the women who were pregnant to them.

Whilst on service in New South Wales twelve marines appeared to have married — nine to convicts, although none of the convict women married to those who returned in the *Gorgon* accompanied them.[22] (See Table 8.) Until the *Gorgon*'s departure, one-eighth of the detachment's strength, or twenty-seven marines, had died on service.[23] (See Table 9.)

Land and Discharge

Phillip's initial instructions from the British government failed to give direction about allocating land to members of the detachment whilst they were still serving. Even after they had finished serving, land was to be granted to non-officers only. Early in March 1788, officers approached

Table 8 Marine marriages, 1788–1792

	Rank	Husband	Wife	Place	Date	Wife's previous status
1.	Pte	Thomas Browne	Elizabeth Barber	Sydney	17.2.88	Convict
2.	"	James Mapp	Susannah Creswell	"	24.2.88	Widow of Pte Creswell
3.	"	William Duglass?	Mary Graves [Groves]	"	1.6.88	Convict
4.	"	William Nash	Maria Haynes	"	1.2.89	Convict
5.	Sgt	William Perry	Ann Scoble	"	1.2.89	De facto
6.	Pte	Thomas Smith	Sarah Willis	Parramatta	5.9.90	Convict
7.	"	John Browne	Martha Daniels	Sydney	10.11.90	Convict
8.	"	Thomas Jones	Elizabeth Leatherby [Litherby]	Parramatta	22.2.91	Convict
9.	"	Thomas Smith	Ann Colepitts	Parramatta	25.9.91	Convict
10.	"	Daniel Standfield	Ellen Harmsworth	Sydney	15.10.91	Widow of Pte Harmsworth
11.	"	John Browne	Rebecca Chapman [Chipman]	Parramatta	10.6.92	Convict
12.	"	Thomas Tynan	Ann Innes	"	27.6.92	Convict

Source: Index to Marriages in New South Wales, 1788–1801, H.J. Rumsey, ML-B1171

Table 9 Marine deaths, 1787–1791

1.	30 April November 1787	Pte	Daniel Creswell (at sea)
2.	30 April 1788	Pte	Thomas Armsworth
3.	15 June 1788	"	John Batchelor (drowned)
4.	21 June 1788	"	John Gammon or Gannon
5.	23 June 1788	Sgt	Henry Petrie
6.	10 October 1788	Pte	John Jones
7.	26 October 1788	"	James Rogers (lost in woods)
8.	11 November 1788	"	Thomas Bullmore (result of fight)
9.	3 February 1789	Capt.	John Shea
10.	25 February 1789	Pte	Wm Edmondson
11.	27 March 1789	"	Luke Haynes
12.	" "	"	James Baker
13.	" "	"	James Brown ⎫ hanged
14.	" "	"	Richard Askew ⎬
15.	" "	"	Richard Dukes ⎭
16.	" "	"	Thomas Jones
17.	1 April 1789	"	Wm Wall
18.	3 October 1789	"	Thos. Scott
19.	4 May 1790	"	Wm Dowling or Doulon ⎫ lost in woods
20.	4 July 1790	"	Edward Odgers ⎭
21.	23 July 1790	"	Thos Harp ⎫ drowned
22.	" "	"	John Bates ⎭
23.	24 July 1790	"	Joseph Stephens
24.	15 August 1790	"	George Slater
25.	6 September 1790	"	Patrick McKeon
26.	20 January 1791	"	Wm Symonds
27.	26 September 1791	"	John Chapple

Source: Records of Birth, Deaths and Marriages, 1787–1791, T.D. Mutch, ML B1644

Phillip for land grants but he told them he lacked the authority and instead gave them gardens and land for feeding stock "but not as grants of land".[24] The officers took this unfavourably and later gave it as a reason for not electing to stay in the colony.[25] As rations became sparse some officers and marines developed gardens to supplement their rations and probably to exchange the superfluity of crops. Had land grants been available to them — as had been the case in other colonies[26] — they could have provided for their convict mistresses and children when the officers left for England.[27] Officers who were given land to farm were also given convicts to do the manual work, but Phillip complained to Lord Sydney that few officers reaped any great advantage from this benefit because they failed to supervise the convicts[28] — a self-defeating policy when applied to an officer's own land. Convict labourers were also allocated to non-officers of the detachment to do the farming, but Phillip condemned the practice because the convicts became overfamiliar when they mixed with soldiers. As an alternative he suggested to Lord Sydney that military personnel be given a quantity of grain to support their livestock,[29] but nothing seems to have come from his suggestion.

By 1790, with moves well under way for the relief of the detachment, the British government was keen to keep the marines in the colony. Lord Grenville therefore offered the three options: they could return home and be discharged, they could settle in New South Wales, or they could join the New South Wales Corps. He was particularly keen for as many as possible to become settlers, and to encourage them to do so, NCOs were to be granted one hundred acres, and privates fifty acres. Both were also to receive subsistence from the public store in clothing and food for a year, seed and tools as required. Rent was to be free for ten years after which it would be nominal at a shilling for every ten acres, and the services of convict labour were to be given free of cost.[30] No such grant was to be along the harbour foreshore so that all could have a "convenient share" of that.

Captain Hill of the New South Wales Corps pointed out in a letter on 26 July 1790 that in America, officers had received land grants in proportion to their rank, but at New South Wales where the marines had borne every hardship "they had no such thing". He regarded the situation as "impolitic".[31] However, the British government maintained its opposition to land grants to officers at New South Wales until July 1792 — by which time most of the marine officers were back in England.[32]

The land grants were attractive to some. In October 1791, two corporals and twenty-seven marine privates were discharged to become settlers at Norfolk Island. These lifted the total marine settlers there to thirty-one,[33] but within a year Lieutenant Governor King was reporting that nine of them had quit their grant and were returning to Sydney to join the New South Wales Corps. He described them as being "very idle settlers" but good soldiers.[34] They were returned to Sydney by the *Atlantic* in September 1792.[35]

Those eight marines who received land grants at Sydney did so on the south side of the harbour on flat land named by Phillip as the Field of Mars.[36] (See Table 10.) These eight marine settlers joined thirty-seven other settlers then farming in the Parramatta area.[37] Phillip had made fifty-eight other grants before he left in December 1792, by which time 513 acres in addition to those granted to the marines had been granted.[38]

Table 10 Land grants to marines in Sydney

1. James Manning	80 acres
2. John Carver	80 "
3. Alexander McDonald	130 "
4. Thomas Swinerton	80 "
5. Thomas Tining	80 "
6. Thomas Cotterel	80 "
7. Isaac Archer	80 "
8. John Colethread	80 "
	690 acres

Source: Journal of the Royal Australian Historical Society, vol 2, part 2 1925, 96

Uniforms worn by British Marines 1755–1807
(Published by permission of Stamps Publicity Ltd, Worthing, UK. Copyright C.C. Stadden)

1. Sergeant, the Marine Corps, 1755
2. Drummer, the Marine Corps, 1758
3. Officer, the Marine Corps (with colour), 1760
4. Officer (Grenadier Company), the Marine Corps, 1773
5. Grenadier, the Marine Corps, 1775
6. Sergeant (Grenadier Company), the Marine Corps, 1780
7. Surgeon, the Marine Corps, 1773
8. Private, the Marine Corps (Light Company), 1775
9. Grenadier, the Marine Corps, 1789
10. Sergeant, the Marine Corps, 1790
11. Officer, the Marine Corps, 1795
12. Officer, the Marine Corps (in greatcoat), 1798
13. Sergeant, Royal Marines, 1805
14. Drummer, Royal Marines, 1807

A marine marksman, 1799
(Published by permission of Stamps Publicity Ltd, Worthing, UK. Copyright C.C. Stadden)

An officer of marines, 1799
(Published by permission of Stamps Publicity Ltd, Worthing, UK. Copyright C.C. Stadden)

Lord Sydney, 1787
(*Published by permission of the Dixson Galleries, State Library of New South Wales*)

Governor Phillip, 1787
(*Published by permission of the Mitchell Library*)

Captain John Hunter
(Published by permission of the Mitchell Library)

David Collins, Judge Advocate of New South Wales
(Published by permission of the Mitchell Library)

Captain Watkin Tench
(*Courtesy the Misses Grylls of Wimbledon, London*)

Lieutenant (later Lieutenant Colonel) George Johnston
(*Published by permission of the Mitchell Library*)

Alicia Clark
(*Published by permission of the Mitchell Library*)

Entrance of Port Jackson, 27 January 1788. A sketch by First Fleeter William Bradley. *(Published by permission of the Mitchell Library)*

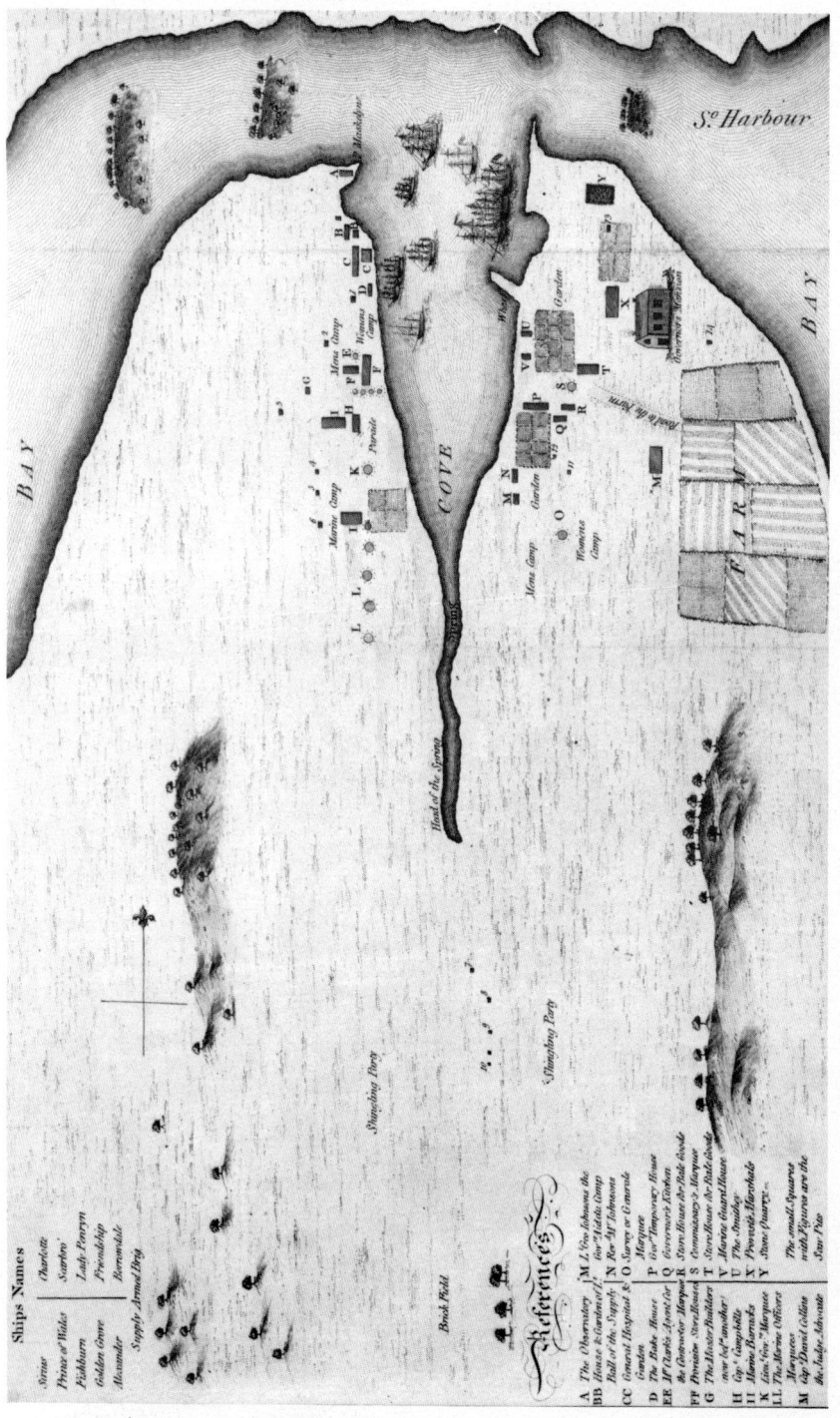

Settlement at Sydney, 16 April 1788. A sketch attributed to Francis Fowkes from the Rex Nan Kivell Collection.

Sydney Cove, Port Jackson, 1788. A sketch by First Fleeter William Bradley.
(*Published by permission of the State Library of New South Wales*)

An Aboriginal woman and her child. A sketch supposedly of John Hunter, David Collins, Lieutenant Johnson, Governor Phillip, and Surgeon White, drawn by Hunter.

Governor Phillip's house at Sydney, 1791
(Published by permission of the Mitchell Library)

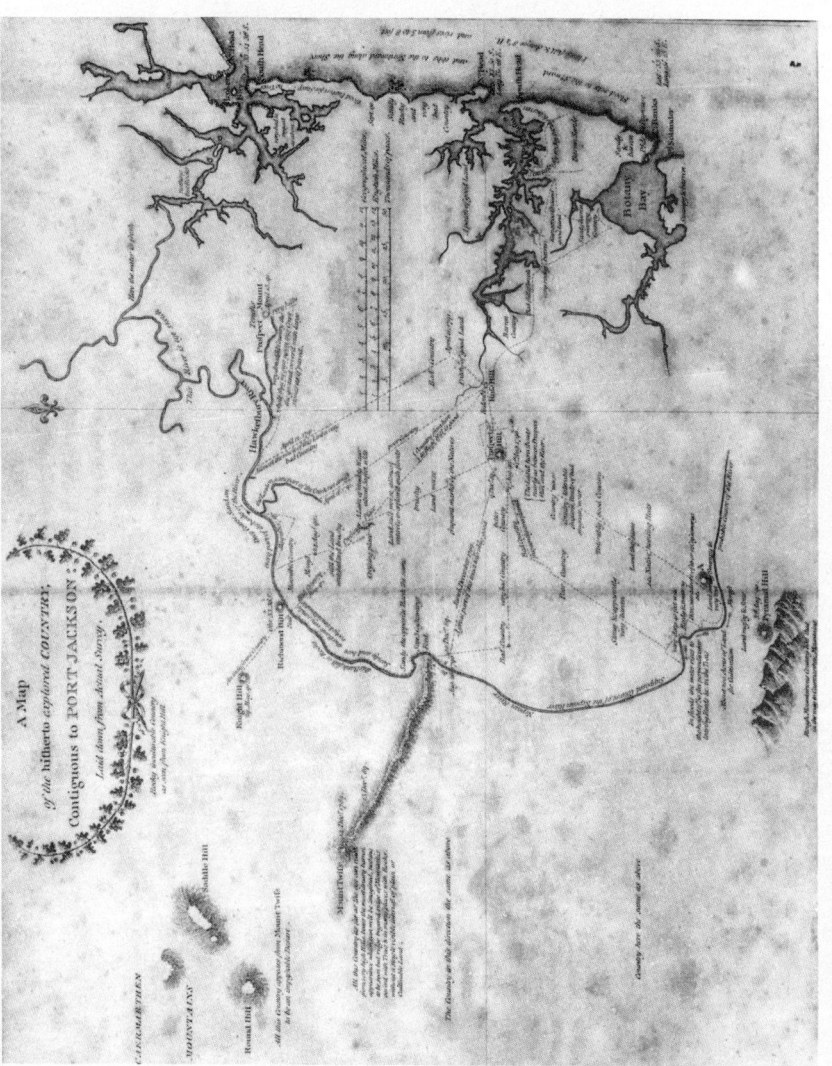

A map of the explorations of the Sydney Plain, drawn by Watkin Tench

Table 11 Some of the marines who joined the New South Wales Corps

Captain	Henry Clements
George Johnston	Benjamin Cusley
	Peter Dargin
Sergeants	Andrew Fishbourn
Richard Clinch	Stephen Gilgert
James Plowman	Charles Green
Joseph Radford	James Grant
	James Hailey
Corporals	John Jones
Thos Lucas	Wm King
Wm Goodall	Thomas Knight
John Wixstead	James Lee
	Wm Mitchell
	Wm Nash
Drummers	Gabriel Nation
Joseph Abbott	Henry Parsons
John West	John Pugh
	James Redman
Privates	John Rice
James Angell	Laurence Richards
Wm Baxter	John Roberts
Thos Bramwell	Thos Rowden
Ralph Brough	Wm Segar-Jones
George Chesley	James White

Source: Public Records Office, London, 417 W012/1128, ML, New South Wales Corps Muster Roll, 25 December 1791–24 June 1792

The third alternative which the British government had offered was for marines to join the New South Wales Corps. This would, of course, have saved the government the trouble and expense of transporting soldiers for that Corps to Sydney. The government offered considerable inducements: those who joined the Corps would receive £3 bounty, and after five years' service they were to receive double the amount of land granted to expirees, as well as tools and seed, and provisions for a year.[39] They were to be free of all taxes and rents for fifteen years, and thereafter to pay a nominal rent of one shilling for every fifty acres.[40] The marines who took up this offer were grouped into a company commanded by Captain George Johnston, and this became one of the companies of the Corps. Some of those who transferred are shown in Table 11.[41] Most of this company's members had taken their discharge by 1797. Captain Johnston served on and eventually became the unit's commanding officer, in which position he arrested Governor Bligh in 1808.

15

Major Robert Ross

Ross and the Civil Authority

No one in the colony caused Phillip more trouble than Major Ross. Of all Phillip's problems, including those of the terrible famine of 1789 and 1790, probably none was so harassing as the persistent antagonism, both covert and open, which Ross pursued against him. It was as well for Ross, and for the colony too, that Phillip was so long-suffering in handling Ross's tantrums, for had he conducted his conspiracies with a governor of less tolerance and resignation, the results for the colony might have been even more serious than they were. Phillip was always single-minded in his service to the colony; and if the colony's interests demanded forbearance from him, then he gave it unstintingly and suffered Ross's contumacy with an impressive dignity.

Long before Phillip reached Sydney, Ross had shown the beginnings of a hostility which was demonstrated in two incidents. The first of these occurred whilst the fleet was preparing at Portsmouth. Ross wrote a letter to Phillip on 22 December 1786 requesting certain items of camp equipment.[1] It was possibly his first letter to Phillip, but the forthrightness of its tone, which bordered on terseness, was unusual in eighteenth century correspondence from a subordinate to a superior, for such correspondence was typified by excessive deference. In the letter, Ross used terms such as, "You will be pleased to demand camp equippage"; "I must again request your attention"; and "I as commanding officer of the detachment". The tone of these statements suggests more an implied order than a subordinate's request. On the evidence of this letter alone the contention would be unsustainable, but letters by Ross to other superiors are available for comparison. For example, when Ross asks Nepean if he would like copies of the ship's roll on 14 March, Ross's tone is cordial, using such terms as, "I have great pleasure in informing you"; and "You have only to let me know". Moreover, a comparison of identical sentiments in the two letters shows that each is phrased very differently: thus to Phillip, Ross writes, "I submit it to you, Sir, that" whereas in Nepean's letter, that statement is rephrased to become, "I likewise beg to observe to you"; and whilst Ross could use the word "beg" to Nepean, he could in no way use it to Phillip. Later letters from Ross to Nepean are couched in similarly cooperative and amiable terms. Accordingly, his letter of 22 April requested a preferment for Captain Campbell, and his sentiments included expressions such as "You, my dear sir" , as well as "I have to return you my best thanks". And if further evidence is needed, his letter five days later amply illustrated the contrast: "Adieu, my dear sir, and with real esteem and regard, believe me"[2] But it is not only in his letters to Nepean that the difference is seen. In his letter to Stephens of 13 April in which he complains about something as serious as unsatisfactory marine accommodation on the ships, he can write, "I beg leave to observe".[3] And lest his brusqueness to Phillip be justified on the grounds that it was a military letter to a military superior, and as such would be in the terms of formal and precise military form, his letter of 12 May to their Lordships of the Admiralty "for their wonted goodness and attention to everything", and their "very particular and flattering attention which they have been pleased to pay us on all occasions",[4] does not support such a claim. Consequently, the contention of an early antipathy by Ross to Phillip long before the fleet left England seems strongly supported.

It does not seem possible to discover what caused that antipathy, but it might well explain the government's later decision not to allow Ross to act as Governor in the event of Phillip's death. Instead the British government waited for six months after Ross's appointment to the lieutenant governorship and then gave a dormant commission to Captain John Hunter empowering him, and not Ross, to assume the governorship in the event of Phillip's death or incapacity.[5] This six months' hesitation would have given time for Ross's suitability to be assessed, which, resulting in certain deficiencies being revealed in him, gave the dormant commission to Hunter instead. It seems irregular that a person who had been granted a lieutenant governorship should be denied the right to act as governor if the occasion arose, but it is quite possible that Ross's antipathy to Phillip, and his peevish temperament, had already been noticed and had denied him the right of succession. It is significant therefore that even his commission did not state specifically that he was to assume the governorship in the event of Phillip's death or incapacity,[6] although after Hunter left Sydney for England on 27 March 1791, Surgeon White stated that the administration of the colony would then pass to Ross in the event of Phillip's demise.

The second incident which illustrated Ross's bitterness towards Phillip before they arrived in New South Wales has already been reported: Ross was peeved that Phillip did not confer with him before deciding to split the fleet shortly after leaving Cape of Good Hope. By then, hopes for amicability were not good.

It did not take long after the fleet arrived at Sydney for the first of Phillip's problems with the Marine Corps to occur, and immediately upon landing, its officers suddenly refused to supervise the convicts in any way. They would do no more than a soldier's normal duty.[7] Although Phillip made it clear that all he wanted was for them to "occasionally encourage" the diligent or chide the indolent, they still declined, justifying their stand by the terms of a letter sent from the Admiralty to the commanding officers at Plymouth and Portsmouth in which no extra duty was mentioned.[8] It should be noted that Phillip was not asking them to do additional duty in terms of added hours; he wanted them merely to encourage or chide, expecting no more than that they listen to any appeal from the overseer and pass it on to Phillip or the Judge Advocate.[9] Ross was not involved in this refusal, and Phillip said Ross had shown every "attention that could be expected of him".[10] However, Phillip's acquittal of Ross in this matter seems unjustified. The officers were under Ross's command and had he ordered them to carry out Phillip's wishes they would have been required to do so. The officers' refusal meant that Phillip had to appoint overseers from the better of the convicts, though they lacked the standing of an officer, and feared to exert authority.[11]

Contrary to reasonable expectations, the first real tumult in the colony came not from convicts but from the officers themselves. On the evening of Sunday 16 March 1788, Private William Dempsey of Captain Meredith's company was going to the communal cooking place to boil the contents of a pot when he saw convict Jane Fitzgerald talking to a marine. As Dempsey passed them, Jane enquired about his health, and as he was replying, Private Joseph Hunt came up and hit him with a stick. Dempsey asked Hunt why he had done so, and, according to Dempsey, Hunt said that it was for speaking to a woman who had come out on his ship. Private Thomas Jones — who, like Hunt, was from 15 Company — then intruded into the incident and asked Dempsey his reasons for the assault. When he heard them, Jones called Hunt a "Portsmouth Rascal" and told him to get out of his sight, a directive with which Hunt thought best to comply, and so returned to his tent.[12] Such was the simple evidence Dempsey presented to Hunt's trial when Hunt was charged with disorderly behaviour on the Tuesday following.[13] However, from an incident so simple, serious repercussions were to flow.

Jones was called to give evidence at the court martial but his story differed from Dempsey's. Jones claimed that he did not see any blows struck. He did not mention either his castigation of Hunt nor his telling him to quit the area. Thus his evidence was more favourable to Hunt, but as both he and Hunt were from 15 Company, it is possible that soldierly mateship might have prevailed, particularly as the next witness, Private James Wedman of 5 Company, confirmed that Hunt had first struck Dempsey on the shoulders with a small stick, and that when Dempsey had objected, Hunt had then hit him on his head twice with his fist. Hunt then cross-examined Wedman about the advice Hunt had given Dempsey that he ought not to speak to a woman of Hunt's ship. Wedman denied that he had heard any such comment. Hunt then questioned Dempsey as to whether he had struck him with the open hand or the clenched fist but Dempsey was not sure which had been used. In summarizing his defence, Hunt admitted that he had struck Dempsey, but not with the intention of inflicting any hurt. He denied that he had had any conversation about women in his ship, and called as character referees Lieutenants Poulden and Timins who testified to his character as a good soldier.

The court, which consisted of Captain Tench as president, and Lieutenants Kellow, Davey, Poulden, and Timins, decided that Private Hunt had transgressed Article 18 of Section 14 of the Articles of War, and that, accordingly, his sentence should be that either he ask for Dempsey's pardon before the whole battalion, or else receive one hundred lashes from the drummers on his bare back. Tench then took this dual sentence to Ross for confirmation, but Ross refused to confirm it. Ross said he could not concur with it on the double grounds that it left the nature of the punishment to the choice of the guilty party, and also because it took from the Commanding Officer his power of either confirming or mitigating the court's sentence. Later, in his report to Stephens, Ross explained that in his opinion, the passing of a dual sentence was inconsistent with martial law.[14]

In giving a choice of sentences to Hunt the court had, in effect, given no court sentence at all. Consequently, the convicted man was being asked by the court to pass sentence on himself; Ross saw the absurdity as well as the irregularity, and asked Tench for the court to reconsider the verdict, which it did, but saw no reason to alter its sentence.

Ross then directed Adjutant Long to write to Tench ordering him to reconvene the court to reconsider its sentence in the light of his objections and refusal to ratify. It met immediately and at four o'clock its members sent their reply to Ross refusing to rescind their sentence on the grounds that they had twice considered it and were forbidden by Article 10 of the relevant act to sit a third time, such article stipulating "that no sentence given by any court-martial, and signed by the President thereof, is liable to be revised more than once". This letter was signed by all five members of the court. At about five o'clock that afternoon Ross again ordered the court (through the Adjutant) to sit and finish the case by passing "only one sentence for one crime".[15]

Ross by now was losing patience and he meant the officers to be under no doubt that they would have to change their decision, for in the same letter, according to his later report to Stephens, he told Long to warn them that that letter would be the last he would write, and if his order were refused, he would regard it as the offence of disobedience. According to Ross however, Long, for reasons best known to himself failed to include the warning.[16]

The reason Long omitted to send this threat ought to be thought about. It is unlikely that he forgot to include it, or that in some way his failure to do so was inadvertent: that was not his way, for we can only conclude from the fact that he remained Ross's adjutant for the entire tour of duty that he was an efficient and capable officer. It is therefore unlikely that an officer of such competence — and particularly an adjutant who as the chief administrative officer of the detachment would be particularly alert to the ramifications of what Ross intended — would have forgotten to include such a gravely significant order from his commanding officer. Moreover, if his failure to do as he was told was caused by negligence, it is reasonable to assume that he would have reported so to Ross, but he gave no explanation and, according to Ross, kept his reasons to himself. Implicit in that admission is that Long's failure, far from being the result of human negligence, was deliberate — deliberate because, working as close to Ross as any adjutant works with his commanding officer, he saw the obdurate frame of mind in which Ross was operating; an obduracy later noted by Phillip in his statement that any reconciliation offered, was declined. And if consideration is given as to why Ross allowed Long to hide his reason for not delivering the warning, it is very likely Ross judged that the reason might well be one critical of his own action.

However, whatever Long's motives, the court again considered Ross's demand and at 7 p.m. sent him an identical refusal. Ross had been confronted, and he was faced now with a number of alternatives: either he tacitly accept a dimunition of his authority as a commanding officer by yielding to the court's constancy; or he could wait and refer the matter to Phillip; or he could take the precipitous action of suspending the court and arresting its members for disobedience of orders. He chose the last, and that night all five officers were arrested.

It had been a hectic day at Sydney Cove; letters had plied

back and forth; tension had risen as two implacable forces had refused to yield; and at the end of it, almost a third of the detachment's officers had been stood down under arrest. In such a situation they could not perform any duty for detachment or colony, and their loss of service would seriously constrict the capacity of the unit to perform its role within the colony. Consequently, the detachment's crisis was the colony's crisis, and yet Phillip, the colony's leader, was unaware of any problem: whilst the day's extraordinary events had been played out at Sydney Cove, he was miles away exploring the countryside. Ross had precipitated the crisis by failing to wait for Phillip's return to refer the matter to him; instead he had created a fait accompli which could only exacerbate the problem and make its resolution infinitely more difficult for Phillip. Ross stated that his motive in arresting the court was to lessen the injury to the service, because when Phillip returned, he would solve the problem. This rationale was either the result of defective reasoning, or for a more sinister objective. If Ross's real intention was for Phillip to solve the problem, it must have been obvious to an officer of his experience that this could be achieved far more readily if unilateral action was deferred. The matter then could be decided by Phillip without the additional complication of having to uphold a commanding officer's order. But Ross's action compromised Phillip and reduced his scope for manoeuvre by locking him into a position in which he would have no alternative but to support his lieutenant governor by endorsing the arrests. To do otherwise would be to seriously harm, if not destroy, the standing of his deputy.

Phillip returned that night but even then Ross did not inform him of the crisis till next morning when he gave Phillip the court martial papers together with the two letters from the officers, and a verbal account of what had happened. Phillip saw immediately the stark threat to the colony which Ross's action posed, for it very considerably reduced the unit's capacity to maintain law and order and protect the colony either from a convict uprising or an Aboriginal attack. Therefore Phillip's immediate aim had to be to restore not only the harmony of the detachment but also the unit's viability by preventing a general court martial of so many officers, the "inconveniences" of which were obvious to him.[17] If those consequences were obvious to Phillip, they ought to have been equally obvious to Ross, and yet it was to be Phillip who noted that one intolerable result would be the need to place sergeants in charge of guards if the five officers were stood down awaiting trial.

Faced with this sudden crisis, Phillip reacted calmly and, according to Ross, "very humanely".[18] He simply asked Ross to leave the papers and he would call for Tench and "endeavour to accommodate the matter" by altering a few words in the decision to make it a "proper" one.[19] But Tench stood firm and Phillip was not able to sway the decision. Earnestly searching for some solution to the impasse, Phillip then proposed to the court a compromise whereby the question of the sentence would be referred to other officers, or even to any one officer.[20] The officers rejected the proposal and said they were only too keen to appear before any general court martial that Major Ross would like to convene,[21] and failing that, the only other way in which they would be satisfied was by a public apology from him "for the indignity done them".[22]

When Phillip received these two demands, he told Ross that if he intended proceeding with the general court martial, he should first apply for it to Phillip in writing. In requiring this, Phillip was taking the wise precaution of tying Ross to specific charges, for it was now obvious that there would be a sequel to face. Ross obliged and asked Phillip to take steps to ensure the maintenance of good order and military discipline which he felt was "absolutely necessary" in the present "critical" situation.[23] On 20 March, after Phillip had considered the positions of both sides, he wrote a General

Order (equivalent to the present Summary of Evidence used in military law) in which he outlined the offence and the officers' two demands, but stated that any general court martial was impossible because, with current officer strength down to thirteen, there were insufficient officers for duty. He ordered that all correspondence on the matter be forwarded to the Judge Advocate so that, when sufficient officers became available, the court martial could then be held. In the meantime, he ordered the five officers to return to duty. In this way, Phillip gained a temporary resolution.

His order took Ross by surprise; according to Ross, Phillip did not notify him of it, and the first he knew of it was when Adjutant Long brought it to him in the Log Book. Phillip's failure to deal directly with Ross on so critical a matter appears an unusual course to follow, but he might have wished to avoid a confrontation: to have first sent the order to Ross might have aroused further trouble from him. Ross was therefore bypassed. Ross ordered Long to show Phillip's order to the five officers; they saucily responded by giving Long a note for Ross which stated that they were still firm in their demand for a general court martial to redress the indignity which he had put upon them. This in effect amounted to a demand for a Redress of Wrongs which they apparently intended pursuing more as a mechanism for reprisal against Ross than for the clearing of their injured reputations. Theirs was a not too subtle threat to Ross that he was going to be brought to account by his subordinates for what he had done to them. They returned to duty, but not before they had thanked Phillip in quite gracious terms for the "friendly and handsome part" he had played in his attempt to resolve their differences with Ross.[24]

Ross now realized that the Admiralty would eventually judge his handling of the incident, and he set about preparing the grounds of his own case. In his despatch to Stephens on 9 July 1788, he complained that some of his officers were so young and inexperienced that they were easily manipulated by others and joined cliques and factions. This had destroyed unit harmony and impaired "good order and military discipline". He made a special complaint about Tench, whose attitude to him he described as "mortifying" and against whom Ross would have taken action had it not been for a desire to keep the officer dissensions from the marines. Referring to his arrest of the five officers, he told Stephens that after he had done so, he sought the opinion of Captain Campbell, who had thirty-one-years' service. Campbell supported Ross's action and gave the opinion that even if the officers disagreed with Ross's order, they had chosen the wrong way to show it, for it was their duty first to comply, and then send their grievance to the Admiralty.[25]

Ross stressed that his remarks did not apply to all officers, most of whom performed their duties well on a tour of duty which was "more severe" than any other; but apparently relationships were so strained that Ross felt unequal to improving them, for he implored the Admiralty to take decisive steps to restore harmony.[26] Militarily, Ross's request was extraordinary, for he was asking a superior authority to restore morale in his own unit — surely a most serious admission of failure by any commanding officer.

However, Phillip had avoided the ramifications which would have flowed from holding a general court martial; the five officers went about their duty, and the colony returned to normal.

Ultimately the whole matter was solved by the effluxion of time. On 18 March 1791, four of the five officers wrote to Phillip pointing out that it was three years since Ross had placed them under arrest, and that the Marine Act stated that no marine could be brought to trial for an offence committed more than three years before a warrant was issued to convene such a trial. As no warrant had been issued, they asked for their arrests to be lifted, not because they feared the outcome of any trial, but because of their indignation at the novelty and disgrace of a situation "unexampled in

British Military Annols [sic]". In an unforgiving mood, they reiterated their readiness to face Ross, their accuser, as Meredith and Tench later were to do. (See chapter 20.) For the sake of maintaining harmony in the colony, they pointed out that they had held their silence for three years in the hope that some way would be found to hold a general court martial, but as time had expired, they desired that their "present degraded situation" be concluded. Finally, in a most courteous paragraph, they thanked Phillip for the patience, kindness and attention which he had always shown to them.[27]

Apportioning blame for the crisis is difficult: on the one hand, Ross's haste in arresting the five during Phillip's absence negated the beneficial effects which Phillip's standing and moderating influence would have supplied; on the other, Campbell's view — that the officers mishandled the situation by not obeying first and complaining afterwards — was in line with normal military practice. Therefore it appears that both sides allowed animosity to dictate their actions.

In the meantime, by July 1788 Phillip was facing mounting problems from the detachment: officers had complained about the necessity to serve on the Criminal Court and were asking for land grants. Consequently he thought it as well to alert London and did so in his letters of 16 May and 10 July.[28]

Also in July 1788, Ross sent his first despatch to Stephens,[29] beginning a process of both criticizing Phillip, and undermining information which Ross assumed Phillip would be transmitting in his own official despatches. After advising that Lieutenant Gidley King's party had gone to Norfolk Island, he implied a criticism of Phillip by stating that no one had told him anything about its departure.[30] On the Sydney colony's potential, he advised that as the soil was infertile, the country was destitute of "any commercial potential" and would never answer the government's expectations of it. And then, to reinforce his charge of Phillip's failure to consult, he stated that the foregoing opinion was his own for he could not be familiar with Phillip's because Phillip had not done him the honour of informing him of it, "or asking me for mine". According to Ross (though not according to Collins) Phillip did not communicate his intentions with anyone.[31] Ross had yet another criticism: when the Navy Board had reduced the marine ration to equal that of the convicts, Ross had complained to Phillip. Ross now reported that Phillip had promised to write home about it only after Ross's prompting. The truth was that Phillip had applied for additional rations for the marines before the fleet left England but had been ignored. Giving the impression that Phillip was indifferent to the welfare of the detachment, Ross asked the Admiralty to take the detachment "under their protection" so that it could be properly fed.[32] He further condemned Phillip for failing to construct defences though "in justice to myself", he had repeatedly urged Phillip to do so,[33] but then proceeded to destroy his own charge by advising that the possibility of an attack was remote.

Phillip had, in fact, thought about the settlement's defence. As he told Lord Sydney in July, he had planned a fort with defence works, but had been unable to find a spring on the high ground near the hospital to the west. Such a location would provide good fields of fire. However he had had to abandon the project because it was beyond the settlement's manpower capacity.[34]

In July, Ross sent a despatch to Nepean and in what can only be described as unctuous petulance, he said he was unsure whether Lord Sydney expected correspondence from him because Phillip had not "consulted" him on the subject and, as with everybody else, kept Ross "in the dark". Feigning innocence, he went on to say that in any case he could hardly report to Lord Sydney the way Phillip treated him as lieutenant governor — or, for that matter, how he treated the detachment generally — without complaining about

Phillip, which, he hastened to assure Nepean, was far from his intention. But Ross had not yet completely expended his incrimination of Phillip: he told Nepean that no military stores could be obtained without application to Phillip, who was so parsimonious with them that those who sought them were made feel uncomfortable by Phillip giving the impression that the issues were not being given by right but as a mark of his personal favour. Implied in that thinly veiled accusation was the charge that Phillip was acting improperly, although Ross would have known as well as anyone else that the depleted stocks had to be distributed stintingly. Closing his day of jaundiced correspondence, he concluded with the gloomy prediction that it would take a hundred years to establish the colony, and that it would be cheaper for the home government to feed the convicts on "turtle and venison" at the best tavern in London, than meet the cost of sending them to Sydney. And handing his two letters of malignity and gloom to Lieutenant William Collins, they were conveyed to his masters in England by those ships of the first fleet which left in late July.[35]

While Ross was writing his letters, Phillip was also writing a despatch giving an entirely different picture. His letter to Lord Sydney said that so good was the land that the farmers ought to be self-sufficient in two or three years, and that the colony would surely become "a valuable acquisition to Great Britain . . . Time would remove all difficultys [sic]".[36] The colony's chaplain wrote to Nepean agreeing with this view.[37]

By now relations between Ross and Phillip had soured considerably and the animosity was being noticed by others. Ralph Clark felt the conditions were so severe that the British government might move the settlement elsewhere.[38] Obviously the open breach between the colony's two top officers was becoming public knowledge.

But Ross was not alone in his discrete undermining of Phillip; he had now acquired an accomplice in Captain Campbell. Writing a private letter to the Earl of Ducie on 12

July 1788, Campbell claimed that the task of establishing the colony called for a man of greater capacity than Phillip. In that letter, he launched into an attack more vitriolic than any mounted by Ross. After alleging Phillip's secrecy, Campbell expressed the opinion that the entire three kingdoms of Britain could not produce a man so "totally unqualified for the business he has taken in hand as this man is". To illustrate the confusion which he alleged Phillip had created, he went on to say that there was hardly a day in which the previous day's orders were not contradicted: "Men are taken from one piece of work before it is begun and sent to another which is left in the same state — I must here except such things as are actually carrying on for himself which he never suffers to be interfered with — everything that can be got hold of is appropriated to his own use. He is selfish beyond measure . . . there is not a man but what despises him . . . so much for a vile subject."[39]

The sentiments of that letter so closely resembled those of Ross to Nepean two days previously that it is difficult to avoid the judgment of collusion. This is strongly reinforced when, at the same time Ross was writing his second condemnation of Phillip to Nepean in November 1788 (to expose the imagined perfidy of Phillip in concealing the utter lack of any potential for the colony), Campbell was again echoing his treacherous complaints. Accusing Phillip of deceit in advising the home government that a sound future lay ahead for New South Wales, Campbell told the Earl of Ducie that he did not know "how far this man has let the people at home into a proper knowledge of the true state of this vile country . . . but from the general tenor of his conversation, I much, very much fear the contrary".[40]

When Major Ross went to Norfolk Island his attacks on Phillip diminished, but Campbell persisted in his clandestine operation. Captain Campbell, the detachment's second-in-command, was Phillip's most bitter, vitriolic critic. Writing to Doctor Farr on 24 March 1791, he repeated his allegation that "those at home have been deceived in the accounts they have received from this country" — "this vilest of countries" — but artfully he asked Doctor Farr to be careful to whom he passed on the criticisms as he did not want to be revealed as their source, for, "as the truth must come out some day or other, let them who have withheld it so long, answer".[41]

In the face of this combined opposition from both the Commanding Officer and the second-in-command, Phillip's achievements are extraordinary.

But let us return to Ross's November letters both written on the 16th: one was official, the other private. In his official despatch to Stephens, Ross despaired of completing the barracks for all except Campbell's company, saying Phillip had allotted tradesmen to tasks which Phillip regarded as being of more importance than housing the detachment or getting it under proper cover.[42] This charge however was not entirely truthful, because, as has been seen, Ross had a month earlier blamed the commanders of the unhoused companies for their "shameful inattention" to erecting their companies' quarters.[43] And it had been Phillip who had, in response to Ross's request, urged them to finish the job.[44] From Phillip's point of view, it was wasteful to have tradesmen standing idle simply because marine officers were not attending to the construction of barracks with any urgency. Consequently, he had allocated the tradesmen elsewhere. Ross also blamed Phillip for employing the blacksmiths on other tasks, so much so that weapon maintenance has fallen behind to the extent that they had two "rifles" for three months and done nothing to them.[45]

Ross's second letter written on 16 November 1788 was a private one to Nepean. Such a form was quite improper because it perfidiously criticized Phillip for a lack of communication with anyone but his secretary, Judge Advocate David Collins. Ross accused Phillip of lying if he had described the land favourably, for to Ross it was a "vile country" and the worst place in the world with its infertile soil and timber fit only for fires. He suggested that Phillip's descriptions be disregarded and no more inhabitants sent.[46] This letter was treacherous, inaccurate, and deceitful, for Ross's method was anathema to normal military forms and transgressed the chain of command. Phillip was not to hear of Ross's three seditious letters until February 1790, and when he did, he sat down in angry resentment to answer their allegations together with the other problems which by then Ross had amassed. But 1788 still had some months to run, and in that time there surfaced a serious problem involving officers and general courts martial.

On 13 October 1788, Ross charged his quartermaster, James Furzer, with neglect of duty, contempt, and disrespect to his commanding officer.[47] Ross then applied to Phillip for a trial. Phillip issued the convening order and the court martial assembled when, to everyone's surprise, Judge Advocate Collins gave an opinion to the court's president, Captain Campbell, that marine officers could not legally sit under a warrant from the Governor "as no power had been delegated to him for that purpose, either by Parliament or the Admiralty".[48] This arose from the special circumstance peculiar to the Marine Corps whereby they were regarded "as an integral or constituent part" of the fleet.[49] Consequently, a special Act of Parliament was necessary to regulate their disciplinary forms when they were serving on shore. When they served ashore with the army in the American War of Independence, a special act had been passed in 1775 to bring them under the provisions of the Army's Mutiny Act. Unfortunately, according to Collins, no such act had been passed to provide for the marines' shore-side service at New South Wales.

Consequently, it was Collins' opinion that Phillip lacked the power to convene general courts martial for marines serving on land. However Collins went on to suggest that considering the time which would elapse before any remedy could be supplied and because it had been clearly "the intention of every branch and department of His Majesty's Government that there should be such a tribunal in this country", that the officers should sit under the auspices of Phillip's commission and then ask the Admiralty for an indemnification for their action.[50] In view of this advice, Captains Tench, Shea and Campbell, and ten other officers signed a letter to Phillip pointing out that as they in their commission oath had sworn not to assemble as a general court martial without a warrant from the Admiralty, they therefore refused to sit under Phillip's commission.[51] Their refusal was on legal grounds and not out of any disrespect to Phillip, as Ralph Clark explained in a letter to Dr Kempster.[52]

Collins' opinion was later upheld by Lord Grenville, who agreed that, as the Marine Act had been amended in the American war, the same would have been necessary for New South Wales. However, as by then the Marine Corps was shortly to be relieved, it was too late to make the necessary amendment.[53] The officers had been correct therefore in refusing to sit on a general court martial convened by Phillip's warrant and no such court was held in New South Wales till 1793.[54]

In any case, Furzer had long resolved the immediate situation by apologizing to Ross and recanting his inflamatory statements.[55] The more important problem, however, had not vanished, for Phillip was now powerless to try any member of the detachment above the rank of a non-commissioned officer.

Early the following year, Ross made another attempt to undermine Phillip's authority and in so doing threatened the stability of the colony. On 3 February 1789, Captain Shea died and was buried with full military honours at a funeral attended by all officers. Phillip told Ross that he assumed the vacancy would be filled by his aide-de-camp, First Lieutenant

George Johnston, who was the "oldest" lieutenant in the detachment. Ross avoided a direct reply, and, acting with a measure of deceit and treachery, sent for Phillip's secretary, David Collins. Ross offered him Shea's company, telling Collins that the offer was made upon a direction of Lord Howe given privately to Ross before leaving England. Ross advised Collins that if he accepted the post, he would relinquish his position as judge advocate. In effect, Ross was purloining Phillip's principal law officer and secretary without the courtesy or propriety of telling Phillip. Such was Ross's deceit in this matter that when he told Phillip next day of the promotions he had made, he did not mention his underhand approach to Collins. Even some days after, when he asked Phillip to approve his nine-year-old son being given a second lieutenant's commission,[56] Ross still remained secretive. Although Phillip withheld his approval, Ross went ahead and appointed the boy.[57]

Fortunately Collins declined Ross's offer out of loyalty to Phillip and because he detested Ross.[58] Had he not done so, a confrontation was inevitable, for implicit in Phillip's statement that "interference on my part was unnecessary", was his intention to call Ross to account had that been necessary.[59] Reporting this incident to Nepean, Phillip pointed out the serious repercussions which could eventuate when officers sent out in civil capacities could resign their civil appointment at will, even though they could not be replaced.[60] He felt certain that, though Howe had given Ross the right to fill vacancies from available officers, Ross had misused it by carrying it into execution without consulting the Governor. This type of misuse he felt certain was never intended by Lord Howe.

In the Collins Affair, Ross had sought to establish the military's superiority over the civil authority by arrogating to the military a power to make appointments for officers from the civil branch of government. For though Collins was an officer of marines, it was not in that function that he was employed in the settlement. His appointments as judge advocate and as Phillip's secretary were entirely civil appointments, and to emphasise the civil nature of his appointment as judge advocate, he wore civilian dress, whereas officers who were on the Criminal Court wore military uniform, sash, and sword.[61] Ross's action had been a significant piece of dangerous arrogance. As for the appointments which Ross made following Captain Shea's death: volunteer John Ross was made second lieutenant; Second Lieutenant Clark was made lieutenant; Lieutenant George Johnston was made captain lieutenant; and Captain Lieutenant Meredith was made captain, and took over Shea's company.[62] The Admiralty later confirmed these promotions.[63]

The Collins Affairs was only two months old when it was followed by the Criminal Court Affair in which officers, prompted covertly by Ross, refused to man the Criminal Court. Phillip's first despatch of 16 May 1788 had informed Lord Sydney that because the officers had not been informed of their criminal court obligation before leaving England, they now thought it a "hardship". Phillip's reaction had been to chide them by stating that a young colony required something more from officers than garrison duty.[64] However, although they did not like the court duty, the officers continued to perform it until the following incident which occurred in April 1789.

Mary Turner, a convict who had given evidence at the trial of the six marines hanged a few weeks previously for stealing from the public store, had for a short time thereafter been kept in custody under suspicion of having committed perjury. "After mature consideration", Collins had ordered her release because of insufficient evidence.[65] On 25 April, Campbell sent the Provost Marshal to Collins to ask why he had released Turner, and Collins gave him his reason, adding by letter that if Campbell had any evidence to implicate her, Collins would assemble the court a few days later to hear the case. However, Campbell took the view that as Turner had been held in custody she had to be brought to trial. Adopting an indignant approach, he told Collins that as Collins had seen fit to release her, he would no longer sit as a member of any court of which Collins was a part. He then urged Collins to retain copies of all the correspondence on the topic "as I assure you I shall of mine". Collins prepared a report for Phillip recording the facts of the case and emphasizing that Turner had been released only after he had considered that no case existed against her, and that no other member of that court had requested she be tried except Campbell. However, as Campbell persisted in the view that she had been held in custody by order of the late court and ought therefore to be dealt with by the law, Collins decided to arrange for her to appear before the next sitting of the Criminal Court on a charge of wilful perjury. Phillip's commission under the Act of Parliament 27 Geo 111 15/87 authorized him to convene the Criminal Court to consist of the Judge Advocate and any six officers, but in spite of the clarity of this directive, Campbell chose to express the opinion that Major Ross had no power to compel his officers to serve on the court when they felt disinclined to do so. Campbell therefore requested Ross to instruct the Adjutant not to list his name in future panels, thus demonstrating his retaliation for Collins' letter to him which he contrived to interpret as being "insulting", hurtful to his feelings, and damaging to his character as a gentleman. Still not satisfied with his misrepresentation of Collins' intention, he then misconstrued Collins' invitation — to provide any incriminating evidence — as an attempt to manoeuvre him into the position of being Turner's prosecutor, something which the letter did not purport.

After receiving Campbell's objection, Ross called a meeting of Lieutenants Poulden, Shairp and John Johnson in Campbell's hut at eleven o'clock on the morning of 27 April. These quite junior officers considered the Collins-Campbell correspondence which, in reality, had nothing to do with them, and then sent a letter to Phillip in which they said that as the matter involved a point of law and "a private disagreement", they suggested that the correspondence be sent to the Lords of the Admiralty.[66] Campbell then wrote to Ross rejecting the notion that his stand was "a private disagreement", and asked Ross to convey this to Phillip and the Admiralty. Phillip decided that the depredations of Campbell had gone far enough, and he now moved to ascertain the degree of support which Campbell's actions had among the officers. He requested Ross to convene the officers and to obtain their opinions about sitting as members of the court. At the meeting, three questions were put to them: Did they regard criminal court duty as a military duty? Did they regard criminal court duty as an extra duty in compliance with an Act of Parliament? Did they have any knowledge of the duty before leaving England? The replies given by Tench were the replies given by twelve other officers: although they did not know of any such Act of Parliament before leaving England, they always regarded criminal court duty as a military requirement. Only Campbell disagreed with this view.

Up to this stage no covert manipulations by Ross had been revealed, but late in May, Collins began to hear rumours of statements Ross had made at the officer meeting. They were that Ross had said the Governor was "oppressive" in calling on Campbell to sit on the Criminal Court, and that Ross had induced the officers to agree with Campbell's view that service on the court was no part of their duty. To check the accuracy of these rumours, Collins took statements from Tench, Cresswell, George Johnston, Poulden, and Long in answer to three questions put to them. These were: What reason did Ross give for calling the meeting? Did Ross describe Phillip's action as "oppressive"? Did Ross ask the officers to join Campbell? Tench replied that the meeting of 27 April had been held by Ross's order, and to the best of his recollection, Ross twice had described Phillip's conduct as "oppressive" and had told officers that they ought not feel obliged to serve on the court. Although Ross had not specifically asked officers to join Campbell's stand, Tench felt that the whole tenor of Ross's address "pointed that way". Creswell agreed with Tench's evidence, and though he could not confirm absolutely that Ross had used the word "oppressive", he felt that that was what had been meant. Johnston and Poulden did confirm that Ross had used the word "oppressive", and Long said that Ross's exact words were that Phillip's action was "oppressive in the highest degree".

The Governor's reaction was immediate. He pointed out to the officers how much a part of their duty it was to serve on the court, and he told Ross that Collins had meant no offence to Campbell by his letter. Therefore he saw no reason why Campbell could not serve on the court and urged him to consider seriously the consequences of refusal. If he persisted in his refusal, Phillip requested that he put his reasons in writing. Ross lost no time in gaining these from Campbell, and returned them post-haste to Phillip: Campbell's view was that criminal court duty was no part of his military duty. As a court was waiting to be formed, Phillip appointed the next officer on the list, expecting that this would settle the matter. But Ross immediately objected, stating that removal of Campbell's name was unfair to all the other officers who had a similar objection to the duty, and that he knew of no Article of War which could compel them. He was not opposed however to officers volunteering for the task.[67] Phillip pointed out to Ross that the officers' obligation was declared in the Act of Parliament creating his commission in which officers were ordered to obey him, and that an Act of Parliament was superior to any Article of War, or for that matter, to any instruction which Ross might give his detachment. Consequently, it was his opinion that officers were not at liberty to decline his orders at their pleasure. To restore tranquillity, however, he acceded to Ross's "demand" that a court of enquiry be set up to determine the offensiveness or otherwise of Collins' letter. But by now Phillip's patience was strained almost to breaking point by Ross's cantankerous attitude, and in stressing the consequences of refusal of court duty by officers, he threatened that so long as ten loyal men remained in the detachment, officers would be found for the duty.[68] How serious Phillip was in this threat is not known, but had he carried it out, there would have occurred a direct military-civil confrontation as happened between Governor Bligh and the New South Wales Corps in 1808.

When the Court of Enquiry duly assembled, it refused to investigate the matter on the grounds that the letter from Collins to Campbell was a private dispute with which they were not competent to deal. This further infuriated Campbell who asked that the court's members not be given copies of his correspondence with Collins. His peevish reaction was reported by Ross to Phillip who rejected Campbell's request and distributed copies to the officers concerned.

It was obvious that this pantomime should be brought to a sharp conclusion. Phillip therefore adopted normal procedure and ordered the Adjutant to supply to Collins the names of those next on the court panel list; but after attempting to comply, Adjutant Long returned to Phillip and told him that Ross had forbidden the supply of any names until Phillip himself had sent him his request either verbally or in orders. The effect of this was that Ross was declaring that he would deal with Phillip but not with Collins, and as Collins by now had developed the most hearty detestation of Ross, Ross was out to snub and belittle him. Phillip complied with Ross's request to deal directly with him and Ross sent the names of the next panel, but Phillip saw to it that the list included Campbell rather than give him the seal of approval for his refusal. However, before the court sat, Phillip assembled its members and pointed out to them the serious consequences of officers refusing duty, but to his astonishment, they told him they had never doubted their obligation to serve on the Criminal Court, both because of Phillip's commission and the precedence which Acts of Parliament took over Articles of War. This surprised Phillip because their reply was directly opposite to the opinion which Ross had been alleging they held. Phillip suspected Ross of misrepresentation and decided to call his bluff by asking him to assemble all officers on 6 May. But Ross knew that he had been beaten and so reported that all officers now thought court duty part of their own duty. Consequently Campbell sat as a volunteer though still holding to his view that it was not part of his duty to do so. Therefore, although Campbell objected to sitting on the Criminal Court, he never refused and always sat at his turn. "For the quiet of the settlement", Phillip decided to let the matter rest.

Shortly after this Phillip heard that the officers had again been assembled by Ross. At the meeting, he had described Phillip's calling on Campbell to sit even as a volunteer as being "oppressive", and had induced them to join Campbell's stand. Phillip asked an officer for details of this meeting, but the officer declined on the grounds of propriety between officers and their commanding officer. Collins decided to pursue any evidence of Ross's sedition and he attended a meeting of the Adjutant and the detachment's five senior officers who confirmed that Ross had induced them to join Campbell's stand, and that Phillip's conduct had been described as "oppressive". Phillip was dismayed and saw clearly that Ross had brought the settlement "to touch on the moment of a general confusion".[69] In his letter to Lord Sydney on 5 June 1789, he pointed out that no legal enquiry could be made of Ross, but as the Lieutenant Governor and Commander of the detachment, Phillip felt he ought to be able to look to him for support, and rightly expressed the opinion that "the situation of the colony at the time called for an address of a very different nature". When the five officers returned from their meeting with Collins, Ross asked them what had transpired; they suggested he ask Phillip, but as he never did, Phillip thought it best to let the matter "rest in its present state" as he lacked the power to enquire.[70] Consequently, with Phillip trying to find out what transpired at Ross's meetings, and Ross trying to do the same with Phillip's, Ross's deviousness temporarily assuaged itself to await its next opportunity, for by now he so disliked, or in turn was disliked by, Phillip, Hunter, Collins, Tench, and most of his officers that he was becoming a victim of his own incorrigibility. Ultimately, the Attorney General ruled that officers were obliged to serve on the Criminal Court for in so doing, they were acting in a civil capacity and a refusal to sit would constitute a misdemeanour by disobeying Phillips' commission.[71]

Another two months were to pass before Ross's next performance. Phillip received a letter from him saying that he had been insulted as the Lieutenant Governor whilst Phillip had been away at Rose Hill.[72] The circumstances were that on 25 August, Fuller, the carpenter, had revealed that overseer Bazely, acting on Mr Brewer's orders, had told convict Thady to join Mr Bloodsworth's gang. Ross called for Brewer to ask him who had permitted Thady to change gangs and was told that the order had come from Collins. Keen no doubt to exploit any opportunity to confront Collins, Ross sent Brewer to him to seek his reason for relocating Thady. Collins replied that Phillip had left such orders before departing. Ross intoned that he felt himself "hurt by this impropriety", and regarded the affront to him as being of "too serious a nature to pass over" without complaining about it to Phillip. The cause of his anger was that Phillip had seen fit to leave orders about convicts with Collins rather than himself as the Lieutenant Governor, and he now wished to be informed by Phillip as to what his position was in the colony. Collins told Phillip that the whole incident was quite unintentional and in spite of the seriousness which Ross was attaching to it, he felt it hardly worth discussing. But to set the record straight he reminded Phillip that he had received his orders about Thady before the Governor had left for Rose Hill but had failed inadvertently to carry them out till after Phillip's departure. When he had learnt from Brewer that Ross was objecting to his action, he had immediately told Thady to return to his previous gang. Unwittingly now the cause of a major tumult, Collins openly apologized for any trouble he had caused.

Phillip, caught in the middle of this crossfire, wrote in reply to Ross explaining the circumstances, advising him that Collins had intended no insult, and then in a masterly use of punctuation to express disgust at the triviality of the whole business, he concluded: "This, Sir, if admitted, will, I presume, satisfy you that no insult was intended". As to the exaggerated significance which Ross had read into Phillip's leaving orders with Collins, he assured him there was not a shadow of ill-intent in his so doing and suggested that Ross be sensible about it. Convinced that the time had come for plain speaking to Ross, Phillip continued that he did not want the peace of the colony constantly disturbed, but he did want Ross to be more guarded in his comments, reminding him of an injudicious statement he had made recently to a convict whose time had expired to which Ross imprudently had exclaimed, "Would to God my time had expired, Too!" Condemning the comment, Phillip tutored that this attitude could only lead the convict to dissatisfaction with his lot. And then with a dignified admonition, he counselled: "The time cannot be far distant when a legal enquiry can take place, and all complaints will then be attended to. Till then His Majesty's service requires some little forbearance on your part as well as on mine".[73] And so evaporated another crisis instigated by one charged in his commission to take the colony into his "care and charge".

During 1789, it had become the pattern for Ross-inspired commotions to erupt at two monthly intervals; accordingly, the Brewer-Thady Affair of August had hardly subsided when in early November it was succeeded by the Night Watch Affair — an affair in which Ross displayed his continuing intransigence to the civil authority.

The affair arose from the need to curb the enormous frequency of robbery. Such a threat had it become to private property that Phillip and Collins decided to establish a night watch of twelve convicts divided into four parties to patrol, apprehend, and secure trespassers. Regulations governing its conduct were drawn up, and included in regulation 5 was a stipulation that any marine found straggling after taptoo, which signalled the return to barracks, or caught in convict huts, was to be detained and sent to the nearest guardhouse. All regulations, and particularly regulation 5, were agreed to by Ross. The patrols, or "divisions" as they were called by Phillip, were placed under the superintendence of Herbert Keeling who daily at noon was to report all robberies and misdemeanours to the Judge Advocate. Collins described the watch as "the first attempt toward a police in this settlement".[74] According to Tench, its divisions covered the western side of the Tank Stream, the Brick Kiln area to the south, the eastern side of the Tank Stream to the public gardens, and from the hospital north to the observatory.[75] The watch began its operations so successfully that for three months not a single robbery was committed at night.[76]

At nine o'clock on the evening of 7 November, watchman Thomas Oldfield received orders from his superior, Charles Peate, to "take every person up" who was out of bounds, and especially if they were in the female camp. Half an hour later, he saw Private Roberts near a hut being built by Gloucester the carpenter, leaning over a pig sty in which there were three piglets though he was showing no disposition to steal them. When asked what he was doing, Roberts said that he was about to go home; Oldfield however asked him to go to the watchhouse, which he did willingly, and from there Peate directed Oldfield to take him to the sergeant of the guard. Sergeant Hume was told that Roberts had been found "after hours in the Women's Camp". Hume apparently questioned Roberts, who said his reason for being in the women's camp was that he had written a letter to Norfolk Island and had gone to the camp hoping to find a crewman of the *Supply* to deliver it.

These details were collated in a report by Adjutant Long, who passed it to Ross, whose reaction was immediate and volcanic: he sent Long to Collins with a message charging that a convict had confined an innocent soldier in the guardhouse — an action which Ross regarded as an insult offered to the whole detachment. He added that the troops would not allow themselves to be treated in such a way, and, lifting his tirade to a military threat, he warned that the troops would not be controlled by convicts "while they had bayonets in their hands".[77] This sabre-rattling was an intolerable threat to the civil authority. Its implications were so serious that Collins, rightly or wrongly, thought it as well to keep the statement from Phillip. (Though when told of it later, Phillip saw it to be "so pointed a menace" that had he known of it, he would have refused to withdraw regulation 5.) Collins only relayed Ross's charge of "insult" to Phillip. Phillip, to placate Ross, requested he come and discuss the problem. Ross rejected this request, adding contempuously that he would not come till the following day, and would be accompanied by two of his officers. The stage therefore had been reached whereby Ross would obey Phillip's requests only on his own conditions. Militarily, this amounted to the offence of disobedience, for military law has never permitted subordinates to lay down terms to superiors. In involving two of his officers, Ross was approaching the offence of mutiny, and in demanding the withdrawal of regulation 5, he was reneging on his previous concurrence with it. Phillip apparently wrote to Ross pointing out three matters: that there had been no robberies since the watch had been established; that previously soldiers had committed robberies; and that the only way to stop them was to catch them in the act. Ross did not deny these claims but simply repeated his charge that the detachment had been insulted by being put under the command of convicts. Phillip denied this, but because an explosive situation had developed — Ross had told the troops of the stand he had taken — Phillip had no alternative but to grant soldiers immunity from the regulation. To have done otherwise would have been, as he explained to Lord Sydney, to run the risk of disputes between the marines and the watch. Regulation 5 had served the public good and it was a distasteful choice imposed on a care-worn Phillip by an incorrigible malcontent: the fact that originally Ross had personally agreed to the regulation denied him the slightest skerrick of credit in the matter.

Although Phillip had been forced to yield to the duress imposed upon him, he was not prepared to be supine. Accordingly, he sent for Adjutant Long and asked him to convey to Ross that although it was impossible to see that any insult had been offered, he was still prepared to discuss the matter, and that as Ross had said that he would bring two officers to any meeting with Phillip, Phillip now "desired" that he place no restriction on officer attendance but bring them all. Phillip was perspicacious enough to realize that any two officers Ross would being would be prejudiced in Ross's favour. Ross was now cornered; his brinkmanship and bluff had again been called. He undoubtedly realized that whilst he could control a deputation of two personally selected officers, such was the animosity towards him by most of the others that he would have no support from many of them in his sordid squabble with a man for whom they had deep respect. He therefore sent a message to Phillip that he did not wish any further enquiry.[78] A logical conclusion is that once again Ross had been misrepresenting the officers' view and using them as pawns.

In this Night Watch Affair, Ross had brought the settlement closer to a military-civil confrontation than it had ever been before. He had been rude to Phillip and had defied a request from him, but more serious was the ominous development in Ross's attitude whereby he now tried to involve the Marine Corps detachment in his confrontations with civil authority. No governor could long ignore the dangerous portents of this, for Ross was acting as if he possessed an independent command — as if Phillip was in command of the convicts only whereas Ross was in unfettered command of the military.[79]

It was after a year of enduring these recurring crises that Phillip decided to take action about Ross's complaints to England in July and November 1788. That Ross should have been so treacherous, angered and disgusted him. There was a limit to the torture he was prepared to suffer, and it had now been reached. He therefore made two decisions, the first of which he proceeded with immediately: it was to report Ross's actions to both Nepean and Lord Sydney and to compile his own defence against Ross's allegations.[80] He wrote the letters on 1 and 13 February 1790, and admitted that he was writing to Nepean "in haste", by which he undoubtedly meant in anger and frustration, for problems early in 1790 were pressing in upon Phillip with relentless force. He was wrestling with the famine; an upsurge in convict stealing was requiring added vigilance and severity; explorations which sought to find good soil failed to do so except at Rose Hill; there had been no communications from England for three years; "gloom and dejection overspread every countenance";[81] Aborigines, displaced from their normal hunting grounds, were setting fire to the bushland to smoke out possums for food; and then, in mid February, heavy rains damaged the convict huts and filled the trenches which had been dug for the foundations of buildings. The colony was struggling for its very existence, and yet Ross was insensitive to the situation and lacked any spirit of cooperation for the general good. By contrast, Phillip, with the most admirable optimism in the midst of such adversity, could write that, given three years, settlers then arriving would have plenty.

Phillip began his letter to Nepean by saying that five months after Ross had complained he had been insulted by Collins, Ross was complaining that Phillip had not given proper attention to the complaint. By now Ross had developed a pathological hatred of Collins,[82] possibly because as a mere captain of marines, he held a superior legal post, and as Phillip's secretary, he enjoyed Phillip's confidence in a way that Ross did not. Referring to Ross's conduct in the Criminal Court Affair as confirmed by several of his officers, Phillip expressed the view that it had brought the settlement to "the moment of a general confusion", which was close to saying that the settlement was close to civil strife.[83] Concerning Ross's complaint that troops had had to go without necessities, Phillip advised that repeatedly had he asked Ross to name those deficiencies but Ross's stock answer had been that the Admiralty had told him the detachment would be made comfortable after the landing. Phillip's view was that, bearing in mind the nature of the service for which they had volunteered, they were well off; personally therefore, he doubted the truthfulness of Ross's complaint. In answer to Ross's accusation that stores belonging to the detachment were being withheld from it, Phillip pointed out that those stores had been held in the detachment's Q store, and not the Commissary's, and the unit had plentiful access to its own Q store. The truth was that the marines had also been issued with a considerable part of the stores intended for convicts, so much so, that a majority of the stores brought out from England were now in the possession of the detachment. In writing "the charge has not a shadow of truth to support it",[84] Phillip was saying that Ross was lying. To the charge that Phillip had kept Ross "in the dark" about what he expected of him as the Lieutenant

Governor, Phillip advised that some months after landing, Ross had complained that he was entitled to more information and confidence than Phillip had given him. Phillip asked him to come next day and he endeavoured to remove so groundless a cause of discontent by every means in his power. Ross left the meeting appearing satisfied and when some days later he told Phillip he was ready to give him every assistance, Phillip gave him charge of the convicts on the western side of the cove and always acknowledged his assistance. But such was Ross's bad temper that the rapprochement between them cooled, forcing Phillip to limit his contacts with Ross to those as commander of the detachment only. Even so, Phillip had not in any way restricted Ross's authority, but had let it be widely known that any order by Ross had Phillip's authority. As an example of this, anything ordered from the public store by Ross was given him without reference to Phillip, so as to enhance the status of his appointment. In refutation of the charge that Phillip was often away "on parties of pleasure", Phillip pointed out that such was his health now that he went to places out of a sense of duty, not pleasure, though others who initially were keen to go on expeditions had now lost the inclination to do so. This was one of Ross's more cruel allegations, for Phillip was in pain for most of his time in the colony, though he kept it to himself as much as possible. Ross also complained that Phillip had requested Ross not to disturb the peace of the settlement. In answer to this, Phillip explained why he had made the request, saying, "Has not his representation or complaint been too frequent?" And to illustrate the perfidious nature of Ross's attitude, he reported that, because of a seditious comment Ross made to a convict, the man thereafter so misbehaved that the Criminal Court had to punish him severely. During the trial, Ross's rudeness to Hunter was so gross and so public that Hunter had informed Phillip that he wished never again to act as a magistrate because he wished to avoid a repetition of such treatment."[85]

And in the same line of objection, Collins himself had requested that he also be able to resign his magistracy because of the publicly insulting treatment he had received from both Ross and Campbell in the presence of convicts and others — for Ross used Campbell as an accomplice in his vendetta against Collins. Added to these dissensions were the deep and irreconcilable dissensions within the detachment which Phillip on a number of occasions had attempted to heal.[86]

Consequently, on 1 February 1790, Phillip asked Lord Sydney to replace the Marines Corps detachment with some other unit.[87] Unknown to Phillip, the decision to recall them had already been made in London nine months earlier. After Lord Grenville — who succeeded Lord Sydney on 5 May 1789[88] — had learned from Phillip's second despatch of the discontents which prevailed in the detachment and the desire of most officers to return home, he had directed that they be replaced by a corps of infantry to be known as the New South Wales Corps.[89] The high hopes which Ross held for the detachment prior to leaving England had been dashed in official circles by his own fractious and disgraceful conduct at Sydney, and although at Norfolk Island his attitude towards Phillip was to be more regular and acceptable, it was for his performance at Sydney that Lord Grenville was later to censure him in severely condemnatory terms.[90]

Relations with the Detachment at Sydney

A commanding officer can be judged on a variety of criteria, but pre-eminent among these is his unit's performance and his man-management. A unit's performance is judged on efficiency and effectiveness; what a unit accomplishes will largely depend on the administrative expertise and efficiency of its commander. In the area of his administrative performance, Ross was never questioned nor found wanting. Of all the complaints which Phillip, Collins and others made about him, none involved his capacity or military knowledge. These were tested fully by the detachment's rigorous and pioneering service at Sydney where from an area of native bushland, Ross had to organize the laying of a military foundation on which successors were able to build. The detachment's early responsibilities fell into two main areas: general military duties and the construction of military accommodation. The latter was not new to the Marine Corps; in the American war it is most probable that the construction of living quarters and defence works would have been a normal part of the marines' service, particularly as a Plymouth order of 29 October 1778 stated that "Entrenchments, roads, making posts, and clearing grounds are part of a soldier's duties and are not paid; building forts and fortresses and any other public works are paid at the rate of nine pence per hour".[91] Consequently, the construction of the barracks at Sydney and Parramatta were normal Marine Corps tasks. However, it was in the area of general military duties that requirements existed which, as Ross noted, were out of the line of normal marine service. Although these included such diverse activities as gardening and exploring, as well as the administrative organization of the many military activities in a new and strange social and physical environment, the demands which these created were quite within Ross's administrative and organizational capacity.

Starting from scratch, he promulgated a system of standard operating procedures to administer the detachment's tasks. These were communicated through the Orders Book. Thus to supervise the conduct of the marines as they strolled about the settlement in their off duty hours, he appointed the Adjutant, Lieutenant Long, to the post of Town Adjutant. Long's selection was a successful one which Phillip commended as being "very useful".[92] Rosters had to cover the various recurring duties of the detachment's personnel, and these were prepared by the Adjutant and submitted to Ross for approval. They included the duty officers' roster, and rosters for the main guard, the public store, the eastern side guard, and guards for special occasions such as hangings. Returns for London were also part of Ross's administrative responsibility and covered such matters as sickness and mortality states, paysheets and stoppages, and non-recurring matters such as the return of personnel who desired to remain in the colony after the detachment departed.[93] As well, returns were compiled of marines used as tradesmen on public works so that they could receive additional pay for their endeavours.[94] These military communications with London were mainly in the form of despatches sent in the care of some officer returning home.

The efficiency of a unit's administration can also be tested by its reaction to stress, and the long famine undoubtedly tested the detachment's quartermastering administration, particularly as the Quartermaster's store held over half of everything brought out from England,[95] and the conserving of resources was essential for the unit's survival.

In this extensive administration, particularly during his service on Norfolk Island, Ross displayed a competence which no doubt derived in large measure from his thirty-two years' service. Even when faced with calamity at Norfolk Island after the loss of the *Sirius*, his military knowledge and efficiency were equal to all occasions. Phillip recognized this when he made him a justice of the peace so that he could sit in judgment of convicts when he was at Rose Hill.[96]

However it was in the area of his man-management that his record was not favourable, for though morale amongst his troops appears to have been satisfactory, the same cannot be said of his officers. "No troops", according to Ross, "ever had more severe duty", and when one considers the famine which afflicted them, the shortages of essential items which plagued them, and the lack of news from home which depressed them, the main thrust of his opinion is convincing. Even so, Ross recorded that in spite of the harshness of their service, the troops were approaching it with "alacrity", which indicates that amongst the ranks, morale was satisfactory.[97] Theirs was service for which they had volunteered, and they knew before leaving England that it would be service "out of the usual line of [marine] duty".[98] Some duties such as guards and patrols at Sydney and Parramatta were performed as part of the detachment's regimental formation, whereas those marines who acted as protectors of the various exploration parties performed a more individualized role which called for personal ingenuity. Although direct evidence is scant, incidents such as that at Wolli Creek on 14 December 1790 — when some of Tench's party were rescued from the mud by other marines[99] — suggests that the ordinary marines and their NCOs possessed a reliable competence. The morale of the private soldiers is not described by Southwell, Scott, or Easty, but, as they do not complain, it is reasonable to assume that at best they enjoyed their service and were happy in performing it, and at worst they suffered it in silence. Although very few of the privates elected to remain as settlers after the detachment returned to England, poor morale was not given as a reason. The evidence suggests a reasonable state of morale, but this probably had more to do with the company commanders than Ross because of their immediacy to the men themselves. This was just as well, considering Ross's propensity to upset those with whom he had close dealings.

Morale amongst the officers, however, was far from sound. They lacked harmony, and the feelings of those who recorded their attitudes towards Ross ranged from Clark's opinion that Ross was "without exception, the most disagreeable Commanding Officer" he had ever known,[100] to David Collins' regret that Ross had not perished with the *Sirius* when it was wrecked.[101] During the voyage from England, Ross had on occasion arrogantly and publicly censured his officers, to which an officer such as Clark took exception; and in this tactlessness were sown the seeds of officer antipathy, an antipathy which erupted in the stand taken by them at the court martial of Private Hunt in March 1788. The resentment of those officers towards Ross never ceased, and was still festering three years later when their requests to Phillip to be released from their arrest contained the most barbed references to Ross. After only six months of service in the colony, almost every officer asked in July 1788 to be relieved at the end of the tour, and Ralph Clark asserted that not even promotion to captain would induce him to stay in the colony a day longer than necessary.[102]

As for Ross, his continuing dislike of service at Sydney and its consequent lack of job satisfaction, probably fuelled the peevishness and bad temper to which Phillip and others alluded. He had a quick temper which was prone to give quick offence to those on whom it was vented. Thus within a fortnight of arriving at Sydney, he had, according to Doctor Bowes, arrested his adjutant for "some words which passed between them",[103] and in August 1788 he had a temporary falling-out with his hitherto firmest friend, Captain Campbell. Both Ross and Campbell were from the west country of England and they appear to have known each other before coming to New South Wales;[104] but their previous association did not prevent Ross from quarrelling so violently with Campbell in front of other officers in the Officers Mess that both had to leave. Clark observed that for some time they would pass each other in disaffection without speaking except on official matters. Their petulance however passed and they shortly became "as close as ever", which Clark and the other officers regretted, for apparently the mess had been more enjoyable without them.[105]

Clark and probably the other officers observed a favoured relationship between Ross and Campbell, and evidence of this went as far back as before the fleet left England. In April 1787, when Nepean had appointed Ross to the Vice-Admiralty Court, Ross lamented that Campbell had received no similar appointment and he asked Nepean "for God's sake" to find one for him.[106] Then from Sydney in October 1788, when Ross was adversely reporting to Stephens all his company commanders except Campbell for their "shameful inattention" to the erection of barracks for their companies, he was fulsome in his praise of Campbell at Rose Hill where he was pleased to report that operations were under the care "of your old friend Campbell . . . whose perservence and attention . . . to the public service . . . is too well known to require my saying on that head". After continuing his praise of Campbell for his "most sedulous attention to the success of this settlement", Ross again importuned Nepean to give Campbell "that for which he has served so long for [sic]".[107] Ross was probably justified in praising Campbell at this time, particularly as the other company commanders had placed their own comfort before that of their men by giving priority to the erection of their own houses and those of their servants, and even to the tending of their own stock.[108] Their indifference meant that their men would not be housed for two or three months whereas Campbell's would be moving into their quarters within a week. In front of Campbell, Ross criticized Captain Shea for the lack of progress on his company's barracks, but in reply Shea told him that it was no part of his duty to be a works supervisor. Ross asked him to at least complete the construction which he had started, but Shea refused to do even that.[109] Ross mentioned this to Phillip, who was astonished that any officer could be so callous; he visited Shea and asked him to provide for his company's accommodation, but even so, Shea twice refused Phillip's request before ultimately capitulating to it after Phillip adopted the stratagem of ordering all officers to expedite the erection of company accommodation.

These incidents make a number of suggestions about Ross's management of his officers. Firstly, his relationship with his company commanders was a curious one: he had had to ask Phillip to get three of them to do something which his own request had failed to achieve. And secondly, his readiness to report his most senior subordinates both to London and to the Governor illustrated a fault in his own command of them. Furthermore, his strenuous importuning on Campbell's behalf probably arose less from any altruistic reason than from the obligation which Ross felt to Campbell for his support in condemning Phillip to people in high places at home. But if Ross's relationship with Campbell was deviously pragmatic, and that with Shea was too short lived to be fully judged, that with the other two company commanders, Tench and Meredith, was less than harmonious, for Ross ordered the court martial of both.

In Tench's case, it arose out of a trivial incident on 11 September 1788 when Provost Marshal Brewer, the convict overseer, was faced with two marine carpenters who had apparently received conflicting orders from Ross and Tench. Brewer complained to Ross, and in the enquiry which followed, Tench denied giving the order but admitted that he had not read out Ross's orders of 31 August to his company. These orders stated that marine carpenters and sawyers were subject to Brewer's orders. Ross reported Tench's failure to Stephens, saying that every company commander knew that a commanding officer's orders were to be conveyed to the troops. Tench had not apologized, and Ross felt this demonstrated an intention to be perverse. He therefore asked the Admiralty to recall Tench, possibly to face a court martial which was not possible in the settlement.[110] This, together with the fact that Ross would have liked the three charges of disobedience, neglect of duty, and contempt of his commanding officer levelled against Tench, indicated an overreaction by Ross. Perhaps Tench's learning and culture put him ill at ease. Tench already had one court martial to face — that hanging over from the Hunt trial. The possibility of another should the Admiralty accede to Ross's request caused Ross to express doubts about the legality of an officer being tried by one court martial before the previous one was finalized.[111] It was not till after Tench returned to England, as will be later described (chapter 20), that the matter was settled.

Meredith's difference with Ross arose from his arrest and his subsequent request to Stephens that the matter be decided by court martial.[112] Ross in April 1790 had suspended Meredith from duty for conduct which Ross felt merited a general court martial, but from the moment he was charged, Meredith was so confident of his innocence that with every degree of assurance he welcomed the trial as a means of vindicating that innocence.[113] As detailed later (chapter 20), the trial was held after the detachment returned to England, and as with that of Tench, proved a sour experience for Ross.

Of Ross's relationships at Sydney with the more junior officers, only those with Lieutenants Robert Kellow, James Furzer and Ralph Clark have been recorded in any detail. Kellow was stood down because of an incident whilst he was on service on Norfolk Island, as will be seen in Chapter 16. Furzer was charged in October 1788 with neglect of duty and other offences but after he apologized to Ross the charges were withdrawn.[114] Clark, although describing Ross as the most disagreeable commanding officer he ever knew,[115] managed to stay on good terms with him by being wary of his caprice. Thus when Ross tried to endanger Clark's friendship with Campbell by falsifying something which Campbell had said, Clark did not react but Campbell was angered and called Ross a "time server" . . . "too much attached to self interest".[116]

Thus it can be seen that overall, the officers were not a happy bunch: by November 1788, Clark was describing them as "the most unsociable set that ever was",[117] and their unsociability was not confined to each other in the detachment. Doctor John Harris, writing of Lieutenant Timins, described him as haughty and "very disagreeable"; and even after Timins' friend arrived from Norfolk Island and the two became "inseparable companions", they soon quarrelled and became the "bitterest enemies".[118]

David Collins, who, as has been seen, had special cause to dislike Ross, became so exasperated with his incorrigibility that he rejoiced at Ross's departure for Norfolk Island, and wrote to his father at Plymouth, that since Ross had gone, "tranquillity may be said to have been our guest, but whenever he returns, Discord will again drive out Tranquillity. Oh! that the 'Sirius' when she was lost, had proved his — but no more of that. While here, he made me the Object of his Persecution — and a day will come — a day of Retribution".[119] Collins later asked his father not to believe the lies of "Mr" Ross — of whom he would only say that he did not believe that there was a worse man living.[120] Even the placid Richard Johnson looked forward to Ross's departure so that the colony would become more peaceful,[121] whilst as already seen, Hunter and Collins requested that they be relieved of the magistracy rather than submit again to Ross's publicly insulting rudeness.[122] It was only too obvious therefore to an officer of Phillip's perception that deep and irreconcilable dissensions plagued the detachment; they were, however, beyond his power to heal.[123]

The evidence against Ross in the area of personnel management and personal relationships is strongly detrimental. His conflicts with his company commanders could only have had an adverse effect on junior officers; tensions at times in the Officers Mess were almost unbearable; Ross's inclination to report his officers to others, and especially to London, could only have exacerbated ill-feeling and caused the factions of which he complained; whilst his favoured relationships with Campbell and his own son John would have added to the cauldron of dissension often so visibly evident.

Such is the evidence, and it throws much light on the cause of Ross's problems in personal relationships. Ross otherwise was an officer of acceptable administrative capacity. Regrettably, this was not matched by an acceptable personality or an attractive sociability. At Port Jackson, his dealings with others were bitter, petulant, perverse, and obstructionist; and yet this attitude could not have been a long standing one for otherwise it would have gone against him when he was being considered for command of the detachment in 1786. His friendship with Nepean during the American war and his appointment to the successful command of a company suggest that he had displayed an acceptable personality there; but at New South Wales, he became the anti-social ogre of Port Jackson. It was at Port Jackson that he was objectionable. It was at Port Jackson that he was the malignant quibbler, the incorrigible malcontent, the disturber of tranquillity. The problem lay in the interaction of two defects: defects in Ross's personality, and defects in Port Jackson's form of government.

Hitherto throughout Ross's service, any latent propensity for perverse obstructionism had been suppressed by the rigidity of the military command system in which he operated and of which he was a subordinate part. He had always been in a position in which he had had a single superior; never before had he had a duality of higher authority to which he was responsible or to which he could appeal; he had always known his role and he had always "known his place". At Port Jackson he knew them too, for both his own commission and that of Phillip's spelt out to him the spirit of both — but therein lay the weakness of the Port Jackson government. The spirit of the home government's intention was clearly that all in the new colony should, by good intentions, labour for the colony's good; but in any constitutional arrangement, an absolute and overriding power must exist in a single office to deal with those occasions when constitutional intentions are thwarted. At Port Jackson, the office of governor did not contain ultimate or overriding power, and it was this defective form of government imposed on Phillip and on his three successors which placed them helplessly in the power of the military. During the terms of four governors the British government failed to see this, and in the case of Phillip, it thought that by relieving the Marine Corps the problem would be eradicated. But by merely replacing one military unit with another, the problem was perpetuated because the source of the problem remained untouched. The governor needed absolute power, not just nominal power; but the first four governors had the shadow of power whilst the military held the substance. In practice, a duality existed by which local power was shared between the civil governor and the military commander, and although this was not the home government's intention as embodied in Phillip's commission, it never-the-less came to be the case. This came about because the Admiralty, to whom Ross chose to feel he owed his primary responsibility, had failed to issue a directive stipulating that, whilst in New South Wales, the governor alone would be his ultimate superior. Because the Admiralty contended with the governor to retain control of the marines, Ross had two superiors, by which he was able to be in direct communication with the home government and from which an area of friction between himself and Phillip was created. Accordingly, Ross was able to refuse Phillip's request for the marines to supervise convicts on the grounds that the Marine Corps detachment would be guided by the Admiralty's instructions to the commanding officers at Plymouth, Portsmouth and Chatham, which nominated their role to be a garrison one only. By the same line of reasoning, and in spite of the terms of Phillip's commission, the Marine Corps officers relied upon Admiralty regulations to provide their reason for refusing to recognize Phillip's power to convene general courts martial. Consequently, collision between the civil power and the military was continually imminent at Port Jackson.

However, the extent to which this defect would result in problems for the colony depended upon the personalities of both leaders: if a disposition to cooperate for the benefit of the colony's welfare dominated all considerations, friction would have been minimal or even non-existent. For Phillip this presented no difficulty, for as has been demonstrated, he was guided by one aim only — to do what was best for the colony, even if this involved self-abnegation. Ross was not actuated by such nobility of purpose. He saw that because of the defect in the constitutional arrangement, he possessed an independence which could be used to enhance his own standing in the scheme of things at Port Jackson; and because he disliked almost everything associated with the colony, and regretted his service in it, his disgruntlement developed a crankiness and a disaffection which fed an obsession to obtain for himself a notoriety to which his rank and position did not entitle him. He became pathologically jealous of his official position, which he regarded apparently as being essential to his personal prestige, and this dependence on position for personal status and recognition produced in him a dislike of anyone who was, either by office or influence, superior to him. Like Cassius, he was not at mind's ease whenever he beheld a greater than himself. Consequently he was a jealous person whose jealousy drove him to vendettas of personal tyranny against those who, in the civil administration, he saw as being his superior. Thus Phillip he discomfited, and Collins and Hunter he savaged, not only because they were, in one way or another, his superiors, but also because they were participants in the civil government which he saw as the only body which overshadowed his status in the colony.

Thus Ross was an officer strong in perversity, limited in vision, too concerned with self and too little with others, whose squalid triumphs over those who had to suffer him denied him that place in Australian history which, with more grace, he may well have shared with Phillip.

No one knew him better or longer than Campbell. As a kindred spirit, Campbell's assessment of Ross is therefore pertinent: "A time server", wrote Campbell, "too much attached to self-interest".[124]

16

Norfolk Island

Early in February 1790, Phillip's patience with Ross came to an end. By then, the threat which Ross's intransigence posed to the peace and good government of the settlement at Sydney demanded that Phillip end his policy of long suffering: consequently, Phillip reported in detail to both Lord Sydney and Nepean, not only the misdemeanours of Ross, but also his refutation of Ross's allegations against him. Then, on 17 February, Phillip told Ross to proceed to Norfolk Island with Meredith and Johnston's companies. He was to relieve King who had been not only the Commandant there since February 1788,[1] but also the Lieutenant Governor since 28 January 1789.[2]

Phillip gave Lord Sydney three reasons for this relief: one was that as the detachment was now divided between Sydney and Rose Hill, it would be advantageous to send the Sydney portion away;[3] another was that as King had spent two years at Norfolk Island, he was best qualified to report directly upon its state; and the other was that by sending King to London, he could "give such information as cannot be conveyed by letters".[4] It does not take much imagination to deduce that that information would include a direct exposure of Ross's misconduct.

Nevertheless, in spite of the intimations that Phillip would

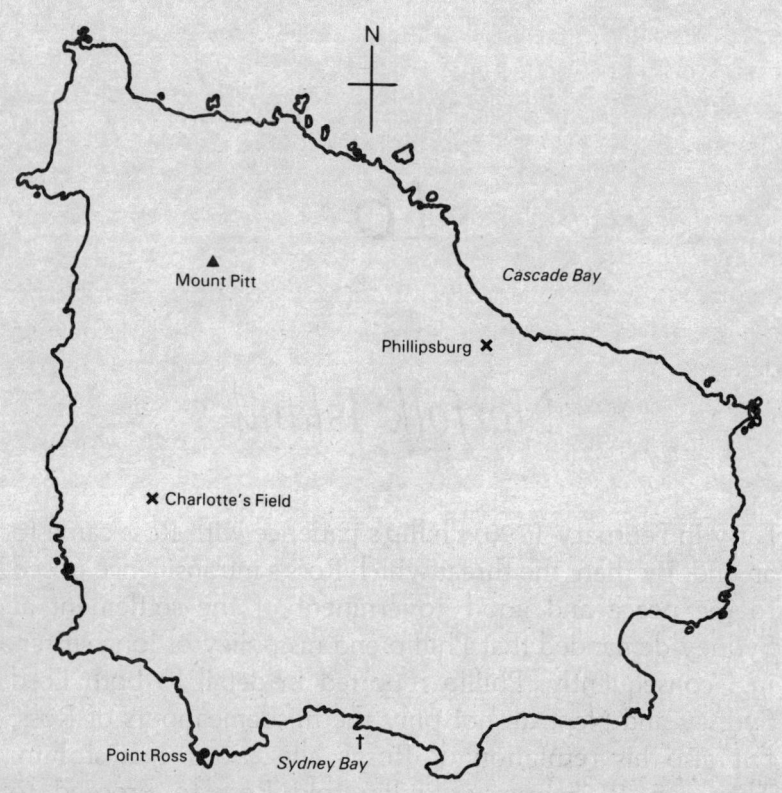

Norfolk Island showing locations of Charlotte's Field and Phillipsburg. Wreck location of *Sirius* indicated as †.

have been only too relieved to see Ross leave Sydney, he told the colony that his reason for sending the marines and convicts to Norfolk Island was that conditions there were superior to those at Port Jackson.[5] Clark and Bradley confirm Phillip's report by stating that Norfolk Island had a better food supply from fish and birds, and that reduction of Sydney's population was essential.[6] The Sydney store would contain only thirteen weeks' provisions after 1 March 1790.[7]

Having been told of his transfer on 17 February, Ross apparently realized that the loneliness felt by all executives would shortly become his own unpleasant experience, and to avoid this as far as possible, he decided to cultivate the friendship of Ralph Clark. That same day, Ross approached

Clark to ask him if he would like to go to Norfolk Island.[8] At first Clark declined, until Ross told him that he himself would be going, and this was, it seems, sufficient persuasion. Having taken Clark into his confidence in a quite uncharacteristic way — he asked Clark to keep his approach secret — Ross revealed that the two companies for the island would be those of Johnston and Meredith, and the lieutenants would be Shairp, Faddy, John Ross, and Clark. Clark however intensely disliked Shairp: he was a man whom he detested "from the bottom of my soul". In his fulsome desire to remove any obstacle to Clark's joining the group, Ross dined with Clark next day and told him that although he had initially overlooked the animosity which existed between the two, he had now repaired this oversight by replacing Shairp with J. Johnson. Ross continued his assiduous cultivation of Clark by having him to both dinner and tea on the 19th, by walking with him for two hours on the 23rd,[9] by spending the day with him on the 24th, and by asking him in which ship he would like to travel to Norfolk Island. Clark replied in terms of the new bonhomie which had now blossomed to bless their relationship, and said that he preferred to travel with Ross, to which Ross touchingly replied "that that was as he would like it".[10]

One is tempted to reflect on the reasons for Ross's new-found sociability. Perhaps he was feeling the loneliness of comparative ostracism by the other officers — something which would be all the more difficult to bear at the outpost of Norfolk Island. Or perhaps his cultivation of Clark's friendship was a personal ploy to gain Clark's support — a support which Ross was beginning to realize might be needed on the island. For the tables were being turned on Ross: the loneliness and vulnerability which his acerbity had made the unpleasant lot of Phillip at Port Jackson was now to become his own situation at Norfolk Island, and no one knew better than Ross how those in authority could be discomfited by incorrigible subordinates. A cultivated and mainly contrived alliance with Clark, therefore, was to be his insurance against such isolation and misery.

With the *Sirius* almost ready for sea, Phillip ordered Ross to prepare his troops for the move and Private Easty on 19 February recorded that Ross issued his warning order for the two companies to prepare for departure aboard the *Sirius* and *Supply* on 5 March 1790.[11] Phillip sent instructions to King to hand over to Ross and return to Port Jackson before leaving for England via Batavia (to which port he was ultimately conveyed by the *Supply*).[12] Meanwhile at Port Jackson, the detachment completed its preparations for departure: Clark, after ensuring that his bed was placed aboard the *Sirius* and that the detachment's colours were safely stowed, accepted the invitation of Ross and Campbell to dine with them on both days preceding departure. By now Clark had much changed his opinion of Ross: he had previously described him as the most disagreeable commanding officer he had ever known;[13] but now he was saying that "Ross's friendship to me is what I call real and sincere".[14] Embarkation was completed when 186 were aboard the *Sirius* and 25 on the *Supply*; Ross, Kellow, Johnson, Clark, John Ross, and 20 NCOs and marines were to travel by *Sirius*, and Captain Johnston, Lieutenant Faddy, and 30 NCOs and marines were to travel on the *Supply*.[15] The two ships moved out from Sydney Cove at six o'clock on the morning of 5 March but so strong a sea was raging at the harbour's mouth that they moored inside the Heads till six o'clock next morning when in the attempt to reach the open sea, the *Sirius* was almost driven on to the rocks of North Head.[16] However, once at sea they made such progress that by noon the two ships were out of sight of land. Their departure was the first dismemberment of the little settlement at Port Jackson and this was felt profoundly by those left behind. The marines' barracks assumed a deserted appearance: where once all had been troops and bustling activity, there now dwelt desertion and loneliness to accentuate the isolation and pangs of homesickness felt by those who remained. Collins observed that "every man seemed left to brood in solitary silence".[17] It was as if famine had thinned the colony of half its members and left those remaining to a dreary prospect.

The *Sirius* and *Supply*, after passing Lord Howe Island and a rock outcrop known as Balls Pyramid on the 9th, reached Norfolk Island on the 13th, only eight days after leaving Sydney. After ten o'clock that morning, many of the male convicts from the *Sirius* were landed to the care of those marines who had been on the island under Lieutenant Creswell's command since 14 June 1789.[18] These included the two marines who had accompanied King in February 1788,[19] the seven who arrived there by the *Golden Grove* in October 1788,[20] and the fourteen who had arrived on 14 June 1789 with Creswell in the *Supply*.[21] As soon as many of the convicts were ashore, the marines began landing that afternoon at half past one at Cascade Bay through a dangerous surf, during which Clark felt that Hunter acted uncivilly to Ross in "pushing" him off into a boat loaded with poultry and pigs.[22] Reception arrangements ashore were non-existent, and after Clark and others had walked five miles into town, they found that the houses which Ross had said would be waiting to accommodate them did not exist.[23] Consequently the troops had to be billeted — Clark himself stayed for two nights at the home of Dr Jamieson. He found this unpleasant and asked Ross if he could be removed, whereupon Ross had a bed prepared for him at the Lieutenant Governor's residence where Ross himself and his son were staying.[24] As soon as he landed, Ross took command of the island and gave the convicts a week to erect their huts.[25] These inferior reception arrangements were to be far different to those which Ross would have in place for the reception of the New South Wales Corps some fifteen months later when its troops would move immediately into completed huts.[26] Although Ross took immediate command of the marines on the island, he asked King to continue as the

Lieutenant Governor till his departure on 24 March.[27]

On 19 March at noon, while attempting to land the stores, Hunter was manoeuvring the *Sirius* in Sydney Bay when treacherous winds took control of the ship and wrecked it on Ross Reef.[28] It was a disaster of major proportion: stores were jettisoned in the hope that she would be refloated. Many of the stores did float ashore, but the ship failed to budge. Clark took a raft through the heavy surf to save people. He was nearly drowned when a panic-stricken convict who could not swim held on so tightly to him that the two almost perished, for which, when they reached shore, Clark took a cane from one of the sergeants and gave the half-drowned convict a thrashing, warning him that he would receive a daily repetition whenever Clark saw him during the next month.[29]

This calamity now made their position extremely precarious: flour was the basis of the staple diet and yet for the five hundred people ashore, there was only six thousand pounds of it, to which Lieutenant Ball added a further five thousand pounds from stock aboard the *Supply*. At once, all were struck with the gravity of their situation. Clark asked, "Gracious God, what will become of us". He possessed only what he stood in and felt that the only prospect facing everyone was starvation.

Instant action therefore was essential and Ross, with commendable presence of mind, supplied it by calling a council of all naval and military officers. This council unanimously determined that martial law should be proclaimed.[30] This remained in force till August 1790 when supplies arrived by the *Justinian* and *Surprize*,[31] though the martial law was more precautionary than repressive: only one convict was court martialled and even he received only five lashes for stealing a female convict's mattress.[32] Phillip agreed with the imposition of martial law and directed Ross to continue it as long as he felt it necessary.[33] Under martial law, the courts martial were composed of seven officers, a majority of whom was needed for corporal punishment, but five of the seven had to concur in a sentence of capital punishment.[34] At the same council meeting, it was decided that all stock except poultry was to become state property, and that there were to be two keys to the public store — one held by a person appointed by Hunter on behalf of the seamen, and the other by someone appointed by the marines. These resolutions were read to all, who confirmed their agreement by walking under the Union Jack flown for the purpose.[35] Such was the reverence for the flag that in Clark's opinion that was as good as swearing on the Bible itself.[36]

On 23 March, Hunter gave two convicts, James Branigan and William Dring, permission to swim out to the *Sirius* to retrieve what cargo they could. They pushed much overboard for it to float to shore, including the animals and fowls, but then they began drinking spirits, and, feeling cold, lit a fire. Those on shore feared that this would set the ship on fire and destroy the remaining stores which were so essential for their survival. They watched powerlessly because of the heavy surf until another convict offered to swim out. After an epic swim he reached the ship and made the culprits extinguish the fire before sending them ashore where Ross put them in irons.[37] All off-duty marines were summoned to prevent the pillage of items washed ashore, and several casks of food were saved in this way. Jettison parties were sent to the wreck daily and these saved a good quantity of necessities. Fortunately, the island abounded in mutton birds and, according to Clark, by 1 May 15,386 of these had been caught and eaten.[38] To enable officers to cope with their additional duties, Ross gave brevet rank to certain of them including Clark, whom he made assistant quartermaster general (AQMG) and keeper of the public store. Clark hoped that these added responsibilities would bring him a higher duty allowance from which he could pay for his losses because all that he had been able to save from the shipwreck was an old coat and four shirts.[39]

Once the cargo that could be saved had been retrieved, the marines settled down to duty on the island. The hardship which had faced them at Port Jackson was to be hardly lessened at Norfolk Island: rations were critically short; all officers had lost personal effects; and Ross had lost his papers.[40] On 20 April, responding competently and decisively to the crisis, Ross and the council reduced the meat ration by half a pound to 3½ pounds (1.6 kg) per man per week. The inhabitants were allowed however to make up the loss by capturing birds.[41] A full stocktake of all rations revealed that only twelve weeks' stocks existed.[42] Ross issued a proclamation in May fixing the weekly ration at 3 pounds (1.4 kg) flour, 1½ pounds (680 g) beef or 17 ounces (480 kg) pork and 1 pound (454 g) rice. Children over one year received half rations, and those under one year received only 1½ pounds flour and 1 pound rice per week.[43] Although this was about half the ration being issued at Port Jackson,[44] its effects were not as severe because at Norfolk Island there was plenty of fish and birds, and crops were more flourishing than those at Sydney.

Thus when Clark went fishing on 21 April, he caught 56 large schnapper which he distributed among the marines and the officers of the *Sirius*;[45] and in the fortnight from 8 to 22 May, 1,867 large schnappers were caught, enabling everyone on the island to be supplied "with a great allowance of fish".[46] Convicts and marines took it in turns to receive whatever fish was caught. Mutton birds also supplemented the meagre ration; on 9 May for example, 4,783 were brought in which made the total to that date over 41,000 birds.[47] This figure rose by the middle of June to 136,000.[48] It is strange therefore that in spite of this abundance of food a good number of marines, seamen and convicts became sick. However, the prospect of starvation, which had been so real in March, was to pass gradually by May.[49] Crops were quickly established and they prospered in the temperate climate — an acre producing 167 bushels of potatoes.[50] Not all seasons however were as prolific, and plagues of caterpillars frequently destroyed crops.[51] When this happened, items of the staple diet were short: Clark mentioned that in one period of six months neither he nor Ross had had a cup of tea or a glass of wine; breakfast consisted of dry bread and coffee made from burnt wheat, but they did not grumble for they felt themselves lucky "even to be able to get that".[52]

The marines were used in a variety of field pioneering duties, for Ross embarked on an extensive development programme. They constructed a trench to bring water nearer the town; they brought in thatch to cover barrack roofs; they dried out powder saved from the *Sirius*, and they felled timber for fashioning at the sawpits. Marines who were carpenters erected the corn mill to grind flour, whilst others prepared ground for the planting of potatoes and corn, and for the erection of huts.[53] An indication of the extent of marine labour can be gained from the fact that almost every man in Captain Johnston's company in the month from 19 June to 17 July 1790, worked twenty-two days clearing and cultivating ground at Charlotte's Field.[54] The produce from these exertions kept starvation at bay, though nothing could restore the basic food items and necessities of life lost from the *Sirius*, and shortages of these continued for almost the whole term on the island. However, this was not permitted to deny observances of royal occasions on the island: on the King's birthday of 4 June 1790, in spite of the recent loss of *Sirius*, the people were allowed a holiday. The marines fired a feu de joie; the gentlemen dined with Major Ross; and "the greatest good cheer and harmony" existed among everyone.[55] (Such was the loyalty to the crown that even when advance elements of the New South Wales Corps later arrived, both they and the marines fired volleys from their respective parade grounds.)[56]

As late as February 1791, Ross, with every justification, was bringing examples of marine shortages to Phillip's attention. "Not one of them have a shoe to their feet, nor scarce a shirt to their backs", he advised, and neither was there a fit bed nor a blanket among them. Not a drop of spirits had been issued for eight months, and so few cooking utensils had been saved from the *Sirius* that each pot was shared by twelve men on a rotational basis; consequently it was often well into the night before some could cook their meal. So severe was their distress that more discontent and grumbling was evident than Ross had ever observed before.[57] Such deprivations affected health, and Collins recorded that in the case of Lieutenant J. Johnson, so ill did he become that he had to be evacuated by the *Supply* on 26 February 1791.[58]

Throughout this trying period, Ross only once succumbed to his former ill-humour when, in his letter to Phillip of 11 February 1791, he expressed the opinion that shortages should be shared equally by Sydney and Norfolk Island.[59] Phillip lost no time in scotching this misinformation. Replying to Ross on 1 March, he put the record straight by pointing out that when Ross left for Norfolk Island, he had taken with him a full quantity of all necessities, little of which had been lost in the *Sirius*. Consequently, if Phillip was correct, it would appear that Ross had underestimated his requirements when he set out for Norfolk Island. But Phillip went on to point out that immediately the *Juliana* had arrived from England in July 1790, he had despatched two ships "with all possible expedition" to Norfolk Island, and that these had carried full cargoes of food, clothing, and implements. He had then sent the *Supply* shortly after to ascertain from Ross not only what else he required, but also to inform him that the *Supply* would return with them. As for the complaint that the supply of spirits had been exhausted after a few months, Phillip pointed out that enough had been sent to last three years. He acknowledged that it had been, by necessity shared with the stranded crew of the *Sirius*, and to make restitution of this, he was holding at Port Jackson a quantity equal to the seamen's portion which would be available to the marines during their voyage home. He thought it better for men to drink water on shore than at sea, and also because the ship conveying them might not have sufficient of its own stocks to satisfy the detachment. However, the marines at Sydney had asked for their three months' portion there and then, and to this, Phillip had consented, but only after a three months' portion had been put away for those marines from Norfolk Island and the crew of *Sirius*. In all this, Phillip had been scrupulously fair, and he further supported his decision not to send alcohol to Norfolk Island because space on the little *Supply* should, he felt, be reserved for more urgent and important items. He admitted that the marines at Norfolk Island had been severely in need of necessities, especially shoes, which, although there had been an original issue, heavy use had destroyed before they were time-expired. He concluded by assuring Ross that there was no intention to deny those at Norfolk Island that which could be sent to them, and he advised him that at Sydney, even NCOs had been forced to wear shoes sent out for the convicts.[60] Ross accepted Phillip's explanation, for nothing more was raised on the subject.

As was the case at Port Jackson, the most common convict crime at Norfolk Island was stealing from gardens. This involved the marines when, as members of the council, they had to sentence the offenders to curtailment of rations or lashing. Thus when convict Thomas Finnesy ran into the woods after stealing cabbages from Lieutenant Creswell's garden and then a few days later was caught trying to steal potatoes from a convict, he was brought before the council, which included Captain Johnston and Lieutenants Johnson and Clark. They reduced his rations to 2 pounds (900 g) of flour per week for ten weeks, and to work in irons during that time. Clark recorded many of the crimes and sentences.

Some sentences were severe, and those advanced in years were not excluded from them: when the seventy-year-old John Mortimore was caught stealing wheat and neglecting work — from which his advanced years apparently had gained him no respite — he was given one hundred lashes.[61] Likewise when Jeffrey Bolton "an old grey headed man" was sentenced for stealing beans from the store, he received fifty lashes and the loss of 3 pounds (1.4 kg) of flour for three months.[62] Bolton was from the *Mary Ann*, which had recently arrived from Port Jackson. He was also the fifth of the *Mary Ann*'s arrivals to be punished, and it is very probable that hunger rather than wantoness drove him and the others to it. Other punishable offences included evasion of duty. This was necessary because survival depended upon everyone's labour being given in the fullest degree possible; consequently when William Cool left his work without permission, the council sentenced him to a ration of only 2 pounds (900 g) of flour per week for a month.[63] Though card playing by convicts was permitted, it was not permitted on Sundays, and when John Laurell and William Robinson were caught doing so, they were sentenced to one hundred lashes.[64] In comparison with the punishments which King began ordering after his return to the island late in 1791, those inflicted by the council were less severe; King ordered two convicts to receive eight hundred lashes each for thieving crops.[65]

The marines were not themselves immune from crime and Clark was driven to exclaim that there was no difference between soldier, sailor or convict when it came to stealing, for not only had Captain Hunter's own marine servant been thieving the good captain's rum, but also Ross's servant, John Ascott, had stolen from his master as well. "There [sic] six of one and half a dozen of the other", lamented Clark.[66] Ascott might well have not been responsible for his misdemeanour, because his unrequited love for a convict woman shortly sent him so insane that his violence necessitated his being placed in a straightjacket before being chained to a gun.[67]

The "grumbling" amongst the troops to which Ross had earlier referred continued to increase until 9 April 1791 when it culminated in an ugly scene bordering on mutiny. It arose over what the marines felt was an inequity in their food supply compared with that enjoyed by the convicts. In the previous January, Ross had cut the male convict ration by two pounds of flour a week and at the same time had reduced the full weekly ration to troops by a quarter. The convicts made up their loss from the vegetables which were growing prolifically in their gardens; the troops were reluctant to garden and consequently had to compensate their ration shortfall by buying vegetables from the entrepreneurial convicts — a situation which increasingly irritated the troops. Such was the groundswell of smouldering discontent that on the 9th, after an inflamatory address had been given by four ringleaders, the troops decided to refuse to collect their weekly rations from the public store on the grounds that the convicts were better off than they were. When it was pointed out that this was their own fault for not gardening, they merely murmured and uttered vague excuses which led Ralph Clark to believe that their real intention was to test the authority of Major Ross. If that was so, Ross was not daunted by their challenge. He ordered Captain Johnston to tell the men that he would not again ask them to collect their rations and that at 1.30 p.m., Johnston would call a ration parade to march to the store so that he could see "which man would dare to refuse". Ross also ordered Johnston to take the added precaution, bearing in mind the sullen temper of the men, of disarming them before they set out. At 1.30 p.m. the test came: Johnston, accompanied by Clark, Faddy and Creswell, went to the barrack yard, and ordered the men to obtain their ration bags and then fall in on parade. This display of determination was sufficient for some of the men, and they went to Johnston to tell him not only that they would obey his orders, but also that they regretted their previous refusal. Very quickly, the others capitulated and what Clark felt would have concluded in a great deal of blood, was avoided. It had been a close thing, for the men were the "most mutinous" with whom Clark had served; to him it had been one of the "most critical" days of his life and his response to the fright he had received was to confide to his diary that if he could be despotic for three hours, he would hang the ringleaders and have the others draw lots to select every fifth man to suffer the same fate. The incident highlighted the growing strain which the long and severe service was having on morale, and Clark identified this as the underlying cause, for he felt the sooner they left the island, the better.[68]

Even so, marine discipline appears to have been better than that of the New South Wales Corps, whose Norfolk Island advance party of three officers and twenty-one men[69] brought with it a noticeable rise in military offences. In the five month period from May to October 1791, the New South Wales Corps was forced to court martial eight soldiers, six of whom were found guilty. In the same period, only four marines were convicted, even though the marine strength of two companies greatly exceeded that of the New South Wales Corps elements.[70] So unsatisfactory was the discipline of the relieving New South Wales Corps that it caused Clark to report that since its troops had arrived "they have had nothing but Courts Martial".[71]

Relationships between the marine officers continued to show the strains which had been evident at Sydney. But the disharmony in Sydney had been the result of the long period of having been together, the rigour of the service, the increasing debilitation arising from the famine, and the depressing effect of no news from home. At Norfolk Island, the friction between officers came from two causes, which unfortunately involved all the officers.[72] Both disputes began early in the tour of duty; neither were resolved before its conclusion. Consequently, in the confinement which the tiny island offered, it was impossible to escape the presence of those involved, and the result was a continuing tourniquet placed on officer relationships which, in the case of Ralph Clark, brought him near to breaking point.

Clark recalled that the first of these disputes began on 26 July 1790 between Lieutenants Kellow and Faddy.[73] It originated one evening after Faddy had dined with Ross and Clark. After the dinner had broken up, Faddy stayed to tell Ross of statements which Kellow had made about Ross. Ross was alarmed by their nature, and sent for Kellow, who denied having uttered such statements. Ross responded by telling Clark, who was the mess secretary, that as one of them had to be lying, he would refuse to dine with either of them until the culprit confessed. When Clark informed Kellow, Kellow asked his advice, and Clark suggested he arrange a pistol duel with Faddy. When Clark notified Faddy of Ross's embargo, Faddy so firmly reasserted that Kellow had used the reported words, that Clark was convinced of Kellow's guilt. Next morning, Faddy returned from Charlotte's Field and after much huffing and puffing about the selection of seconds, it was decided to fight the pistol duel at the nearby camp. However, when Captain Johnston heard of it, he disapproved and not only ordered both Kellow and Faddy to be confined to their quarters, but also placed them under arrest. Ross reacted by ordering an enquiry consisting of Johnston, Creswell, Clark, and John Johnson to ascertain who was guilty. The enquiry was held but both officers stuck to their respective stories. Ross then asked the enquiry to try again but before its members met, Kellow and Faddy already had gone to Turtle Bay, near the settlement, and fired one shot of the duel. The Naval Agent to the First Fleet, Lieutenant Shortland of the *Supply*, was present and questioned Kellow. Kellow modified his previous stance to the extent that he admitted part of the alleged statement and maintained that he could not recollect the other words. Shortland then put it to him that, as he was now claiming a temporary loss of recollection that he had used certain words, it was possible he might indeed have used them. Kellow agreed and Shortland stopped the further firing so that the group could return to town with news of Kellow's partial admission. Johnston was told of Kellow's concession, and the enquiry committee reconvened to examine again the whole boring business.

Kellow repeated his part admission and this, together with his demeanour, convinced the committee of his guilt. He now stood not only in personal disgrace but also in breach of an officer's code of conduct in that, by being prepared to put a fellow officer's life at stake whilst knowing his own guilt, he had acted neither as an officer nor as a gentleman. Under these circumstances, the other officers asked Ross not to force them to do duty with an officer so "really infamous" and he agreed by placing Kellow under open arrest, suspending him from all duties and from any interference with the colony's affairs. Ross then ordered that Kellow be returned to England by the first available ship. Kellow's reaction was to adopt an attitude of complete indifference. He endured his being "sent to Coventry" for fifteen months, until he returned to Sydney where he thought better of his transgression and apologized to his brother officers. They in turn asked Ross to cancel their complaint against him which he did and reinstated him to duty, though Clark felt that a repetition of the offence was quite possible if Kellow recommenced drinking.[74]

The second cause of strained officer relationships was Major Ross's ill-considered policy of favouring Ralph Clark. This became clearly observed by the others, particularly as Clark and Ross frequently went on walks together.[75] It was a policy which could only arouse a justified resentment and cause, ultimately, an unenviable discomfiture to Clark himself. A few months after arriving, such was the jealousy it created that Clark wanted to leave the island because he felt the other officers would like to do him harm. Such was his unhappiness that his diary entry for 10 September 1790 lamented, "Do come good 'Gorgon' for I wish to be away".[76] Nor did Ross lessen his partiality towards Clark even though an officer of his experience would have known and observed its effect on morale, for six months later Clark was still complaining of its effect on his relationships with Creswell, whose growing antipathy towards him was producing a reciprocated antipathy in Clark. Creswell's attitude was fuelled by fears that Clark would gain promotion or preferment, and the intensity of Clark's own bitterness urged him to express the private threat that should Creswell "start anything", the world would be "too small" for both of them. However, his threat was more emotional than real for when Creswell and Johnston left for Sydney in the *Supply* on 9 May 1791, Clark bore them no ill-will and forgave their unkindness to him.[77]

Clark himself laboured unsparingly to develop the settlement. Partly because he was deputy assistant quartermaster general, and partly because of his favoured relationship with Ross, Ross gave him the oversight of building a town at Charlotte's Field. This "nettled" the other officers, but Clark had not solicited the appointment and claimed that he would have helped any of them if they themselves had gained it.[78] He set about with impressive energy and resolved to build the town complete with roads, houses, and other buildings. He began the project on 30 November 1790; within ten days, the third house was under construction. He became so caught up in his own industry that he expected others to do likewise, and when two convicts absconded to town rather than work at their allotted tasks, he had both of them flogged. His achievements were impressive: by the end of December, the frame of the tenth house was erected; he had informed the carpenters on the method to be used in constructing a bridge; he set men to work making bricks; and he presented the quarterly accounts for Ross to sign.[79] By March 1791, he was able to send over thirteen thousand cobs of corn to market,[80] and had discovered that grapes and potatoes thrived on the island. When the road reached a swamp, he used both marines and convicts to surmount the problem,[81] and such was his wholehearted enthusiasm for his task, that he spent days marking out the streets and the town's marketplace.[82] When the settlement gained the appearance of a town, it was named Queensborough in honour of Her Majesty. But now that the fields were fully productive, convicts, and especially convict women, began to plunder them. At first Clark thought of having a set of stocks made "for the d . . . B . . . of women", the incorrigibility of whom drove him to cursing and swearing;[83] but Ross empowered him to use Richardson, the flogger, to give as many lashes as were necessary to deter the thieving. Clark sentenced Catherine White to fifty lashes but she could only bear fifteen before fainting, whereupon the doctor intervened; Mary Higgins was sentenced to a similar number but when she had received twenty-six, it was Clark who intervened and forgave her because of her age; when Mary Teut fainted during her lashing, Clark forgave her the balance.[84]

This semblence of compassion for convict women was a new attitude in Ralph Clark, for it was a considerable departure from his hitherto hard-line policy towards them. As an illustration of the change, he had noted that although Charlotte White, punished on 20 October 1790, was a liar and a great thief, she was nevertheless "a good looking woman".[85] He ordered her to receive six lashes only, the smallest number ordered by him. His praise of her was the first he had ever recorded about any convict woman. The reason for this mellowing might well have resided in the fact that he was attracted to a nineteen-year-old convict, Mary Branham, who would shortly fall pregnant to him. The news of the pregnancy must have mortified this man whose condemnation of convict women — albeit the incorrigible among them — had been so persistent and so scathing. Nor could his anguish have been eased when he recalled his previously declared intentions to maintain, in spite of all enticements to the contrary, an unspotted matrimonial fidelity. This is not to pass judgment; rather does it highlight his moral dilemma; and as suffering purifies human nature and is eminent in the reduction of arrogance, Clark's own fall from grace, like that of the prodigal son, gave him a new-found understanding of erring humanity — an understanding which could cause him not only to write on Christmas Day 1790, "I wish a merry Christmas to all the world",[86] but also to pity the convict women of Charlotte's Field as they were issued with cloth to make shifts: "Poor things", he wrote, "they want things bad enough, God Knows".[87] His child, a daughter, was duly born in July 1791 and he named her Alicia, after his wife. Like most of the others, he did not take her back with him to England, but she was christened, whether by his request is unknown but probable, at St Phillips, Sydney, two days before he sailed for England.[88]

Clark had learnt of his impending return to England in August 1790 when the *Justinian* and *Surprize* had called at the island and had brought him six letters from Alicia and Ralph.[89] From them, he learnt that Alicia had sent him supplies by the *Guardian* which had subsequently been wrecked off Cape Town.[90] Clark's love for her continued though he now expressed it less mawkishly: he sent her a box of stuffed birds;[91] he yearned for the *Gorgon* to take him "to everything that is dear to me on earth";[92] and after recalling how awful 1789 and 1790 had been to him and how deeply he wished to be reunited with his family, he wished his wife a happy birthday via his diary entry for her day.[93] Their reunion was still more than a year away.

Towards the end of their time on the island, some thirty-one marines elected to stay and in consequence received land grants (see Table 12) of sixty acres (about 24 ha) each.[94] The grants to Privates Samuel King and Charles Heritage (and presumably to the others) were free from fees, taxes, and quit rent (the rent which would have been owing if the

Table 12 Land grants of 60 acres to marines on Norfolk Island, 1791

5 APRIL 1791			
Grant no. 14.		Pte	Charles Heritage
15.		"	Samuel King
17 AUGUST 1791			
Grant no. 45.		Pte	William Mitchell
46.		"	Thomas Bramwell
47.		"	Thomas Bishop
48.		"	John McCarthy
49.		"	Lawrence Richards (married with two children)
50.		"	John Munday (married with three children)
51.		"	Thomas Chipp
52.		"	William Strong
53.		"	James McManus
54.		"	Thos O'Bryen
55.		"	Richard Knight
56.		"	Abraham Hand
57.		"	William Dempsey
58.		"	Thos Sculley
59.		"	John Barrisford (married with two children)
60.		"	James Redmond
61.		"	Wm Tonks
62.		"	Thos Halfpenny
63.		"	Wm. Standley
64.		"	John Gowen
65.		"	Thos Dukes
66.		"	James ? Williams
67.		"	Daniel Standfield (married with three children)
68.		"	John Roberts
69.		"	Wm. Simms
70.		"	John Foley
71.		"	Patrick Connell
72.		"	John Redman
73.		"	Thos. Spencer

Source: *New South Wales Archives Office*, Sydney, AO 4/1634; *Public Records Office*, London, PRO Reel 3554; ML T/L 703

grantee quit the property within the ten year period) for ten years; thereafter charges would be one shilling a year. These settlers had to reside on the land and cultivate it; half an acre was to be cleared for them by convicts, and these marine-settlers were to be issued free with clothing, two palliasses, two blankets, one iron pot, and other necessities.[95] By

December 1791, there were thirty-one marine-settlers compared with the seventy-one others who by then were farming on the island.[96] Some of the marine-settlers had applied to King to marry the "best behaved" of the convict women with whom they had already been living. When the Reverend Johnson visited, the weddings proceeded, and the men undertook to take the women off the public store a year after their marriage.[97] These marine settlers however did not impress King and within a month or two of their taking up their grant, he told Phillip that they were being troublesome and two had had to be sentenced. It was his opinion that they would soon tire of their task once the novelty wore off.[98]

This chapter will close with an attempt to evaluate the performance of Major Ross at Norfolk Island. He had gone there with a questionable reputation from his less than satisfactory behaviour at Port Jackson, but whereas at Sydney he had been a second-in-command, at Norfolk Island the command was his. To that extent he held an unusual position: he was the Lieutenant Governor of Norfolk Island, but his rank was only that of a major, and yet he had to issue orders to Hunter whose rank as a naval captain was superior. It was therefore from the power of his appointment as Lieutenant Governor that he had to operate. Thus Clark records that when Hunter led a party to fell trees on Mount Pitt, Ross stopped him on the grounds that, as the greater part of the settlement's subsistence came from birds, the trees were to remain and none was to be cut down without his permission.[99] Again, when he discovered that the crew of the *Sirius* had been drawing candles from the public store, he told them to cease the practice and draw from their purser's stocks;[100] later he ordered the *Sirius* crew to grub land so as to plant a garden for themselves.[101] Hunter never questioned

Ross's authority. At first, Hunter was loud in his praise of him, writing to Stephens in August 1790, "We [the crew of *Sirius*] have great right to remember with gratitude the kindness of our good friend Major Ross . . . He, poor unfortunate man, lost most of his things . . . which he bears with surprising magnanimity".[102] Hunter's praise was a far cry from his refusal to continue his magistracy at Port Jackson because of Ross's intolerable rudeness, and he recognized that it was largely Ross's decisiveness after the loss of the *Sirius* which had saved the settlement. No sooner had Ross coped with the shipwreck than he turned his energy and talents to tackling the task of subsistence, and when difficulties arose, he was capable of providing the solution; and when opportunities arose, he grasped them.

In early June 1790, a reconnaissance party discovered land which could be cleared in a tenth of the time it was taking nearer the West Point township. Ross examined it, and, noting its light cover, immediately saw it as being the main area for cultivation. He estimated that it would need only the same number of men to clear five acres there as one acre back at the settlement. He called the new area Charlotte's Field, and within five days, he not only had a road construction party making a road from it to West Point, but also had huts built there to house the work parties from Captain Johnston's company, the members of which he ordered to be paid tradesmen's rates. Work began daily at seven o'clock and to encourage the effort, Ross would send fish to the men, with the result that such was their morale, they had to be stopped working when it rained, according to Clark.[103] Ross did not interfere by harassing them, and allowed a month to pass before making his first visit.[104] He was pleased with what he saw: potatoes, corn, and such a variety of other crops had been sown that, when the *Justinian* and *Surprize* called a month later, a boatload of cabbages, turnips and greens was sent to them as being surplus to the settlement's requirements.[105] The island's sufficiency became such that in

February 1791, Ross was able to tell Phillip that if Port Jackson could not send any food, Norfolk Island would not feel any "distress"; and when advance elements of the New South Wales Corps arrived at about the same time, one of its NCOs reported that his troops were "flourishing . . . digging thirty bushels of potatoes, and picking vast quantities of french beans".[106] Consequently, in spite of the loss of *Sirius*, only two convicts died naturally in the first six months.[107]

Whilst at Norfolk Island, Ross's manner changed for the better: his former fractiousness was, in the main, replaced by agreeableness. He was happier, more industrious, and praised convicts who were energetic and hard-working — a service which, it ought to be noted, he had forbidden his troops to perform for Phillip at Port Jackson. When Arscott, the convict carpenter, and Richard Philamore were deserving of praise, he commended them; when he wrote to Phillip it was, with one exception, in the terms of a friendly correspondence.[108] He adopted a policy of judicious compassion towards erring convicts: thus when Thomas Strick, a convict who had escaped eight months earlier, was eventually apprehended, Ross forgave him because of the suffering, lack of clothes, and loneliness which he had endured.[109] When convict John Howard was sentenced to five hundred lashes for selling the slops issued to him from the public store, and then lied to Ross about it, he received eighty lashes initially because that was all he could then bear, and Ross forgave the balance.[110] He dispensed the same good fortune to Thomas Brown,[111] and when Ross handed over to King on 13 November 1791, he requested that all prisoners in confinement be pardoned.[112] He could show restraint to convicts even in the face of considerable provocation: in May 1790, he was told that some convicts were catching birds at Mount Pitt, and if they were with egg as yet unlaid, they would cut the egg out and then let the poor bird fly away. (This was the cruellest thing Ralph Clark had ever heard.) In addition, convicts were destroying birds wantonly by sending dogs against them. Ross ordered all convicts to be mustered for the announcement of his orders against these practices, and pointed out the island's dependence on birds when the seas were too rough to catch fish. His restrained admonition concluded the practice.[113] Soldiers were not excluded from his clemency and he forgave a New South Wales Corps private one hundred lashes because of his previous good behaviour.[114]

As seen, his policy contrasted very favourably with that which King reinstituted upon his return, even though Ross faced a more critical time. As an example of King's more severe rule, when convict Resby's time had expired, Resby, with some justification, refused to work. King placed him on three day's rations per week, and ordered him to Port Jackson without his wife even though he had been married only the day before.[115]

In administration, Ross displayed a notable competence which ran into matters of administrative detail as well as to matters necessitating executive decision. When he saw the abundance of birds on Mount Pitt, and when the fish were prolific, he ordered that the standbys of salted beef and pork should be conserved and not issued till further notice. After the *Sirius* crisis, he discovered that salvage items alleged to be coming into Clark's store were in effect not doing so. He therefore told Clark to issue receipts for exact deposits only.[116] When the *Justinian* and *Surprize* arrived with stores, he realized that the extent of the logistics demanded more than a deputy assistant quartermaster general. So he upgraded the position to a deputy commissary, to which he appointed a civilian, Mr Freeman, who superseded Clark.[117] Such was Ross's administrative ability and clear-headedness that when he fell ill in July 1791, Clark feared that if he died, a "scene of confusion" would result.[118]

In spite of the aforesaid commendations, Ross had his detractors, chief of whom was Phillip Gidley King. King apparently had formed a dislike of Ross during the voyage of the First Fleet. In a memo written before leaving England for his return to Norfolk Island, King wondered whether he ought to have a dormant commission to deal with the contingencies of Phillip being dead by the time of his return to Port Jackson and Ross refusing to relinquish the government of Norfolk Island.[119] But surely King's fears were unfounded, for if Phillip had died, Ross would have replaced him at Sydney, in the higher post. King's prognostications suggested a prejudgment — coloured no doubt by the reports on Ross which Phillip had asked him to convey to his masters in England.

When King returned to Norfolk Island on 4 November 1791, he reported "discord and strife in every person's countenance, and in every corner of the island". He went on to say that upon landing "a general murmuring and discontent at Major Ross's conduct" assailed him from every description of people, and 158 convicts presented him with a signed petition against Ross's plan to force them to be self-sufficient by March 1792. Stripped of its verbiage, the convicts' complaint was against Ross's eagerness for the island to be self-supporting — a not too heinous ambition. But what was really worrying King was that unless Ross changed "from the language he now holds", he would pass on to London favourable accounts of his stewardship[120] which would conflict with those which King had so recently supplied. Yet Ross was entitled to do so for even King admitted that the crops wore "a most promising aspect", and within a month a wheat harvest of a thousand bushels had been gathered.[121] That there was animosity between the two is illustrated both by Clark's report that they "had words" a few days after King's return,[122] and by King's peevish dismantling of a large storehouse which Ross had erected for the harvest, but which King disliked.[123] Consequently, King's criticisms of Ross's administration ought to be judged against the background of his antipathy.

The effect on Ross of King's bitterness would have been minimal because they were together on the island for one month only. After almost a year with Hunter (who returned to Port Jackson per *Supply* on 11 February 1791), relations had soured to an icy bitterness. The Officers Mess had been a composite mess for both marine and naval officers, but so constant was the bickering within it that the naval officers boycotted it in early 1791 and established their own. It is possible that Hunter and the other naval officers anticipated the break up of the composite mess, because during the whole time that the second captain of *Sirius* messed with Ross, he did not produce the wine he had saved from the ship. Yet when the naval mess was established, he both produced it and used it during the remainder of their stay, well knowing that Ross had nothing better to drink than water.[124] Another instance was publicly displayed when the naval officers, including Hunter, boycotted Ross on the King's birthday. When Hunter was leaving the island for Port Jackson, Ross, in a conciliatory gesture, sent him some fowls. Hunter refused to accept them. Ross was deeply hurt and sent Ralph Clark to find out whether Hunter's complaint against him was a private or public one. Hunter replied "neither" and told Clark to tell Ross that if they ever met again, he hoped it would be on grounds of civility. Such an acidic reply was uncharacteristic of Hunter — he was not reported anywhere as having made a similar statement to anyone else. Clark pressed him, and Hunter revealed that young John Ross had told Mr Parker, the *Sirius* carpenter, that Major Ross was reporting Hunter to his seniors in the Admiralty at London. Clark felt that this was not so and when he returned, he told Ross, who questioned his son, who denied it.[125] Hunter's reason sounds flimsy and quickness to take offence was not a trait in his character; the real reason was probably the insult that Ross had given him in Sydney. In simple terms, it is probable that Hunter abhorred the man.

Others were also critical of Ross. It was the opinion of Doctor Harris that things would proceed much better at Norfolk Island if it were not for Ross, whom he found to be such a dominating character "that he will allow no one under him to be comfortable".[126] Meanwhile, at Port Jackson another doctor, Surgeon Jamieson, was defaming Ross's character. (When Ross later confronted him about it, he was evasive.) Clark thought Jamieson to be a "cunning villain",[127] but undoubtedly the scandal he had spread was accepted at Sydney as being the truth. A convict, Francis Folks, also attempted secretly to report Ross for cruelty: when told to copy some official books for Ross, he wrote a secret letter to Judge Advocate Collins in Sydney reporting Ross not only of cruelty and oppression, but of "every other crime that is possible for man to be guilty of". Ross discovered his misdemeanour and confined him in irons.[128]

Periodically, sections of the New South Wales Corps arrived from 15 April 1791.[129] They brought increasing troubles to the settlement, but probably none so vexing for Ross as Captain Hill and his arrogant detestation for Ross. Hill quarrelled with Ross almost from the day he arrived, and it was not only Ross with whom Hill could not agree. By late August, Faddy and Hill had not spoken for over two months, and both refused to sit on their horses together. Yet Clark found Hill to be a "genteel and well behaved man".[130] Relationships between the marines and the corps were so strained by then that Ross decided to send the corps some distance away to Phillipsburgh. This move gladdened Clark, who disliked their attempts — admittedly unsuccessful — to sow disaffection amongst the marine officers.[131] His opinion of the corps was not flattering, for he found its personnel to be "without exception, the most selfish set of men".[132] As an example, at Phillipsburgh a New South Wales Corps garrison court martial decided on 18 October to take no action against a soldier who appeared before it charged with an offence. Ross regarded this decision as unsatisfactory and sent Faddy to Hill with the offer of a marine court martial to assist in examining the proceedings. When Faddy relayed it to Hill, Hill abused him and threatened to take Faddy's sword and put him under arrest. Faddy reported Hill's extraordinary reaction to Ross, who decided that it merited a court martial and Hill was advised accordingly. However, there were not enough officers on the island, so the matter could not be heard till he returned to Port Jackson.

Possibly realizing that Ross's time on the island had almost expired, Hill now embarked on a campaign of insubordination. On 16 November 1791, a few weeks before Ross's departure, a group of disaffected convicts complained to Hill about Ross. Without informing Ross, and quite covertly, he eagerly took up their cause and recorded their evidence on oath before the Reverend Johnson (who had recently arrived from Port Jackson on the *Atlantic*) and Surgeon Balmain — both of whom disliked Ross. Whether or not these two knew that the convicts were lying is not recorded; certainly Clark did, for he described them as "rascals who would sell their father's life if they could gain by it".[133] In any case, Hill's covert action constituted another military offence, indicating that he felt no contrition for his previous behaviour, and that his dislike of Ross verged on hatred.

This was confirmed the very next day (17th) in the Hume Affair. Mr Hume, the Superintendent of Convicts, reported to Hill that Ross had forced him to sign a statement under duress. He advised that witnesses to Ross's misdemeanour were Faddy, Clark and Sergeant Kennedy. When Ross heard of the allegation, he arranged for all three to be examined on oath before the chaplain and Balmain; they denied Hume's allegation. Clark records that when Hume was confronted with this, he "crumbled", and revealed his duplicity.[134] The point of the incident was that it revealed the eagerness with which Hill would seize upon any allegation, no matter how insecure, in his vendetta against Ross.

In many ways, Ross's last days at Norfolk Island reversed his own last days at Port Jackson before he went to the island — days in which he had so disturbed Phillip and the colony as to bring it to the verge of a "general confusion". Now the position was reversed, for it was Ross who was the object of another's vitriol. Whereas Phillip had had to endure Ross's incorrigibility over a long period, Ross's discomfiture was to be relatively short-lived, for the marines' tour of duty at Norfolk Island was almost at an end.

The first element of their relief, the New South Wales Corps, had arrived on the *Supply* on 15 April 1791.[135] These had been followed by those on the *Mary Ann* on 15 August,[136] the *Salamander* on 16 September,[137] the *Atlantic* on 26 October,[138] and the *Queen* on 2 November.[139] After the relief of the two units, Ross and his marines departed on the *Queen* for Port Jackson where they arrived on 5 December prior to embarking on HMS *Gorgon* eight days later.[140]

And so ended the Norfolk Island period of their tour of duty. It had not been easy; it had started in near tragedy but gradually by the efforts and leadership of Ross, Clark and the marines generally, adversity had been turned into achievement. From the days in August 1790 when the unsupplemented stocks available on shore were 6,835 pounds flour, 320 pounds beef, 3,253 pounds pork, 500 pounds rice, and 200 bushels of wheat — all to feed 506 mouths[141] — to those of their departure when even the piqued Governor King grudgingly had to acknowledge the promising aspect of crops and a wheat harvest of a thousand bushels, the marines' achievement in providing subsistence had been significant. When there is added to this the construction of two towns and their attendant infrastructure, the tour had been of signal service to the island. Their one weakness had again been in the area of human relations. The army-navy rivalry and, to a lesser extent than at Port Jackson, Ross's propensity to upset his own officers, had provided the unfortunate ingredients. On balance, however, Ross and the marines had been most successful at Norfolk Island.

17

Phillip's Dispute with Dawes

Lieutenant William Dawes had travelled to the colony on the *Sirius*, and probably because it contained the only artillery in the early days of the settlement, he had remained aboard until 23 May 1788 when he joined the marine battalion on shore to replace Lieutenant William Collins,[1] who was about to be invalided to England.[2] Before landing, public orders had appointed him an artillery and engineer officer and as such the artillery ordnance of the colony was then placed under his charge. In late April, he began constructing a small artillery redoubt on the eastern side of Sydney Cove (at Bennelong Point) — the first military fortification in the country.[3]

The redoubt was begun in July 1788 and completed in November. A flagstaff was erected at it and two pieces of "iron ordnance" were placed in it.[4] On 1 January 1789, Collins recorded that the colours were flown from it,[5] and by the next month, Dawes had completed the construction of the fort's magazine and the ammunition of the settlement was then placed safely within its walls.[6] From the next King's birthday, the colony's artillery was fired from this fort at Bennelong Point until it was replaced in 1791 by a fort of eight embrazures constructed by Dawes at what is now Dawes Point.[7] These defence works had followed his construction of the observatory on the west point of the Cove, in which he stored the Astronomer Royal's instruments and began his prolific scientific and longitudinal observations. During the next few years Dawes served the colony unstintingly, not only in his scientific and military work, but also in exploration with Watkin Tench. As well, he surveyed allotments for settlers, supervised engineer tasks, and visited La Perouse at Botany Bay in February 1788 on Phillip's behalf, and in all these ways was valuable to Phillip, who wanted him to stay in the colony.[8] Dawes himself was keen to stay because no other astronomer had been appointed to replace him to continue the valuable work he had begun, and his father memorialized Lord Grenville to compensate his son for the heavy additional duties involved in his triple capacity as the colony's engineer, artillery officer, and astronomer.[9]

But Dawes was not only a scholar and a useful man; he was also a very religious man and a man of immovable principles. Southwell described him as being studious, kind to everyone, esteemed and respected, and "truly religious without any appearance of formal sanctity".[10] His intellectual frame of mind led him to form an obvious friendship with that other scholar of the settlement, Watkin Tench, and the two enjoyed each other's company and probably never more so than on their demanding and extensive expeditions of discovery. He possessed a pleasant personality which appealed to Elizabeth Macarthur, and with his friend Tench, he was a welcome and frequent member of her circle of friends.[11]

An indication of his strength of conscience was to be given on 13 December 1790. A few days earlier Mr McEntire, Phillip's gamekeeper, had been mortally speared by Aborigines whilst accompanying a marine party to the north arm of Botany Bay. As the Bid-ee-gal tribe of that area had been responsible for killing most of the seventeen whites since January 1788, Phillip — in his only departure from his normal humanitarian approach to Aborigines —

ordered a punitive (or deterrent) expedition of over forty men which was to be led by Tench and to include the duty officer, Lieutenant Dawes. At first Dawes refused to obey the order, and sent his refusal by letter to Captain Campbell. Campbell tried to dissuade him but Dawes remained adamant and Campbell was forced to inform Phillip who also, unsuccessfully, tried to gain Dawes' compliance rather than have him placed under arrest. In a severe struggle with his conscience, Dawes consulted the chaplain, and, taking his advice, then accompanied the party. However, upon his return he informed Phillip that he not only regretted having participated, but would not obey a similar order in future.[12] Phillip at first overlooked this insubordination by allocating Dawes to non-combat duties, but his attitude was a factor in his quarrel with Phillip a year later.

That quarrel occurred on 5 November 1791. Lord Grenville had suggested that Dawes, because of his usefulness, remain in the colony.[13] Phillip offered the extension to Dawes, on condition that Dawes acknowledge three improprieties and undertake no recurrence of them. These were: his purchase of convict rations contrary to repeated orders against the practice; his initial refusal to obey the Bid-ee-gal order of the previous December; and his unofficerlike behaviour to Phillip in front of Adjutant Long.[14] Dawes firmly denied all three charges. In answer to the first, he said that the flour he had purchased from the convict baker was flour that the baker had received as a personal perquisite. Consequently it was not the baker's ration but his own property which he was free to dispose of as he wished. He denied that he had ever purchased a convict's ration. Phillip dismissed this defence by revealing that a convict on oath before the magistrates had declared that he had made a practice of bartering flour for sugar from Dawes; moreover Major Ross had previously had to remind Dawes of the impropriety of purchasing peas from convicts.[15] Consequently Phillip's rebuttal is a strong one. To the second charge, Dawes confirmed his decision never to obey such an order; and to the third, that of impropriety to the Governor in the presence of the Adjutant by way of answering Phillip's accusation of leaving the observatory without sufficient cause, he had not meant any disrespect and apologized for it. To this explanation Phillip stated that expressions which Dawes had used were such that he could have been court martialled for them.[16] Phillip passed the matter to Lord Grenville who seems not to have taken it very seriously, for Dawes went on to become Governor of Sierra Leone.

That men as dedicated and honourable as Phillip and Dawes should have clashed was a sad outcome and the real cause was probably unstated in the correspondence. Both men had laboured unceasingly in a hostile and uncompromising new land and probably both were worn out by their exertions. Though Dawes did not acknowledge any physical fatigue, Phillip certain did. He had first asked to return temporarily to England on 15 April 1790 to attend to his private affairs, believing that the colony was sufficiently well established to permit his temporary absence.[17] However, in February the following year Grenville asked him to delay his return because of his value to the colony.[18] A similar offer by Ross to delay his return had been ignored. By March however Phillip's health had so deteriorated as to make his return an urgent necessity and he revealed to Lord Grenville that he had endured daily a pain his side for two years.[19] In the following November, within a fortnight of his clash with Dawes, Phillip wrote to Sir Joseph Banks: "My health is gone, and I am worn out by a pain which affects the left kidney. It is no longer in my power to go about as I have done". For this reason, he wanted to get to London to gain "some relief".[20] He felt constrained therefore to be permitted to resign.[21] It was not till 15 May 1792, however, that Grenville's successor, Lord Dundas, granted Phillip's request,[22] and following this, Phillip left New South Wales on the *Atlantic* on 11 December 1792. Shortly after arriving in

London, he was forced to resign the governorship because of continuing ill health.[23] It is probable therefore that Phillip's broken health, combined with Dawes' heightened sense of personal and social justice, contributed to what was a most regrettable breach.

18

The Second Fleet

While two companies of the marines were toiling at Norfolk Island, the other two were continuing their service at Port Jackson.[1] At both places, service was severe, but whereas those at Norfolk Island enjoyed ultimately a plentiful food supply, a change of surroundings, and a more equitable climate, life for those at Sydney continued to be dreary, hungry, and lonely. Impoverishment was all pervasive; the ration barely sustained subsistence; troops were shoeless and in tatters; life seemed as though it could hardly be worse — and yet worse it was to become when news of the loss of the *Sirius* broke upon them on 5 April. Thereupon, the severe measures which Phillip took to save the colony demanded an increased vigilance by the marines, for every morsel was precious and stood between the community and starvation. May 1790 was a terrible month: despair was on every countenance and hunger tortured every stomach. The ration was now so miserable that one elderly convict, probably Joseph Owen, whilst waiting at the store for his subsistence, collapsed from hunger, and died.[2] An autopsy revealed that his stomach was "quite empty".[3] Another convict, Joseph Elliott (alias Trimby) was caught stealing potatoes worth two pence halfpenny. Extreme hunger had forced his crime but such was the desperate need to conserve every ounce of food that he received three hundred lashes on his bare back with a cat-o'-nine-tails, his flour ration was stopped for six months, and he was chained for the same period to two other delinquents — all three being employed on road work.[4] Hunger drove others to similar acts of desperation, and when a goat owned by Surgeon White destroyed some vegetables growing in the garden of convict John Fuller, the court presided over by David Collins recommended that White make good Fuller's loss.[5] Collins recorded that so great was "the villainy of the people, or the necessities of the times", that a prisoner lying at the hospital from the effects of part of his five hundred lashes, removed the irons from one leg, and though still partly encumbered by the other, went out and robbed a farm. On being returned, "he received another portion of his punishment".[6] But not only convicts were driven to steal food: Private Thomas Paul, "a man of infamous character", whilst acting as guard over a garden, robbed from it and received five hundred lashes for his crime.[7] That it was hunger which drove men to steal was highlighted by the fact that the stealing was confined to Sydney Cove; at Rose Hill, where vegetables were more freely available, no thefts occurred.[8] Very little labour could be forced from the convicts because of their physical debility, and yet the wheat and barley required for the next season still had to be sown by them though it fell far short of what the colony required. By April and May, the famine was at its most serious; distress everywhere was excrutiating. Four months' flour and three months' supply of pork at half rations was all that remained. Surgeon White railed at what he felt was the British government's neglect: "Surely they have quite forgotten or neglected us" he wrote; to him New South Wales only merited "execrations and curses", and he felt the only possible course of action left was to "withdraw the settlement".[9]

But June 1790 was to bring changed fortune, and June 1790 was to be the turning point in the colony's fight for survival. The weather on 3 June was as miserable as the plight of the colony itself; it was cold; it rained constantly; and the wind blew tempestuously. Enduring its suffering with that forlorn numbness which derives from abject hopelessness, the colony was sheltering from so foul an afternoon when at half past three, "to the inexpressible satisfaction of every heart in the settlement",[10] the shout went out, "the flag's up".

Tench was sitting in his hut musing on his fate when he heard a clamour in the street. He got up, went to the door, opened it, and saw women with their children running about and kissing them. Every face had changed: countenances which previously had been furrowed by despair were now radiant with joy. Needing no further indication that the Second Fleet was probably off the Heads, he ran to a hill with his spy-glass, and with a fellow officer, saw that the South Head flag was up. They looked at each other: "We could not speak; we wrung each other by the hand, with eyes and hearts overflowing". Tench ran to the jetty; high talk and unabashed excitement reigned everywhere. Phillip was boarding his boat to meet the ship and Tench asked if he could accompany him; Phillip agreed, and as their boat neared the Heads, they saw the *Lady Juliana*, commanded by Lieutenant Thomas Edgar, entering. Phillip transferred to a fishing boat and returned to Government House, but Tench pushed his boat through the wind and rain until at last he saw that "blessed word — London". His boat's crew shrieked, "Pull away, my lads; she is from Old England . . . hurrah for a belly full of news from friends". Shortly they boarded the ship. Breathlessly, they asked a thousand questions; letters were produced and torn open with agitated and trembling haste; news burst upon them "like meridian splendour on a blind man".[11]

The news included the illness of George III and his subsequent restoration to health; the French Revolution; the imminent arrival of the New South Wales Corps commanded by

Major Francis Grose, and the disaster which had befallen the *Guardian* in hitting an iceberg on 23 December 1789 off the Cape of Good Hope and her subsequent demise in its harbour. Had she avoided the mishap, Phillip would have been saved much anguish, for she contained the answers to many of his requests which he had sent back by the First Fleet: answers such as convict supervisors, fruit trees, and special convict craftsmen. Moreover, her arrival in January or February would have prevented the 1790 famine and the loss of the *Sirius*. But the excitement of the occasion superceded all conjecture and on the following Wednesday, Phillip suspended all labour; everyone in the colony attended church to give "a general thanksgiving to Almighty God" not, as one would have expected, for their own deliverance, but for the King's recovery — surely a remarkable selflessness. The chaplain preached on the text from Proverbs 8:15 — "By me Kings reign and Princes decree justice", and after the service the officers dined with the Governor. That evening, an address to the King pledging their "zeal and fidelity" to him was agreed upon and presented two days later to Phillip for transmission to London.[12]

However, the joy which was diffused by the *Lady Juliana*'s arrival was considerably checked by other unwelcome news which she brought: she had aboard 222 females — "a cargo so unnecessary and unprofitable", remarked Collins, "instead of a cargo of provisions".[13] In addition, she had brought so little food that the ration could be increased by only one-and-a-half pounds of flour a week. The other alarming news she brought was that three other transports, the *Neptune*, *Surprize*, and *Scarborough* (on its second voyage to Port Jackson) with 1,000 convicts would arrive any day. The *Lady Juliana* convicts were disembarked on 11 June 1790, for such had been the fury of the weather that it had taken three days for her to travel from the Heads to Sydney Cove. It was then seen that though they had been well treated, many were infirm with old age and "utterly incapable of any exertion toward their own maintenance".[14] One ray of joy however was shed when the storeship *Justinian* arrived on 29 June. She had actually arrived off Sydney Heads a day before the *Lady Juliana*, but such had been the winds and the current that she had been driven as far north as Port Stephens where she was very nearly lost in the frightful gale. What her loss would have done to the colony is unthinkable, for her cargo was full and valuable, and, for a while, restored the colony to its former plenty.

Towards the end of June, the rest of the Second Fleet arrived: the *Surprize* on the 25th, and the *Neptune* and *Scarborough* on the 28th. On board the *Neptune* was Lieutenant John Macarthur of the New South Wales Corps with his young wife and child; but the rest of the three ships' convict passengers were mainly ill and emaciated from neglect by the ships' commanders, and quite unfit for work. "Naked, filthy, dirty, lousy wretches, many of them unable to stand",[15] their condition was not only cruel to themselves, but to the colony as well. One female convict who had arrived in the *Lady Juliana* wrote in a letter to a friend in England, "Oh! if you had but seen the shocking sight of the poor wretches that came out in the three ships, it would make your heart bleed. They were almost dead; very few could stand, and they were obliged to sling them as you would goods, and hoist them out of the ship. They were so feeble, and they died 10 or 12 a day after they landed." She went on to say that Phillip was angry with the ships' captains and threatened to report them to London for murder, for they had withheld food so as to make a greater profit on the voyage, and this had reduced so many of their convict passengers to death or its proximity.[16] By noon on 28 June, after two hundred sick had been landed from the different transports, Collins described the appalling scene:

> The west side [of Sydney Cove] afforded a scene truly distressing and miserable; upward of 30 tents were pitched in front of the hospital, all of which, as well as the hospital and the adjacent huts, were filled with

people, many of whom were labouring under the complicated diseases of scurvy and the dysentery, and others either in the last stages of those terrible disorders, or yielding to the attacks of an infectious fever.

The appearance of those who did not require medical assistance, was lean and emaciated. Several of those miserable people died in the boats as they were rowed to shore, or on the wharf as they were lifting out of the boats; both the living and the dead exhibiting more horrid spectacles than had ever been witnessed in this country.[17]

Many had been confined in irons and chained together in water feet deep; only a few at a time were permitted on deck, and this had encouraged disease. On the *Neptune* some had died in chains and their neighbours had concealed the dead bodies so as to gain the extra rations until such time as the stench caused the corpse's place to be found by someone in authority.

The cause of this outrage lay in the contract let by the British government to the London merchants Calvert, Camden, and King, by which they were paid £17.7s.6d for each convict embarked. This permitted the ships' captains to pocket profit and consequently they had no interest in keeping the convicts alive, for, as Collins noted, "the dead were more profitable than the living".[18] The enormity of the horror can be judged from table 13, which is based on that prepared by Tench.[19] The figure for deaths and those landed ill compares with the First Fleet statistics of 24 dead on the voyage and 30 landed sick. Moreover, of those landed sick from the Second Fleet, 124 later died in hospital. Consequently, 26 per cent died on the voyage and when to this is

Table 13 Death and sickness rates of Second Fleet convicts, June 1790

	No. Embarked	No. died on voyage	No. landed sick	Percentage dead
Neptune	530	163	269	31%
Surprize	252	42	121	17%
Scarborough	256	68	96	27%
	1038	273	486	26%

Source: Tench, *Sydney's First Four Years*, 230.

added the subsequent deaths in hospital, the mortality figure rises to 37 per cent. In a display of the grossest bad taste, several of the perpetrators of this ghastly outrage, the ships' captains, opened shops on shore which sold, at extortionate prices, the rations which had been withheld from their starving convict passengers.[20]

In what way the Marine Corps responded to the sudden calamity is not stated, but it is reasonable to assume that marines assisted the parties sent into the woods to collect the medicinal berry juice which surgeons used as an antiscorbutic.[21] And no doubt the marines in some way helped to erect the canvas prefabricated hospital brought out on the *Justinian*,[22] and the many tents of which the chaplain stated there were ninety to a hundred.[23] To cope with the 1,715 people now at Port Jackson, Lieutenant Long again was appointed to act as town adjutant till further orders.[24]

However, the stores brought by the Second Fleet eased the stringent situation in the colony — the battle for survival had been won. The weekly ration was increased to 8 pounds (3.6 kg) of flour, and either 7 pounds (3.2 kg) of beef or 4 pounds (1.8 kg) of pork,[25] and this was in spite of the 1790 drought which had ruined the winter crops of potatoes and wheat. The number of convicts at Sydney Cove was reduced as more were sent to Rose Hill where, by November, two hundred acres (more than 80 ha) had been cleared. Forty-one houses had been erected there, each consisting of two rooms and a chimney; as well, the barracks, a store, Government House, and stone barracks for the officers, had also been constructed. The marine detachment there in November was not a large one: to guard the five hundred convicts, a guard of only two officers and twenty-seven troops was necessary.[26] Consequently, the marine presence could not have been oppressive.

Tench was interested in the farming achievements of James Ruse and visited him at Rose Hill in November. He had just sown wheat and maize and as this was the first time he had planted maize, he expressed apprehension about its outcome. Tench noted that his method was to clear land, burn trees, dig in the ashes and grass from a compost pit, and hoe eight or nine rods a day. He had only his wife to help him at the time, she being the convict Elizabeth Perry of the *Lady Juliana* whom he had married on 5 September 1790. He confided to Tench that his greatest problem was not the heavy labour but the nightly robbing of his crops by convicts.[27]

19

The New South Wales Corps

The Second Fleet brought the first contingent of the New South Wales Corps. The balance would arrived in HMS *Gorgon* on 21 September 1791, and (with Major Grose) on the *Pitt* on 14 February 1792. Phillip, in his despatch to Nepean way back on 9 July 1788, had criticized the marine officers for not helping with the convicts and for objecting to Criminal Court duty. Phillip had suggested that the successor force should have a strength of from four hundred to six hundred.[1] The first official indication that the marines would not be replaced by another unit of the Marine Corps was in a draft on 14 May 1789 from the Secretary of War which stated that they were to be succeeded by an infantry unit from the British Army, specially raised for service in the colony, and whose commanding officer was to be taken from the list of majors. The reason for not replacing the marines with marines was not given till Lord Grenville wrote to Phillip on 19 June 1789, revealing the cause to be the discontents of the officers and the desire of most of the marine detachment to return home.[2] Consequently, the wish expressed in 1787 by Ross to Nepean before the First Fleet left Portsmouth that creditable service by the marines would enhance the corps' standing, had been unfilfilled.[3] They were to be replaced not by a Marine Corps unit, but by a unit from the marines' historical opponent — the Army.

Some comparisons between the New South Wales Corps and the Marine Corps are appropriate. The New South Wales Corps, at a strength of 319,[4] was to be a third larger than the marine detachment, as it would have to provide for the larger population now resident at Port Jackson and Norfolk Island. Its commander and company commanders had raised their own companies for which they had received a bounty of £3.3s per recruit.[5] By contrast, the marine detachment had been raised by voluntary enlistment without the involvement of its officers, and so heavy had been the response that the marine divisional commanders had been able to select a better quality soldier. When the decision to raise the New South Wales Corps was made, Sir George Young of the War Office on 8 June 1789 appointed Major Francis Grose of the Twenty-ninth Foot Regiment as its commanding officer; recruiting then began and full strength took three months to achieve, whereas the Marine Corps detachment had been filled in two weeks.[6] Recruit specifications were that ensigns were not to be under sixteen years, all recruits were to be at least 5 feet 4½ inches (about 1.64 m), and were not to be younger than sixteen nor older than thirty.[7] Such strictures do not appear to have been placed on the marines, all of whom were eager volunteers.

The same eagerness to enlist was not experienced by the New South Wales Corps, for Grose found it necessary to complete his enlistments from deserters in London's Savoy Military Prison, rationalizing his action on the grounds that desertion would be impossible from Botany Bay.[8] Some enlistments came from defaulters who joined the corps rather than face an army court martial from which sentences of up to one thousand lashes could be imposed. Thus Private William Dyson of the Queen's Dragoon Guards, when sentenced by a regimental court martial in 1791, opted to avoid the lash by agreeing to serve in the New South Wales Corps for life.[9] Marine recruitment was not subject to any such parleying; its service was not an alternative to something less desired or less dreaded. Because its Botany Bay detachment was filled in six days and because the large numbers who applied permitted culling of undesirables, it did not have to enlist any soldiers from jails. Nor did it have to issue any order such as Grose received, that soldiers were only to be allowed ashore during the voyage in the company of NCOs who were to be answerable for their conduct.[10] To at least one sergeant, the prospect of such service lacked appeal: his party arrived at Port Jackson without him — "he having deserted on their leaving England".[11] And yet in spite of these early suggestions that the quality of the new unit's troops might not be the equal of the Marine Corps', the Army's attitude of an assumed superiority over the Marine Corps persisted. In a letter from Captains Hill and Patterson of the New South Wales Corps written to Sir George Young on 16 September 1789, they imply that the purity of the Army ought not to be sullied by any influx of marines into it; consequently they expressed some indignation at the temerity of Captain Nepean, a marine, claiming seniority in the Army, and pointed out that even no less a person than Lord Percy was refused a request to bring a marine friend of his into a line regiment.[12] Obviously the old rivalry was still alive.

As the troops of the New South Wales Corps disembarked, they moved into the marine quarters left ready for them after the two marine companies had transferred to Norfolk Island three months earlier. Straightaway, a subaltern's detachment was sent to Rose Hill to serve in conjunction with the marines there.[13] One of its officers was Lieutenant John MacArthur, and he and his wife Elizabeth quickly gathered around them a circle of friends, of whom Tench and Dawes were valued members.[14] Another officer, Captain Hill, complained repeatedly even though he moved into an established military barrack — a luxury not available to marines upon their arrival. He objected to living in a "miserable thatched hut" with no kitchen or garden; he disliked living on salted meat and had not had "a mouthful of fresh meat"; there were no condiments, and the price of everything was exorbitant.[15] Disciplinary offences soon occurred: two NCOs were reduced to the ranks for irregular behaviour;[16] a soldier was court martialled for disobeying Tench in a punitive expedition against Aborigines at Botany Bay;[17] but when Private Francis MacKewen sold some of his personal issues to two convicts, it was they who were punished and not he.[18]

Although any comparisons of the two corps are limited by the shortness of the time that both spent together in the colony, the inheritance by the New South Wales Corps of an established military station was an undeniable advantage which materially lightened its service. Not only was hut accommodation immediately available but military routine had been established, and the marines could obviously help the new soldiers become acclimatized. Geographically, the Marine Corps explorations had revealed the possibilities of the Sydney Plain, thereby reducing the need for their successors to mount the exacting expeditions of exploration which had been so necessary in the colony's early days. Commerce, though rudimentary in form, was functioning in shops, and in an increasing variety and availability of goods, particularly as traders were now coming from India and America. Correspondence with home was now available through the regular arrivals and departures of ships for England. This made life for the new men more bearable than it had been for their pioneering predecessors, but the greatest boon enjoyed by the New South Wales Corps was food. That one commodity which had been so cruelly denied the marines was now more assured. There was little likelihood the famine or the two-and-a-half years' isolation experienced by the marines would happen again, for the situation had greatly changed. Whereas no ships from

England had arrived in that lonely period, no less than eleven had arrived from England in the first four months of the new corps' service at Port Jackson. Consequently, the new corps' tour of duty could hold promise of being easier and more pleasant; whether it would prove more beneficial to the colony than that of the marines, remained to be seen.

20

Homeward Bound

By late 1791, the marines' tour of duty was drawing to its close. Their excitement had run high at the thought of going home ever since HMS *Gorgon* had arrived at six o'clock on the morning of 21 September. She was so heavily laden with six months stores for the marines that she touched bottom during her tow by *Supply* up the harbour to Sydney Cove.[1] Tench could not contain his joy: "If I be allowed to speak of my own feelings ... we hailed it with rapture and exultation".[2] However, their departure was still three months away and half the detachment was still at Norfolk Island. Dawes, Tench, Shairp, J. Johnson, and G. Johnston were still undecided whether to stay or go home with the rest of their comrades: now that the settlement had become a more pleasant place than it had been a year previously, it was developing an attractiveness for them. But as the day of departure approached and thoughts of home became stronger, all bar George Johnston and Judge Advocate Collins were to return. Collins learnt from his wife that he would be passed over for promotion in the marines and placed on half pay when the Marine Corps returned home. This decision was Nepean's and was made on the basis that Phillip would be offering Collins a company in the New South Wales Corps. Phillip twice made the offer but Collins refused it on four grounds.

Firstly, he would have to serve under Captain Nepean, who was his junior. Secondly, it would create conflict between his civil and military duties. Thirdly, it would keep him in New South Wales, a place of which he was "heartily tired". And finally, he very much disliked the type of officer in the New South Wales Corps. Collins also said that although he was keen to return to his family in England and to do so in the company of those marines who travelled in the *Gorgon*, he so disliked Major Ross that he preferred to stay rather than travel in the same ship. Moreover, he felt an obligation to remain with Phillip as his secretary out of the respect which he held for him, by which he was "blended in every concern".[3]

There were two groups of marines who would not be returning with the main body. The first group, the sixty men commanded by Poulden and assisted by Davey and Timins,[4] was held by Phillip until the last of the New South Wales Corps arrived with Major Grose on the *Pitt* in February 1792. These sixty ultimately went home on the *Atlantic* in December 1792.[5] The other group was the marine-settlers who had decided to stay. These included the twenty-eight privates who left Port Jackson on 26 October to become settlers at Norfolk Island,[6] and the eight settled at the Field of Mars in Sydney. On 31 October, Lieutenant Creswell embarked the marines' advance party of twenty-three on the *Gorgon*[7] and by 15 November the ship was ready to sail as soon as Major Ross and his marines arrived from Norfolk Island.

In the meantime, the ship's master, Captain Parker, and Mrs Parker were entertained graciously by Phillip, and Mrs Parker formed a high opinion of the love which so many had for him. This she expressed in a revealing tribute: she likened him to the monarch of Great Britain in that he could justly be called, "the Father of his people". She observed that the convict who had forsaken his crimes looked up to him with reverence and enjoyed the rewards of his industry "in peace and thankfulness".[8] Meanwhile, all sorts of Australiana were being loaded aboard the *Gorgon*: possums, kangaroos, shrubs, birds, and one hundred tubs of plants together with the two or three cases of wine sent by Phillip to be drunk by the officers when the ship was off Cape Horn.

At the same time the *Supply* too was almost ready for her return voyage to England. She had been shield and buckler to the tiny colony through all the days of its vicissitudes, and deep feelings were felt at her approaching departure. She left on 26 November, and the feelings of those who saw her move down the harbour were captured by Tench. "It was impossible to view our separation with insensibility: — the little ship which had so often agitated our hopes and fears; which ... we had learned to regard as part of ourselves; whose doors of hospitality had ever been thrown open to relieve our accumulated wants, and chase our solitary gloom!"[9] She arrived at Portsmouth on 21 April 1792 carrying Lieutenant Creswell and Phillip's despatches.[10]

Eventually the *Queen* arrived from Norfolk Island bearing Ross and the long-awaited contingent. Ross's return had been awaited with apprehension, for it rekindled memories of his former turbulence and disturbance to the settlement. The chaplain feared a recurrence; David Collins wrote that it was the prayer of everyone in the colony that Ross's stay would be as brief as possible.[11] And as if Port Jackson was designed now to bring out the worst in him, Ross fought a duel with Captain Hill of the New South Wales Corps on 13 December, just before he and the rest of the marines boarded the *Gorgon*.[12] Scott records that the marines were accompanied by their twenty-one wives, forty-three children, and four convict children.[13]

It was probably as well for the settlement that on 17 December, all farewells completed, the *Gorgon* weighed anchor and moved out to the stream. Shortly, however, two convict stowaways were detected and returned on shore, and at seven o'clock on Sunday night, 18 December, she sailed further down the harbour, finally clearing the Heads at eight o'clock next morning.[14] By Christmas Day, the ship was off Lord Howe Island where the sea was calm enough to enable Sergeant Scott to row a boat to the shore in a vain attempt to catch some birds — a failure for which he compensated by buying a pair of live pigeons from someone more successful.[15] On 5 January 1792, they passed the northern tip of New Zealand and saw a great number of whales and albatross. Apparently Ralph Clark had lost his sea legs because he was seasick for the first few weeks out of Port Jackson while he prepared the marines' accounts.[16] The thoughts of home-coming which throughout the five long years of his absence had never left him, were now strongly upon him and on 3 February he remembered Alicia's birthday with a love which, in spite of his affair with Mary Branham, had been his mainstay and constant solace. Cape Horn was passed on 8 February in weather which was stormy and so close to freezing that several penguins visited the ship shortly after. Huge ice fields were seen: Clark sighted one iceberg which was eighteen miles long; and so extensive was the ice field that Scott was still counting nineteen icebergs twelve days later.[17] Shortly after, the ship was hit by terrible gales which split sails and caused it to be laid to. On 12 March they reached the Cape of Good Hope where Clark, hoping that their stay would not be a long one because of his urgent wish to get home, received a letter "from my beloved . . . for which I return the thanks of a fond husband".[18] At the Cape they took aboard the convict escapee Mary Bryant and her child. Bryant, her husband, and a small party had escaped two years earlier from Port Jackson on their epic voyage via Batavia. Mary and the child were the last survivors at the Cape, though the child was to die a month later.[19] On 6 April the *Gorgon* left for England, and though it was rumoured that she would call at Ascension, Clark earnestly hoped against it for he wished "every day more and more to get home".[20] Although his wish was not granted, the ship stayed at Ascension for only two days. On 1 May, an incredible coincidence was reported by Clark: a shark was caught from which, when opened, a Book of Common Prayer was retrieved, quite undefaced and owned by Francis Carty, a convict who had sailed on the First Fleet to Botany Bay almost five years before.[21] By now Clark's impatience was developing an increasing intensity, for though he had never been a user of profane language, he now could utter, "I wish to Christ a breeze would spring up and let us get home".[22]

But the hearts of those aboard were filled with a mingled joy — joy at the prospect of home-coming hourly closer, but sadness at the wives and children who had died since before arriving at the Cape of Good Hope. The first had been that of Judith Doherty on 21 February who left three small children. From then onwards, nine children of marines died until the last recorded death was that of Sergeant Hume's wife on 20 May. Clark attributed the cause of the child deaths to excessive heat, and when the youngest child of Sergeant Gilbourne died, Clark was deeply saddened: "poor little John", he wrote, had been a "fine child" but the temperatures which had been as "hot as hell" had been "playing the devil with the children".[23] This melancholy end to a tour of duty so close to its completion was made all the more tragic by the recollection that those taken had survived such difficulties at Port Jackson. The *Gorgon* completed its long voyage at Spithead on 19 June 1792 with Clark's heart gladdened to learn that as the *Supply* had arrived, his Betsy would have received the letters he sent by it, for which he thanked God.[24]

Those marines still detained in Port Jackson then left by the *Atlantic* at 7 a.m. on 11 December 1792.[25] Phillip accompanied them and had been farewelled with every display of genuine sincerity and respect. As he boarded his boat from the east side with the three marine officers who were to accompany him, the New South Wales Corps paid him "the honours due to his rank and situation in the colony".[26] He had personally directed every undertaking in the colony since its formation[27] and had tended it with infinite tact, foresight, and forbearance. He had been guided by discretion and the most humanitarian of principles, and had insisted that there could be no slavery in a free land: convicts had been neither treated nor regarded as slaves. His position had been one of lonely isolation; he had had no one to turn to; no confidante. He had gained strength from his own resolve, expressed to Sir Joseph Banks, never to swerve from a line of conduct "which I laid down for myself the day I embarked and which had the good of the service on which I am employed for its object. I have in no one instance ever consulted my own."[28] The *Atlantic*, after clearing the Horn on 17 January 1793 and the Falkland Islands three days later, called at Rio de Janeiro, and spent most of February there. At six o'clock on the evening of 19 May, she made a brief call at Falmouth, where Phillip left her on the 22nd, and next day she anchored off Spithead. On 24 May, the marines landed, as Easty sensitively described it, "to our unspeakable joy in old England",[29] and with those who elected to serve on rather than be discharged, Easty rejoined his division after six years' absence. Those who were discharged from ill health or who were "unserviceable", as the marine regulation put it, were allowed to keep their clothing and uniform unless it had been issued less than eight months before, whereupon coats and hats were recalled for the use of recruits.[30]

Very soon after arrival, Ross began to endure the retribution which his actions at Port Jackson had been so steadily accumulating. Attacks sprang from those who had savoured for so long their thirst for revenge. First among them was Meredith, who lost no time in mounting his onslaught. Within days of the *Gorgon*'s return, he reminded the Admiralty that in March 1790 Ross had ordered him to be court martialled for "behaving highly improper as an officer", and for "the subversion of all subordination to military discipline".³¹ When Phillip had forwarded the papers to London, in April 1790, Meredith had told him that he wanted the general court martial to be held as soon as possible after his return to England because of his innocence and his ability to justify his conduct.³² Now that he was back in England, he moved with speed and a determined persistence to use the general court martial not only to clear his reputation, but also as a device to destroy and humiliate Ross. Such was his determination that within a fortnight of his return, he had written two letters to the Admiralty and one to Ross, all requesting a speedy hearing, and by 30 June 1792, Stephens of the Admiralty ordered Ross to prepare his evidence. Without awaiting the outcome of the trial, the Admiralty on 5 July, in an extraordinary vote of confidence in Meredith, made Meredith's promotion to captain substantive.³³ On 17 July, Stephens told Ross (who was then serving in London) to lose no time in getting to Plymouth for the trial; but on 1 August, Ross sought to delay the case by expressing doubts as to the capacity of General Collins, commander of the Plymouth division, to hold the trial because some of Ross's witnesses were still at Port Jackson.³⁴ Meredith's response to this was swift: on 4 August, he wrote to Collins expressing his keenness for the court martial to be held.³⁵ General Collins referred both letters to Stephens, who replied that the Admiralty had ordered Meredith's trial to proceed without delay.³⁶ It began on 3 September with Colonel Thomas Duval as president, and after being adjourned to the 18th, it found from the evidence that Ross's charge was not only groundless but malicious.³⁷ The charge was groundless because, the court found, Ross had been unable to prove his allegation, which the court felt was of so trivial a nature as to have been satisfied by Meredith's apology at the time. The court announced that not only was the apology "ample atonement", but also that Ross's charge was "an unjustifiable assertion". As for the charge being malicious, the court so described it because of the unconcionable duration of Meredith's arrest (three years), and the "unusual and unnecessary severity of it". Meredith was then honourably acquitted and removed of any imputation against his character or reputation. Moreover, the court advised that it "unreservedly" agreed with the "very respectable" character references submitted on Meredith's behalf, and that as recompense for the "injustice" done him, it recommended to General Collins that not only should Meredith's acquittal be read in open court, but also its declaration as to his exemplary character.[38]

Meredith's exoneration was complete; Ross on the other hand had been exposed and crushed by a damning indictment announced with barely concealed relish. He appears to have foreseen the outcome and tried to avoid being present when the verdict was announced: a few days before the verdict, he asked for leave of absence to return to London ostensibly to complete the detachment's unfinished business but the Admiralty firmly rejected his requests.[39] And so Meredith emerged with the "respect of his corps" and went on to become a major general. Ross received neither promotion nor recognition from his masters: even his brevet rank was not made substantive. The most the Admiralty would do for him was, upon his transfer to the Chatham Division, to credit him with the sea duty time which had accrued to him in the Plymouth Division.[40]

But before Ross could recover from the humiliation which the terms of the court's decision had heaped upon him, Tench then moved for his share of retribution by also applying to General Collins for a general court martial to clear his reputation of the stain of Ross's comments at Meredith's court martial. He then went further: he asked that Ross be charged with "tyranny and oppression" for his own three-year arrest in March 1788. Tench was specific in his request: he wanted Ross charged under Article 21, Section 4, of the Articles of War.[41] It now appeared that unless the Admiralty acted firmly, there was no knowing how many courts martial would be requested; it therefore resiled from opening a Pandora's box and asked Tench to be "sensible" now that over three years had passed, or that if he was determined to prosecute Ross, he must specify the details and instances of his charges before the Admiralty would consider granting his request. Tench did not proceed. Like so many other of the Botany Bay officers, he went on to promotion, becoming a lieutenant general; Dawes became governor of Sierra Leone; Davey and David Collins became lieutenant governors of Tasmania.

Ross thereafter appears to have been shunted around: when he had returned from Sydney, he had been posted first to London, and then to Plymouth. Sagging under the combined weight of Lord Grenville's official censure and that of Meredith's court martial, he apparently became bitterly resentful: when he was appointed to rejoin his division at Chatham on 22 November 1792 he failed to do so till 13 December when he was ordered to St Alban's as its recruiting officer.[42] He spent a mere month there before being sent to Brentford in the same capacity. After seven months there he was shifted again on 25 August 1793 to Ipswich as its recruiting officer, and it was in that posting that he died at Brompton on 9 June 1794.[43] His death was recorded in the Ipswich Journal of 28 June:

> On the 9th instant, died at Brompton, Major Robert Ross of the Chatham Division of Marines, and late Lieutenant Governor of New South Wales.[44]

Similar announcements appeared in *The Times* of 19 June 1794; and the *Morning Chronicle* of 21 June,[45] and *The Scots Magazine* of 1794. However his death certificate given by two doctors was dated 7 June 1798.[46] Moreover, the staff major of marines who completed Ross's record of service, though stating that Ross died on 9 June 1794, at home, whilst posted on recruiting service at Ipswich, proceeded to date the return as having been compiled three months previously — that is, on 6 March 1794. However, both these dates must be taken as errors, especially as Major General Tupper, general officer commanding at Chatham, advised the Admiralty of Ross's death as having occurred on 9 June 1794.[47]

As for Ralph Clark, after his return to England he was appointed to 100 Company, Chatham, and on 1 May 1793, boarded HMS *Tartar* with son Ralph for the West Indies. Shortly after his departure, his beloved wife Alicia died whilst giving birth to a stillborn child. But, probably before he could be given the news, his son Ralph died of yellow fever, and on the same day, he himself was killed on the same ship fighting the French at Haiti in 1794. Thus the small family for which he had suffered so much in New South Wales came to an end.

Many of those marines who came to New South Wales would have lived to see with satisfaction their corps recognized by royal order on 29 April 1802 as the Royal Marine Corps. The order, from George III, was signed by one of the corps' most staunch supporters — Evan Nepean, who by 1802 had become Secretary to the Admiralty.[48] By this honour, parity with the army had been recognized at last.

Conclusion

An Evaluation

Thus the marines' tour of duty had run its course. For four years they had been the guardians of the struggling community during which all but the most resolute optimists despaired of success. During this vital period, they had provided the indispensable backbone of discipline and order whilst their officers, in conjunction with Governor Phillip and his small civil staff, had laid the foundations of an organized society. They had shared its wants, known its hardships, endured its isolation, and suffered its disappointment. They had been aware of shortcomings within their own ranks; of tensions between the officers; of their commanding officer's turbulent leadership; and of unpleasant differences between him and the Governor. And to their disappointment, they had learnt that such was their reputation in London that they had been replaced with a unit not from their own corps, but from their opponents' — the Army. The more thoughtful among them must have wondered how their service would be judged. Would their tour be seen as a success or a failure? How would they fare in any evaluation? Today, with the benefit of intervening history, a judgment ought fairly to be made if only to test the hazy, unconsidered view which lingers with many who, in confusion, apply the New South Wales Corps' reputation to the Marine Corps. An evaluation of the marines' service cannot sustain that contention.

As it is usual for an evaluation of military performance to be made by assessing achievement against the aims originally set, the aims given to the marines ought to be recalled. As given by Lord Sydney they were: that the detachment was to form a military establishment on shore for the dual purpose of protecting the settlement against Aborigines, and preserving good order.[1] In considering those limited objectives, one is struck by the extent to which the marines liberally exceeded them, for marine service was given to far more facets of colonial life than these. They had explored the Sydney Plain and revealed its agricultural potential, its river-pattern, and likely communication pattern for future construction. Such exploration dispelled ignorance of the settlement's hinterland and notified the colony both of its potential and of the setting in which it was located. Moreover, neither at Port Jackson nor at Norfolk Island had the marines sought a privileged position in the issue of rations, for they had accepted Phillip's demand that there be no distinction between theirs and that of the convicts. During the famines in both places, they had contributed to their own maintenance by growing crops, and at Sydney even officers had established gardens and stock to reduce the demand on the public store. Their service at Norfolk Island had materially alleviated the growing supply crisis at Sydney and thereby contributed to Sydney's early viability, as had their service at the Rose Hill–Parramatta outstation. Nowhere had they exercised their authority repressively; there was no terrorizing, as was later to occur under their successors — for example when New South Wales Corps soldiers destroyed the home of John Baughan in 1796.[2] Nor was there a tyrannical attitude adopted by the military generally towards civil officers — about which Hunter was later forced to complain.[3] In fact, such had been the moderation of their yoke that it had permitted the birth of a distinctive social identity in which an air of independence and an irreverant attitude to authority was making its first, though timid, appearance.

Marine relationships with the Aborigines had likewise been restrained in spite of the invidious position in which the marines had been placed in carrying out patrols against them on the orders of others. But even when so ordered, massacres and brutalities were not committed, and on the one occasion they were asked to so act, it was from a marine officer, Dawes, that the objection came. The detachment itself, as distinct from Ross, cooperated with the civil authority; no attempt was made to overturn that authority as was made by the New South Wales Corps in 1808, and had Ross attempted to do so, it is most likely that he would have failed for want of support from his officers because of their dislike of him, their respect for Phillip, and the standard of their character as exemplified in officers such as Tench, Dawes and Clark. The general quality of the marine who came to New South Wales was, from his behaviour in the colony, superior to his counterpart in many parts of the Army. Thus there were no murders committed by marines; they attended church parades without demur and showed a respect for religion which Marsden was later to find wanting in their successors;[4] and by their general demeanour, they made for a cohesiveness of society rather than the divisiveness created by their successors. Consequently, no complaint was made against them as was made against their successors by the Hawkesbury settlers to Bligh in 1806.[5]

The evidence indicates that their service to the colony was sound. The colony had progressed during their time: Tench wrote about its feeling "consequential" enough to envisage the construction of imposing buildings around a "magnificent square";[6] and Private Easty, as he boarded the *Gorgon*, felt that the state of the colony was "far better" than it had ever been: its wheat was ready for harvest; the hard work of clearing land had now made much country fit for cultivation; the clay made fine bricks so that building construction was fast; and huts were "everywhere". His only regret was the lack of a church.[7] Phillip agreed and, writing at the time of the marines' departure, acknowledged that though flour was temporarily short, crops were flourishing.[8] The marines had not been the farmers, but they had helped in the colony's orderly development.

The question remains as to why, with their performance so sound, they were not replaced by a unit of their own corps. In some way the Marine Corps reputation had been tarnished. Major Ross had wanted the detachment to enhance the corps' reputation, to give such creditable service as to lift the corps from that "subordinate obscurity" which had hitherto been its status.[9] As it was to the Army that the corps had been "subordinate", the replacement of it by an Army unit indicated that the Corps had muffed its opportunity to eclipse its opponent to become "an active Corps" which the government could, with confidence, use in the future.[10] Grenville had told Phillip in June 1789 that the reasons for recalling the marines were the "discontents" which had surfaced in the unit, and the widespread desire of its personnel to return home.[11] Two years later, however, in acknowledging Phillip's complaint about Ross and Campbell, Grenville severely condemned the pair of them. He told Phillip that their behaviour had been "ill calculated to promote that good understanding so essentially necessary for securing the prosperity of the colony". He expressed the opinion that it was reasonable to expect that officers would "avoid any nice distinctions in point of duty", and warned that the future prospect of officers would be judged on the way they conducted themselves when confronted by those occasions in which details were not expressly stated in instructions.[12] This censure reached Phillip before Ross left for England but we do not know whether he passed it on to Ross.[13] The government's disapproval, therefore, though falling primarily on Ross and Campbell, fell also on the detachment generally — and it was that injustice which hurt its other members: the writer of a letter to *The Bee* in March 1791, after acknowledging the differences which had occurred between Ross and Phillip, expressed the general disappointment that their altercation had deprived the detachment of the credit due to it for its achievements. He expressed his indignation with candour: "It is a grievous hardship that unconcerned individuals . . . should be . . . deprived of that merit which is so dearly bought by their services in this country".[14] He hoped that those marines whose reputation had been injured would receive justice upon their return to England by those in authority investigating matters to bring out the truth. The evidence justifies his complaint, for in spite of poor leadership the detachment had successfully served the colony's interests. Unfortunately Ross had failed his unit's reputation and in so doing had caused those in official places to deny it that credit justifiably due to it. But distance from the colony had misplaced the government's criticism; those at Sydney knew the real position and showed it. Consequently, after the *Gorgon* had sailed, Collins lamented that with her had gone "a valuable portion of our friends";[15] a year later the same public approbation was accorded the rear party as it boarded the *Atlantic*, for Easty recorded that "amidst all the acclamations of a large concourse of people, every mark of joy and respect" was shown after a tour of duty ashore which he computed as being four years, ten months, and eight days.[16] The people of the colony would have known before the marines left for England that the discontent and chagrin which had already broken out in the New South Wales Corps did not augur well for their own future: as one correspondent wrote, those in charge of the colony were "heartily sorry" for the exchange.[17]

Thus the intention of the marine soldiers as expressed in their memorial before leaving England in 1787 to be "loyal subjects of the King and worthy members of society"[18] was achieved in spite of Ross's poor example. And there lies the paradox: that in spite of his faulty leadership, the contribution to the colony made by those subordinate to him was widely recognized by those within it. It was from official circles only that the detachment's reputation became obscured by the reputation of its commander. Of those who judged the detachment, Collins was probably the one best placed to provide a cogent opinion for as a marine, he knew its ethos completely, and yet as Judge Advocate, he was sufficiently distanced from it to assess its quality without the duty of biased loyalty. His judgment consequently is significant:

"As valuable a corps as any in His Majesty's service".[19]

Appendix A

Children of Marines 1787–1792

Name	Father	Mother*	Date of baptism	Status	Surname taken	Remarks and fate after father's return to England
ALLEIN (ALLEN), Rebekah	Pte John BROWNE	Susannah ALLEIN (c)	25.10.1789	Illegitimate	Mother's	The child's mother died at childbirth (17.10.89) and was buried the same day. Collins and Hunter sitting as magistrates placed Rebekah under the care of Frances Davis but the child died and was buried on 1.2.1790.
BACON, Elizabeth	Sgt Samuel BACON	Jane BACON	10.2.1788	Legitimate	Father's	returned with parents on *Gorgon*.
BACON, John Dingle	Sgt Samuel BACON	Jane BACON	8.12.1791	Legitimate	Father's	Born 3.6.1790 (a twin) died on *Gorgon's* return voyage at Ascension Island on 24.4.1792.
BACON, Robert	Sgt Samuel BACON	Jane BACON	8.12.1791	Legitimate	Father's	Born 3.6.1790 (a twin died on *Gorgon's* return voyage at Cape of Good Hope on 6.4.1792.
BAGLEY, Maria	Cpl James BAGLEY	Sarah BAGLEY	Arrived on First Fleet	Legitimate	Father's	Appears on Victualling List 26.2.88–17.11.88. Returned with parents on *Gorgon*.
BAKER, Elizabeth	Sgt William BAKER	Susannah HOFFNALL (c)	1.1.1789	Illegimate	Father's	Remained in colony.
BARRISFORD, Joseph	Pte John BARRISFORD	Hannah BARRISFORD	14.6.1789	Legitimate	Father's	Went to Norfolk Island in 1790 where their father remained as a settler. They left for the Derwent River in 1807.
BARRISFORD, Mary	Pte John BARRISFORD	Hannah BARRISFORD	8.9.1790	Legitimate	Father's	
BEADSLEY, Harriott	Pte John McCARTY	Ann BEADSLEY (c)	1.3.1789	Illegitimate	Mother's	Remained in colony.
BLAKE, James	Pte James BLAKE	Ann TEASDEL (alias CHESHER (c)	28.11.1790	Illegitimate	Father's	Remained in colony.
BRIXEY, William	Cpl Charles BRIXEY	Ann WRIGHT (c)	18.12.1790	Illegitimate	Father's	At William's christening, Cpl Brixey was named as the putative father. He returned with both parents on *Gorgon*.
CHAPMAN, Elizabeth	Cpl Thos. CHAPMAN	Jane CHAPMAN	Born in England	Legitimate	Father's	Accompanied her parents to Port Jackson on *Prince of Wales*. On 10.9.1789, aged 8, she was raped by Pte Henry Wright. Returned with parents on *Gorgon*.
CHAPMAN, Jane	Cpl Thos. CHAPMAN	Jane CHAPMAN	Born in England	Legitimate	Father's	Arrived with parents on *Prince of Wales* and returned with them on *Gorgon*.
CHAPMAN, Maria	Sgt Thos. CHAPMAN	Jane CHAPMAN	11.4.1790	Legitimate	Father's	Returned with parents on *Gorgon*.
CHEW, John	Pte John CHEW	Mary PILE (c)	5.7.1789	Illegitimate	Father's	Remained in colony after 1791.
CLARK, Alicia	Lt Ralph Clark	Mary BRANHAM (c)	16.12.1791	Illegitimate	Father's	Born 23.7.1791 at Norfolk Island; brought to Port Jackson December 1791. Remained in colony.
COLE, Thomas	Pte William ELLIS	Elizabeth COLE (c)	9.8.1789	Illegitimate	Mother's	The mother worked at Norfolk Island from 1790–1796 but

Name	Reputed father / Father	Mother	Date	Legitimacy	Whose child	Notes
COLETHREAD, James COLETHREAD (?) COLETHREAD, John	Pte John COLETHREAD (c)	Ann COLEPITS (c)	8.1.1789	Illegitimate	Father's	settled at the Field of Mars in 1792. Buried 20.4.1789
COTTERILL, Thomas	Pte Thomas COTTERILL	Ann LYNCH (c)	18.10.1789	Illegitimate	Father's	His father was a settler at Field of Mars, 1792.
(GREEN) DARLING, Charles Green	Pte Charles GREEN	Margaret DARLING (c)	1.2.1789	Illegitimate	Mother's	In March 1790, his mother went to Norfolk Island where she met Owen Cavenough, a marine, who settled there till 1796 when the family returned to the Hawkesbury River.
DAVIS, Mary DAVIS, Thomas	Pte John DAVIS Pte John DAVIS	Martha DAVIS Martha DAVIS	3.9.1791 9.8.1788	Legitimate Legitimate	Father's Father's	Returned with parents on *Gorgon*. Returned with parents on *Gorgon*.
DOCKERTY (?) DOUGHERTY, Ann	Pte Arthur DOUGHERTY	Judith DOUGHERTY	13.4.1789	Legitimate	Father's	Returned with parents on *Gorgon* but her mother died at sea 21.2.1792.
DOUGHERTY, Daniel	Pte Arthur DOUGHERTY	Judith DOUGHERTY	19.8.1787	Legitimate	Father's	Baptised on *Prince of Wales* at Rio — born 10.7.1787 at Rio. Returned per *Gorgon*. Mother died at sea 21.2.1792.
DOUGHERTY, Margaret	Pte Arthur DOUGHERTY	Judith DOUGHERTY	23.8.1791	Legitimate	Father's	Although she is not listed on *Gorgon's* passenger list, she undoubtedly sailed in it with the rest of her family.
(? DEVAN) DWAN, Dennis	Sgt Edward DWAN	Jane DWAN	8.9.1791	Legitimate	Father's	Sailed with family on *Gorgon* but died at sea 3.5.1792.
(? DEVAN) DWAN, Edward	Sgt Edward DWAN	Jane DWAN	20.4.1787	Legitimate	Father's	Returned with parents on *Gorgon*.
(? DEVAN) DWAN, Mark Turner	Sgt Edward DWAN	JANE DWAN	7.11.1789	Legitimate	Father's	Sailed on *Gorgon* with family but died at sea 25.4.1792.
FURZER, James Patrick	Lt James FURZER	Ann PARSLEY (c)	24.10.1791	Illegitimate	Father's	Remained in colony.
GILBORN, John Watkins	Pte Andrew GILBORN	Margaret GILBORN	8.12.1791	Legitimate	Father's	Born 19.1.1791. Returned with parents on *Gorgon* but died 26.4.1792 at sea.
GILBORN, William Prideaux	Pte Andrew GILBORN	Margaret GILBORN	1.9.1788	Legitimate	Father's	Returned with parents on *Gorgon*.
GOUGH, Joseph	Cpl Thomas GOUGH	Johannah GOUGH	Born in England	Legitimate	Father's	Arrived on *Prince of Wales*. His parents returned on *Gorgon* though his name does not appear (? omitted).
HARDIMAN, (?) Mary Maria	Reputed father: Pte William BLACKBURN	Elizabeth HARDIMAN	19.7.1791	Illegitimate	Mother's	Remained in colony.
HARMSWORTH, Ann	Pte Thomas HARMSWORTH	Alice (?) HARMSWORTH	Born in England	Legitimate	Father's	
HARMSWORTH, John	Pte Thomas HARMSWORTH	Alice (?) HARMSWORTH	Born in England	Legitimate	Father's	
HARMSWORTH, Daniel	Cpl Daniel STANFIELD	(?) Alice Ellis HARMSWORTH	25.4.1790	Illegitimate	Mother's	Father died 30.4.1788 — mother married Cpl Stanfield on 15.10.1791 and settled with her family at Norfolk Island.
HARMSWORTH, Thomas	Pte Thomas HARMSWORTH	Alice (?) HARMSWORTH (widow)	Born in England	Legitimate	Father's	Died 24.2.1788 at Port Jackson.
HUME, Mary	Sgt John HUME	Sarah HUME	22.11.1789	Legitimate	Father's	Returned with parents on *Gorgon* but died at sea 19.5.1792.
JOHNSTON, George	Capt-Lt George JOHNSTON	Esther ABRAHAMS (c)	4.3.1790	Illegitimate	Father's	Remained in colony.

* (c) = convict

Name	Father	Mother*	Date of baptism	Status	Surname taken	Remarks and fate after father's return to England
KELLOW, Joanna	Lt Robert KELLOW	Catherine HART (c)	12.12.1791	Illegitimate	Father's	Remained in colony.
KELLOW, Robert	Lt Robert KELLOW	Catherine Hart (c)	1.1.1790	Illegitimate	Father's	
LONG, Johanna	Lt John LONG	Mary HARRISON (c)	3.11.1791	Illegitimate	Father's	Born 29.10.1790. Remained in colony.
McDONALD, James	Pte Alexander McDONALD	Mary PHILLIPS (c)	5.9.1789	Illegitimate	Father's	Father settled at Field of Mars.
MAPP, William	Pte James MAPP	Susannah MAPP	8.11.1790	Legitimate	Father's	Sailed in *Gorgon* but died at sea 1.5.1792.
MEREDITH, James	Capt James MEREDITH	Mary HUGHES (c)	9.5.1790	Illegitimate	Father's	Remained in colony.
MEREDITH, Mary	Capt James MEREDITH	Mary HUGHES (C)	22.9.1792	Illegitimate	Father's	
MITCHELL, William	Cpl William MITCHELL	Jane FITZGERALD (c)	28.10.1788	Illegitimate	Father's	Settled at Norfolk Island in 1791 but returned to Sydney in 1793.
MITCHELL, James	Cpl William MITCHELL	Jane FITZGERALD (c)	28.10.1788	Illegitimate	Father's	
MUNDAY, Edward	Pte John MUNDAY	Ann MUNDAY	Born in England	Legitimate	Father's	
MUNDAY, Elizabeth	Pte John MUNDAY	Ann MUNDAY	22.6.1788	Legitimate	Father's	Settled at Norfolk Island 1791.
MUNDAY, John	Pte John MUNDAY	Ann MUNDAY	14.11.1790	Legitimate	Father's	
NASH, John	Pte William NASH	Mariah NASH	15.1.1792	Legitimate	Father's	Father transferred to New South Wales Corps in 1792.
NASH, William	Pte William NASH	Mariah NASH (Nee Haynes) (c)	25.5.1788	Illegitimate	Father's	Parents married 1.2.1789. Father transferred to New South Wales Corps in 1792.
PARFETT, Geoffrey	Drummer John PARFETT	Sarah PARFETT	14.11.1789 Born on First Fleet	Legitimate	Father's	
PARFETT, James	Drummer John PARFETT	Sarah PARFETT	Possibly born in England	Legitimate	Father's	Returned with parents on *Gorgon*.
PARFETT, Sarah	Drummer John PARFETT	Sarah PARFETT	15.1.1792 Possibly born in England	Legitimate	Father's	
PARFETT, Tiffany	Drummer John PARFETT	Sarah PARFETT				
PERRY, Kezzia	Sgt William PERRY	Ann PERRY	8.9.1791	Legitimate	Father's	Returned with parents on *Gorgon*.
PERRY, Thomas	Sgt William PERRY	Ann PERRY	30.6.1789	Legitimate	Father's	Returned with parents on *Gorgon* but died at sea 3.6.1792.
POULDEN, John	Lt John POULDEN	Mary MITCHELL	30.11.1791	Illegitimate	Father's	Born 14.4.1790. Remained in colony.
(? ROSSON) RAWSON, Joseph	Drummer Joseph ABBOTT	Isabella RAWSON (c)	15.2.1789	Illegitimate	Mother's	Died Port Jackson, 12.11.1789.
(? REDMUND) REDMAN, James	Pte Michael REDMAN	Elizabeth REDMAN	20.7.1788	Legitimate	Father's	Returned with parents on *Gorgon*.
RICHARDS, Sam	Pte Laurence RICHARDS	Mary RICHARDS	Born on First Fleet	Legitimate	Father's	Father settled at Norfolk Island 1791.
RICHARDS, William	Pte Laurence RICHARDS	Mary RICHARDS	25.12.1790	Legitimate	Father's	
RUSSELL, Ann Maria	Pte John RUSSELL	Elizabeth RUSSELL (? above)	13.9.1790	Legitimate	Father's	Returned with parents on *Gorgon*.
RUSSELL, Henry M.	(? above)	(? above)	Not recorded			
RUSSELL, Mary	(? above)	(? above)	Not recorded			
RUSSELL, Thomas	Pte John RUSSELL	Mary RUSSELL	12.8.1787	Legitimate	Father's	Baptised on *Friendship* at Rio — born deformed.

SCOTT, William Boxsell	Sgt James SCOTT	Jane SCOTT	1.7.1790	Legitimate	Father's	Returned with parents on *Gorgon*.
SCOTT, Elizabeth	Sgt James SCOTT	Jane SCOTT	3.9.1787	Legitimate	Father's	
(?) STEWARD STEWARD, Charles Johnstone	Sgt Peter STEWARD	Margaret STEWARD	3.1.1790	Legitimate	Father's	
(?) STEWARD STEWARD, John	Sgt Peter STEWARD	Margaret STEWARD	Born in England	Legitimate	Father's	Returned with parents on *Gorgon*.
THOMAS, Charles Frank	Pte Samuel THOMAS	Ann THOMAS	20.4.1789	Legitimate	Father's	Returned with parents on *Gorgon*.
THOMAS, James	Pte Samuel THOMAS	Ann THOMAS	Born on voyage 3.2.1788	Legitimate	Father's	Died 1.4.1788 at Port Jackson.
THOMAS, William	Pte Samuel THOMAS	Ann THOMAS	11.12.1791	Legitimate	Father's	Born 30.9.1791. Returned with parents on *Gorgon*.
TURNER, Elizabeth	Pte John TURNER	Susannah TURNER	20.6.1790	Legitimate	Father's	Returned on *Gorgon* but died at sea 4.5.1792.
TURNER, Mary	Pte John TURNER	Susannah TURNER	15.6.1788	Legitimate	Father's	Returned with parents on *Gorgon*.
WALL, Pheobe	Pte William WALL	Grace BROWN (c)	15.1.1792	Illegitimate	Father's	Did not return by *Gorgon*.
WILLIAMS, Sarah	Pte Robert RYAN	Frances WILLIAMS (c)	16.7.1789	Illegitimate	Mother's	Father settled on Norfolk Island 1791.
WRIGHT, Mary Ann	Pte Mathew WRIGHT	Mary WRIGHT	Born on First Fleet	Legitimate	Father's	Shown on *Gorgon* passenger list.
WRIGHT, Elizabeth	Pte Mathew WRIGHT	Mary WRIGHT		Legitimate	Father's	Returned with parents on *Gorgon*.
WRIGHT, Hannah	Pte Mathew WRIGHT	Mary WRIGHT	4.9.1791	Legitimate	Father's	
YOUNG, John	Sgt Thomas YOUNG	Elizabeth YOUNG	Born in England	Legitimate	Father's	Returned with parents on *Gorgon*.
YOUNG, Thomas	Sgt Thomas YOUNG	Elizabeth YOUNG	? Born in England	Legitimate	Father's	

* (c) = convict

Appendix B

Officer Biographies

MAJOR ROBERT ROSS

Born 1740; commissioned 17 June 1756 as second lieutenant 86 Company, Chatham; 25 June–26 July 1758, at seige of Louisbourg; 12 September 1759, at capture of Quebec; 27 October 1759, promoted first lieutenant 36 Company, Chatham; 21 September 1763, transferred to 11 Company, Portsmouth; 1 March 1773, promoted captain-lieutenant 6 Company, Plymouth, then despatched to America and appointed commander 5 Company 1 Battalion; 17 June 1775, appointed commander 39 Company vide Captain Ellis; 17 August 1779, taken prisoner of war by French in English Channel but later released; 1781–82, in Mediterranean and West Indies; 19 March 1783, promoted brevet major; 12 October 1786, appointed commandant NSW Marine Corps detachment; 24 October 1786, appointed lieutenant governor of New South Wales; March 1790–December 1791, commandant and lieutenant governor Norfolk Island; 18 December 1791, departed Sydney on HMS *Gorgon*; 19 June 1792, arrived Spithead, England; 22 November 1792, appointed to rejoin Chatham Division; 13 December 1792, appointed recruiting officer St Albans; January 1793 recruiting officer Brentford; 25 August 1793, recruiting officer Ipswich; 9 June 1794, died at Brompton.

CAPTAIN JAMES CAMPBELL

Commissioned 15 March 1757 in 92 Company, Chatham; 27 March 1778, promoted captain; 1 August 1783, posted to 48 Company, Plymouth; ?1786, posted to HMS *Carnatic*; November 1786, posted to NSW Marine Corps detachment; 12 May 1787, departed on First Fleet for New South Wales; 18 December 1791, departed Port Jackson on HMS *Gorgon*; 19 June 1792, arrived Spithead, England, 1794, promoted brevet major; 1795, apparently died as death recorded in Officer List published 1 January 1796.

CAPTAIN JOHN SHEA

Eldest son of Lieutenant Richard Shea, killed at Bunker's Hill 17 June 1775; commissioned 14 January 1773 in 30 Company, Plymouth; 1774, served in America; 4 January 1775, promoted first lieutenant; 1 January 1779, appointed adjutant, Plymouth; 8 September 1779, promoted captain-lieutenant in 12 Company; 1 January 1781, promoted captain in 119 Company, Plymouth; 1 September 1783, placed on half pay; 1 December 1786, restored to full pay in 61 Company, Portsmouth; 10 December 1786, posted to NSW Marine Corps detachment as company commander; 12 May 1787, departed Plymouth for New South Wales; 2 February 1789, died Port Jackson.

CAPTAIN-LIEUTENANT JAMES MEREDITH

Born 1753; commissioned 16 January 1776 into 8 Company; 17 March 1778, promoted first lieutenant in 59 Company; 4 September 1782, promoted to captain-lieutenant; 12 May 1787, commanded aboard *Friendship* on First Fleet voyage; 1811, promoted major general; 1821, promoted lieutenant general; 1838, promoted general; 7 July 1841, died at Monmouth, aged 88.

CAPTAIN-LIEUTENANT WATKIN TENCH

Born 1758; commissioned 1776 into 18 Company, Plymouth; 1777–79, sea service off North America; 25 March 1778, promoted first lieutenant in 30 Company; between 1778 and 1782, a period ashore in Maryland as a prisoner of war of the French after his ship *Mermaid* driven ashore there; 9 September 1782, promoted captain-lieutenant in 24 Company commanded by Major Collins (father of David Collins, future judge advocate of New South Wales); 1 May 1786, placed on half pay; 12 December 1786, restored to full pay and posted to NSW Marine Corps detachment; 12 May 1787, departed on *Charlotte* for New South Wales; 18 December 1791, departed Port Jackson on HMS *Gorgon*; 19 June 1792, arrived Spithead, England; 1792, promoted brevet major; 1793–94, served with Channel Fleet aboard HMS *Alexander*; captured by French and prisoner of war for six months; 1801–02, Channel service; 1816, promoted major general (temp.); 1819–27, commanded Plymouth Division; 1821, promoted lieutenant general; 1827, retired with the substantive rank of lieutenant colonel; 1833, died.

FIRST LIEUTENANT GEORGE JOHNSTON

Born 19 March 1764 at Annandale, Dumfriesshire, son of Captain George Johnston, ADC to Lord Percy, later Duke of Northumberland; commissioned 6 March 1776 in 45 Company; 1777–78, served at New York and Halifax; 1779–80, recruiting officer in England; 1781, service in East Indies aboard HMS *Sultan*, severely wounded in action; posted 59 Company, Portsmouth; 28 November 1786, joined NSW Marine Corps detachment, boarded *Lady Penrhyn* and sailed to New South Wales; ADC to Governor Phillip; February

1789, promoted to local rank of captain-lieutenant (vide Shea); 1791, transferred to New South Wales Corps and remained in colony; 1793, granted 100 acres at Petersham; formed an association with Esther Abrahams, convict, with whom he had three sons and four daughters; 1800, arrested for illegal trading in spirits and sent to London for trial but no trial held; returned to Port Jackson and promoted brevet major; 1808, arrested Governor Bligh; June 1811, cashiered; 12 November 1814, married Esther Abrahams when he was fifty and his eldest son twenty-four years of age; 1817, granted further 1,500 acres at Lake Illawarra: total land held 4,162 acres; 5 January 1823, died and buried at Petersham.

FIRST LIEUTENANT JOHN CRESWELL

Commissioned 13 June 1776 in 26 Company; 1778, promoted first lieutenant; 12 May 1787, departed in *Charlotte* with First Fleet marines for New South Wales; 18 December 1791, departed Port Jackson on HMS *Gorgon*; 19 June 1792, arrived Spithead; 1792, promoted captain; 1 August 1798, injured in action aboard HMS *Alexander* at the Battle of the Nile; 1802, promoted major; 1804, died.

FIRST LIEUTENANT THOMAS DAVEY

Born 1758; father was a mill owner who after "sturdy begging" in 1778 gained a commission for Thomas in the Royal Marines; 1779, served on HMS *Vengeance* in America; 1780 served on HMS *Preston* in West Indies; promoted first lieutenant; invalided to England; 30 November 1786, joined NSW Marine Corps detachment; 18 December 1791, returned to England on HMS *Gorgon*; 19 June 1792, arrived Spithead; 1795, promoted captain; 1797, retrieved a ship from naval mutineers at the Mutiny of the Nore; 1808, promoted brevet major; 1812, used Lord Harrowby as his patron to obtain lieutenant governorship of Tasmania; Macquarie, disliked his dissipated morals and buffoonery;

1816, replaced as lieutenant governor; 2 May 1823, died intestate, leaving only £20.

FIRST LIEUTENANT JAMES FURZER

Appointed second lieutenant 62 Company, 10 November 1776; 7 August 1778, promoted first lieutenant; 1 December 1786, appointed quartermaster to the Botany Bay detachment and travelled with headquarters aboard *Sirius*; 18 December 1791, returned aboard HMS *Gorgon* to England but was not promoted; 1794–95, served aboard *Carnatic*; 1799, died in West Indies.

FIRST LIEUTENANT JAMES MAXWELL

Appointed second lieutenant in 36 Company, 16 February 1776; 11 April 1778, promoted first lieutenant; 12 May 1787, departed with NSW Marine Corps detachment aboard *Lady Penrhyn*; July 1788, left Port Jackson to be invalided home sick; 2 March 1792, died at Stonehouse.

FIRST LIEUTENANT ROBERT KELLOW

Commissioned 9 November 1776 into 6 Company; 6 August 1778, promoted first lieutenant in 104 Company; 12 May 1787, travelled with NSW Marine Corps detachment on *Scarborough*; at Port Jackson, formed an association with convict Catherine Hart, with whom he had a son and a daughter; March 1790, transferred to Norfolk Island where he offended his brother officers who thereafter ostracized him; 1792, arrived in England but was not promoted; last listed as a marine officer in 1815.

FIRST LIEUTENANT JOHN POULDEN

Commissioned 10 December 1776 in 60 Company; 17 December 1778, promoted first lieutenant; 1779, assisted at the capture of the French ship *Conte d' Artois*; 12 December

1786, joined NSW Marine Corps detachment and travelled aboard *Charlotte*; 1792, returned to England; 1794, promoted captain; last listed as a marine officer in 1814.

FIRST LIEUTENANT JOHN JOHNSON

Commissioned 28 January 1779 in 39 Company; 30 November 1786, joined marine detachment for New South Wales travelling in *Alexander*; 1792, returned to England and ultimately reached rank of lieutenant colonel.

SECOND LIEUTENANT WILLIAM JOHN FADDY

Appointed second lieutenant 29 July 1780; 23 December 1786, joined *Friendship* to travel with marine detachment to New South Wales; 1792, returned to England; 1797, promoted captain-lieutenant; 1 August 1798, killed whilst serving aboard HMS *Vanguard* commanded by Nelson at the Battle of the Nile.

SECOND LIEUTENANT JOHN LONG

Commissioned 27 September 1779 into 139 Company; 1 December 1786, appointed adjutant of NSW Marine Corps detachment; travelled in *Sirius*; 1792, returned to England; 1808, promoted brevet major; 1814, transferred to British Army and promoted lieutenant colonel; last listed as an officer in 1825.

SECOND LIEUTENANT THOMAS TIMINS

He came from a military family; two of his brothers were commanders in the Royal Navy, and another was serving with the East India Company; he himself as a midshipman had seen action off The Lizard in 1778 in which year he was commissioned into the Royal Marines 105 Company at Portsmouth; 1779, transferred to 4 Company, went to America; 12 May 1780, present at capture of Charleston,

South Carolina; 1781, present at the action at Chesapeake Bay, and promoted first lieutenant; 1775–83, present at the capture of many ships during American war; 1783, transferred to 86 Company at Chatham and placed on half pay; 1786, joined 63 Company which was the company ordered to produce the NCOs for the Botany Bay detachment; 14 December 1786, joined NSW Marine Corps detachments, and served there till he returned to England by *Atlantic* in 1793; 16 June 1795, promoted captain-lieutenant; 1796, promoted captain; 1802, joined 65 Company; fought at Trafalgar on 21 October 1805 aboard HMS *Dreadnought*; although ninety-two marine officers served at Trafalgar, Timins was the only marine officer rewarded when he was awarded brevet major rank; 1807, his wife, whom he married after his service in New South Wales, died leaving him six daughters, the youngest of whom was two months old; 1810, his rank of major was made substantive; 1812, received brevet rank of lieutenant colonel; 1811–13, inspecting field officer, Manchester; 1823, made substantive lieutenant colonel; 23 October 1828, died at Southsea. A memorial to him was placed in the south aisle of the Portsmouth Garrison Church.

FIRST LIEUTENANT JAMES MAITLAND SHAIRP

Appointed second lieutenant in 55 Company, Portsmouth, 12 June 1778; 25 October 1780, promoted first lieutenant in 57 Company; 1783, placed on half pay; 1784, returned to full-time service; 20 December 1786, joined *Alexander* at Woolwich as a member of Botany Bay detachment; 19 June 1792, returned to England on HMS *Gorgon*; 7 May 1795, promoted captain; 1796, probable year of death as he was superseded on the Officer List.

SECOND LIEUTENANT RALPH CLARK

Probable year of birth, 1755; 25 August 1779, commissioned into 27 Company; 1 August 1783, transferred to 6 Company; 7 December 1786, joined *Friendship* as member of Botany Bay detachment; 5 March 1790, proceeded to Norfolk Island where he was appointed deputy assistant quartermaster general and superintendent of works at Charlotte Field; during his tour of duty, he wrote his valuable journal of events; July 1791, from a relationship with convict Mary Branham, a daughter Alicia born; 5 December 1791, arrived at Port Jackson with Mary Branham and daughter; 16 December 1791, Alicia baptised St Phillips Church; 18 December 1791, departed for England, without Mary or Alicia, on HMS *Gorgon*; 19 June 1792, arrived Spithead; appointed to 100 Company, Chatham; 1 May 1793, boarded HMS *Tartar* with son Ralph for West Indies; shortly after his departure, his wife died whilst giving birth to a stillborn child; but, probably before he could be given the news, his son Ralph died of yellow fever, and on the same day, he himself was killed on the same ship fighting the French at Haiti in 1794. Thus the small family for which he had suffered so much in New South Wales came to an end.

SECOND LIEUTENANT WILLIAM DAWES

Born 1762; 2 September 1779 commissioned in the Royal Marines; 1787, joined NSW Marine Corps detachment. He was a man of wide learning, "the scholar of the expedition", an astronomer, surveyor, and well versed in artillery and engineering. Before leaving England, he was equipped by the Astronomer Royal, the Reverend Dr Maskeleyne, with various instruments so as to observe a comet last sighted in 1661 but which Dr Maskeleyne felt would reappear in the southern skies in 1789. Phillip ordered that Dawes was always to be present when the clock of the *Sirius* was wound daily at noon. He was appointed to travel in the *Sirius* and command the reserve of marines aboard, but this was unattractive to him and he sought permission to travel in one of the transports, a request which the Admiralty refused. In the colony, his duties as artillery officer set him apart from the detachment, and he did not therefore become embroiled in its affairs. In 18 December 1791, he returned to England aboard HMS *Gorgon*; he twice became governor of Sierra Leone, was mathematics master at Christ's Hospital School 1799–1800, and died in the anti-slavery cause in Antigua in 1836.

SECOND LIEUTENANT ALEXANDER JOHN ROSS (local rank)

The son of Major Ross, he accompanied his father to New South Wales. He was not officially an officer whilst in New South Wales, but when Lieutenant Maxwell was evacuated to England in July 1788, Major Ross gave the boy the local rank of second lieutenant. After he returned to England aboard HMS *Gorgon* in 1792, this was confirmed and he was posted to 6 Company, Plymouth. In 1794, he transferred to 70 Company and saw action at Corigior; 1799, appointed adjutant, Plymouth; 29 January 1801, died at Brentford.

Appendix C

Order of Battle

New South Wales Marine Corps Detachment, July 1788

HEADQUARTER STAFF

Commandant	Maj. Robert Ross
Adjutant	2nd Lt John Long
Quartermaster	Lt James Furzer
Engineer Officer	Lt William Dawes

COMPANY COMMANDERS

Capt. James Campbell	Capt. Lt James Meredith
Capt. John Shea	Capt. Lt Watkin Tench

SUBALTERNS

Lt George Johnston	2nd Lt Ralph Clark
Lt Robert Kellow	2nd Lt John Faddy
Lt John Poulden	2nd Lt John Creswell
Lt Thomas Davey	2nd Lt William Collins
Lt Thomas Timins	2nd Lt John Ross (local rank)
Lt John Johnson	
Lt James Maitland Shairp	
Lt James Maxwell	

CAPTAIN CAMPBELL'S COMPANY

Sergeants
Isaac Knight
James Scott
Edward Devan

Corporals
Andrew Gilborne
Samuel Bacon
Charles Brexey

Drummers
John West
Benjamin Cook

Privates

Luke Haynes
Daniel Standfield
James Baker
John Brannon
Henry Wright
Isaac Archer
Charles Reynolds
James Lee
John Brown
Wm. Dowlan
James White
James Brown
Richard Asky
John Rice
Alexr. M'Donald
Wm. Godfrey
Thos. Bramwell
Thos. Bishop
Wm. King
Joseph Hunt
Francis Mee

Michael Redman
Peter Dargin
Thomas Jones
Thos. Woodhouse
Edwd. Overton
Patrick Connell
John Davis
Thomas Knight
Thomas Bullmore
Thomas O'Brien
Richard Dukes
Wm. Simmons
Edwd. Dinger
Joshua Coward
John M'Carthy
John Colethread
James Grant
Wm. Edmonds
George Flemming
Thomas Scott

CAPTAIN SHEA'S COMPANY

Sergeants
John Kennedy
Wm. Clayfield
Richard Clinch

Corporals
Richd. Nicholas
Thomas Gough
Thomas Chapman

Drummers
John Parfett
Joseph Abbott

Privates

Robt. Willmott
Thos. Tynan
John Jones
Joseph M'Calder
Joseph Lewis
Gabriel Nation
Thomas Phillips
Thomas Lucas
Thomas Nevitt
William Nash
William Seedhouse
John Watts
Robt. Stephens
John Russell
Wm. Douglas
Wm. Browning
Thos. Rowden
Stephen Gilbert
John Kennedy

Patrick M'Keon
John Hailey
Andrew Fishburn
James Kirby
John Thatcher
John Munday
Thos. Spencer
William Wall
John M'Cann
James Hailey
John Escott
Henry Parsons
Thos. Haswell
Robert Ryan
Edward Thomas
Lawrence Richards
Alexander Ross
Isaac Farr
William Smith

CAPTAIN-LIEUTENANT MEREDITH'S COMPANY

Sergeants
John Hume
Thomas Young
Peter Stewart

Corporals
John Winxstead
Martin Connor
James Plowman

Drummers
Alexr. Freeborne
Joseph Cox

Privates

Mathew Wright
John Roberts
George Winwood
James Reiley
Morty Lynch
Humphrey Evans
William Goodall
Thomas Harp
Thomas Scully
William Baxter
Ralph Bagnall
John Jones
John Turner
William Mason
John Griffiths
Samuel Thomas
Thomas Williams
James Hurdle
Thomas Cottrell
Edward Odgers

James Rogers
Arthur Dougherty
George Cheslett
William Dempsey
John Howell
James Wise
Thos. Bramage
Wm. Ellis
John Pugh
John Folly
Thos. Martin
John Clayton
John Woods
Barney M'Avenaugh
Thos. Jackson
Benjn. Cusley
John Hayes
Abraham Hand
John Easty
James Angell

CAPTAIN-LIEUTENANT TENCH'S COMPANY

Sergeants
William Perry
Edward Campion
William Baker

Corporals
Thomas Smith
Alexr. Anderson
James Bagley

Drummers
William Hughes
Robt. Mount Stephens

Privates

James M'Manus
John Wilkins
William Roberts
Ralph Brough
Mark Hurst
Richard Knight
Anthony Reed
William Chadwick
William Segar Jones
Michael Tolan
Henry Rosser
William Norris
William Bull
Joseph Harpur
John Carver
John Barrisford
James Mapp
Henry Clements
Walter Strong
George Gunn

John Brown
Robert Thompson
James Manning
Thos. Swinerton
Charles Green
Thomas Chipp
John Chew
William Dew
Wm. Mitchell
Wm. Stoulton
John Redman
Wm. Edmonstone
James Redman
William Hallam
John Lewis
Elias Bishop
William Cable
Joseph Radford
Phillip Goodwin
James Wherritt

Notes to the Text

Abbreviations

ADB	Australian Dictionary of Biography
ADM	Admiralty references
AO	Archives Office of New South Wales
BJS	British Journal of Sociology
CO	Colonial Office
HO	Home Office
HRA	Historical Records of Australia
HRNSW	Historical Records of New South Wales
JAS	Journal of Australian Studies
JRAHS	Journal of the Royal Australian Historical Society
ML	Mitchell Library
PRO	Public Records Office
WO	War Office

Historical Introduction

1. *Privy Council Register*, 4, Charles II, 28 October 1664.
2. Gillespie, *An Historical Review*, 1.
3. Previous occasions were 1664, 1702 and 1739.
4. Gillespie, *An Historical Review*, 120.
5. Blumberg, *Royal Marine Records*, 2.
6. Gillespie, *An Historical Review*, 84.
7. Shortly after being commissioned in the British Marines, Wolfe transferred to the Twelfth Regiment of Foot in the British Army.
8. Gillespie, *An Historical Review*, 148.

9. Ibid., 188.
10. Ibid., 191.
11. Ibid., 234. The commendation appeared in Orders on 9 June 1776.
12. Longford, *Wellington*, 321.
13. Gillespie, *An Historical Review*, 208, 272.
14. Haswell, *The British Army*, 58.
15. Ibid., 52.
16. Ibid.
17. Blumberg, *Royal Marine Records*, 1.
18. Ibid.
19. Ibid.
20. Ibid.
21. Company numbers were used instead of regimental numbers until 1882. See Blumberg, *Royal Marine Records*, 19.
22. Ibid., 9.
23. Ibid., 23.
24. Examples of marine officers promoted from the ranks were: Sergeant Major John Christian was promoted second lieutenant in Forty-seven Company on 27 October 1756. Sergeant Major C. Olive was promoted second lieutenant in Thirty-one Company on 9 September 1772. Sergeant Major Harry Rudd was promoted second lieutenant on 29 March, 1774. See *Blumberg, Royal Marine Records*, 17.
25. Blumberg, *Royal Marine Records*, 3.
26. Ibid., 8.
27. Ibid., 3.
28. Field, *Britain's Sea Soldiers*, 134. The figures quoted by Field are based on Millan's Succession of Colonels, 1743, but the Director of the Royal Marines Museum feels there was little change by 1788.
29. Admiralty letter of 28 September, 1764, Blumberg, *Royal Marine Records*, 10.
30. Ibid., 5.
31. Gillespie, *An Historical Review*, 84.
32. Blumberg, *Royal Marine Records*, 7.
33. Ross to Nepean, 27 April 1787, *HRNSW*, vol. 1, part 2, 93.
34. Ibid.
35. Cobley, *Sydney Cove 1788*, 190.
36. Clark, *Journal*, 208.
37. Blumberg, *Royal Marine Records*, 27.
38. Ibid.
39. *HRNSW*, vol. 1, part 2, 1-8.
40. Blumberg, *Royal Marine Records*, 38.
41. Ibid., 31.
42. Ibid.
43. Ibid., 32.
44. Aldington, *The Duke*, 179.
45. Longford, *Wellington*, 321.
46. Ibid.
47. Parsons, "The Social Composition of the Men of the New South Wales Corps", *JRAHS*, vol 50, part 4, 298.
48. Ibid.
49. Bateson, *Convict Ships*, 26.
50. Atkinson, "John Macarthur Before Australia Knew Him", *JAS* 4 (June 1979): 28.
51. Razzell, "Social Origins of Officers in the Indian and British Home Army 1758–1962", *BJS*, 14 (1963): 255.
52. Letter from Secretary of State, 9 November 1784, PRO, ADM 1/4151, 1784–85.
53. Haswell, *The British Army*, 68.
54. Worgan, *Journal*, 74.
55. Marine Order of 28 December 1784, Blumberg, *Royal Marine Records*, 31.

56. Ibid., 32.
57. Ibid.
58. HRNSW, vol. 2, 369.
59. Blumberg, *Royal Marine Records*, 33.
60. Ibid., 33. The orders were issued on 10 April 1786.
61. Ibid., 16. This fund, still in existence, was established at Plymouth on 6 November 1766.
62. Ibid., 34.
63. Ross to Nepean, HRNSW, vol. 1, part 2, 93.

Chapter 1   Preparations for the Great Adventure

1. Eldershaw, *Phillip of Australia*, 17.
2. HRNSW, vol. 1, part 2, 2.
3. Frost, *Convicts and Empire*, 6.
4. Martin, ed., *Founding of Australia*, 68.
5. *Gentleman's Magazine* 56 (1786): 260.
6. Eldershaw, *Phillip of Australia*, 19. Eldershaw entertains no doubt that it was Lord Sydney who made the proposal.
7. HRNSW, vol. 1, part 2, xxxvi.
8. *Bonwick Transcripts*, Box 56, 208, ML.
9. Eldershaw, *Phillip of Australia*, 12.
10. Shaw, *Convicts and the Colonies*, 43.
11. *Bonwick Transcripts*, Box 56, 209, ML.
12. Ibid., 212.
13. Ibid., 218.
14. Ibid., 221.
15. HRNSW, vol. 2, 737.
16. Martin, ed., *Founding of Australia*, 169.
17. Ibid., 175.
18. Ibid., 198.
19. Frost, *Convicts and Empire*, 115, 119.
20. Ibid.
21. HRNSW, vol. 1, part 2, 14.
22. Ibid., 15.
23. Ibid., 17.
24. Ibid., 18.
25. Ibid., 22.
26. Bateson, *Convict Ships*, 94.
27. Bradley, *A Voyage*, 1. Bradley confirms that five of the ships had been chartered by 12 September 1786.
28. Bateson, *Convict Ships*, 95.
29. Eldershaw, *Phillip of Australia*, 34.
30. Phillip took command of HMS *Sirius* on 25 September 1786. See Bradley, *A Voyage*, 1-2.
31. King, *Journal*, 5.
32. HRNSW, vol. 1, part 2, 24.
33. Lord Howe to Lord Sydney, 3 September, 1786, Ibid., 22.
34. Ibid., 189. See also W.S. Campbell, "Arthur Phillip", *JRAHS* 21 (1936): 264.
35. Stephens to Colonel Tupper, 8 October 1786. HRNSW, vol. 2, 368. Colonel Tupper, Major General Collins and Lieutenant Colonel Hughes commanded the Portsmouth, Plymouth, and Chatham divisions respectively.
36. Ibid., 369.
37. Ibid., 369-70.

38. Blumberg, *Royal Marine Records*, 197.
39. Easty, *Memorandum*, 2.
40. Letters relating to marines, PRO ADM 2/1177, 1785–86, 540. Letters relating to marines, PRO ADM 2/1178, 1786–88, 16.
41. Correspondence of RM Commandant, Plymouth, for 5 February, 1787 (page unnumbered), PRO ADM 1/3290, 1787.
42. Parsons, "Courts Martial: The Savoy Prison and the New South Wales Corps", *JRAHS*, vol. 63, part 4, 248-62.
43. *HRNSW*, vol. 2, 372.
44. Letter from the Admiralty to Lord Sydney, 12 October 1786. Ibid., vol. 1, part 2, 24.
45. Letter of 27 October 1786 relating to marines, PRO ADM 2/1177, 1785–86, 525.
46. *HRNSW*, vol. 2, 370.
47. Ibid., 371.
48. Ibid.
49. Letter to the Board of Ordnance, 15 November 1786, PRO ADM 2/1177, 1785–86, 548.
50. *HRNSW*, vol. 2, 372.
51. Ibid., 373.
52. Scott, Remarks, 37.
53. *HRNSW*, vol. 1, part 2, 29.
54. Ibid., 15, 18.
55. *HRNSW*, vol. 1, part 2, 284; PRO ADM 2/1178, 1786–88, 1. Wives of convict men were not permitted to accompany them until the Second Fleet.
56. *HRNSW*, vol. 1, part 2, 29.
57. Ibid., 109.
58. Letters relating to marines, 21 November 1786, PRO ADM 2/1178, 1786–88, 1.
59. Privy Council Minutes of 24 November 1786, *Bonwick Transcripts*, Box 56, 243, ML.
60. Easty, *Memorandum*, 2. It is probable that this was the same detachment of which Easty was a member and which marched from Chatham to Woolwich on 1 December 1786. *See also* Bateson, *Convict Ships*, 98.
61. From an article in the *London Chronicle*, 23 June 1789, *Bonwick Transcripts*, Box 57, 122, ML.
62. Letters relating to marines, 1786–88, PRO ADM 2/1178, 17.
63. Bradley, *A Voyage*, 2.
64. *HRNSW*, vol. 1, part 2, 32.
65. Ibid., vol. 2, 43.
66. Ibid., vol. 1, part 2, 32-33; and *HRNSW*, vol. 2, 376.
67. Admiralty letters from Phillip, PRO ADM 1/2308, 1785–89, section 12; also *HRNSW*, vol. 1, part 2, 41.
68. Phillip had raised the matters with Nepean on 1 March 1787 (*HRNSW*, vol. 1, part 2, 54), and with Lord Sydney on 12 March 1787 (Ibid., 56).
69. *HRNSW*, vol. 1, part 2, 50.
70. Ibid., 42.
71. Correspondence of RM Commandant, Portsmouth, 13 January 1787, PRO ADM 1/3290. *See also* Easty, *Memorandum*, 3.
72. Correspondence of RM Commandant, Portsmouth, 15 January 1787. This letter states that those marines who travelled aboard *Sirius* and *Supply* were to be in addition to the strength of the detachment's four companies. PRO ADM 1/3290.
73. *HRNSW*, vol. 2, 378.
74. *HRNSW*, vol. 1, part 2, 43-44.
75. PRO ADM 2/1178, 1786–88, 83; and *HRNSW*, vol. 2, 377.
76. Letter to author from the Director, Royal Marines Museum, Eastney, Hants, UK, 11 December 1981.
77. Letter to author from the Director, Royal Marines Museum, 10 February 1981.
78. PRO ADM 1/2308 , 1785–89, section 12.

79. Easty, *Memorandum*, 3.
80. Admiralty letter from Phillip, 7 February 1787, *PRO* ADM 1/2308, 1785–89, section 12.
81. *HRNSW*, vol. 1, part 2, 48.
82. *HRNSW*, vol. 2, 380.
83. Bradley, *A Voyage*, 9.
84. Easty, *Memorandum*, 3.
85. Ibid.
86. Bradley, *A Voyage*, 9, though Easty (*Memorandum*, 4) gives the dates as 15 and 16 March.
87. White, *Journal*, 229.
88. Clark, *Journal*, 1.
89. *HRNSW*, vol. 2, 368.
90. Gillespie, *An Historical Review*, 192.
91. Ibid., 191.
92. *ADB*, vol. 1, 397.
93. Ibid., 397-98.
94. Meredith was commissioned in 1776 and promoted to major in 1794.
95. Tench was commissioned in 1776 and promoted to major in 1794.
96. The officers not promoted to substantive rank were Ross, Kellow, Campbell, and Furzer.
97. Atkinson, "British Whigs and the Rum Rebellion", *JRAHS*, vol. 66, part 2, 74-90. Also see *ADB*, vol. 2, 20, for comments on Johnston.
98. *Bonwick Transcripts*, Box 57, 121, ML.
99. Royal Marines Museum Archives, Eastney, Hants, UK, ARCH 9/2/C, as per director's letter of 26 October 1984. The biographical details listed in *HRNSW*, vol. 2, 417, are not those of the Captain James Campbell who came to New South Wales. They are of an officer of the same name who became Major General Sir James Campbell.
100. *HRNSW*, vol. 1, part 2, 84.
101. Campbell to Dr Farr, 24 March 1791, *ML* Document 1174.
102. Best, "Captain John O'Shea", *Descent* vol. 4, part 1, 1968, 9-13. *See also* Collins, *An Account*, 544n.
103. Tench, *Sydney's First Four Years*, introduction by Fitzhardinge, xv.
104. Southwell, *Correspondence*, *HRNSW*, vol. 2, 719, *letter to his mother of 27 July 1790*.
105. *HRNSW*, vol. 2, 498.
106. *Bonwick Transcripts*, A2000-4, vol. 4, 888-95, ML.
107. *HRNSW*, vol. 2, 384.
108. Phillip, *The Voyage*, 7.
109. White, *Journal*, 49.
110. *HRNSW*, vol. 1, part 2, 50.
111. Ibid., 55.
112. Ibid., 56.
113. Ibid., 58.
114. Correspondence to RM Commandant Portsmouth, 28 April and 4 May 1787, *PRO* ADM 1/3290, 1787.
115. *HRNSW*, vol. 1, part 2, 78.
116. Ibid.
117. *HRNSW*, vol. 2, 386.
118. Clark, *Journal*, 241-45.
119. *HRNSW*, vol. 1, part 2, 69-70.
120. Clark, *Journal*, 247.
121. Bowes, *Journal*, 13.
122. From the *Dublin Chronicle* of 5 May 1787, *Bonwick Transcripts*, Box 57, section 103, 59, ML.
123. *HRNSW*, vol. 1, part 2, 101-2.

124. Ibid., 102.
125. Bradley, *A Voyage*, 11.
126. *HRNSW*, vol. 1, part 2, 104.
127. White, *Journal*, 58.
128. Admiralty letters from Phillip, *PRO* ADM 1/2308, 1785–89, section 12.
129. Ibid.

Chapter 2   The Voyage Out

1. Bradley, *A Voyage*, 12.
2. Tench, *Sydney's First Four Years*, 11.
3. Ibid., 14. (Milton's *Paradise Lost* X11, line 645.)
4. Tench, *Sydney's First Four Years*, 14.
5. Scott's, *Remarks*, 1.
6. Bradley, *A Voyage*, 17.
7. Clark, *Journal*, 11.
8. Easty, *Memorandum*, 6.
9. White, *Journal*, 52.
10. Clark, *Journal*, 11.
11. Ibid., 65.
12. Ibid., 49.
13. Easty, *Memorandum*, 7.
14. Bradley, *A Voyage*, 12.
15. Clark, *Journal*, 13.
16. Ibid., 14.
17. Ibid., 68.
18. Ibid., 13.
19. Ibid., 14.
20. Ibid., 15.
21. Easty, *Memorandum*, 11.
22. Phillip, *The Voyage*, 18.
23. Easty, *Memorandum*, 11.
24. Clark, *Journal*, 16.
25. Scott, *Remarks*, 3.
26. Ibid., 4.
27. *HRNSW*, vol. 1, part 2, 107.
28. Ibid., 111, 119.
29. Clark, *Journal*, 17.
30. Easty, *Memorandum*, 12.
31. Tench, *Sydney's First Four Years*, 17; and *HRNSW*, vol. 2, 518 (King's journal).
32. King, *Journal*, 11.
33. Tench, *Sydney's First Four Years*, 16-17. Bradley (*A Voyage*, LIX) says the Governor received less than fifteen hundred.
34. Tench, *Sydney's First Four Years*, 17-18; and Collins, *An Account*, LXIII-LXIV.
35. Scott, *Remarks*, 3.
36. Clark, *Journal*, 19.
37. Ibid., 22.
38. Ibid., 19.
39. Scott, *Remarks*, 4.
40. Clark, *Journal*, 20.
41. White, *Journal*, 63.
42. Scott, *Remarks*, 6.
43. Ibid.
44. Scott, *Remarks*, 8.

45. Clark, *Journal*, 25-26.
46. Ibid., 26.
47. Ibid., 23.
48. Easty, *Memorandum*, 17-18. (Footnote says Shea fell ill on 3 July.)
49. Clark, *Journal*, 24.
50. Ibid., 25.
51. Bowes, *Journal*, 13.
52. Clark, *Journal*, 22.
53. Clark, *Journal*, 59.
54. Ibid., 28.
55. Ibid., 32.
56. Cobley, *Sydney Cove 1788*, 210.
57. Clark, *Journal*, 36.
58. Scott, *Remarks*, 7.
59. Easty, *Memorandum*, 21.
60. Clark, *Journal*, 29.
61. Ibid., 25.
62. Scott, *Remarks*, 10.
63. Ibid., 12.
64. Bradley, *A Voyage*, 35-36.
65. Clark, *Journal*, 34.
66. Ibid., 40.
67. Ibid., 35.
68. Ibid., 39.
69. Ibid., 32.
70. Scott, *Remarks*, 13.
71. Easty, *Memorandum*, 27.
72. Ibid., 30-31.
73. Ibid.
74. White, *Journal*, 76.
75. Clark, *Journal*, 37.
76. Ibid.
77. Scott, *Remarks*, 13.
78. The parties were held on 20, 21, 24, 30 August, 16, 28, 30 September, 7, 10 October.
79. Clark, *Journal*, 40-42, 46, 49-50, 53, 66.
80. Ibid., 66.
81. Ibid., 84.
82. White, *Journal*, 73.
83. Ibid., 74.
84. Clark, *Journal*, 37.
85. Ibid.
86. Ibid., 38.
87. Scott, *Remarks*, 13.
88. Bradley, *A Voyage*, 37.
89. *HRNSW*, vol. 1, part 2, 112.
90. Clark, *Journal*, 46.
91. Scott, *Remarks*, 14.
92. Ibid., 13.
93. *PRO* ADM 1/2308, 1785–89, section 12, 2 September 1787.
94. Collins, *An Account*, vol. 1, LXXV.
95. Ibid.
96. *PRO* ADM 1/2308, 1785–89, section 12, 2 September 1787.
97. *HRNSW*, vol. 1, part 2, 112.
98. Clark, *Journal*, 48.
99. Scott, *Remarks*, 16.

100. Clark, *Journal*, 44.
101. Ibid., 45.
102. Ibid., 51.
103. *HRNSW*, vol. 2, 741.
104. Bradley, *A Voyage*, 41.
105. Scott, *Remarks*, 19.
106. Cobley, *Sydney Cove 1789–1790*, 317.
107. Easty, *Memorandum*, 47.
108. PRO ADM 1/2308, 1785–89, section 12, 10 November 1787.
109. Clark, *Journal*, 55-58.
110. Ibid., 61.
111. Ibid., 63.
112. Scott, *Remarks*, 20; Clark, *Journal*, 259.
113. *HRNSW*, vol. 1, part 2, 119.
114. Scott, *Remarks*, 21.
115. Easty, *Memorandum*, 50.
116. Scott, *Remarks*, 21.
117. Ibid.
118. Clark, *Journal*, 259.
119. Ibid., 252.
120. Ibid., 260.
121. Ibid.
122. Easty, *Memorandum*, 51.
123. Scott, *Remarks*, 21.
124. Ibid.
125. Collins, *An Account*, vol. 1, LXXX.
126. Collins, *An Account*, vol. 1, LXXIX.
127. Scott, *Remarks*, 23, 24.
128. Clark, *Journal*, 66.
129. Ibid., 259.
130. Collins, *An Account*, vol. 1, LXXXVI.
131. Scott, *Remarks*, 24.
132. Clark, *Journal*, 67.
133. Ibid., 265.
134. White, *Journal*, 102.
135. Clark, *Journal*, 69.
136. Ibid., 54.
137. Ibid., 260.
138. *HRNSW*, vol. 1, part 2, 169.
139. Ibid., 26.
140. Collins, *An Account*, vol. 1, LXXXVII.
141. Ibid.
142. Clark, *Journal*, 74.
143. Scott, *Remarks*, 27.
144. Bowes, *Journal*, 46.
145. Easty, *Memorandum*, 70; King, *Journal*, 26-27.
146. Clark, *Journal*, 75.
147. Ibid., 88.
148. Ibid., 283.
149. Ibid., 77, 79.
150. Scott, *Remarks*, 28.
151. Ibid., 29.
152. Bowes, *Journal*, 51.
153. Clark, *Journal*, 82.

Chapter 3 Botany Bay to Sydney Cove

1. Collins, *An Account*, vol. 1, LXXXVIII.
2. Easty, *Memorandum*, 79.
3. *HRNSW*, vol. 1, part 2, 121.
4. Scott, *Remarks*, 31.
5. Clark, *Journal*, 86.
6. *HRNSW*, vol. 1, part 2, 539 (King's journal).
7. Ibid.
8. Collins, *An Account*, vol. 1, 1.
9. King, *Journal*, 33.
10. Clark, *Journal*, 91.
11. Scott, *Remarks*, 33.
12. King, *Journal*, 33.
13. Bateson, *The Convict Ships*, 114.
14. PRO ADM 1/2308, 1785–89, section 12, 28 September 1789.
15. *HRNSW*, vol. 1, part 2, 108.
16. Tench, *Sydney's First Four Years*, 11.
17. *HRNSW*, vol. 1, part 2, 57.
18. Clark, *Journal*, 91.
19. *HRNSW*, vol. 2, 662.
20. Easty, *Memorandum*, 90.
21. Bradley, *A Voyage*, 59.
22. King, *Journal*, 34-35.
23. Clark, *Journal*, 91.
24. *HRNSW*, vol. 2, 662.
25. Bradley, *A Voyage*, 61.
26. Collins, *An Account*, vol. 1, 2.
27. Hunter, *Journal*, 43.
28. PRO ADM 1/2308, 1785–89, section 12, 10 July 1788.
29. Worgan, *Journal*, 29.
30. Bowes, *Journal*, 57.
31. Clark, *Journal*, 91.
32. White, *Journal*, 199.
33. Clark, *Journal*, 92.
34. King, *Journal*, 36.
35. Bradley, *A Voyage*, 63.
36. Collins, *An Account*, vol. 1, 3.
37. Bowes, *Journal*, 63.
38. Collins, *An Account*, vol. 1, 534-35n (from J. Dunmore, *French Explorers in the Pacific*, Oxford, 1965, 275; and La Perouse, *A Voyage Round the World*, London, 1807, vol. 3, 141-42).
39. Cobley, *Sydney Cove 1788*, 34.
40. Bowes, *Journal*, 63; Clark, *Journal*, 92.
41. *HRA*, vol. 1, introduction xx.
42. White, *Journal*, 113.
43. King, *Journal*, 36.
44. Collins, *An Account*, vol. 1, 4.
45. Bradley, *A Voyage*, 65.
46. Collins, *An Account*, vol. 1, 4-5.
47. Clark, *Journal*, 93.
48. Ibid.
49. Bowes, *Journal*, 64; Tench, *Sydney's First Four Years*, 38; King, Journal, 36; Milton, *Paradise Lost* I lines 252-53; Collins, *An Account*, vol. 1, 4.
50. Scott, *Remarks*, 36; Tench, *Sydney's First Four Years*, 41.

Chapter 4   Sleeping on the Ground

1. Clark, *Journal*, 93-4.
2. Bowes, *Journal*, 33.
3. Easty, *Memorandum*, 94.
4. Tench, *Sydney's First Four Years*, 38.
5. King, *Journal*, 97.
6. Bowes, *Journal*, 33.
7. Clark, *Journal*, 94.
8. Bowes, *Journal*, 65.
9. Scott, *Remarks*, 35.
10. Easty, *Memorandum*, 94.
11. Clark, *Journal*, 94.
12. King, *Journal*, 37.
13. Easty, *Memorandum*, 95.
14. Cobley, *Sydney Cove 1788*, 45.
15. Clune, *Norfolk Island*, 7.
16. Bowes, *Journal*, 69.
17. Ibid., 66.
18. Clark, *Journal*, 94.
19. Ibid., 95.
20. Ibid., 94.
21. King, *Journal*, 37.
22. Clark, *Journal*, 95.
23. Cobley, *Sydney Cove 1788*, 50.
24. King, *Journal*, 40.
25. Clark, *Journal*, 95.
26. *Banks Papers*, Brabourne Collection, vol. 3, 1786-1800, A78-2, ML FM 4 1747.
27. Clark, *Journal*, 95.,
28. Tench, *Sydney's First Four Years*, 39.
29. Ibid.
30. Bowes, *Journal*, 67.
31. Clark, *Journal*, 95-96.
32. Bradley, *A Voyage*, 80.
33. Clark, *Journal*, 96.
34. Southwell, *Correspondence*, in *Bonwick Transcripts*, Box 57, 217, ML.
35. White, *Journal*, 114; Tench, *Sydney's First Four Years*, 41.
36. Bowes, *Journal*, 68.
37. Collins, *An Account*, vol. 1, 6-7.
38. Bowes, *Journal*, 34.
39. Clark, *Journal*, 96.
40. Cobley, *Sydney Cove 1788*, 63.
41. Clark, *Journal*, 97.
42. Tench, *Sydney's First Four Years*, 39.

Chapter 5   Early Crimes and Punishments

1. Longford, *Wellington*, 321.
2. Bowes, *Journal*, 70.
3. Clark, *Journal*, 97.
4. Tench, *Sydney's First Four Years*, 100n.
5. Clark, *Journal*, 96.

6. Bowes, *Journal*, 69.
7. Haswell, *The British Army*, 68.
8. Clark, *Journal*, 100.
9. Ibid., 101.
10. Cobley, *Sydney Cove 1788*, 149.
11. Ibid., 174.
12. Scott, *Remarks*, 39. Scott calls him Payton.
13. White, *Journal*, 143.
14. Tench, *Sydney's First Four Years*, 62.
15. Cobley, *Sydney Cove 1788*, 218.
16. Ibid., 263.
17. Cobley, *Sydney Cove 1789-90*, 4.
18. Ibid., 7.
19. Minutes of Magistrates Court, 15 August 1789, 210-17. (Quoted by Heney, *Australia's Founding Mothers*, 56.)
20. Cobley, *Sydney Cove 1789-90*, 81-94.
21. Ibid., 101.
22. Ibid., 111.
23. Tench, *Sydney's First Four Years*, 134.
24. White, *Journal*, 162-63.
25. Collins, *An Account*, vol. 1, 95.
26. *HRA*, vol. 1, 185.
27. Cobley, *Sydney Cove 1788*, 243.
28. Collins, *An Account*, vol. 1, 123.
29. *Banks Papers*, Brabourne Collection, 1786-1800, A78-2, ML FM 4, 1747.
30. *HRNSW*, vol. 2, 758.

6 The Manly Aborigine

1. *HRNSW*, vol. 1, part 2, 89-90.
2. "Articles of Charge Against Warren Hastings, Esq., Late Governor General of Bengal", as contained in The Works of the Right Honorable Edmund Burke, London 1887, vol. 9, 383: quoted by Atkinson, *The Ethics of Conquest in 1786, Aboriginal History*, vol. 6, no. 2, Dec. 1982.
3. *Morning Chronicle*, 16 October 1786; *Daily Universal Register*, 27 September 1786; *Public Advertiser*, 28 September, 6 October 1786.
4. *HRNSW*, vol. 1, part 2, 129.
5. Worgan, *Journal*, 33.
6. *HRNSW*, vol. 1, part 2, 129.
7. Worgan, *Journal*, 33.
8. Bradley, *A Voyage*, 66.
9. Ibid., 67.
10. Ibid., 75.
11. Bowes, *Journal*, 66.
12. Worgan, *Journal*, 33.
13. Bradley, *A Voyage*, 83-4.
14. Bowes, *Journal*, 77.
15. Ibid.
16. Bradley, *A Voyage*, 96.
17. Ibid., 94.
18. Collins, *An Account*, 18.
19. Bradley, *A Voyage*, 99.
20. Ibid., 104.
21. Ibid., 111.

22. Worgan, *Journal*, 51.
23. White, *Journal*, 134.
24. Worgan, *Journal*, 51.
25. White, *Journal*, 135.
26. Ibid., 165.
27. Collins, *An Account*, vol. 1, 34.
28. Tench, *Sydney's First Four Years*, 137.
29. Ibid.
30. Ibid., 139-40.
31. Ibid., 139.
32. Ibid.
33. Ibid., 140.
34. Scott, *Remarks*, 44.
35. Tench, *Sydney's First Four Years*, 140.
36. Scott, *Remarks*, 48.
37. Tench, *Sydney's First Four Years*, 144.
38. Ibid., 222.
39. Ibid., 200-204.
40. Ibid., 205-6.
41. Ibid., 208.
42. Ibid., 212-13.
43. Ibid., 213.
44. Ibid., 215.
45. Ibid.
46. Hunter, *Journal*, 499; and Tench, *Sydney's First Four Years*, 320n. 15.
47. Tench, *Sydney's First Four Years*, 236.
48. Ibid.
49. Ibid., 240.
50. Ibid., 53.
51. Collins, *An Account*, 137-39.
52. Clark, *Journal*, 109.
53. Ibid., 109-110.
54. *HRNSW*, vol. 1, part 2, 171.
55. Document 1174, ML.

Chapter 7 Little Journeys — Hard Climbs

1. Bradley, *A Voyage*, 76.
2. Collins, *An Account*, vol. 1, 12.
3. Bradley, *A Voyage*, 87-94 and *HRA* vol. 1, 20-21.
4. Collins, *An Account*, vol. 1, 15.
5. Ibid.
6. Wood, G.A., article in *JRAHS*, vol. 12, 1926, 3.
7. White, *Journal*, 121.
8. Admiralty letters from Phillip, *PRO ADM* 1/2308, 1785-89, section 12.
9. White, *Journal*, 127-30.
10. Bowes, *Journal*, 43.
11. *HRNSW*, vol. 1, part 2, 134.
12. Ibid.
13. White, *Journal*, 156.
14. Hunter, *Journal*, 151-52.
15. Milton, *Paradise Lost* II, line 197.
16. Tench, *Sydney's First Four Years*, 154.
17. Ibid.

18. Hunter, *Journal*, 152-53.
19. In 1794, Nepean (1751–1822) became Under Secretary of State for War. He was created a baronet in 1802, and appointed Governor of Bombay in 1812.
20. *HRA*, vol. 1, 156.
21. Hunter, *Journal*, 160-62; and Tench, *Sydney's First Four Years*, 155.
22. Tench, *Sydney's First Four Years*, 158.
23. *JRAHS*, vol. 27, part 1, 1941, 245-75.
24. Tench, *Sydney's First Four Years*, 174-75.
25. Ibid., 223.
26. Ibid., 234.
27. Ibid., 235.
28. Tench, *Sydney's First Four Years*, 237-38.
29. Campbell, J.F., article in *JRAHS*, vol. 12, 1926.
30. Tench, *Sydney's First Four Years*, 237.
31. *Globe and Laurel*, vol. 5, No 27, 7 January 1898, 51, Lt. Col. Parkins Hearle, RMLI.

Chapter 8   Hardship in Sydneytown

1. Clark, *Journal*, 244.
2. Bowes, *Journal*, 74.
3. *HRNSW*, vol. 1, part 2, 171.
4. Ibid., 144.
5. *Banks Papers*, Brabourne Collection, vol. 3, 1786–1800, A78-2, ML FM 4, 1747.
6. Clark, *Journal*, 101-3.
7. Ibid., 264.
8. Ibid., 268.
9. Tench, *Sydney's First Four Years*, 75.
10. *HRNSW*, vol. 2, 761.
11. Admiralty letter from Phillip, 10 July 1788, PRO ADM 1/2308, 1785–89, section 12.
12. Hunter to Stephens, 3 January, 1789, *HRNSW*, vol. 1, part 2, 225.
13. Collins, *An Account*, vol. 1, 7.
14. Banks Papers, Brabourne Collection, vol. 3, 1786–1800, A78-2, ML FM 4, 1747.
15. Collins, *An Account*, 7.
16. Ibid., 535.
17. *HRNSW*, vol. 1, part 2, 470n.
18. Collins, *An Account*, vol. 1, 113.
19. Ibid.
20. *HRNSW*, vol. 1, part 2, 147.
21. Easty, *Memorandum*, 100.
22. Tench, *Sydney's First Four Years*, 134.
23. Ibid., 57.
24. Phillip, *The Voyage*, 119.
25. *HRNSW*, vol. 1, part 2, 172.
26. *HRA*, vol. 1, 81.
27. Collins, *An Account*, vol. 1, 30.
28. *HRA*, vol. 1, 74.
29. Phillip, *The Voyage*, 79.
30. *HRNSW*, vol. 1, part 2, 218.
31. Collins, *An Account*, vol. 1, 46.
32. Heney, *Australia's Founding Mothers*, 85.
33. Cobley, *Sydney Cove 1788*, 248.
34. Cobley, *Sydney Cove 1791–92*, 130.
35. Bradley, *A Voyage*, 97.

36. Tench, *Sydney's First Four Years*, 59.
37. White, *Journal*, 157-58.
38. Bowes, *Journal*, 78.
39. Collins, *An Account*, vol. 1, 541n. Lieutenant William Collins recovered from his illness and lived to be 77, dying on 26 September 1842, still a lieutenant.
40. Bowes, *Journal*, 76.
41. *HRA*, vol. 1, 64.
42. Cobley, *Sydney Cove 1788*, 176.
43. *HRA*, vol. 1, 64.
44. Collins, *An Account*, vol. 1, 27.
45. *HRNSW*, vol. 1, part 2, 166.
46. Scott, *Remarks*, 45.
47. *HRNSW*, vol. 1, part 2, 144.
48. Scott, *Remarks*, 45.
49. *HRNSW*, vol. 1, part 2, 155.
50. Ibid., 193.
51. Ibid., 155.
52. Bowes, *Journal*, 24.
53. *HRNSW*, vol. 1, part 2, 324; also Easty, *Memorandum*, 108; and Scott, *Remarks*, 45.
54. *Index of Burials in New South Wales 1787–1800*, H.J. Rumsey, ML B1186.
55. Clark, *Journal*, 99-100.
56. Bradley, *A Voyage*, 108.
57. Clark, *Journal*, 111-14.
58. Bradley, *A Voyage*, 188.
59. Scott, *Remarks*, 52.
60. Ibid., 43.
61. *HRA*, vol. 1, 202; also Tench, *Sydney's First Four Years*, 174; and Scott, *Remarks*, 53.
62. The Southwell Papers, *HRNSW*, vol. 2, 713.
63. Southwell Papers, *Correspondence*, in Bonwick Transcripts, Box 57, ML 360.
64. Tench, *Sydney's First Four Years*, 179; also Collins, *An Account*, vol. 1, 110-11.
65. Tench, *Sydney's First Four Years*, 152.
66. Ibid., 79 and 161.
67. Bradley, *A Voyage*, 186.
68. Tench, *Sydney's First Four Years*, 163.
69. Clark, *Journal*, 113.

Chapter 9 The Reluctant Hangman

1. Bowes, *Journal*, 75.
2. Worgan, *Journal*, 38.
3. Bowes, *Journal*, 75.
4. Tench, *Sydney's First Four Years*, 44.
5. Clark, *Journal*, 102.
6. Ibid., 103.
7. Collins, *An Account*, vol. 1, 22.
8. Tench, *Sydney's First Four Years*, 59.
9. Collins, *An Account*, vol. 1, 43.
10. Bradley, *A Voyage*, 104.

Chapter 10 Rations and Supplies

1. *HRNSW*, vol. 2, 413.
2. PRO ADM 1/3824; ML PRO Roll 412, 65.

3. Ibid., 66.
4. Ibid.
5. Tench, *Sydney's First Four Years*, 166.
6. *HRNSW*, vol. 2, 761.
7. PRO ADM 1/3824; ML PRO Roll 412.
8. *AO 4/1634*.
9. *HRNSW*, vol. 1, part 2, 15, 18.
10. *HRA*, vol. 1, 44.
11. Scott, *Remarks*, 37.
12. *HRNSW*, vol. 1, part 2, 143.
13. Ibid., 151.
14. Ibid., 174.
15. White, *Journal*, 132.
16. *HRNSW*, vol. 1, part 2, 142.
17. Ibid., 175.
18. Ibid., 149. The cattle which strayed in July 1788 were found by Hunter at Cowpastures in November 1795. By then they had increased to upwards of sixty head (Collins, *An Account*, vol. 1, 436). Scott (*Remarks*, 38) suggests that the loss of the cattle was deliberate and says that the cattle "was drove or strayed" — the word "strayed" he added as an afterthought.
19. Cobley, *Sydney Cove 1788*, 234.
20. ML PRO REEL 3551; PRO TI/671, 209.
21. PRO ADM 1/3824, 32; ML PRO Roll 412.
22. Ibid., 28.
23. Scott, *Remarks*, 42-4.
24. Hunter to Admiralty, 3 January 1789. PRO ADM 1/1909, 1788–92, section 12.
25. Tench, *Sydney's First Four Years*, 158.
26. *HRNSW*, vol. 1, part 2, 326.
27. Tench, *Sydney's First Four Years*, 164.
28. Collins, *An Account*, vol. 1, 85.
29. *HRNSW*, vol. 1, part 2, 327.
30. Tench, *Sydney's First Four Years*, 158.
31. *HRA*, vol. 1, 168.
32. Vergil, *The Aeneid*, book XII, line 59.
33. Cobley, *Sydney Cove 1789–90*, 165.
34. *HRNSW*, vol. 1, part 2, 327.
35. Collins, *An Account*, vol. 1, 88.
36. Ibid., 82.
37. Cobley, *Sydney Cove 1789–90*, 168. Johnson to Fricker, 9 April 1790.
38. Collins, *An Account*, vol. 1, 88; and *HRA*, vol. 1, 167.
39. Tench, *Sydney's First Four Years*, 220.
40. Collins, *An Account*, vol. 1, 91.
41. Tench, *Sydney's First Four Years*, 220.
42. Collins, *An Account*, vol. 1, 90.
43. Cobley, *Sydney Cove 1789–90*, 175.
44. Cobley, *Sydney Cove 1791–92*, 53.
45. Tench, *Sydney's First Four Years*, 167.
46. Cobley, *Sydney Cove 1791–92*, 51.
47. Ibid., 88.
48. Collins, *An Account*, vol. 1, 90.
49. Cobley, *Sydney Cove 1791–92*, 68.
50. Collins, *An Account*, vol. 1, 91.
51. Ibid., 92.
52. Cobley, *Sydney Cove 1791–92*, 69.
53. Collins, *An Account*, vol. 1, 135.
54. Ibid., 144.
55. Ibid., 128-30.

Chapter 11   Marines under the Lash

1. Tench, *Sydney's First Four Years*, 134.
2. Stanley, "The Push From the Bush" in *"The 80th Regiment 1838", Bulletin of Social History* no. 11 (November 1981), 11-14.
3. Collins, *An Account*, vol. 1, 49.
4. Easty, *Journal*, 111.
5. Tench, *Sydney's First Four Years*, 145.
6. Collins, *An Account*, vol. 1, 49.
7. Bradley, *A Voyage*, 163.
8. Easty, *Journal*, 111.
9. Ibid., 119.
10. Cobley, *Sydney Cove 1789–90*, 277.
11. Scott, *Remarks*, 55.
12. Cobley, *Sydney Cove 1791–92*, 84.
13. Easty, *Journal*, 129-30; Collins, *An Account*, vol. 1, 141.
14. Collins, vol. 1, 141.
15. White, *Journal*, 166-67.
16. *HRNSW*, vol. 1, part 2, 220.
17. Scott, *Remarks*, 42.
18. Clark, *Journal*, 96.
19. Easty, *Journal*, 99.
20. Cobley, *Sydney Cove 1789–90*, 93.
21. Collins, *An Account*, vol. 1, 66.
22. Clark, *Journal*, 182; and Collins, *An Account*, vol. 1, 549n.
23. From an uncatalogued newspaper cutting in the Mitchell Library marked "Royal Marines".

Chapter 12   Parramatta

1. *HRNSW*, vol. 2, 394.
2. Ibid., vol. 1, part 2, 189.
3. *HRA*, vol. 1, 296-97.
4. Scott, *Remarks*, 41-2.
5. Cobley, *Sydney Cove 1788*, 235; or *HRNSW*, vol. 1, part 2, 192.
6. *HRNSW*, vol. 1, part 2, 536.
7. Ibid., 470.
8. Ibid., 557.
9. Newton Fowell's letter of 31 July 1790, ML, CO 201/5, Reel 3, vols 5-7, 287.
10. Collins, *An Account*, vol. 1, 67.
11. *HRNSW*, vol. 1, part 2, 470.
12. Collins, *An Account*, vol. 1, 127.

Chapter 13   God Save the King

1. Collins, *An Account*, vol. 1, 25.
2. Easty, *Journal*, 103.
3. Bowes, *Journal*, 53.
4. Ibid.
5. Easty, *Journal*, 103; and White, *Journal*, 256. Vice-regal clemency was often dispensed

on royal occasions even to pardoning those in irons for stealing food. (See Collins, *An Account*, vol. 1, 137.)
6. White, *Journal*, 140, 256; also Cobley, *Sydney Cove 1788*, 158-59; and Bowes, *Journal*, 53.
7. White, *Journal*, 256.
8. Tench, *Sydney's First Four Years*, 60.
9. Worgan, *Journal*, 54.
10. Worgan, *Journal*, 55; and Cobley, *Sydney Cove 1788*, 160.
11. Cobley, *Sydney Cove 1788*, 168.
12. Worgan, *Journal*, 55.
13. Collins, *An Account*, vol. 1, 30.
14. Easty, *Journal*, 105.
15. Collins, *An Account*, vol. 1, 30.
16. Clark, *Journal*, 269.
17. White, *Journal*, 154.
18. Clark, *Journal*, 269; and White, *Journal*, 160.
19. Tench, *Sydney's First Four Years*, 152.
20. Collins, *An Account*, vol. 1, 96.
21. Clark, *Journal*, 139.

Chapter 14 Staying On: Family and Land

1. *HRNSW*, vol. 1, part 2, 109.
2. ML, PRO Reel 3551, PRO TI/671.
3. *HRA*, vol. 1, 144.
4. *HRNSW*, vol. 1, part 2, 326.
5. Collins, *An Account*, vol. 1, 144.
6. Tench, *Sydney's First Four Years*, 164.
7. *HRNSW*, vol. 2, 413.
8. Letter of 14-22 April 1789, 2, ML PRO, ADM 1/3824, Roll 412.
9. Scott, *Remarks*, from the front cover.
10. Ibid.
11. Ibid., 83.
12. Ibid.
13. Ibid., 36-37.
14. *HRNSW*, vol. 1, part 2, 142.
15. Ibid.
16. Cobley, *Sydney Cove 1791–92*, 67.
17. In recording the births, deaths and marriages of the marines, absolute accuracy is not possible in all cases because of vagueness in some of the original records. The information given therefore is as accurate as possible.
18. *HRNSW*, vol. 1, part 2, 109.
19. Based on the list of Fidlon and Ryan in *The First Fleeters*.
20. AO Reel 2125, Card 5, entry 112/180.
21. AO Reel 2125, Card 7.
22. *Index to Marriages in New South Wales, 1788–1801*, H.J. Rumsey, ML B1171.
23. *Record of Births, Deaths, and Marriages, 1787–1797*, T.D. Mutch, ML B1644.
24. Bradley, *A Voyage*, 95.
25. *HRA*, vol. 1, 35.
26. Collins, *An Account*, vol. 1, 555n.
27. Ibid.
28. Phillip to Lord Sydney, 13 February 1790, AO 4/1634.
29. Ibid.
30. *HRA*, vol. 1, 122-25.

31. *HRNSW*, vol. 1, part 2, 370.
32. Ibid., 632.
33. Scott, *Remarks*, 68; Easty, *Journal*, 133.
34. P.G. King's Letter Book, Norfolk Island, 1788-99, ML C187.
35. Collins, *An Account*, vol. 1, 197.
36. Ibid., 167; J.F. Campbell, "The Dawn of Rural Settlement in Australia", *JRAHS*, vol. 2, part 2, 1925, 96.
37. Phillip to Grenville, 15 December 1791, AO 4/1634.
38. *JRAHS*, vol. 2, part 2, 1925, 97.
39. *HRA*, vol. 1, 122.
40. Tench, *Sydney's First Four Years*, 171.
41. New South Wales Corps Muster Roll, 25 December 1791 to 24 June 1792, PRO 417 WO12/11028, ML. Field (*Britain's Sea Soldiers*, 177) indicates that sixty-three marines transferred to the New South Wales Corps. The thirty-eight listed in this chapter are those whom the author was able to trace in the corps' Muster Rolls.

Chapter 15   Major Robert Ross

1. *HRNSW*, vol. 1, part 2, 40.
2. Ibid., 83, 92-93.
3. Ibid., 78.
4. Ibid., 104.
5. Ibid., 94.
6. Ibid., 26.
7. Ibid., 138.
8. Ibid., 208.
9. Ibid.
10. *HRA*, vol. 1, 35.
11. *HRNSW*, vol. 1, part 2, 138.
12. Ibid., 140.
13. Ibid., 156.
14. Ibid., 159.
15. Ibid., 160.
16. Ibid., 157.
17. Ibid., 139.
18. Ibid., 157.
19. Ibid.
20. Ibid.
21. Ibid., 164.
22. Ibid., 158.
23. Ibid.
24. Ibid., 164.
25. Ibid., 158.
26. Ibid., 159.
27. *HRA*, vol. 1, 260-62.
28. *HRNSW*, vol. 1, part 2, 153.
29. Ibid., 170.
30. Ibid., 172.
31. Ibid., 173.
32. Ibid., 174.
33. Ibid., 171.
34. Ibid., 148.
35. Ibid., 176.
36. Ibid., 177.

37. Ibid., 181.
38. Clark, *Journal*, 263.
39. ML Document Ac 145.
40. ML Document 486 of November 1788.
41. ML Document 1174.
42. *HRNSW*, vol. 1, part 2, 218.
43. Ibid., 195.
44. Ibid., 196.
45. Ibid., 218.
46. Ibid., 212-13.
47. Ibid., 215-17.
48. Collins, *An Account*, vol. 1, 35.
49. Samuel, *An Historical Account*, 676.
50. *HRNSW*, vol. 1, part 2, 216.
51. PRO, ADM 1/3824, 49.
52. Clark, *Journal*, 272.
53. *HRA*, vol. 1, 121.
54. Ibid., 740n.
55. Apparently, it was not unusual for officers to be given a second chance: Grose would have done so with an officer "if he had seen fit to acknowledge his errors". (*HRNSW*, vol. 1, part 2, 404.)
56. Scott, *Remarks*, 45.
57. *HRA*, vol. 1, 106.
58. Collins, *An Account*, vol. 1, 544n.
59. *HRNSW*, vol. 1, part 2, 228-29.
60. *HRA*, vol. 1, 106.
61. Collins, *An Account*, vol. 1, 9.
62. Ibid., 43-44.
63. *HRNSW*, vol. 2, 485.
64. *HRNSW*, vol. 1, part 2, 139.
65. *HRNSW*, vol. 2, 112.
66. Ibid., 115.
67. Ibid., 108.
68. Ibid.
69. Ibid., 150.
70. Ibid., 110.
71. *HRNSW*, vol. 1, part 2, 462.
72. *HRA*, vol. 1, 151.
73. Ibid., 154.
74. Collins, *An Account*, vol. 1, 63.
75. Tench, *Sydney's First Four Years*, 156.
76. *HRNSW*, vol. 1, part 2, 288.
77. *HRA*, vol. 1, 135.
78. Ibid., 136.
79. Field, *Britain's Sea Soldiers*, 174.
80. *HRNSW*, vol. 1, part 2, 288-91, 302-4.
81. Tench, *Sydney's First Four Years*, 162.
82. *HRNSW*, vol. 1, part 2, 301.
83. Ibid., 303.
84. Ibid., 304.
85. Ibid., 303.
86. *HRA*, vol. 1, 136-37.
87. *HRNSW*, vol. 1, part 2, 291.
88. Ibid., 288n.
89. Ibid., 254.
90. *HRA*, vol. 1, 217.

91. Blumberg, *Royal Marine Records*, 24.
92. Cobley, *Sydney Cove 1791-92*, 189.
93. *HRNSW*, vol. 1, part 2, 201.
94. Ibid., 172.
95. Ibid., 304.
96. Cobley, *Sydney Cove 1788*, 258.
97. *Banks Papers*, 1747.
98. *HRNSW*, vol. 1, part 2, 93.
99. Tench, *Sydney's First Four Years*, 212-13.
100. Clark, *Journal*, 263.
101. Collins, *An Account*, vol. 1, 53.
102. Clark, *Journal*, 264.
103. Bowes, *Journal*, 73.
104. ML Document 1174, 24 March 1791. In a letter written by Campbell to Dr Farr, Physician to the Royal Hospital, Plymouth, he refers to the west country association both he and Ross enjoy.
105. Clark, *Journal*, 273, 269.
106. *HRNSW*, vol. 1, part 2, 84.
107. Ibid., 213.
108. Ibid., 195.
109. Ibid., 196.
110. Ibid., 197-200.
111. PRO ADM 1/3824; ML PRO Roll 42, 14.
112. *HRA*, vol. 1, 164.
113. *HRNSW*, vol. 1, part 2, 324.
114. *HRNSW*, vol. 1, part 2, 202-3.
115. Clark, *Journal*, 263.
116. Cobley, *Sydney Cove 1791-92*, 98.
117. Clark, *Journal*, 274.
118. Papers of Doctor John Harris, 20 March 1791, ML Document CYA 1597.
119. Collins, *An Account*, vol. 1, 53.
120. Cobley, *Sydney Cove 1791-92*, 195.
121. Ibid., 190.
122. *HRNSW*, vol. 1, part 2, 303.
123. *HRA*, vol. 1, 136-37.
124. Cobley, *Sydney Cove 1791-92*, 98.

Chapter 16 Norfolk Island

1. *HRNSW*, vol. 1, part 2, 136. Creswell replaced Meredith as commander of Meredith's company.
2. Ibid., 287.
3. *HRA*, vol. 1, 201. Phillip advised Stephens that 128 marines remained at Port Jackson and 79 at Norfolk Island on 17 July 1790.
4. *HRNSW*, vol. 1, part 2, 326.
5. Collins, *An Account*, vol. 1, 78.
6. Clark, *Journal*, 113; and Bradley, *A Voyage*, 188.
7. *HRNSW*, vol. 1, part 2, 708. Private Southwell in his letter to Rev. J. Butler states that the marines were sent to Norfolk Island in March 1790 to relieve the food shortage at Port Jackson and also alludes to differences between Ross and Phillip.
8. Clark, *Journal*, 111.
9. Ibid., 113.
10. Ibid., 115.
11. Easty, *Journal*, 114.

12. *HRNSW*, vol. 1, part 2, 383. P.G. King arrived in London on 21 December 1791 (*HRNSW*, vol. 1, part 2, 428).
13. Clark, *Journal*, 263.
14. Ibid., 116.
15. Bradley, *A Voyage*, 188. Bradley's figures vary with those of Phillip. Bradley's total for marines conveyed to Norfolk Island in March 1790 is sixty-two, whereas Phillip's figure is sixty-five in *AO* 4/1634, Phillip to Secretary of State, 5 March 1790.
16. Clark, *Journal*, 117.
17. Collins, *An Account*, vol. 1, 81.
18. *HRNSW*, vol. 2, 628.
19. Ibid., vol. 1, part 2, 124.
20. Ibid., 185, and PRO TI/668, Roll 3551, *ML*, Treasury Board Papers, no. 1550–1749, p. 1789. The marines on Norfolk Island during 1788 were Privates Charles Heritage and Sam King (arrived on the *Supply*, February 1788); Privates Thos. Smith, John Gowen, Sam Wigsall, James Williams, Thos Dukes, John Williamson, John Batchelor (arrived on the *Golden Grove*, October 1788). Private Batchelor, who was drowned on 15 June 1788, was the first to be buried on Norfolk Island (*HRNSW*, vol. 2, 575).
21. *HRNSW*, vol. 1, part 2, 268 (King's Journal).
22. Clark, *Journal*, 120.
23. Ibid.
24. Ibid., 121.
25. Ibid., 120.
26. Ibid., 204.
27. King, *Journal*, 341.
28. PRO ADM 1/5329, 1791–92 for 19 April 1792. Upon his return to England, Hunter faced a court martial for losing the *Sirius*. It was held aboard HMS *Brunswick* at Portsmouth on 19 April 1792. He was honourably acquitted.
29. Clark, *Journal*, 122.
30. Collins, *An Account*, vol. 1, 85.
31. Bradley, *A Voyage*, 211.
32. Clark, *Journal*, 159; and *HRNSW*, vol. 1, part 2, 439.
33. Phillip to Secretary of State, 10 April 1790, *AO* 4/1634.
34. Letter by Newton Fowell from Batavia dated 31 July 1790, ML CO 201/5, Reel 3, vols 5-7, 290.
35. Collins, *An Account*, vol. 1, 85.
36. Clark, *Journal*, 123.
37. Ibid., 124.
38. Ibid., 130.
39. Ibid., 123.
40. Ibid.
41. Ibid., 128.
42. *HRNSW*, vol. 1, part 2, 391.
43. Clark, *Journal*, 335.
44. *HRNSW*, vol. 1, part 2, 327.
45. Clark, *Journal*, 128.
46. Ibid., 132.
47. Ibid.
48. Ibid., 140.
49. Ibid., 141.
50. Ibid., 133.
51. *HRNSW*, vol. 1, part 2, 435.
52. Clark, *Journal*, 179.
53. Ibid., 138 and 141.
54. ML CO 201/5, Reel 3, vols 5-7, 279.

55. Clark, *Journal*, 139.
56. Ibid., 202.
57. *HRNSW*, vol. 1, part 2, 435-36.
58. Collins, *An Account*, vol. 1, 124.
59. *HRNSW*, vol. 1, part 2, 436.
60. Ibid., 466-67.
61. Clark, *Journal*, 207.
62. Ibid., 210.
63. Ibid., 143.
64. Ibid., 211.
65. Ibid., 224.
66. Ibid., 129.
67. Ibid., 212.
68. Ibid., 192.
69. Monthly returns, NSW Corps 1791–92, dated 24 March 1791, ML PRO WO 17/2294.
70. Clark, *Journal*, 199, 200, 202, 208, 217, 220 for NSW Corps courts martial and 189, 203, 206 for marine detachment courts martial.
71. Clark, *Journal*, 297.
72. Ibid., 287.
73. Ibid., 149-50.
74. Ibid., 112-13.
75. Ibid., 170-72.
76. Ibid., 162.
77. Ibid., 197.
78. Ibid., 172.
79. Ibid., 177.
80. Ibid., 183, 186.
81. Ibid., 187.
82. Ibid., 219.
83. Ibid., 178.
84. Ibid., 197.
85. Ibid., 166.
86. Ibid., 176.
87. Ibid., 185.
88. *ADB*, vol. 1, 1788–1850, 226.
89. Clark, *Journal*, 158, 162.
90. Ibid., 157.
91. Ibid., 161.
92. Ibid., 162.
93. Ibid., 180.
94. AO 4/1634; PRO Reel 3554, ML T/L 703.
95. P.G. King Letter Book, Norfolk Island 1788–1789, letter from King to Port Jackson 22 October 1791, ML-C187.
96. Phillip to Grenville, 15 December 1791, AO 4/1634; PRO Reel 3554, ML T/L 703.
97. P.G. King Letter Book, ML-C187; King to Phillip, 17 November 1791, PRO Reel 3554, ML T/L 703, 80.
98. King to Phillip, 29 December 1791. PRO Reel 3554, ML T/L 703, 86.
99. Clark, *Journal*, 135.
100. Ibid., 129.
101. Ibid., 142.
102. *HRNSW*, vol. 1, part 2, 399.
103. Clark, *Journal*, 145.
104. Ibid., 147.
105. Ibid., 160.
106. Banks Papers, Brabourne Collection, vol. 3, 1786–1800, A78-2, ML FM 4, 1747.

107. Clark, *Journal*, 136, 165. (Ann Farmer died 24 May 1790, and . . . Price, a male convict, died 10 October 1790.)
108. *HRNSW*, vol. 1, part 2, 434-50.
109. Clark, *Journal*, 201.
110. Ibid., 220.
111. Ibid., 217.
112. Ibid., 223.
113. Ibid., 136.
114. Ibid., 200.
115. Ibid., 224.
116. Ibid., 129.
117. Ibid., 158.
118. Ibid., 206.
119. *HRNSW*, vol. 1, part 2, 474.
120. Ibid., 562.
121. Ibid., 572.
122. Clark, *Journal*, 222.
123. .*HRNSW*, vol. 1, part 2, 572.
124. Clark, *Journal*, 288.
125. Ibid., 291.
126. Harris Papers, ML Documents CYA, 1597, 12.
127. Clark, *Journal*, 196.
128. Ibid., 220.
129. Ibid., 194.
130. Ibid.
131. Ibid., 208.
132. Ibid., 299.
133. Ibid., 224.
134. Ibid.
135. Ibid., 194.
136. Ibid., 208.
137. Ibid., 213.
138. *HRNSW*, vol. 1, part 2, 554.
139. Ibid., 538.
140. Ibid., 569.
141. Clark, *Journal*, 283.

Chapter 17   Phillip's Dispute with Dawes

1. *HRA*, vol. 1, 46.
2. Phillip to Admiralty, 10 July 1788, PRO ADM 1/2308, 1785-79, section 12.
3. Collins, *An Account*, vol. 1, 20.
4. Pooley, "Defenders and Defences of Australia", *JRAHS*, vol. 1, part 7, 1903.
5. Collins, *An Account*, vol. 1, 42.
6. Ibid., 45.
7. *JRAHS*, vol. 1, part 7, 1903.
8. *HRNSW*, vol. 1, part 2, 543.
9. Ibid., vol. 2, 423.
10. *Bonwick Transcripts*, Box 57, 351, ML. (Southwell to Rev. Butler, 27 July 1790.)
11. *HRNSW*, vol. 2, 498.
12. *HRA*, vol. 1, 294.
13. *HRNSW*, vol. 1, part 2, 415.
14. Ibid., 534-44.
15. Ibid., 545.

16. Ibid., 545-46.
17. Ibid., 329.
18. Ibid., 463-64.
19. Ibid., 484.
20. Cobley, *Sydney Cove 1791–92*, 158.
21. *HRNSW*, vol. 1, part 2, 559.
22. Ibid., 625.
23. Ibid., 666n.

Chapter 18   The Second Fleet

1. For the Returns of both groups, see *HRA*, vol. 1, 201.
2. Cobley, *Sydney Cove 1789–90*, 195.
3. Collins, *An Account*, vol. 1, 89.
4. Ibid., 90.
5. Cobley, *Sydney Cove 1789–90*, 197.
6. Collins, *An Account*, vol. 1, 91.
7. Ibid., 90; and Court of Criminal Jurisdiction, Minutes of Proceedings, February 1788 to December 1797, 186.
8. Collins, *An Account*, 91.
9. *Gentleman's Magazine* 61, part 1, 1791, 79.
10. Collins, *An Account*, 93.
11. Tench, *Sydney's First Four Years*, 169-70.
12. *HRA*, vol. 1, 176.
13. Collins, *An Account*, vol. 1, 96.
14. Ibid., 97.
15. C.M.H. Clark, *A History of Australia*, vol. 1, 123.
16. Letter from a female convict dated 24 July 1790, *Banks Papers*, ML FM 4, 1747.
17. Collins, *An Account*, vol. 1, 99.
18. Ibid., 100.
19. Tench, *Sydney's First Four Years*, 230.
20. Collins, *An Account*, vol. 1, 99.
21. Ibid., 100.
22. Tench, *Sydney's First Four Years*, 264.
23. Cobley, *Sydney Cove 1789–90*, 264.
24. Ibid., 235; and *HRNSW*, vol. 1, part 2, 365.
25. Tench, *Sydney's First Four Years*, 192.
26. Ibid., 199.
27. Ibid., 197.

Chapter 19   The New South Wales Corps

1. *HRNSW*, vol. 1, part 2, 153.
2. Ibid., 254.
3. Ibid., 93.
4. M. Lewis to Nepean, 28 September 1789. Letter Book 1789 (April–December), 347, PRO WO 4/138.
5. Ibid., 51-52, of 20 May 1789.
6. Lewis to Nepean, 28 September 1789, HO 50/381, f.489.
7. Young to Grose, 8 June 1789, NSW Corps Letter Book, PRO WO 4/845, 2-5.
8. Grose to Lewis, 15 June 1789, Letters of Secretary at War, 1789, G-M, 45-47, PRO WO 1/1042.

9. PRO WO 4/608, 286. Letter of Lewis to Grose, 11 July 1791, as quoted by T.G. Parsons in *JRAHS*, vol. 63, part 4, March 1978, 248-62.
10. Miscellany Book 1789–93, 14, (15 October 1789) PRO WO 26/34.
11. Collins, *An Account*, vol. 1, 145. (No member of the marine detachment was reported as having failed to report for the First Fleet's departure in 1787).
12. Letter from Hill and Paterson to Sir George Young, 16 September 1789, Secretary at War, 1789, G-M, 205-6, PRO WO 1/1042.
13. Collins, *An Account*, vol. 1, 103.
14. Cobley, *Sydney Cove 1791–92*, 22.
15. Cobley, *Sydney Cove 1789–90*, 251.
16. Scott, *Remarks*, 55.
17. Cobley, *Sydney Cove 1789–90*, 310.
18. Cobley, *Sydney Cove 1791–92*, 102.

Chapter 20   Homeward Bound

1. Collins, *An Account*, vol. 1, 148.
2. Tench, *Sydney's First Four Years*, 245.
3. Cobley, *Sydney Cove 1791–92*, 128.
4. NSW Corps Monthly Returns, 1791–92 for 13 December 1791, PRO WO 17/2294.
5. *HRNSW*, vol. 1, part 2, 542, 555.
6. Ibid., 554.
7. Cobley, *Sydney Cove 1791–92*, 138; and Easty, *Journal*, 133.
8. Cobley, *Sydney Cove 1791–92*, 197.
9. Tench, *Journal*, 245.
10. Bonwick Transcripts, Box 12, BT12, 19, ML.
11. Cobley, *Sydney Cove 1791–92*, 157.
12. Ibid., 191.
13. Scott, *Remarks*, 69.
14. Cobley, *Sydney Cove 1791–92*, 197-98.
15. Scott, *Remarks*, 70.
16. Clark, *Journal*, 224.
17. Scott, *Remarks*, 73.
18. Clark, *Journal*, 230.
19. Ibid., 230 and 234.
20. Ibid., 232.
21. Ibid., 233.
22. Ibid., 236.
23. Ibid., 233.
24. Collins, *An Account*, vol. 1, 221; Clark, *Journal*, 238.
25. Easty, *Journal*, 142.
26. Collins, *An Account*, vol. 1, 211.
27. Ibid., 110.
28. Cobley, *Sydney Cove 1789–90*, 274.
29. Easty, *Journal*, 174.
30. Royal Marine Library Catalogue, No 252(a) (Regulations and Instructions Relating to the Marine Forces when on Shore, Regulation XXI).
31. *HRNSW*, vol. 2, 481.
32. Ibid., vol. 1, part 2, 324.
33. Ibid., vol. 2, 472.
34. Ibid., 477.
35. Ibid.
36. Ibid., 478.
37. *Globe and Laurel*, vol. 15, 12.

38. *HRNSW*, vol. 2, 481.
39. Ibid.
40. Ibid., 484.
41. Ibid., 482.
42. *Bonwick Transcripts*, vol. 4, A2000-4, 1017, ML.
43. Ibid.
44. Ibid., 1016.
45. Ibid., 1021.
46. Ibid., 1015.
47. Ibid., 1020. *The Gentleman's Magazine*, vol. 91, mentions that Ross's daughter, Charlotte, married Thomas Baldock on 28 July 1821.
48. ML envelope entitled "Royal Marines" (uncatalogued).

Conclusion

1. *HRNSW*, vol. 1, part 2, 17.
2. Ibid., vol. 3, 15.
3. Ibid., 179.
4. Ibid., 440.
5. Ibid., vol. 6, 191.
6. Tench, *Sydney's First Four Years*, 246.
7. Easty, *Journal*, 143.
8. *HRNSW*, vol. 1, part 2, 570.
9. Ibid., 93.
10. Ibid.
11. Ibid., 254.
12. *HRA*, vol. 1, 217-19.
13. Grenville's letter arrived at Port Jackson on 5 November 1791; Phillip acknowledged it on 15 December 1791, and sent it to London by *Gorgon* three days later.
14. *HRNSW*, vol. 2, 788.
15. Collins, *An Account*, vol. 1, 159.
16. Easty, *Journal*, 141.
17. *HRNSW*, vol. 2, 788.
18. Ibid., vol. 1, part 2, 101.
19. Collins, *An Account*, vol. 1, 159.

Bibliography

A. Books

Aldington, Richard. *The Duke, A Life of Wellington.* New York: Viking Press, 1943.

Australian Dictionary of Biography. Vols 1 & 2. Melbourne: Melbourne University Press, 1966.

Bateson, Charles. *The Convict Ships, 1787–1868.* Sydney: A.H. & A.W. Reed, 1974.

Blumberg, H.E. *Royal Marine Records from 1755–1914.* Eastney, Hanks, UK: Royal Marine Historical Society, 1934.

Bowes, Arthur, *Journal 1787–1789.* Sydney: Australian Documents Library, 1979.

Bradley, William. *A Voyage to New South Wales, 1786–1792.* Sydney: New South Wales Public Library, 1969.

Clark, C.M.H. *A History of Australia.* Vol. 1, Melbourne: Melbourne University Press, 1962.

Clark, Ralph. *The Journal and Letters of Lieutenant Ralph Clark, 1787–1792.* Sydney: Australian Documents Library, 1981.

Cobley, John. *The Crimes of the First Fleet Convicts.* Sydney: Angus & Robertson, 1970.

Cobley, John. *Sydney Cove 1788.* Sydney: Angus & Robertson, 1962.

———. *Sydney Cove 1789–1790.* Sydney: Angus & Robertson, 1963.

———. *Sydney Cove 1791–1792.* Sydney: Angus & Robertson, 1965.

———. *Sydney Cove 1793–1795.* Sydney: Angus & Robertson, 1983.

Clune, Frank. *The Norfolk Island Story.* Sydney: Angus & Robertson, 1967.

Collins, David. *An Account of the English Colony in New South Wales, 1798.* Sydney: A.H. & A.W. Reed, 1975.

Easty, John. *Memorandum of the Transactions of a Voyage from England to Botany Bay, 1787-1793*. Sydney: Public Library of New South Wales, 1965.
Eldershaw, M. Barnard. *Phillip of Australia*. Sydney: Angus & Robertson, 1938.
Fidlon, P.G. and Ryan, R.J. *The First Fleeters*. Sydney: Australian Documents Library, 1981.
Field, Colonel Cyril. *Britain's Sea Soldiers*. Vols 1 & 2. Liverpool: Lyceum Press, 1924.
Frost, Alan. *Convicts and Empire: A Naval Question*. Melbourne: Oxford University Press, 1980.
Gillespie, Alexander. *An Historical Review of the Royal Marine Corps*. Birmingham: M. Swinney, 1803 (Mitchell Library: Q 355.0942/6).
Haswell, Jock. *The British Army, A Concise History*. London: Thames & Hudson, 1975.
Heney, Helen. *Australia's Founding Mothers*. Melbourne: Nelson, 1978.
Historical Records of Australia. Series 1, vol. 1. The Library Committee of the Commonwealth Parliament, 1914.
Historical Records of New South Wales. Vols 1-3. New South Wales Government Printer, 1892.
Hunter, John. *An Historical Journal, 1787-1792*. Sydney: Angus & Robertson, 1968.
King, P.G. *The Journal of Philip Gidley King, Lieutenant RN, 1787-1790*. Sydney: Australian Documents Library, 1980.
Knight, Frank. *Captain Cook and the Voyage of the Endeavour 1768-1771*. Melbourne: Nelson, 1968.
Longford, Elizabeth. *Wellington, The Years of the Sword*. London: Weidenfeld & Nicolson, 1969.
Macintosh, Neil K. *Richard Johnson, Chaplain to the Colony of New South Wales*. Sydney: Library of Australian History, 1978.
Martin, Ged, ed. *The Founding of Australia*. Sydney: Hale & Iremonger, 1978.
Phillip, Arthur. *The Voyage to Botany Bay*. London: John Stockdale, 1789. Facsimile edition, Melbourne: Hutchinson Group, 1982.
Ryan, A.J. *Land Grants 1788-1809*. Sydney: Australian Documents Library, 1981.
Samuel, E. *An Historical Account of the British Army and the Law Military*. London: Clowes, 1816.
Scott, James. *Remarks on a Passage to Botany Bay 1787-1792*. Sydney: Public Library of New South Wales, 1963.
Shaw, A.G.L. *Convicts and the Colonies*. Melbourne: Melbourne University Press, 1977.

Tench, Watkin. *Sydney's First Four Years*. Sydney: Library of Australian History, 1979.
Tolchard, Clifford. *The Humble Adventurer*. Melbourne: Lansdowne Press, 1965.
White, John. *Journal of a Voyage to New South Wales 1790*. Sydney: RAHS and Angus & Robertson, 1962.
Worgan, G.B. *Journal of a First Fleet Surgeon*. Sydney: Library of Australian History, 1978.

B. Journals and Articles

Atkinson, A.T. "John Macarthur Before Australia Knew Him." *Journal of Australian Studies* no. 4, June 1979.
————. "British Whigs and the Rum Rebellion." *Journal of the Royal Australian Historical Society* vol. 66, part 2.
————. "The Ethics of Conquest", *Aboriginal History*, vol. 6, no. 2, December 1982.
Best, Evan C. "Captain John O'Shea." *Descent* vol. 4, part 1, 1968.
Campbell, J.F. "The Dawn of Rural Settlement in Australia." *Journal of the Royal Australian Historical Society* vol. 2, part 2, 1925.
————. Article in *Journal of the Royal Australian Historical Society* vol. 12, 1926.
Campbell, W.S. "Arthur Philip." *Journal of the Royal Australian Historical Society*, vol. 21, 1936.
Journal of the Royal Australian Historical Society, Sydney. Vols 1, 2, 6, 9, 11, 12, 17, 18, 21, 22, 24, 25, 37, 44, 50, 57, 66.
Parsons, T.G. "The Social Composition of the Men of the New South Wales Corps." *Journal of the Royal Australian Historical Society* vol. 50, part 4.
————. "Courts Martial: The Savoy Prison and the New South Wales Corps." *Journal of the Royal Australian Historical Society* vol. 63, part 4.
Pooley, Grace Hendy. "Defenders and Defences of Australia." *Journal of the Royal Australian Historical Society* vol. 1, part 7, 1903.
Razzell, P.E. "Social Origins of Officers in the Indian and British Home Army 1758–1962." *British Journal of Sociology* vol. 14, 1963.
Stanley, Peter. "The Push from the Bush" in "The 80th Regiment 1838" *Bulletin of Social History* no. 11, November 1981.
Wood, Professor, G.A. Article in *Journal of the Royal Australian Historical Society* vol. 12, 1926.

C. Magazines and Newspapers

Daily Universal Register, The. 27 September 1786.
Gentleman's Magazine, The. London. Vol. 56 (1786); vol. 57 (1787); vol. 58 (1788); vol. 59 parts 1 & 2 (1789); vol. 60 (1790); vol. 61 part 1 (1791).
Globe and Laurel, The. "A Journal of the Corps of Royal Marines." Vol. 5, no. 27, 7 January 1898.
Morning Chronicle, The. 16 October 1786.
Newcastle Herald, The. 24 January 1959. For article by Arthur McMartin: "Marines Found Commonwealth".
Public Advertiser, The. 28 September, 6 October 1786.

D. Archival Material

Increasing copies of Public Records Office material are arriving on microfiche at Mitchell Library, Sydney.

Archives Office of New South Wales (AO), Sydney

AO Reel 2125, AO 4/1634.

Mitchell Library (ML), Sydney

Mitchell Library Documents. 486; 1174; AC145; CYA 1597; C187.
Banks Papers, The. Brabourne Collection, vol. 3, 1786–1800, (ML FM 4).
Bonwick Transcripts, The. Boxes 12 and 57.
Index of Burials in New South Wales, 1787–1800. H. J. Rumsey, (ML B1186).
Index of Marriages in New South Wales, 1788–1801. H. J. Rumsey, (ML B1171).
Record of Births, Deaths, and Marriages, 1787–1797. T. D. Mutch, (ML B1644).
Southwell, Daniel. *Correspondence.* The Bonwick Transcripts, Box 57.

Privy Council Register

Vol. 4, Charles II (Extract photocopy).

Public Records Office (PRO), London

Admiralty References (ADM). ADM 2/1116 (1781–89); ADM 2/1177 (1785–86); ADM 2/1178 (1786–88); ADM 2/1179 (1788–89); ADM 2/1180 (1789–90); ADM 2/1181 (1790–91); ADM 2/1182 (1792); ADM 1/3290 (1787); ADM 1/3824 (XCA13091); ADM 1/4151 (1784–85); ADM .36/11120 (XP4954); ADM 1/2308 (1785–89); ADM 1/1909 (1788–1792); ADM Pro Reel 3551 (PRO TI/671-ML); ADM 1/5329 (1791–92).
Colonial Office (CO). CO 201/5 (Reel 3, vols 5–7, ML); CO 201/3.
Home Office (HO). HO 50/381.
Marine Pay Office. ADM 96/154 (1781–1790); ADM 96/155 (1791–95); ADM 96/484 (1783–88).
War Office (WO). WO 1/1042; WO 4/138; WO 4/608; WO 4/845; WO 12/11028; WO 17/2294; WO 26/34.

Royal Marines Museum, Eastney, UK

Royal Marine Archives. ARCH 9/2/C; 9/2/J; 9/2/C3; 9/2/T; 9/2/S; 9/2/D; 9/2/RI.
Royal Marines Museum. Letters to author of various dates.

Index

Abbott, Drummer Joseph, 104
Aborigines
   attacks by, 111-13, 115-18
   contacts with, 77-82, 109-15, 117, 119, 121
   policy towards, 109, 111
   reactions of, 116, 119-22
Abrams, Henry, 106
Acres, Thomas, 98
Admiralty, 2, 8, 9, 201
alcohol, 44, 173-74, 236
Alexander, 23, 29, 32, 39-40, 51, 67, 70, 74, 78, 98
allowances, 30-31
Alt, Augustus, 102
American Independence, War of, 4-6, 18
ammunition, 29, 41, 64, 69
Anson, Lord, 7
Anstruther, Colonel, 9
Arabanoo, 114-16
Arden, Pepper, 20
Arndell, Doctor Thomas, 51-52, 58-62, 66, 78
Ascension Island, 278
Ascott, John, 238
Askew, Private Richard, 51
Atlantic, 180, 255, 259, 275, 278-79
Austrian Succession, War of, 2

Badajos, battle of, 12, 97
Baker, Corporal James, 47, 61, 100, 160-61
Ball, Lieutenant Henry B., 59, 78, 154, 232
Balloodery, 121-22
Ball's Pyramid, 231
Balmain, Surgeon William, 101, 170, 254
Baneelon, 116-17
Bangai, 119
Banks, Sir Joseph, 18-19, 36, 259
Barangaroo, 116
Barbados, 3
Barber, Elizabeth, 57-58
Barrett, Thomas, 143-44
Barrisford, Private John, 61
Barsby, Samuel, 98-99, 102-3
Bates, Private John, 141
Baughan, John, 285
Bee, The, 288
Begley, Corporal James, 162
Bellamy, Sarah, 103-4
Belle Isle, 3, 33
Bennett, John, 49, 145
Bid-ee-gal tribe, 257-58
Blackburn, David, 81
Blackburn, Private William, 176
Bligh, Governor, 36, 286

Bloodsworth, Private James, 207
Bolton, Jeffrey, 238
Book of Common Prayer, 65, 69, 79, 102, 278
Borrowdale, 24
Botany Bay, 10, 19-21, 77-86, 92, 128, 154
Bowes, Doctor Arthur, 82, 96, 111, 165
Bradley, Lieutenant William, 111, 146
Bramwell, Private, 99
Branham, Alicia, 244-45
Branham, Mary, 244-45
Branigan, James, 233
Brewer, Henry, 144, 207, 221
British Army, 1-2, 5-6, 11-13
Brixey, Private Charles, 175-76
Broken Bay, 124, 126, 129
Brompton, 282
Brown, Private James, 160-61
Browne, Private John, 176
Bryant escape, 157, 277
Bullmore, Private Thomas, 61, 70, 163
Bunker's Hill, 4, 36
Burke, Edmund, 19, 108

Calvert, Camden, and King, 266
Campbell, Captain James, 26, 36, 82, 89, 91, 105, 122, 141, 160, 165, 195-96, 201-7, 220, 222, 258, 287, 295
Camp Cove, 110
Canada, 3, 6
Cape Breton, 3
card playing, 238
Carmarthen Hills, 125, 127
Cascade Bay, 231
Cathcart, Colonel, 22
Cavenaugh, Private Owen, 175
Charles II, 1
Charlotte, 23, 32, 34, 40, 47, 54, 59, 69, 85, 89
Charlotte's Field, 235, 241, 243, 245, 248

Clark, Alicia, 38, 42, 46, 48, 54-55, 60, 68-69, 82, 88, 245, 277-78
Clark, Second Lieutenant Ralph, 283, 300-301
  yearns for family, 42, 46, 48-49, 54-55, 57, 60, 68-69, 73, 76, 79, 82, 277-78
  during voyage, 38, 49, 50-51, 53, 55, 57, 60, 62, 64, 66-68, 73, 76
  at Port Jackson, 11, 81-83, 89, 90-93, 95, 98-99, 122, 133, 140
  relations with Ross, 50, 222, 228-30, 242-43
  at Norfolk Island, 230-33, 237, 239-45, 250
Colbee, 116, 155
Cole, Elizabeth, 175
Collins, David, (Judge Advocate), 4, 74, 282, 288-89
  appointment of, 29-30, 32
  at Port Jackson, 81, 85, 94, 100, 102, 112, 137, 154-55, 160-63, 171, 176, 198-99, 262, 265-66, 274-75
  involvement with Ross, 200-212, 223, 253, 276
Collins, General, 29, 280-81
Collins, Lieutenant William, 38, 84, 133, 138-39, 195
Concord, 4
Connor, Sergeant Martin, 102
Considine, Doctor Dennis, 140
Contades, Marshal, 6
convicts, 15
  in the fleet, 32, 43, 47-48, 51, 53-54, 57, 59, 63, 65, 67, 71, 79
  at Port Jackson, 89-90, 92-93, 96, 98-107, 112-13, 115-16, 134, 137, 139, 154-56, 165
Cook, Captain James, 18, 81
Cook, Drummer Benjamin, 69, 98
Cook's River, 117-18, 128
Cool, William, 238

Cowden, Isaac, 156
Creswell, Private Daniel, 72, 102
Creswell, Second Lieutenant John, 38, 125-26, 160, 203, 231, 239-41, 243, 275-76, 297
Criminal Court, 42, 99, 193, 201-7
Cuba, 3
Cullen, James, 100
Cumberland, Duke of, 7

Daily Universal Register (later *The Times*), 21, 109
Daley, James, 105-6
Das Voltas Bay, 21
Davey, Lieutenant Thomas, 38, 48, 89, 186, 275, 282, 297-98
Davis, Martha, 174
Davis, Samuel, 112
Dawes, Lieutenant William, 32, 38-39, 45, 77-79, 92, 128-30, 138, 256-60, 282, 301-2
Death of Douglas, The, 55
Deedora, 120
defence works, 194, 256
Dempsey, Private William, 185-86
Deptford, 24, 29
Dodd, Henry Edward, 107, 134, 166
Doherty, Judith, 278
Dougherty, Private Arthur, 55, 59, 104, 174
Dring, William, 233
Ducie, Earl of, 195-96
Dudgeon, Elizabeth, 53, 57-58
Dukes, Private Richard, 160-61
Dundas, Lord, 259
Dunkirk, 15
Duval, Colonel Thomas, 280

Easty, Private John, 34, 42, 61, 82, 162-63, 279, 286-88
Eccleston, George, 102
Edgar, Lieutenant Thomas, 263
Elliott (Trimby), Joseph, 261-62
Endeavour, 18
exploration expeditions, 124-30

Faddy, Second Lieutenant John, 38, 56, 61-62, 67, 81, 230, 241-42, 299
Falkland Islands, 279
famine, 152-56, 171
Farmer, Anne, 100
Farquhar, George, 171
Farr, Doctor, 196-97
Ferguson, Midshipman, 141
Finnesy, Thomas, 237
First Fleet, 23-24, 32, 34, 40, 46, 50-53, 59-65, 67-72, 74-75, 79
Fishburn, 24, 47
Fitzgerald, Jane, 185
Folks, Francis, 253
Fowles, Elizabeth, 106, 145, 159
Fox, Charles, 18-19
France, 2-3, 15, 22
Freeman, James, 145
French East India Company, 3
French Revolution, 263
Friendship, 23-24, 32, 34, 40, 53-54, 57, 65, 71, 75, 78, 85, 89
Furzer, Lieutenant James, 32, 34, 38, 70, 75, 101, 160, 175, 198-99, 298

general courts martial, 32
Georges River, 80, 82, 118
George III, 263-64, 283
Gibraltar, 2
Gilbourne, Sergeant, 278
Godfrey, Private William, 99, 163
Golden Grove, 24
Goodall, Private William, 159
Gordon, Daniel, 145
Gorgon, HMS, 33, 175, 255, 274, 276-78
Government House, 89, 132
Green, Private Charles, 99, 175
Grenville, Lord, 179, 215, 258-59
Grose, Major Francis, 264, 270
Guadaloupe, 3
Guardian, 245, 264

Hall, Joseph, 143, 145
Hall, Margaret, 53, 58
Hand, William, 155

Handley, Cooper, 113
hangings, 143-46, 160-61
Harmsworth, Private John, 75, 175-76
Harp, Private Thomas, 141
Harris, Sir James, 22
Harris, Surgeon John, 137, 222, 252
Haslar Hospital, 9
Hastings, Warren, 108
Haswell, Private Thomas, 102
Hawkesbury River, 120, 126
Haynes, Private Luke, 61, 77, 160-61
Hearle, Colonel Parkins, 131
Higgins, Mary, 244
Hill, Captain, 10, 253-55, 271-72, 276
Hood, Admiral Lord, 37
Howe, Lord, 11, 25, 42, 200
Hume, Sergeant John, 55, 173, 210, 254, 278
Hunt, Private Joseph, 159-62, 185-88
Hunt, Robert, 155
Hunter, Captain John, 45, 81, 90, 100, 110-11, 124, 128, 142, 152, 176, 184, 231, 238, 248, 252, 285
Hurst, Private Mark, 162
Hyaena, HMS, 46, 48

India, 2-3, 6
Ipswich Journal, 282

Jackson, Sir George, 81
Jamieson, Doctor Thomas, 231, 253
Johnson, Lieutenant John, 38, 51, 70, 165, 202, 230, 237, 241, 299
Johnson, Reverend Richard, 30, 61, 64, 93-94, 139, 144, 195, 247, 254, 258, 264
Johnston, Lieutenant George, 29, 35, 84, 106, 112-13, 125-26, 160, 181, 201, 203, 227, 230, 237, 239-41, 274, 296-97
Jones, Private Thomas, 160-61, 185-86

Justinian, 245, 248, 265

kangaroos, 276
Keeling, Herbert, 104, 209
Kellow, Lieutenant Robert, 33, 112, 175, 186, 230, 241-42, 298
Keltie, James, 81, 103, 128
Kennedy, Sergeant John, 55, 60-61
Kent, 72
King, Lieutenant Philip Gidley, 52, 77-80, 91-92, 106, 154, 227, 230, 238, 247, 250-51
Knight, Sergeant Isaac, 71, 119-20
Knight, Private Richard, 162

labour superintendents, 106
Lady Juliana, 106, 140, 236, 263-66
Lady Penrhyn, 23, 29-30, 32, 36, 40
Lady Shore, 13
land grants, 179-80, 193, 245-46
Lane, William, 155
La Perouse, Jean-Francois, 83-84, 92
Lemaine Island, (Gambia), 20
Levy, Amelia, 105, 159
London Chronicle, 36
London, lord mayor of, 21
Long, Lieutenant John, 32, 34, 38, 75, 126, 187-91, 203, 210-11, 299
Lord Howe Island, 231, 277
Louisberg, 2
Lovell, Henry, 143, 145

Macarthur, Elizabeth, 37, 257, 271
Macarthur, John, 35, 271
McCormick, Sarah, 57, 59, 66, 104
McDonald, Private Alexander, 99
McEntire Affair, 117-18, 257
McManus, Private James, 162
Manly Cove, 110, 114
Marine Corps, British, 172, 267, 283-89
  history of, 1-5, 7-12, 14-18, 22-24, 26-30, 271
  during voyage, 32, 39-40, 44, 51, 55, 62-63, 67-68, 72, 75, 79

at Port Jackson, 81, 84, 89,
    94-96, 100, 103, 105, 112-13,
    117, 119, 131, 133-47,
    158-59, 161, 163-66, 169-81,
    201, 215, 275
  at Norfolk Island, 227, 235,
    238-40, 245-47, 255
  return voyage of, 275-79
Marine Mutiny Act, 2
Mars, Field of, 275
Marsden, Reverend Samuel, 286
martial law, 232
Martinique, 3
Mary Ann, 238, 255
Mason, Elizabeth, 104
Massey, General, 4
Matilda, 156
Matra, James Maria, 17-20
Maxwell, Lieutenant James, 38, 55,
  69-70, 133, 138-39, 298
Meredith, Captain Lieutenant James,
  36-37, 53, 58, 61-62, 66, 72, 77,
  81, 96, 101, 103-4, 160, 163,
  170, 175, 201, 221-22, 227,
  279-81, 295-96
Miller, Andrew, 137, 151, 172
Minden, 6
Morning Chronicle, 109
Mortimore, John, 238
Mount Twiss, 128
mutton birds, 233-34, 249

Nautilus, HMS, 21-22
Needham, Elizabeth, 99
Nepean, Evan, 10, 17, 20, 30-31,
  36, 39, 127, 194-96, 212-15, 283
Nepean River, 129-30
Neptune, 156, 264-66
Nesbitt, Captain Thomas, 21
Nevan, Captain John, 20-21
Newcastle, Duke of, 7
New South Wales Corps, 1, 10, 14,
  121, 166, 181, 240, 269-73, 275,
  279, 288
non-commissioned officers, 16

Norfolk Island, 91, 106, 171,
  175-76, 227-28, 231-38, 245,
  249, 255
Norris, Private William, 160-61, 163
North, Lord, 18-19
North America, 4, 6
Nova Scotia, 2

Odgers, Private Edward, 141, 159
Officers' Widows' Fund, 16
Okey, William, 112
Oldfield, Thomas, 209
Osborn, Thomas, 155-56
Owen, Joseph, 261

Palmer, John, 153, 159
Paradise Lost, 47, 127
Parker, Mrs, 275
Parramatta (Rose Hill), 107, 132,
  165-67, 262, 271
Peate, Charles, 209
pensions, 16
Perry, Elizabeth, 268
Petrie, Sergeant Henry, 140
Peyton, Samuel, 101-2
Philippines, the, 3, 6
Phillip, Captain Arthur, 24-25, 198,
  220, 278-79
  preparations before sailing, 24,
    31, 39, 42, 44
  during voyage, 63-65, 74-75
  at Port Jackson, 77, 81-84, 94-96,
    104, 111, 113, 118, 124-26,
    129, 141, 152-53, 170, 172
  relations with Ross, 74-75,
    189-96, 201-12, 230
  dealings with Norfolk Island,
    227-28, 236-37
  dispute with Dawes, 256-60
Pitcairne, Major, 4
Pitt, 275
Pitt, the Younger, 19, 30
Pittwater, 124
Plowman, Corporal James, 159
Plymouth, 11, 15
Point Sutherland, 80

Pondicherry, 2
Port Jackson, 10, 81, 85-86, 124
Portsmouth, 11, 39
possums, 276
Poulden, Lieutenant John, 38, 70, 186, 202-3, 275, 298-99
Powers, John, 52-53
Prince of Wales, 23, 32, 40, 48, 60, 67, 69, 85, 98
prison hulks, 17
Privy Council, 29
Public Advertiser, 109
public store, 159-63
Pugh, Private John, 162-63
Pully, Elizabeth, 53, 57-58, 66

Quebec, 3, 6
Queen, 255, 276
Queensborough, 244

rations, 28-29, 39, 65, 72, 147-52, 154-56, 228, 267
Receveur, Abbé Louis, 112
Recruiting Officer, The, 171
Redman, Mrs Michael, 174
regimental colours, 33
Richards, Private Lawrence, 67
Richmond Hill, 120, 125
Rio de Janeiro, 14, 41, 51, 59-65, 279
Roberts, Private John, 160-61, 163
Rocks, the, 137
Rose, George, 25
Rose Hill. *See* Parramatta
Rose Hill Packet, 166
Ross, John, 139, 201, 230, 252, 302
Ross, Major Robert, 10, 34-36, 294-95
    prior to departure from England, 2-5, 10, 17, 30-32, 34-36, 41, 44
    during voyage, 50, 62, 72, 74-75, 77
    performance at Port Jackson, 78-84, 90, 92-94, 105-6, 133, 135, 137-39, 144, 147, 160-61, 163, 165, 173, 182-85
    relationships with others, 122, 187-226, 228-30, 241-43, 275-76
    at Norfolk Island, 227, 230, 232-33, 236, 238, 247-54
    after return to England, 279-83, 287
Ross Reef, 232
routine orders, 90-92
royal occasions, 168-71, 235
Ruglass, John, 145
Ruse, James, 165-66, 267-68
Ryan, John, 143, 145
Ryan, Private Robert, 55

St Johns, 3
Salamander, 255
Sanderson, Thomas, 145
Savoy Military Prison, 13
Scarborough, 23, 32, 37, 40, 48, 75, 77-78, 89, 264
Scott, Sergeant James, 50-51, 54-55, 64, 79, 162, 174
seamen, 45, 48, 81, 98
Second Fleet, 261-67
Senegal, 3
Seven Years War, 3-4
Shairp, Lieutenant James Maitland, 38, 165, 202, 300
Shea, Captain John, 33, 36, 56-57, 139, 220, 295
Shortland, Lieutenant John, 241-42
Sirius, HMS, 24, 29, 31-32, 40, 44, 46, 48, 63, 79, 134, 152, 161, 168-70, 230-34
Smith, Captain Detmer, 157
Smith, Sergeant Thomas, 102
South Head, 132, 142
Southwell, Private Daniel, 79, 84, 141
Spanish Succession, War of, 2
Standfield, Corporal Daniel, 104, 176
standing orders, 16
Stephens, Philip, 25, 27, 31, 187, 191-92, 221

stock, 71, 84, 94, 128
stores, medical, 33
Supply, HMS, 24, 32, 59, 67, 75, 77, 84, 153, 166, 168, 227, 230, 232, 236, 255, 274, 276
Surprize, 245, 248, 264-66
Sydney, Lord, 17, 19-20, 22-23, 39, 194-95, 212-15
Sydney Cove, 84-85, 89, 137

Tank Stream, 82, 85, 89
Tench, Captain Watkin, 26, 34, 36-38, 47, 52, 79, 82, 89, 93, 106, 117-21, 127-31, 133, 153-55, 160-61, 169, 171, 186-93, 203, 209, 221-22, 257, 263, 267, 274, 276, 281-82, 296
Teneriffe, 50-53
Teut, Mary, 244
Thackerly, Elizabeth, 57-58
Thomas, Private Samuel, 93
Thompson, William, 102
Timins, Lieutenant Thomas, 38, 48, 69-70, 186, 222, 275, 299-300
Toulon, Private Michael, 61
Tupper, Major General, 283
Turner, Mary, 201

Union Jack, 83, 85

venereal disease, 51
Vergil, 154
Versailles, Treaty of, 5, 11
Vittoria, battle of, 13

Waaksamheyd, 157
War, Articles of, 186
War, Secretary for, 9, 11
Ware, Charlotte, 53
weapons, 27
Wedman, Private James, 186
Welldon, Colonel, 8
Wellington, Duke of, 4, 12
West Point, 248
whale, 141
White, Catherine, 244
White, Charlotte, 244
White, Surgeon John, 39, 47, 55, 100-101, 106, 119, 170, 174, 262
Wilkins, Private John, 141
Williams, John, 145
Wixstead, Corporal John, 159
Wolfe, James, 3
Worgan, Doctor George, 110, 128, 169-70
Wright, Private Henry, 163-64
Wright, Private Matthew, 69

Yannimaroo, 20
Young, Admiral Sir George, 20, 270